Hands-On Embedded Programming with C++17

Create versatile and robust embedded solutions for MCUs and RTOSes with modern C++

Maya Posch

BIRMINGHAM - MUMBAI

Hands-On Embedded Programming with C++17

Commissioning Editor: Aaron Lazar
Acquisition Editor: Chaitanya Nair
Content Development Editor: Rohit Kumar Singh
Technical Editor: Ketan Kamble
Copy Editor: Safis Editing
Project Coordinator: Vaidehi Sawant
Proofreader: Safis Editing
Indexer: Mariammal Chettiyar
Graphics: Alishon Mendonsa
Production Coordinator: Arvindkumar Gupta

First published: January 2019

Production reference: 1310119

Published by Packt Publishing Ltd.
Livery Place
35 Livery Street
Birmingham
B3 2PB, UK.

ISBN 978-1-78862-930-0

www.packtpub.com

`mapt.io`

Mapt is an online digital library that gives you full access to over 5,000 books and videos, as well as industry leading tools to help you plan your personal development and advance your career. For more information, please visit our website.

Why subscribe?

- Spend less time learning and more time coding with practical eBooks and videos from over 4,000 industry professionals

- Improve your learning with Skill Plans built especially for you

- Get a free eBook or video every month

- Mapt is fully searchable

- Copy and paste, print, and bookmark content

Packt.com

Did you know that Packt offers eBook versions of every book published, with PDF and ePub files available? You can upgrade to the eBook version at `www.packt.com` and as a print book customer, you are entitled to a discount on the eBook copy. Get in touch with us at `customercare@packtpub.com` for more details.

At `www.packt.com`, you can also read a collection of free technical articles, sign up for a range of free newsletters, and receive exclusive discounts and offers on Packt books and eBooks.

Contributors

About the author

Maya Posch is a senior C++ developer with more than 15 years of experience. Discovering the joys of programming early on, and later the joys of electronics, she has always expressed a profound interest in technology, a passion that she gladly shares with others.

Describing herself as a C developer who happens to like C++ and Ada, she likes to seek the limits of what can be done with the minimum of code and hardware to accomplish everything that is cool, new, and exciting.

She also enjoys FPGA development, AI, and robotics research, in addition to creative writing, music, and drawing.

About the reviewers

Frans Faase studied computer science at the University of Twente and received a master's degree in the field of compiler design and formal methods. He worked on some research projects in academia, but mostly worked as a software engineer in industry. He has about 20 years of experience of working with C++, both professional as recreational. He has contributed to several open source projects. Recently, he also gained some experience developing software for micro-controllers, mostly using the Arduino environment.

Patrick Mintram is a software engineer who has made his way up from electronics technician. He has made a career in the world of embedded systems, including developing and testing in a safety-critical environment and line-level repair and maintenance. He is married with two cats, Duke and Daisy, and spends his free time tinkering and running.

Packt is searching for authors like you

If you're interested in becoming an author for Packt, please visit `authors.packtpub.com` and apply today. We have worked with thousands of developers and tech professionals, just like you, to help them share their insight with the global tech community. You can make a general application, apply for a specific hot topic that we are recruiting an author for, or submit your own idea.

Table of Contents

Section 2: Testing, Monitoring

Preface

C++ does not add any bloat, extends maintainability, and offers many advantages over different programming languages, thus making it a good choice for embedded development. Do you want to build standalone or networked embedded systems and make them safety-critical and memory-safe? In this book, you will learn exactly how to do this. You will learn how C++ works and compares to other languages used for embedded development, how to create advanced GUIs for embedded devices in order to design an attractive and functional UI, and how to integrate proven strategies into your design for optimum hardware performance.

This book will take you through various embedded systems hardware boards so that you can choose the best one for your project. You will learn how to tackle complex architectural problems by fully embracing the proven programming patterns presented in the book.

Who this book is for

If you want to start developing effective embedded programs in C++, then this book is for you. Good knowledge of C++ language constructs is required to understand the topics covered in the book. No knowledge of embedded systems is assumed.

What this book covers

Chapter 1, *What Are Embedded Systems?* makes you familiar with what an embedded system entails. By looking at the various categories and examples of embedded systems in each category, a good overview of what is meant with the term *embedded* and the wide variety within that term should be formed. It explores the wide range of historic and currently available microcontrollers and system-on-chip solutions you can find in existing systems as well as new designs.

Chapter 2, *C++ as an Embedded Language*, explains why C++ is actually as nimble as C and similar languages. Not only is C++ generally at least as fast as C, there is no additional bloat, and it offers many advantages with code paradigms and maintainability.

Chapter 3, *Developing for Embedded Linux and Similar Systems*, explains how to develop for Linux-based embedded systems and kin on SBCs and manage the differences between Linux-based and PC-based development.

Chapter 4, *Resource-Restricted Embedded Systems*, deals with planning for and using limited resources efficiently. We will take a look at how to select the right MCU for a new project and add peripherals and deal with Ethernet and serial interface requirements in a project. We will also look at an example AVR project, how to develop for other MCU architectures, and whether to use an RTOS.

Chapter 5, *Example – Soil Humidity Monitor with Wi-Fi*, explains how to create a Wi-Fi-enabled soil humidity monitor with actuator options for a pump or similar. Using the built-in web server, you can use its browser-based UI for monitoring and control, or integrate it into a larger system using its REST API.

Chapter 6, *Testing OS-Based Applications*, looks at how to develop and test embedded OS-based applications. You will learn how to install and use a cross-compilation toolchain, do remote debugging using GDB, and write a build system.

Chapter 7, *Testing Resource-Restricted Platforms*, shows how to effective develop for MCU-based targets. You will also see how to implement an integration environment that allows us to debug MCU-based applications from the comfort of a desktop OS and the tools it provides.

Chapter 8, *Example – Linux-Based Infotainment System*, explains how you can fairly easily construct an SBC-based infotainment system, using voice-to-text to construct a voice-driven UI. We will also look at how we can extend it to add even more functionality.

Chapter 9, *Example – Building Monitoring and Control*, shows how a building-wide monitoring and management system is developed, what its components looks like, and what lessons are learned during its development.

Chapter 10, *Developing Embedded Systems with Qt*, looks at the myriad of ways in which the Qt framework can be used to develop for embedded systems. We will look at how it compares with other frameworks and how Qt is optimized for these embedded platforms, before working through an example of a QML-based GUI that can be added to the previously-created infotainment system.

Chapter 11, *Developing for Hybrid SoC/FPGA Systems*, teaches you how to communicate with the FPGA side of a hybrid FPGA/SoC system and helps you understand how a variety of algorithms are implemented in FPGA and used on the SoC side. You will also learn how to implement a basic oscilloscope on a hybrid FPGA/SoC system.

Appendix, *Best Practices*, runs through a number of common issues and pitfalls that are likely to occur while working on an embedded software design.

To get the most out of this book

A working knowledge of Raspberry Pi is required. You will need C++ compiler, the GCC ARM Linux (cross-) toolchain, the AVR toolchain, the Sming framework, Valgrind, the Qt framework, and the Lattice Diamond IDE.

Download the example code files

You can download the example code files for this book from your account at www.packtpub.com. If you purchased this book elsewhere, you can visit www.packtpub.com/support and register to have the files emailed directly to you.

You can download the code files by following these steps:

1. Log in or register at www.packtpub.com.
2. Select the **SUPPORT** tab.
3. Click on **Code Downloads & Errata**.
4. Enter the name of the book in the **Search** box and follow the onscreen instructions.

Once the file is downloaded, please make sure that you unzip or extract the folder using the latest version of:

- WinRAR/7-Zip for Windows
- Zipeg/iZip/UnRarX for Mac
- 7-Zip/PeaZip for Linux

The code bundle for the book is also hosted on GitHub at https://github.com/PacktPublishing/Hands-On-Embedded-Programming-with-CPP-17. In case there's an update to the code, it will be updated on the existing GitHub repository.

We also have other code bundles from our rich catalog of books and videos available at https://github.com/PacktPublishing/. Check them out!

Conventions used

There are a number of text conventions used throughout this book.

`CodeInText`: Indicates code words in text, database table names, folder names, filenames, file extensions, pathnames, dummy URLs, user input, and Twitter handles. Here is an example: "The C++ class itself is implemented in C as a `struct` containing the class variables."

A block of code is set as follows:

```
class B : public A {
    // Private members.

public:
    // Additional public members.
};
```

When we wish to draw your attention to a particular part of a code block, the relevant lines or items are set in bold:

```
class B : public A {
    // Private members.

public:
    // Additional public members.
};
```

Any command-line input or output is written as follows:

```
sudo usermod -a -G gpio user
sudo usermod -a -G i2c user
```

Bold: Indicates a new term, an important word, or words that you see onscreen. For example, words in menus or dialog boxes appear in the text like this. Here is an example: "Compared to MCUs, SoCs are not as resource-limited, usually running a full **operating system (OS)** such as a Linux-derived OS, VxWorks, or QNX."

Warnings or important notes appear like this.

 Tips and tricks appear like this.

Get in touch

Feedback from our readers is always welcome.

General feedback: Email `feedback@packtpub.com` and mention the book title in the subject of your message. If you have questions about any aspect of this book, please email us at `questions@packtpub.com`.

Errata: Although we have taken every care to ensure the accuracy of our content, mistakes do happen. If you have found a mistake in this book, we would be grateful if you would report this to us. Please visit `www.packtpub.com/submit-errata`, selecting your book, clicking on the Errata Submission Form link, and entering the details.

Piracy: If you come across any illegal copies of our works in any form on the Internet, we would be grateful if you would provide us with the location address or website name. Please contact us at `copyright@packtpub.com` with a link to the material.

If you are interested in becoming an author: If there is a topic that you have expertise in and you are interested in either writing or contributing to a book, please visit `authors.packtpub.com`.

Reviews

Please leave a review. Once you have read and used this book, why not leave a review on the site that you purchased it from? Potential readers can then see and use your unbiased opinion to make purchase decisions, we at Packt can understand what you think about our products, and our authors can see your feedback on their book. Thank you!

For more information about Packt, please visit `packtpub.com`.

1
Section 1: The Fundamentals - Embedded programming and the role of C++

In this section the reader should become familiar with the many embedded platforms out there, along with a basic practical example project.

The following chapters will be covered in this section:

- Chapter 1, *What Are Embedded Systems?*
- Chapter 2, *C++ as an Embedded Language*
- Chapter 3, *Developing for Embedded Linux and Similar Systems*
- Chapter 4, *Resource-Restricted Embedded Systems*
- Chapter 5, *Example - Soil Humidity Monitor with Wi-Fi*

Section 1: The Fundamentals - Embedded programming and the role of C++

What Are Embedded Systems? 1

Essentially , the *embedded* part of an *embedded system* refers to the state of being embedded into a larger system. The system that has been embedded is a computer system of some description, which has one or more very specific functions in the overall system, rather than being a general-purpose component. This larger system can be digital, mechanical, or analog in nature, while the additional integrated digital circuitry tightly interacts with data from and to interfaces, sensors and memory to implement the actual system functionality.

In this chapter, we will look at the following topics:

- Different categories of embedded platforms
- Examples of each category
- Development challenges of each category

The many faces of embedded systems

Every computerized function in today's devices is implemented using one or multiple microprocessors, meaning a computer processor (central processing unit, or CPU) usually contained in a single **integrated circuit (IC)**. The microprocessor comprises at least the **arithmetic logic unit (ALU)** and control circuitry, but logically also registers, and **input/output (I/O)** banks, in addition to more advanced features commonly tailored to a specific product category (wearables, low power sensors, mixed signal, ...) or market (consumer, medical, automotive, ...).

At this point in history, almost all microprocessors are found in embedded systems. Even though people are likely to possess a computer, laptop, and smartphone, maybe even a tablet, the number of embedded microprocessors in a given household far dwarfs the number of general-purpose microprocessors.

Even within a laptop or PC, there are a number of embedded microprocessors in addition to its general-purpose CPU. These microprocessors have tasks like handling keyboard or mouse input, processing touch-screen inputs, converting streams of data into Ethernet packages, or creating video or audio output.

In older systems, such as the Commodore 64, this same pattern can be seen, with a CPU IC, sound IC, video IC, and so on. Whereas the CPU runs whatever code the application developer has written, the other chips in the system have very specific purposes, down to the controller IC for the floppy or hard disk drive.

Outside of general-purpose computers, we find embedded microprocessors everywhere, often in the form of even further integrated MCUs. They control kitchen devices, washing machines, and the engines of our cars, in addition to the higher-level functions and the processing of sensor information.

While the first microwaves were analog devices, using mechanical timers and variable resistors to set power level and duration, today's microwaves contain at least one microcontroller, which is responsible for handling user input, driving a display of some type, and configuring the microwave's systems. The display itself can have its own microcontroller, depending on the complexity of the chosen configuration.

Perhaps more excitingly, embedded systems also provide monitoring, automation and fail-safe features that keep airplanes flying, ensure that guided missiles and space rockets perform as intended, and enable ever-increasing possibilities in areas such as medicine and robotics. The avionics of an airplane constantly monitor countless parameters from a multitude of sensors, running the same code on its triple-redundant configuration to detect any possible glitches.

Tiny yet powerful microprocessors enable the rapid analysis of chemicals and DNA or RNA strands, which would have taken racks of equipment before. With the progress of technology, an embedded system has become small enough that it can be sent through the human body to monitor its health.

Beyond Earth, space probes and rovers on Mars, the Moon, and asteroids are performing a myriad of duties every day, again with the courtesy of well-tested embedded systems. The Moon missions themselves were made possible due to the first major example of an embedded system in the form of the Apollo Guidance Computer. This 1966-era embedded system consisted of wire-wrapped boards full of triple-input NOR logic gates, built for the explicit purpose of handling navigation, guidance, and control of the Command Module and Lunar Module launched by the Saturn V rockets.

The ubiquitous and versatile nature of embedded systems has made them an inseparable part of modern life.

For embedded systems, they are usually distinguished between the following categories:

- **Microcontrollers (MCUs)**
- **System-on-Chip (SoC)**, often as a **Single-Board Computer (SBC)**

Microcontrollers

One of the driving factors of innovation in the field of embedded systems is cost, since they will often be high-volume, cheap consumer products. To that end, it helps to have the entire microprocessor, memory, storage, and input/output peripherals on a single chip, simplifying implementation effort, reducing PCB real estate, all with the added benefit of faster and simpler design and production with higher yield. This led to the development of **microcontrollers** (**MCUs**) during the 1970s: single-chip computer systems that could be added to a new design for a minimal cost.

With the introduction of **Electrically Erasable Programmable Read-Only Memory** (**EEPROM**) to MCUs in the early 1990s, it first became possible to rewrite the program memory of MCUs repeatedly without having to resort to erasing memory content using ultraviolet light through a special quartz window in the MCU's packaging. This allowed for much easier prototyping and further reduced cost and - as far as development and lower-volume production is concerned - in-circuit programming.

As a result of this, many systems that were previously controlled by intricate mechanical and analog mechanisms (like elevators and temperature controllers) now contain one or more MCUs, which handle the same functionality while reducing costs and increasing reliability. By having the features handled in software, developers were also free to add advanced features such as complex preset programs (for washing machines, microwaves, and so on) and simple to complex displays to provide feedback to the user.

TMS 1000

The first commercially available MCU was Texas Instrument's TMS 1000, a general-purpose 4-bit, single-chip system. It was first made available for sale in 1974. The original model had 1 KB of ROM, 64 x 4 bits of RAM, and 23 I/O pins. They could be clocked at speeds from 100 to 400 KHz, with each instruction executing in six clock cycles.

Later models would increase the ROM and RAM sizes, though the basic design remained largely unchanged until production ceased in 1981:

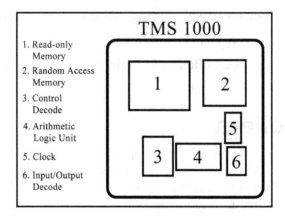

The size of the MCU die was roughly 5 x 5 millimeters, small enough to fit in a DIP package. This type of MCU used mask-programmable ROM, meaning that you could not get a blank TMS 1000 chip and program it. Instead, you would have to send the debugged program to Texas Instruments to have it physically produced using a photolithography mask, resulting in a metallic bridge for each bit.

Being a fairly primitive design (relative to later MCUs), it lacked a stack and interrupts, had a set of 43 instructions and two general-purpose registers, making it quite similar to the Intel 4004 CPU. Some models had special peripherals for driving **vacuum fluorescent displays** (VFD) and for continuously reading inputs to handle user input via a keyboard without interrupting the main program. Its basic pinout looked as follows:

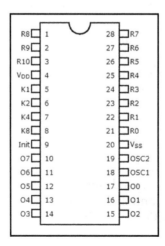

Obviously the pin functions predate the **general purpose input/output (GPIO)** pins we know today - the **K** pins can only be used for input, while output pins are denoted as **O** and control pins are marked with **R**. The **OSC** pins are to be connected to an external oscillator circuit. Much like with discrete logic ICs, the **Init** pin is used to initialize the chip on power-up and has to be kept high for at least six cycles, whereas recent MCUs have integrated Power-On Reset (POR) and a reset pin that needs at most a discrete resistor and capacitor.

According to the original Texas Instruments press release from 1974, these microcontroller could be had for as little as $3 or less if you bought them in large quantity. They would be used in popular toys such as the Speak and Spell, but also just about everywhere else, including household appliances, automobiles, and scientific equipment. By the time production ceased in the early 1980s, many millions had been sold.

It's also interesting to note that while one-time programmable low cost microcontrollers have gone down in price a lot, the class of products has persevered - as an example, the Padauk PMS150C can now be had for $0.03 and whilst offering an 8 bit architecture, its 1K words of ROM and 64 bytes of RAM sound oddly familiar.

Intel MCS-48

Intel's response to Texas Instrument's successful TMS 1000 MCU was the MCS-48 series, with the 8048, 8035, and 8748 being the first models released in 1976. The 8048 has 1 KB of ROM and 64 bytes of RAM. It is an 8-bit design with a Harvard architecture (split code/data memory), introducing a native word size of 8 bits and interrupt support (two single-level) and is compatible with 8080/8085 peripherals, making it a highly versatile MCU. The advantage of wider ALU and register word sizes is still perceivable today, where for example a 32 bit addition is sequentially executed on an 8 bit MCU as a series of 8 bit additions with carry.

The MCS-48 features over 96 instructions, most of them a single byte in length, and allows for external memory to be added in addition to the internal memory. In a community effort, available information on the MCS-48 family has been compiled and released at https://devsaurus.github.io/mcs-48/mcs-48.pdf .

Here we consider the simplicity of the MCS-48 functional block diagram and compare it to that of its successors as follows:

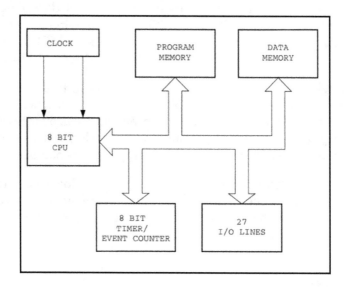

Even for a design that was introduced just a few years after the TMS 1000, the rapid evolution of MCU designs is evident. Since MCU design evolved alongside popular CPU designs of the time, including the 6502, its 16-bit version, and what would eventually become the M68K processor family, there are many similarities to be found.

Due to its flexible design, it remained popular and in production until the 1990s, until the MCS-51 (8051) series gradually replaced it. See the next section for more details on the 8051.

The MCS-48 was used in the keyboard of the original IBM PC as its controller. It was also used with the 80286 and 80386 to perform A20 line gating and reset functions in the case of the former. Later PCs would integrate these features into Super I/O devices.

Other notable uses of the MCS-48 include the Magnavox Odyssey video game console and a range of Korg and Roland analog synthesizers. While masked ROM (up to 2 KB) was an option with the MCS-48 family, the 87P50 used an external ROM module for its programming, and the 8748 and 8749 featured up to 2 KB EPROM, which allowed for the MCU's internal programming to be altered repeatedly.

Like with standalone EPROM modules, this requires the package to contain a fused quartz window, which allows for ultraviolet light to reach the MCU die, as can clearly be seen in the following photograph of an 8749 MCU with EPROM (by Konstantin Lanzet, CC BY-SA 3.0):

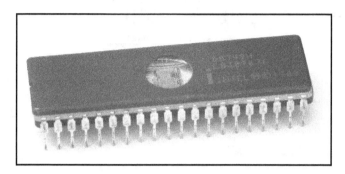

The charge stored in the EPROM cells that defines bits as written dissipates within a 20-30 minute exposure to strong ultraviolet light. The same can be achieved in direct sunlight over the course of a few weeks. The erase cycle usually implies removing the package and putting it in the light tight erasing device. After this, the EPROM can be programmed anew. The specified data retention of an EPROM is about 10-20 years at 85°C, and because the degradation accelerates exponentially with temperature, statements of 100 years or more at room temperature are not uncommon (27C512A: 200 years).

Due to the expense of creating the quartz window and integrating it into the package, one-time programmable EPROMs were used for a while, which allow for the easy programming of an EPROM, but mounted the programmed die in an opaque package so that it could not be reprogrammed any more. Ultimately, EEPROMs became available in the early 1980s, which replaced EPROMs almost completely. EEPROMs can be rewritten about a million times before they begin to develop issues when retaining stored data. Their data retention performance is similar to that of EPROMs.

Intel MCS-51

Recent chips from Cypress CY7C68013A (USB peripheral controller) to Ti CC2541 (a Bluetooth SoC) feature commodity 8051 cores, demonstrating that the Intel MCS-51 family design remains popular to this day. There's a plethora of derived MCUs by other manufacturers as well, even though Intel stopped producing this series of MCUs in March of 2007. First introduced in the 1980s, it's an 8-bit MCU like the 8048, but expands heavily on its feature set.

The functional block diagram as depicted in the Intel 80xxAH datasheet is shown as follows:

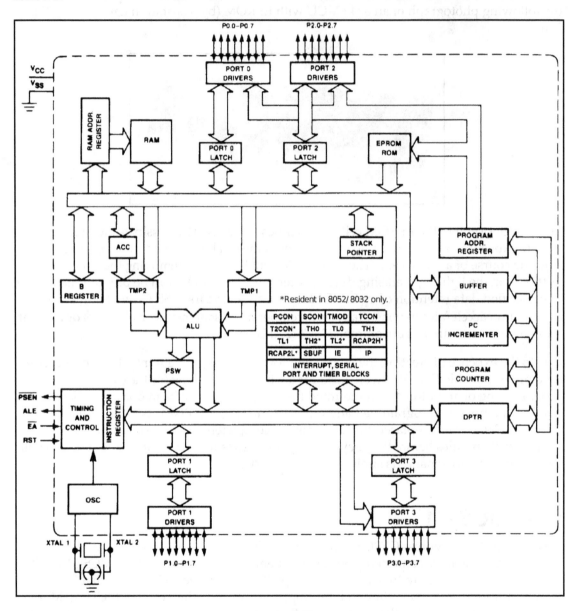

It's very similar to the Atmel (now microchip) AT89S51 which is still in production today.

Datasheets commonly address size and performance metrics in a *Features* list, as quoted below for the AT89S51:

- 4K Bytes of **in-system programmable (ISP)** flash memory
  - Endurance: 10,000 write/erase cycles (was 1,000,000 for EEPROM)
- 4.0 V to 5.5 V operating range
- Fully static operation: 0 Hz to 33 MHz (was 12 MHz)
- Three-level program memory lock
- 128 x 8-bit internal RAM
- 32 programmable I/O lines

but then the list goes on with modern core, peripheral, low power and usability features:

- Two 16-bit timer/counters
- Six interrupt sources
- Full duplex UART serial channel
- Low-power Idle and power-down modes
- Interrupt recovery from power-down mode
- Watchdog timer
- Dual data pointer
- Power-off flag
- Fast programming time
- Flexible ISP programming, byte- and page-mode

The only major changes to the 8051 architecture over the past decades involved migrating from the original **n-type metal oxide semiconductor (NMOS)** transistor technology to **complementary MOS (CMOS)** – usually denoted as 80C51 – and more recently the addition of USB, I2C, and SPI interfaces, as well as advanced power management and debugging interfaces that have become ubiquitous since the beginning of this century. The Atmel application note 3487A doesn't give a concise explanation for the letter S, however the then new in-circuit serial programming (ISP) might thereby be highlighted.

The pinout diagram of the AT89S51 documents the SPI pins (**MOSI, MISO, SCK**):

```
                        PDIP

              P1.0 □ 1          40 □ VCC
              P1.1 □ 2          39 □ P0.0 (AD0)
              P1.2 □ 3          38 □ P0.1 (AD1)
              P1.3 □ 4          37 □ P0.2 (AD2)
              P1.4 □ 5          36 □ P0.3 (AD3)
       (MOSI) P1.5 □ 6          35 □ P0.4 (AD4)
       (MISO) P1.6 □ 7          34 □ P0.5 (AD5)
        (SCK) P1.7 □ 8          33 □ P0.6 (AD6)
               RST □ 9          32 □ P0.7 (AD7)
        (RXD) P3.0 □ 10         31 □ EA/VPP
        (TXD) P3.1 □ 11         30 □ ALE/PROG
       (INT0) P3.2 □ 12         29 □ PSEN
       (INT1) P3.3 □ 13         28 □ P2.7 (A15)
         (T0) P3.4 □ 14         27 □ P2.6 (A14)
         (T1) P3.5 □ 15         26 □ P2.5 (A13)
         (WR) P3.6 □ 16         25 □ P2.4 (A12)
         (RD) P3.7 □ 17         24 □ P2.3 (A11)
             XTAL2 □ 18         23 □ P2.2 (A10)
             XTAL1 □ 19         22 □ P2.1 (A9)
               GND □ 20         21 □ P2.0 (A8)
```

Beyond standalone MCUs, 8051 cores are also integrated into larger systems where a low-power, basic MCU is dedicated to diverse, low speed, real-time or high I/O count tasks. A broad range of chips from the likes of Ti CC2541 (Bluetooth low energy SoC) to Cypress CY7C68013A (FX2LP™ USB peripheral controller) underline the utility and relevance of the 8051 architecture to this day.

In **field-programmable gate array (FPGA)** or **application specific integration circuit (ASIC)** development, 8051-type processors are also commonly deployed as soft cores, where they are adapted and added to VHDL and Verilog HDL projects to handle tasks that lend themselves better to sequential execution without the need for tight timing or large bandwidth. Last but not least, the charm of soft cores lies in the ability to use full-featured development and debugging tools while maintaining tight integration with the remaining hardware design. The equivalent of only a few hundred bytes of program code run by a soft core might well be a large state machine, memories, counters and ALU-like logic, all of which raises the question which implementation is easier to validate and maintain.

PIC

The PIC family of MCUs was first introduced in 1976 by General Instrument, using their new CP1600 16-bit CPU. This CPU was nearly compatible with the PDP-11 series of processors with its instruction set.

In 1987, General Instrument spun off its microelectronics division to create Microchip Technology, which became an independent company in 1989. Microchip technology produces new PIC designs to this day. Alongside the evolution of PIC cores and peripherals, on-chip memory technology development yielded the introduction of light tight encapsulated EPROM for on-time programmable and later EEPROM for in-circuit reprogramming capabilities. Like most MCUs, PIC MCUs have a Harvard architecture. Today, PIC designs range from 8-bit to 32-bit, with a wide range of features. These are the PIC families as the time of writing this book:

Family	Pins	Memories	Details
PIC10	6-8	384-896 bytes ROM, 64-512 bytes RAM	8-bit, 8-16 MHz, modified Harvard
PIC12	8	2-16 KB ROM, 256 bytes RAM	8-bit, 16 MHz, modified Harvard
PIC16	8-64	3.5-56 KB ROM, 1-4 KB RAM	8-bit modified Harvard
PIC17	40-68	4-16 KB ROM, 232-454 bytes RAM	8-bit, 33 MHz, superseded by the PIC18, though third-party clones exist.
PIC18	28-100	16-128 KB ROM, 3,728-4,096 bytes RAM	8-bit modified Harvard
PIC24 (dsPIC)	14-144	64-1,024KB ROM, 8-16 KB RAM	16-bit, DsPIC (dsPIC33) MCUs have digital signal processing (DSP) peripherals built in.
PIC32MX	64-100	32-512 KB ROM, 8-32 KB RAM	32-bit, 200 MHz MIPS M4K with MIPS16e mode, released in 2007.
PIC32MZ EC PIC32MZ EF PIC32MZ DA	64-288	512-2,048 KB ROM, 256-640 KB static RAM (32 MB DDR2 DRAM)	32-bit, MIPS ISA (2013), PIC32MZ DA version (2017) having a graphics core. Core speeds of 200 MHz (EC, DA) and 252 MHz (EF).
PIC32MM	20-64	16-256 KB RAM, 4-32 KB RAM	32-bit microMIPS, 25 MHz, variant optimized for low cost and low power.
PIC32MK	64-100	512-1,024 KB ROM, 128-256 KB RAM	32-bit, 120 MHz, MIPS ISA, variant introduced in 2017. Targeted at industrial control and other forms of deeply integrated applications.

The PIC32 families are interesting in that they're based on an MIPS processor core, and use this **Instruction Set Architecture (ISA)** instead of the PIC ISA that's used by all other PIC MCUs. The processor core design they share is the M4K, a 32-bit MIPS32 core from MIPS Technology. Between these families, the differences are easy to spot when looking at the block diagrams from their respective datasheets.

The decades of development in the PIC line of microcontrollers are perhaps best made tangible in the form of functional block diagrams, so we start by looking at the PIC10:

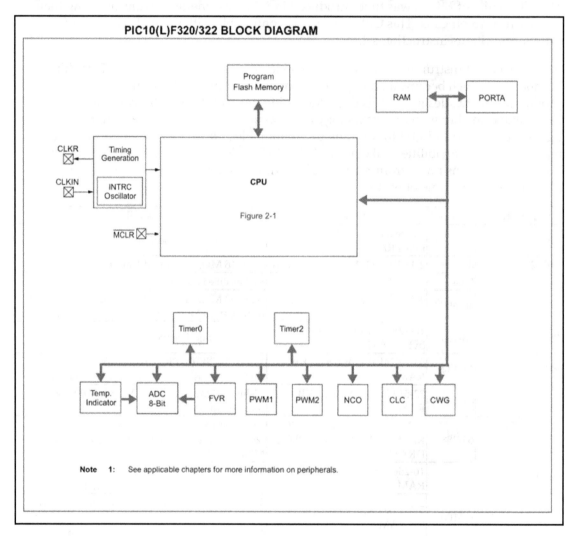

These are very small MCUs, with barely any peripherals around a processor core not more closely defined here—and the referenced table only mentions the memory layout. The I/O port is very minimal and the I2C and UART interfaces we know today are not implemented as peripheral logic. To pick an example for a controller next in line, the PIC16F84 datasheet is very detailed in terms of processor architecture and shows that more power-up and reset circuitry has been added while also expanding GPIO and adding EEPROM for easy integrated non-volatile storage. Self-contained serial peripherals are still absent.

Next, we'll have a look at the PIC18:

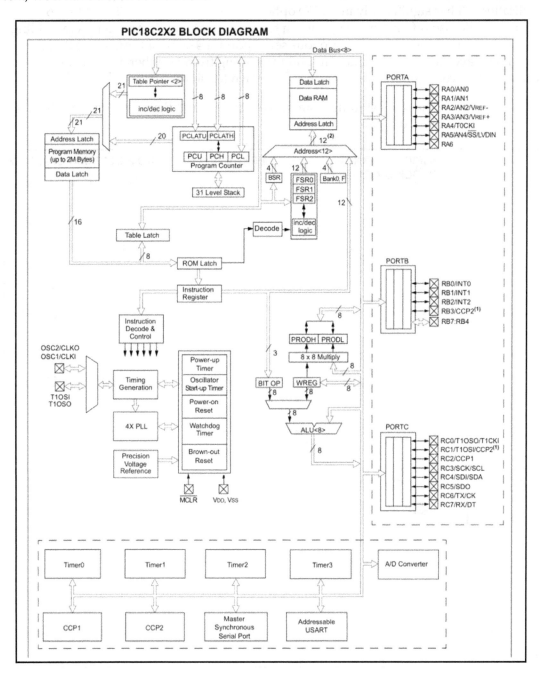

The PIC18 family is the latest 8-bit PIC architecture, with MCUs covering a wide range of applications. It has significantly more I/O options than the PIC10, PIC12, and PIC16 families, while also offering more options in terms of ROM and RAM and now providing USART in conjunction with a synchronous serial port for 4-wire SPI. Also note that the ports now have alternate pin functions and the routing from peripherals to the pins and the corresponding configuration registers are not shown for simplicity.

Next, let's observe the focus shifting from the core to Port and Peripheral capabilities in the PIC24 functional block diagram:

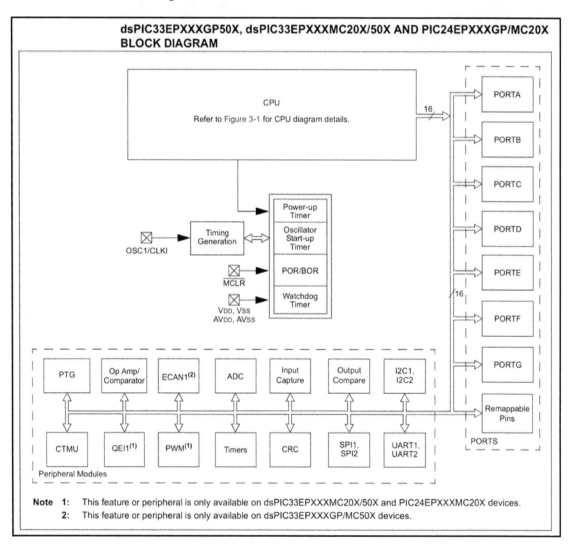

The diagram is similar to that of the PIC10, with the CPU abstracted away as a single block relative to the rest of the MCU. Each of the `PORT` blocks being a set of I/O pins, we're running out of space to display all the possible pin functions.

Each I/O pin can have a fixed function (linked with a peripheral module), or have an assignable function (hardware-level rerouting, or done in software). Generally, the more complex the MCU, the more likely it is that I/O pins are generic and not fixed-function.

Finally we have look at the PIC32:

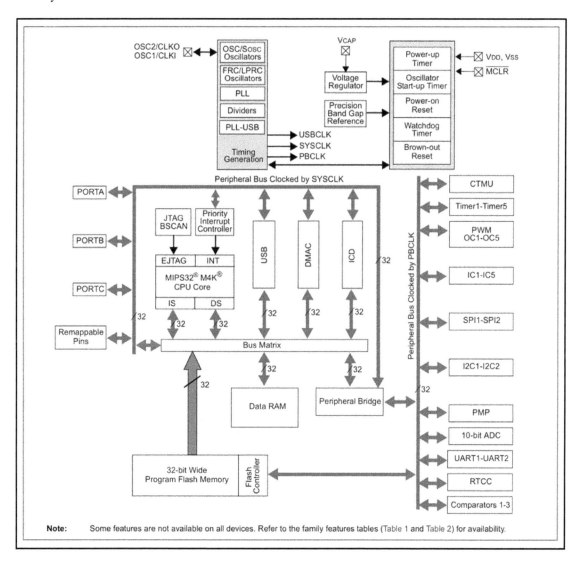

This block diagram is for PIC32MX1XX/2XX devices in the PIC32MX family. It is usually clocked at 50 MHz.

An interesting property of the PIC32 architecture is that it effectively turns the Harvard architecture M4K MIPS CPU into a more John von Neumann-like architecture by having both program instructions and data travel over the System Bus Matrix. Note that the space dedicated to a single processor register in the PIC10 diagram now casually depicts a complex digital or mixed signal peripheral, or the powerful JTAG in-circuit programming and debugging interface.

AVR

The AVR architecture was developed by two students at the Norwegian Institute of Technology, with the original AVR MCU developed at Nordic VLSI (now Nordic Semiconductor). It was originally known as μRISC and available for licensing until the technology was sold to Atmel. The first Atmel AVR MCU was released in 1997.

Today, we can look back on a multitude of 8-bit AVR families:

Family	Pins	Memories	Details
ATtiny	6-32	0.5-16KB ROM 0-2 KB RAM	1.6-20 MHz. Compact, power-efficient MCUs, with limited peripherals.
ATmega	32-100	4-256 KB ROM 0.5-32 KB RAM	
ATxmega	44-100	16-384 KB ROM, 1-32 KB RAM	32 MHz, largest AVR MCUs, with extensive peripherals and performance-enhancing features such as DMA.

There also used to be an 32-bit AVR32 architecture, but it was deprecated by Atmel as it moved to the ARM 32-bit architecture instead (SAM). See the *ARM-based MCU* section for more details on SAM. More detailed information is found in the corresponding `Product Selection Guide`.

Additionally, Atmel used to have so-called **Field Programmable System Level Integrated Circuit (FPSLIC)** MCUs: hybrid AVR/FPGA systems. These essentially allowed you to add your own peripherals and functionality to the hardware of an AVR MCU.

Let's look at the ATtiny family. This is the block diagram of the ATtiny212/412 series of MCUs:

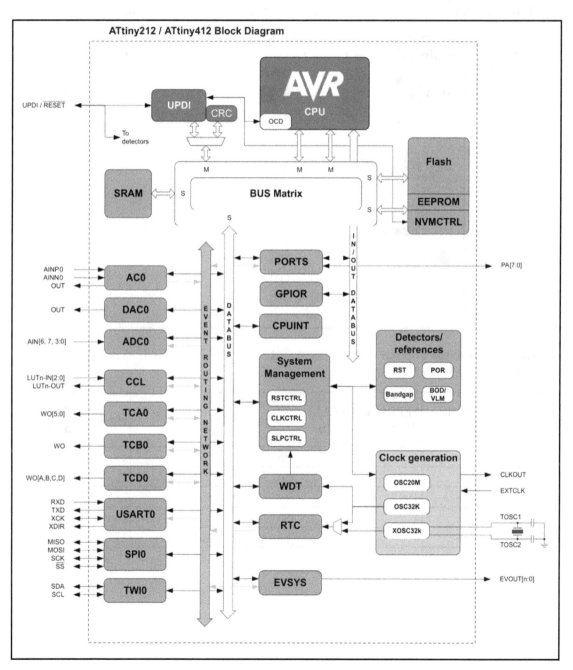

This series of ATtiny MCUs can run up to 20 MHz, with up to 4 KB of Flash ROM and 256 bytes of SRAM, as well as up to 128 bytes of EEPROM, all in an 8-pin package. Despite its small size, it has a large number of peripherals, which can be routed to any supported pin:

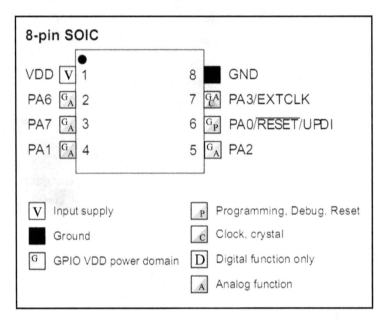

Contrast this with the popular ATmega2560 and related MCUs, which have the following properties:

Device	Flash (KB)	EEPROM (KB)	RAM (KB)	General purpose I/O pins	16-bit PWM channels	UART	ADC channels
ATmega640	64	4	8	86	12	4	16
ATmega1280	128	4	8	86	12	4	16
ATmega1281	128	4	8	54	6	2	8
ATmega2560	256	4	8	86	12	4	16
ATmega2561	256	4	8	54	6	2	8

With GPIO pins numbering in the dozens, the block diagram is correspondingly more complex, with many more port blocks for the I/O pins:

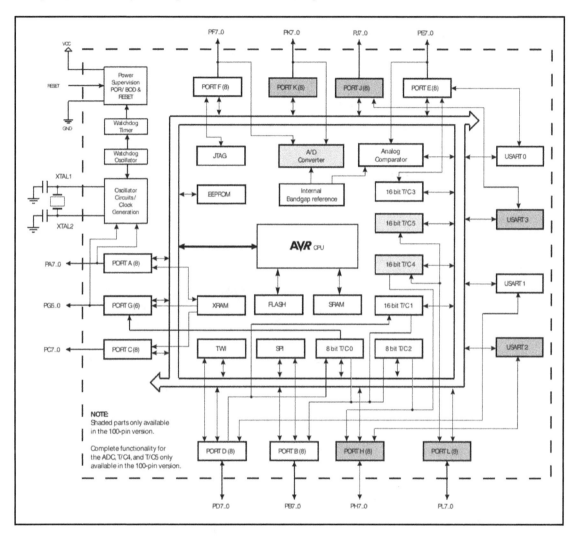

Here, all the incoming and outgoing arrows indicate a single pin or block of pins, most of them general-purpose. Because of the large number of pins, it is no longer practical to use an inline package format (DIP, SOIC, and so on) for the physical chip.

For the ATmega640, 1280 and 2560, a 100-pin TQFP package is used, here with the functionality of each pin indicated as found in its datasheet:

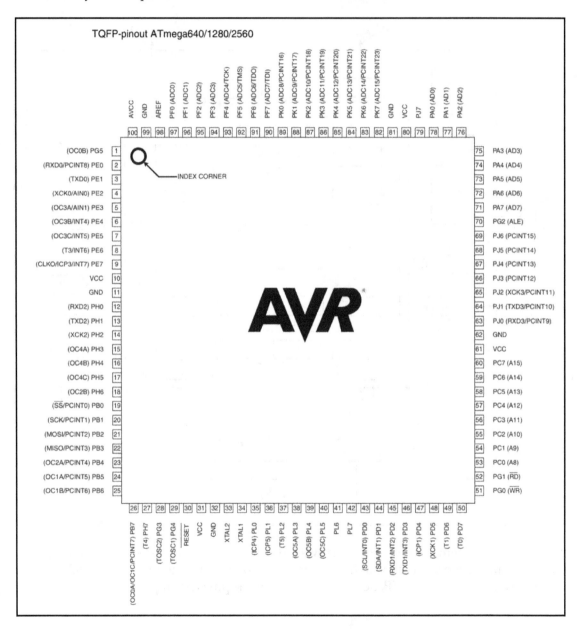

The ATxmega family is very similar to the ATmega, with a similar pinout, mostly differentiating themselves using architectural changes and optimizations, more ROM and RAM, and peripheral options.

Whether to pick an ATtiny, ATmega, or ATxmega MCU depends first and foremost on the requirements you have for your project, specifically the required input and output, types of peripherals (serial, SPI, I2C, CAN, and so on), and the size of both the code and the RAM required to run this code.

M68k and Z80-based

The Zilog Z80 8-bit processor is an Intel 8080-compatible processor, which competed with other microprocessors during the 1980s, powering home computers and gaming systems including the Nintendo Game Boy, Sega Master System, Sinclair ZX80/ZX81/Spectrum, MSX, and Tandy TRS-80.

Zilog introduced an MCU (Z380) based around the Z80 microprocessor in 1994, with various updates over the years, including the Z8, eZ80, and others. Z80 clones are also quite common.

Another popular 1980s era microprocessor is the Motorola 68k (or 68000). It's 16-bit for its ALU and external data bus, but with 32-bit registers and 32-bit internal data bus. After its introduction in 1979, its architecture is still in use today, with Freescale Semiconductor (now NXP) producing a number of 68k microprocessors.

Motorola introduced numerous MCUs based around the 68k architecture, including the MC68320 communications controller in 1989. Current 68k-based MCU designs include the ColdFire, which is a fully 32-bit design.

ARM Cortex-M

A very common type of 32-bit MCU is the ARM Cortex-M family. It includes the M0, M0+, M1, M3, M4, M7, M23, and M33, with a number of them having a **floating point unit** (**FPU**) option for increased floating point performance.

Not only are they used as standalone MCUs, they are also commonly integrated into **System-on-Chip** (**SoC**) devices to provide specific functionality, such as touchscreen, sensor, or power management functionality. As Arm Holdings doesn't manufacture any MCUs themselves, many third-party manufacturers have licensed the designs, sometimes making their own modifications and improvements.

Here is a brief overview of these MCUs:

Core	Announced	Architecture	Instruction set
M0	2009	Armv6-M	Thumb-1, some of Thumb-2.
M0+	2012	Armv6-M	Thumb-1, some of Thumb-2.
M1	2007	Armv6-M	Thumb-1, some of Thumb-2.
M3	2004	Armv7-M	Thumb-1, Thumb-2.
M4	2010	Armv7-M	Thumb1, Thumb-2, optional FPU.
M7	2014	Armv7E-M	Thumb-1, Thumb-2, optional FPU.
M23	2016	Armv8-M	Thumb-1, some of Thumb-2.
M33	2016	Armv8-M	Thumb 1, Thumb-2, optional FPU.

The **Thumb** instruction sets are compact, 16-bit-length instructions, making them ideal for embedded, resource-restricted systems. Other ARM microprocessor families can also support this Thumb instruction set in addition to the 32-bit instruction set.

H8 (SuperH)

H8 family MCUs were commonly used with 8-, 16-, and 32-bit variations. Originally created in the early 1990s by Hitachi, new designs were still being created by Renesas Technology until a few years ago, though the latter recommends new designs use the RX (32-bit) or RL78 (16-bit) families. A notable use of an H8 MCU is in the Lego Mindstorms RCX controller, which uses an H8/300 MCU.

ESP8266/ESP32

The ESP family are 32-bit MCUs that are produced by Espressif Systems, with integrated Wi-Fi (both) and Bluetooth (ESP32) functionality.

The ESP8266 first appeared in 2014, when it was sold by a third-party manufacturer, Ai-Thinker, in the form of a module (ESP-01) that could be used by another MCU or microprocessor-based systems to provide Wi-Fi functionality. The ESP-01 module contained firmware for this purpose, which allowed the module to be addressed using Hayes-style modem commands.

Its system specifications are as follows:

- Tensilica Xtensa Diamond Standard L106 microprocessor (32-bit)
- 80-160 MHz CPU speed
- Less than 50 KB of RAM available for user applications (with Wi-Fi stack loaded)
- External SPI ROM (512 KB to 16 MB)
- Wi-Fi support for 802.11 b/g/n

As the 32-bit MCU on the ESP-01 module was found to be capable of far more than the simple modem task assigned to it, it soon came to be used for more general-purpose tasks, with a range of upgraded ESP8266 modules (with integrated EEPROM chip), as well as breakout boards. Of the latter, the NodeMCU-style board has become very popular, though a number of other third-party manufacturers have made their own breakout boards, which provide different form factors and functionality.

The basic block diagram for the ESP8266EX looks as follows:

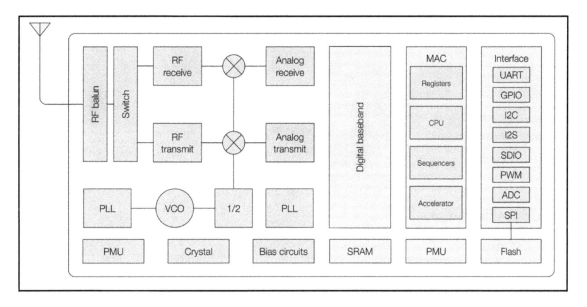

After the immense success of the ESP8266, Espressif Systems developed the ESP32, which used an upgraded, dual-core CPU, among other changes. Its block diagram looks like this:

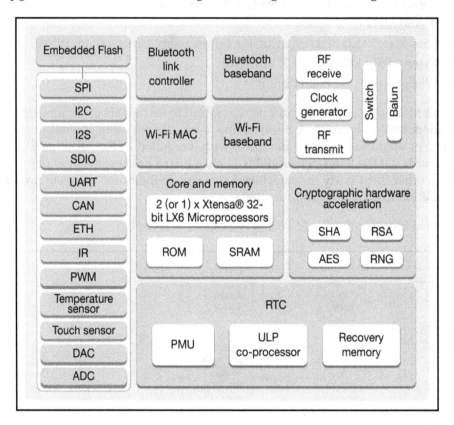

Its specifications are as follows:

- Xtensa 32-bit LX6 (dual-core) microprocessor
- 160-240 MHz CPU speed
- 520 KB of SRAM
- Wi-Fi support for 802.11 b/g/n
- Bluetooth v4.2 and BLE (low energy)

Both the ESP8266 and ESP32 are generally sold as complete modules, with the MCU, external ROM module, and a Wi-Fi antenna either integrated into the board or with an external antenna option:

The metal shielding can covering the board helps to protect the board from electromagnetic interference, benefiting its Wi-Fi (and Bluetooth, in the case of the ESP32) transceiver, but the whole design with a fixed antenna and geometry is required for FCC certification and later use as an approved module. Connecting an external antenna with higher gain may violate local regulations. The FCC ID it comes with is instrumental in getting a product containing such a module approved for commercialization.

Others

In addition to the previously listed MCUs, there is a wide range of MCUs available from a number of manufacturers with different architectures. Some, like the Propeller MCU from Parallax with its multi-core architecture, are fairly unique, whereas most simply implement the usual single-core CPU architecture with a number of peripherals, RAM, and internal or external ROM.

Beyond physical chips, Altera (now Intel), Lattice Semiconductor, and Xilinx provide so-called soft cores, which are MCUs that are meant to be run on a FPGA chip, either as standalone components or as part of a larger design on that FPGA. These can also be targeted by C/C++ compilers.

Challenges

The main development challenges with MCUs lie in the relatively limited resources that are available. Especially with the small, low-pin-count MCUs, you have to have a good idea of how many resources (CPU cycles, RAM, and ROM) a particular piece of code takes up, and whether it's realistic to add a specific feature.

This also means that picking the right MCU for a particular project takes both technical knowledge and experience. The former is required to pick an MCU that will suit the task; the latter is very helpful for the optimal MCU and helps to shorten the time that's required to make a choice.

System-on-Chip/Single Board Computer

Systems-on-Chips (**SoCs**) are similar to MCUs, but distinguish themselves from those types of embedded systems by having some level of integration while still requiring a number of external components to function. They are commonly found as part of a single board implementation (**Single Board Computer** (**SBC**)), including the PC/104 standard, and more recently form factors such as the Raspberry Pi and derivative boards:

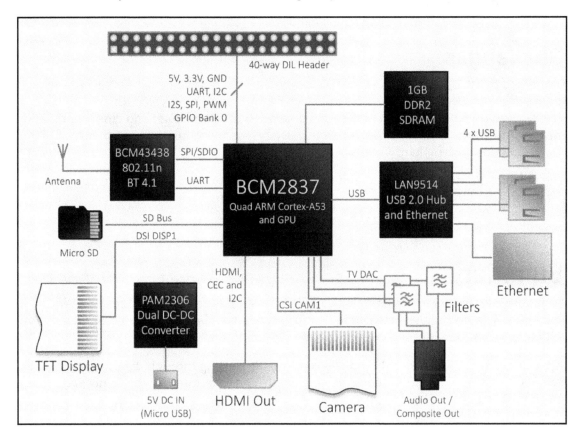

This diagram was used from `https://xdevs.com/article/rpi3_oc/`. It clearly shows how an SBC (in this case, the Raspberry Pi 3) is laid out. The BCM2837 is the ARM-based SoC, providing the CPU core and basic peripherals (mostly broken out into the header section). All of the RAM is in an external module, as are the Ethernet and Wi-Fi peripherals. ROM is provided in the form of an SD (Flash) card, which also provides storage.

Most SoCs are ARM-based (Cortex-A family), though MIPS is quite common as well. SBCs are commonly used in industrial settings.

Other instances are mass produced boards, such as those for smartphones, which do not form a predefined form factor, but still follow the same pattern of having the SoC and external RAM, ROM, and storage, as well as various peripherals. This is in contrast with the MCUs of the previous section, which would always be able to function by themselves, except for the few requiring an external ROM.

Challenges

Compared to MCUs, the development challenges of SoCs tend to be far less severe. Some of them are on the level and have an interface where you can even develop directly on the device, even doing compilation cycles on the device without having to do cross-compilation on a PC and copying over the binary. This is also helped by running a full OS instead of developing for the bare hardware.

The obvious disadvantage is that with this increase in features comes an increase in complexity, and the resulting complications, such as having to deal with user accounts, setting permissions, managing device drivers, and so on.

Summary

In this chapter, we got an in-depth look at what constitutes an embedded system. We learned how to distinguish between the various types of embedded systems, as well as how to determine the basics of picking the right MCU or SoC for a project.

After this chapter, the reader should feel comfortable reading through datasheets for MCUs and SoCs, explaining the differences between both, and determining what is needed for a given project.

The next chapter will look at why C++ is a highly suitable choice for the programming of embedded systems.

2
C++ as an Embedded Language

When it comes to embedded development on resource-restricted systems, it is still common to consider only C and ASM as viable choices, accompanied by the thought that C++ has a larger footprint than C, or adds a significant amount of complexity. In this chapter, we will look at all of these issues in detail and consider the merits of C++ as an embedded programming language:

- C++ relative to C
- Advantages of C++ as a multi-paradigm language
- Compatibility with existing C and ASM
- Changes with C++11, C++14, and C++17

C++ relative to C

The lineages of C and C++ both trace their lineage back to the ALGOL programming language, which saw its first version in 1958 (ALGOL 58), followed by updates in 1960 and 1968. ALGOL introduced the concept of imperative programming—a programming style in which statements explicitly tell the machine how to make changes to data for output and control flow.

A paradigm that emerges rather naturally from imperative programming is the use of procedures. We will start with an example, to introduce the terminology. Procedures are synonymous to sub-routines and functions. They identify the groups of statements and make them self-contained, which has the effects of confining the reach of these statements to the limited scope of the section they are contained within, creating hierarchy and consequentially introducing these procedures as new, more abstract statements. Heavy use of this procedural programming style finds its place in so-called structured programming, alongside loop and branching control structures.

Over time, structured and modular programming styles were introduced as techniques to improve the development, quality and maintainability of application code. The C language is an imperative, structured programming language due to its use of statements, control structures and functions.

Take, for example, the standard Hello World example in C:

```
#include <stdio.h>
int main(void)
{
    printf("hello, world");
    return 0;
}
```

The entry point of any C (and C++) application is the `main()` function (procedure). In the first statement line of this function, we call another procedure (`printf()`), which contains its own statements and possibly calls other blocks of statements in the form of additional functions.

This way we have already made use of procedural programming by implementing a `main()` logical block (the `main()` function), which is called as needed. While the `main()` function will just be called once, the procedural style is found again in the `printf()` statement, which calls the statements elsewhere in the application without having to copy them explicitly. Applying procedural programming makes it much easier to maintain the resulting code, and create libraries of code that we can use across a number of applications, while maintaining only a single code base.

In 1979, Bjarne Stroustrup started work on *C with Classes*, for which he took the existing programming paradigms of C and added elements from other languages, in particular Simula (object-oriented programming: both imperative and structured) and ML (generic programming, in the form of templates). It would also offer the speed of the **Basic Combined Programming Language** (BCPL), without restricting the developer to its restrictive low-level focus.

The resulting multi-paradigm language was renamed to **C++** in 1983, while adding additional features not found in C, including operator and function overloading, virtual functions, references, and starting the development of a standalone compiler for this C++ language.

The essential goal of C++ has remained to provide practical solutions to real-world issues. Additionally, it has always been the intention for C++ to be a better C, hence the name. Stroustrup himself defines a number of rules (as noted in *Evolving C++ 1991-2006*) that drive the development of C++ to this day, including the following:

- C++'s evolution must be driven by real problems
- Every feature must have a reasonably obvious implementation
- C++ is a language, not a complete system
- Don't try to force people to use a specific programming style
- No implicit violations of the static type system
- Provide as good support for user-defined types as for built-in types
- Leave no room for a lower-level language below C++ (except assembler)
- What you don't use, you don't pay for (zero-overhead rule)
- If in doubt, provide means for manual control

The differences relative to C obviously goes beyond object-oriented programming. Despite the lingering impression that C++ is just a set of extensions to C, it has for a long time been its own language, adding a strict type system (compared to C's weak type system at that time), more powerful programming paradigms, and features not found in C. Its compatibility with C can therefore be seen more as coincidence, with C being the right language at the right time to be used as a foundation.

The problem with Simula at the time was that it was too slow for general use, and BCPL was too low-level. C, being a relatively new language at the time, provided the right middle ground between features and performance.

C++ as an embedded language

Around 1983 when C++ had just been conceived and got its name, popular personal computer systems for a general audience, as well as businesses, had specifications like ones listed in the following table:

System	CPU	Clock speed (MHz)	RAM (KB)	ROM (KB)	Storage (KB)
BBC Micro	6502 (B+ 6512A)	2	16-128	32-128	Max 1,280 (ADFS floppy) Max 20 MB (hard drive)
MSX	Zilog Z80	3.58	8-128	32	720 (floppy)
Commodore 64	6510	~1	64	20	1,000 (tape) 170 (floppy)
Sinclair ZX81	Zilog Z80	3.58	1	8	15 (cartridge)
IBM PC	Intel 8080	4.77	16-256	8	360 (floppy)

Now compare these computer systems to a recent 8-bit **microcontroller** (**MCU**) such as the AVR ATMega 2560 with the following specifications:

- 16 MHz clock speed
- 8 KB RAM
- 256 KB ROM (program)
- 4 KB ROM (data)

The ATMega 2560 was launched in 2005 and is among the more powerful 8-bit MCUs available nowadays. Its features stack up favorably against the 1980s computer systems, but on top of that the MCU does not rely on any external memory components.

The MCU core clock speed is significantly faster these days thanks to improved silicon IC manufacturing processes which also provide smaller chip sizes, high throughput, and thus lower cost and what's more, 1980s architectures commonly took 2 to 5 clock cycles to retrieve, decode, execute an instruction and store the result as opposed to the single-cycle execution performance of the AVR.

Current MCU (Static) RAM limitations are mostly due to cost and power constraints yet can be easily circumvented for most MCUs using external RAM chips, along with adding low-cost flash-based or other mass storage devices.

Systems like the **Commodore 64 (C64)** were routinely programmed in C, in addition to the built-in BASIC interpreter (in a built-in ROM). A well-known C development environment for the Commodore 64 was Power C published by Spinnaker:

Power C was one brand of productivity software aimed at C developers. It came on a single, double-sided floppy disk and allowed you to write C code in an editor, then compile it with the included compiler, linker, header files, and libraries to produce executables for the system.

Many more of such compiler collections existed back then, targeting a variety of systems, showing the rich ecosystem that existed for software development. Among these, C++ was of course a newcomer. The first edition of Stroustrup's *The C++ Programming Language* was only being published in 1985, yet initially without a solid implementation of the language to go with it.

Commercial support for C++ however began to appear rapidly, with major development environments such as Borland C++ 1.0 being released in 1987 and updated to 2.0 in 1991. Development environments like these got used in particular on the IBM PC and its myriad of clones where no preferred development language such as BASIC existed.

While C++ began its life as an unofficial standard in 1985, it wasn't until 1989 and the release of the *The C++ Programming Language* in its second edition as an authoritative work that C++ reached roughly the level of features equal to what would first be then standardized by an ISO working group as ISO/IEC 14882:1998, commonly known as C++98. Still it can be said that C++ saw significant development and adoption before the advent of the Motorola 68040 in 1990 and Intel 486DX in 1992, which bumped processing power above the 20 MIPS mark.

Now that we have considered early hardware specifications and the evolution of C++ alongside C and other languages of the time intended to be used on the relatively limited systems that existed back then, it seems plausible that C++ is more than capable of running on such hardware, and by extension on modern-day microcontrollers. However, it also seems necessary to ask to what extent the complexity added to C++ since then has impacted memory or computing performance requirements.

C++ language features

We previously took a look at the explicit nature of changes to data and system state that defines imperative programming as opposed to declarative programming, where instead of manipulating data in a loop such functionality could be declared as mapping an operator to some data, thus spelling out the functionality, not the specific order of operations. But why should programming languages necessarily be a choice between imperative and declarative paradigms?

In fact, one of the main distinguishing features of C++ is its multi-paradigm nature making use of both imperative and declarative paradigms. With the inclusion of object-oriented, generic, and functional programming into C++ in addition to C's procedural programming, it would seem natural to assume that this would all have to come at a cost, whether in terms of higher CPU usage or more RAM and/or ROM consumed.

However, as we learned earlier in this chapter, C++ language features are ultimately built upon the C language, and as such there should in turn be little or no overhead relative to implementing a similar constructs in plain C. To resolve this conundrum and to investigate the validity of the low-overhead hypothesis, we'll now take a detailed look at a number of C++ language features, and how they are ultimately implemented, with their corresponding cost in binary and memory size.

Some of the examples that focus specifically on C++ as a low-level embedded language are taken with permission from Rud Merriam's Code Craft series, as published on Hackaday: `https://hackaday.io/project/8238-embedding-c`.

Namespaces

Namespaces are a way to introduce additional levels of scope into an application. As we saw in the earlier section on classes, these are a compiler-level concept.

The main use lies in modularizing code, dividing it into logical segments in cases where classes are not the most obvious solution, or where you want to explicitly sort classes into a particular category using a namespace. This way, you can also avoid name and type collisions between similarly named classes, types, and enumerations.

Strongly typed

Type information is necessary to test for proper access to and interpretation of data. A big feature in C++ that's relative to C is the inclusion of a strong type system. This means that many type checks performed by the compiler are significantly more strict than what would be allowed with C, which is a weakly typed language.

This is mostly apparent when looking at this legal C code, which will generate an error when compiled as C++:

```
void* pointer;
int* number = pointer;
```

Alternatively, they can also be written in the following way:

```
int* number = malloc(sizeof(int) * 5);
```

C++ forbids implicit casts, requiring these examples to be written as follows:

```
void* pointer;
int* number = (int*) pointer;
```

They can also be written in the following way:

```
int* number = (int*) malloc(sizeof(int) * 5);
```

As we explicitly specify the type we are casting to, we can rest assured that during compile time any type casts do what we expect them to do.

Similarly, the compiler will also complain and throw an error if we were to try to assign to a variable with a `const` qualifier from a reference without this qualifier:

```
const int constNumber = 42;
int number = &constNumber; // Error: invalid initialization of reference.
```

To work around this, you are required to explicitly cast the following conversion:

```
const int constNumber = 42;
int number = const_cast<int&>(constNumber);
```

Performing an explicit cast like this is definitely possible and valid. It may also cause immense issues and headaches later on when using this reference to modify the contents of the supposedly constant value. By the time you find yourself writing code like the preceding, however, it can reasonably be assumed that you are aware of the implications.

Such enforcement of explicit types has the significant benefit of making static analysis far more useful and effective than it is in a weakly typed language. This, in turn, benefits run-time safety, as any conversions and assignments are most likely to be safe and without unexpected side effects.

As a type system is predominantly a feature of the compiler rather than any kind of run-time code, with (optional) run-time type information as an exception. The overhead of having a strongly typed type system in C++ is noticed only at compile time, as more strict checks have to be performed on each variable assignment, operation, and conversion.

Type conversions

A type conversion occurs whenever a value is assigned to a compatible variable, which is not the exact same type as the value. Whenever a rule for conversion exists, this conversion can be done implicitly, otherwise an explicit hint (cast) can be provided to the compiler to invoke a specific rule where ambiguity exists.

Whereas C only has implicit and explicit type casting, C++ expands on this with a number of template-based functions, allowing you to cast both regular types and objects (classes) in a variety of ways:

- `dynamic_cast` `<new_type>` (expression)
- `reinterpret_cast` `<new_type>` (expression)
- `static_cast` `<new_type>` (expression)
- `const_cast` `<new_type>` (expression)

Here, `dynamic_cast` guarantees that the resulting object is valid, relying on **runtime type information (RTTI)** (see the later section on it) for this. A `static_cast` is similar, but does not validate the resulting object.

Next, `reinterpret_cast` can cast anything to anything, even unrelated classes. Whether this conversion makes sense is left to the developer, much like with a regular explicit conversion.

Finally, a `const_cast` is interesting in that it either sets or removes the `const` status of a value, which can be useful when you need a non-`const` version of a value for just one function. This does, however, also circumvent the type safety system and should be used very cautiously.

Classes

Object-oriented programming (OOP) has been around since the days of Simula, which was known for being a slow language. This led Bjarne Stroustrup to base his OOP implementation on the fast and efficient C programming language.

C++ uses C-style language constructs to implement objects. This becomes obvious when we take a look at C++ code and its corresponding C code.

When looking at a C++ class, we see its typical structure:

```cpp
namespace had {
using uint8_t = unsigned char;
const uint8_t bufferSize = 16;
    class RingBuffer {
        uint8_t data[bufferSize];
        uint8_t newest_index;
        uint8_t oldest_index;
        public:
        enum BufferStatus {
            OK, EMPTY, FULL
        };
        RingBuffer();
        BufferStatus bufferWrite(const uint8_t byte);
        enum BufferStatus bufferRead(uint8_t& byte);
    };
}
```

This class is also inside of a namespace (which we will look at in more detail in a later section), a redefinition of the `unsigned char` type, a namespace-global variable definition, and finally the class definition itself, including a private and public section.

This C++ code defines a number of different scopes, starting with the namespace and ending with the class. The class itself adds scopes in the sense of its public, protected, and private access levels.

The same code can be implemented in regular C as follows:

```c
typedef unsigned char uint8_t;
enum BufferStatus {BUFFER_OK, BUFFER_EMPTY, BUFFER_FULL};
#define BUFFER_SIZE 16
struct RingBuffer {
    uint8_t data[BUFFER_SIZE];
    uint8_t newest_index;
    uint8_t oldest_index;
};
void initBuffer(struct RingBuffer* buffer);
enum BufferStatus bufferWrite(struct RingBuffer* buffer, uint8_t byte);
enum BufferStatus bufferRead(struct RingBuffer* buffer, uint8_t *byte);
```

The `using` keyword is similar to `typedef`, making for a direct mapping there. We use a `const` instead of a `#define`. An `enum` is essentially the same between C and C++, only that C++'s compiler doesn't require the explicit marking of an `enum` when used as a type. The same is true for structs when it comes to simplifying the C++ code.

The C++ class itself is implemented in C as a `struct` containing the class variables. When the class instance is created, it essentially means that an instance of this `struct` is initialized. A pointer to this `struct` instance is then passed with each call of a function that is part of the C++ class.

What these basic examples show us is that there is no runtime overhead for any of the C++ features we used compared to the C-based code. The namespace, class access levels (public, private, and protected), and similar are only used by the compiler to validate the code that is being compiled.

A nice feature of the C++ code is that, despite the identical performance, it requires less code, while also allowing you to define strict interface access levels and have a destructor class method that gets called when the class is destroyed, allowing you to automatically clean up allocated resources.

Using the C++ class follows this pattern:

```
had::RingBuffer r_buffer;
int main() {
    uint8_t tempCharStorage;
    // Fill the buffer.
    for (int i = 0; r_buffer.bufferWrite('A' + i) ==
had::RingBuffer::OK; i++)     {
        //
    }
    // Read the buffer.
    while (r_buffer.bufferRead(tempCharStorage) == had::RingBuffer::OK)
    {
        //
    }
}
```

This compares to the C version like this:

```
struct RingBuffer buffer;
int main() {
    initBuffer(&buffer);
    uint8_t tempCharStorage;
    // Fill the buffer.
    uint8_t i = 0;
    for (; bufferWrite(&buffer, 'A' + i) == BUFFER_OK; i++) {
        //
    }
    // Read the buffer.
    while (bufferRead(&buffer, &tempCharStorage) == BUFFER_OK) { //
    }
}
```

Using the C++ class isn't very different from using the C-style method. Not having to do the manual passing of the allocated `struct` instance for each functional call, but instead calling a class method, is probably the biggest difference. This instance is still available in the form of the `this` pointer, which points to the class instance.

While the C++ example uses a namespace and embedded enumeration in the `RingBuffer` class, these are just optional features. One can still use global enumerations, or in the scope of a namespace, or have many layers of namespaces. This is very much determined by the requirements of the application.

As for the cost of using classes, versions of the examples in this section were compiled for the aforementioned Code Craft series for both the Arduino UNO (ATMega328 MCU) and Arduino Due (AT91SAM3X8E MCU) development boards, giving the following file sizes for the compiled code:

	Uno	Due		
C	C++	C	C++	
Global scope data	614	652	11,184	11,196
Main scope data	664	664	11,200	11,200
Four instances	638	676	11,224	11,228

Optimization settings for these code file sizes were set to −O2.

Here, we can see that C++ code is identical to C code once compiled, except when we perform initialization of the global class instance, on account of the added code to perform this initialization for us, amounting to 38 bytes for the Uno.

Since only one instance of this code has to exist, this is a constant cost we only have to pay once: in the first and last line, we have one and four class instances or their equivalent, respectively, yet there is only an additional 38 bytes in the Uno firmware. For the Due firmware, we can see something similar, though not as clearly defined. This difference is likely affected by some other settings or optimizations.

What this tells us is that sometimes we don't want to have the compiler initialize a class for us, but we should do it ourselves if we need those last few bytes of ROM or RAM. Most of the time this will not be an issue, however.

Inheritance

In addition to allowing you to organize code into objects, classes also allow for classes to serve as a template for other classes through the use of polymorphism. In C++, we can combine the properties of any number of classes into a new class, giving it custom properties and methods as well.

This is a very effective way to create **user-defined types** (**UDTs**), especially when combined with operator overloading to use common operators to define operations for addition, subtraction, and so on for the UDT.

Inheritance in C++ follows the following pattern:

```
class B : public A { // Private members. public: // Additional public
members. };
```

Here, we declare a class, B, which derives from class A. This allows us to use any public methods defined in class A on an instance of class B, as if they were defined in the latter to begin with.

All of this seems fairly easy to understand, even if things can get a bit confusing the moment we start deriving from more than one base class. However, with proper planning and design, polymorphism can be a very powerful tool.

Unfortunately, none of this answers the question of how much overhead the use of polymorphism adds to our code. We saw earlier that C++ classes by themselves add no overhead during runtime, yet by deriving from one or more base classes, the resulting code would be expected to be significantly more complex.

Fortunately, this is not the case. Much like with simple classes, the resulting derived classes are simple amalgamations of the base structs that underlie the class implementations. The inheritance process itself, along with the validation that comes with it, is primarily a compiler-time issue, bringing with it various benefits for the developer.

Virtual base classes

At times, it doesn't make a lot of sense for a base class to have an implementation for a class method, yet at the same time we wish to force any derived classes to implement that method. The answer to this problem is virtual methods.

Take the following class definition:

```
class A {
public:
    virtual bool methodA() = 0;
    virtual bool methodB() = 0;
};
```

If we try to derive from this class, we must implement these two class methods or get a compiler error. Since both of the methods in the base class are virtual, the entire base class is referred to as a virtual base class. This is particularly useful for when you wish to define an interface that can be implemented by a range of different classes, yet keep the convenience of having just one user-defined type to refer to.

Internally, virtual methods like these are implemented using `vtables`, which is short for *virtual table*. This is a data structure containing, for each virtual method, a memory address (pointer) pointing to an implementation of that method:

```
VirtualClass* → vtable_ptr → vtable[0] → methodA()
```

We can compare the performance impact of this level of indirection relative to C-style code and classes with direct method calls. The Code Craft article on the timing of virtual functions (`https://hackaday.com/2015/11/13/code-craft-embedding-c-timing-virtual-functions/`) describes such an approach, with interesting findings:

	Uno	Due		
Os	O2	Os	O2	
C function call	10.4	10.2	3.7	3.6
C++ direct call	10.4	10.3	3.8	3.8
C++ virtual call	11.1	10.9	3.9	3.8
Multiple C calls	110.4	106.3	39.4	35.5
C function pointer calls	105.7	102.9	38.6	34.9
C++ virtual calls	103.2	100.4	39.5	35.2

All times listed here are in microseconds.

The same two Arduino development boards are used for this test as for the one comparing compile output size between C code and C++ classes. Two different optimization levels are used to compare the impact of such compiler settings: -Os optimizes for the size of the resulting binary in terms of bytes, where as the -O2 setting optimizes for speed in a more aggressive manner than the -O1 optimization level.

From these timings, we can say for sure that the level of indirection introduced by the virtual methods is measurable, although not dramatic, adding a whole 0.7 microseconds on the ATMega328 of the Arduino Uno development board, and about 0.1 microseconds on the faster ARM-based board.

Even in absolute terms, the use of virtual class methods does not carry enough of a performance penalty to truly reconsider its use unless performance is paramount, and this is primarily the case on slower MCUs. The faster the MCU's CPU, the less severe the impact of its use will be.

Function inlining

The inline keyword in C++ is a hint to the compiler to let it know that we would like each call to a function whose name is preceded by this keyword to result in that function's implementation instead of being copied to the location of the call, thus skipping the overhead of a function call.

This is a compile-time optimization, which only adds the size of the function implementation to the compiler output, once for each distinct call to the inline function.

Runtime type information

The main purpose of RTTI is to allow the use of safe typecasting, like with the dynamic_cast<> operator. As RTTI involves storing additional information for each polymorphic class, it has a certain amount of overhead.

This is a runtime feature, as the name gives away, and thus can be disabled if you don't need the features it provides. Disabling RTTI is common practice on some embedded platforms, especially as it is rarely used on low-resource platforms, such as 8-bit MCUs.

Exception handling

Exceptions are commonly used on desktop platforms, providing a way to generate exceptions for error conditions, which can be caught and handled in try/catch blocks.

While exception support isn't expensive by itself, an exception being generated is relatively expensive, requiring a significant amount of CPU time and RAM to prepare and handle the exception. You have to also make sure to catch every exception, or risk having the application terminate without clear cause.

Exceptions versus the checking of return code for a method being called is something that has to be decided on a case-by-case basis, and can also be a matter of personal preference. It requires a quite different programming style, which may not work for everyone.

Templates

It's often thought that templates in C++ are very heavy, and carry a severe penalty for using them. This completely misses the point of templates, which is that templates are merely meant to be used as a shorthand method for automating the generation of nearly identical code from a single template – hence the name.

What this effectively means is that for any function or class template we define, the compiler will generate an inline implementation of the template each time the template is referenced.

This is a pattern we commonly see in the C++ **standard template library** (STL), which, as the name suggests, makes heavy use of templates. Take, for example, a data structure like a humble map:

```
std::map<std::string, int> myMap;
```

What happens here is that the singular template for an std::map is taken by the compiler, along with the template parameters we provide within the sharp brackets, filling in the template and writing an inline implementation in its spot.

Effectively, we get the same implementation as if we had written the entire data structure implementation by hand just for those two types. Since the alternative would be to write every implementation by hand for every conceivable built-in type and additional user-defined type, the use of a generic template saves us a lot of time, without sacrificing performance.

The standard template library

The standard library for C++ (STL) contains a comprehensive and ever-growing collection of functions, classes, and more that allows for common tasks to be performed without having to rely on external libraries. The STL string class is very popular, and allows you to safely handle strings without having to deal with null terminators and anything similar.

Most embedded platforms support all or at least a significant part of the STL, barring limitations on available RAM and the like that prevent the implementation of full hash tables and other complex data structures. Many embedded STL implementations contain optimizations for the target platform, minimizing RAM and CPU usage.

Maintainability

In the preceding sections, we have seen a number of features that C++ offers, and the viability of using them on a resource-limited platform. A big advantage of using C++ is the reduction in code size you can accomplish through the use of templates, along with the organization and modularization of a code base using classes, namespaces, and the like.

By striving for a more modular approach in your code, with clear interfaces between modules, it becomes more feasible to reuse code between projects. It also simplifies the maintenance of code by making the function of a particular section of code clearer and providing clear targets for unit and integration testing.

Summary

In this chapter, we tackled the big question of why you would wish to use C++ for embedded development. We saw that, due to the courtesy of C++'s development, it is highly optimized for resource-constrained platforms, while providing a large number of features essential to project management and organization.

The reader should, at this point, be able to describe C++'s main features and provide concrete examples of each. When writing C++ code, the reader will have a clear idea of the cost of a particular language feature, being able to reason why one implementation of a section of code is preferable to another implementation, based on both space and RAM constraints.

In the next chapter, we will take a look at the development process for embedded Linux and similar systems, based on **single-board computers** (**SBCs**) and similar.

3
Developing for Embedded Linux and Similar Systems

Small, SoC-based systems are everywhere these days, from smartphones, video game consoles, and smart television sets, to infotainment systems in cars and airplanes. Consumer devices relying on such systems are extremely common.

In addition to consumer devices, they're also found as part of industrial and building-level controller systems, where they monitor equipment, respond to input, and execute scheduled tasks for whole networks of sensors and actuators. Compared to MCUs, SoCs are not as resource-limited, usually running a full **operating system (OS)** such as a Linux-derived OS, VxWorks, or QNX.

In this chapter, we will cover the following topics:

- How to develop drivers for OS-based embedded systems
- Ways to integrate peripherals
- How to handle and implement real-time performance requirements
- Recognizing and dealing with resource limitations

Embedded operating systems

An OS is typically used with an embedded system when you're writing your application directly for the system's hardware, which is an unrealistic proposal. What an OS provides to the application is a number of APIs that abstract away the hardware and functionality implemented using this hardware, such as network communications or video output.

The trade-off here is between convenience and both code size and complexity.

Whereas a bare metal implementation ideally implements only those features it needs, an operating system comes with a task scheduler, along with functionality that the application being run may not ever need. For this reason, it's important to know when to use an OS instead of developing directly for the hardware, understanding the complications that come with either.

Good reasons to use an OS are if you have to be able to run different tasks simultaneously (multitasking, or multithreading). Implementing your own scheduler from scratch is generally not worth the effort. Having the need to run a non-fixed number of applications, and being able to remove and add them at will, is also made significantly easier by using an OS.

Finally, features such as advanced graphics output, graphics acceleration (such as OpenGL), touch screens, and advanced network functionality (for example, SSH and encryption) can be made much easier to implement when you have access to an OS and readily accessible drivers, and the APIs related to them.

Commonly used embedded operating systems include the following:

Name	Vendor	License	Platforms	Details
Raspbian	Community-based	Mainly GPL, similar	ARM (Raspberry Pi)	Debian Linux-based OS
Armbian	Community-based	GPLv2	ARM (various boards)	Debian Linux-based OS
Android	Google	GPLv2, Apache	ARM, x86, x86_64	Linux-based
VxWorks	Wind River (Intel)	Proprietary	ARM, x86, MIPS, PowerPC, SH-4	RTOS, monolithic kernel
QNX	BlackBerry	Proprietary	ARMv7, ARMv8, x86	RTOS, microkernel
Windows IoT	Microsoft	Proprietary	ARM, x86	Formerly known as Windows Embedded
NetBSD	NetBSD Foundation	2-clause BSD	ARM, 68k, MIPS, PowerPC, SPARC, RISC-V, x86, and so on	Most portable BSD-based OS

What all of these OSes have in common is that they handle basic functionality such as memory and task management, while offering access to hardware and OS functionality using programming interfaces (APIs).

In this chapter, we will specifically focus on SoC and SBC-based systems, which reflects in the preceding list of operating systems. Each of these OSes is meant to be used on a system with at least a few megabytes of RAM and in the order of megabytes to gigabytes of storage.

If the target SoC or SBC is not yet targeted by an existing Linux distribution, or one wishes to heavily customize the system, one can use the tools from the Yocto Project (http://www.yoctoproject.org/).

Linux-based embedded OSes are quite prevalent, with Android being a well-known example. It is mostly used on smartphones, tablets, and similar devices, which heavily rely on graphical user interaction, while relying on the Android application infrastructure and related APIs. Due to this level of specialization, it is not well-suited to other use cases.

Raspbian is based on the very common Debian Linux distribution, aimed at basically just the Raspberry Pi series of SBCs. Armbian is similar, but covers a far wider range of SBCs. Both of these are community efforts. This is similar to the Debian project, which can also be used directly for embedded systems. The main advantage of the Raspbian, Armbian, and other similar projects is that they provide ready-made images to be used with the target SBC.

Like Linux-based OSes, NetBSD has the advantage of being open source, meaning that you have full access to the source code and can heavily customize any aspect of the operating system, including support for custom hardware. One big advantage NetBSD and similar BSD-based OSes have is that the OS is built from a single codebase, and managed by a single group of developers. This often simplifies the development and maintenance of an embedded project.

The BSD license (three- or two-clause) offers a major benefit for commercial projects, as this license only requires one to provide attribution instead of requiring the manufacturer to provide the full source code of the OS on request. This can be very relevant if one makes certain modifications to the source code, adding code modules that one wants to keep closed source.

Recent PlayStation gaming consoles, for example, use a modified version of FreeBSD, allowing Sony to heavily optimize the OS for the hardware and its use as a gaming console without having to release this code together with the rest of the OS's source code.

Proprietary options also exist, such as the offerings from BlackBerry (QNX) and Microsoft (Windows IoT, formerly Windows Embedded, formerly Windows CE). These tend to require a license fee per device and require the assistance of the manufacturer for any customization.

Real-time OSes

The basic requirement for a real-time OS (RTOS) is that it can guarantee that tasks will be executed and finished within a certain time span. This allows one to use them for real-time applications where variability (jitter) between the execution times of a batch of the same task is not acceptable.

From this, we can draw the basic distinction between hard and soft real-time OSes: with low jitter, the OS is hard real-time, as it can guarantee that a given task will always be executed with practically the same delay. With higher jitter, the OS can usually but not always execute a task with the same delay.

Within these two categories, we can again distinguish between event-driven and time-sharing schedulers. The former switches tasks based on priority (priority scheduling), whereas the latter uses a timer to regularly switch tasks. Which design is better depends on what one uses the system for.

The main thing that time sharing has over event-driven schedulers is that since it gives far more CPU time to lower-priority tasks as well, it can make a multitasking system seem to run much smoother.

Generally, one would only use an RTOS if your project requirements are such that one must be able to guarantee that inputs can be handled within a strictly defined time window. For applications such as robotics and industrial applications, it can be crucial that an action is performed in exactly the same time span every time, with failure to do so resulting in the disruption of a production line or an inferior product.

With the example project that we will be looking at later in this chapter, we do not use an RTOS, but a regular Linux-based OS, as no hard timing requirements exist. Using an RTOS would impose an unneeded burden and likely increase complexity and costs.

One way to regard an RTOS is to get as close to the real-time nature of programming directly for the hardware (bare metal) without having to give up all of the conveniences of using a full-blown OS.

Custom peripherals and drivers

A peripheral is defined as an ancillary device that adds I/O or other functionality to a computer system. This can be anything from an I2C, SPI, or SD card controller to an audio or graphics device. Most of those are part of the physical SoC, with others added via interfaces that the SoC exposes to the outside world. Examples of external peripherals would be RAM (via the RAM controller) and a **real-time clock** (**RTC**).

One issue that one will likely encounter when using cheaper SBCs such as the Raspberry Pi, Orange Pi, and countless similar systems is that they usually lack an RTC, meaning that when they are powered off, they no longer keep track of the time. The thought behind this is usually that those boards will be connected to the internet anyway, so the OS can use an online time service (**Network Time Protocol**, or **NTP**) to synchronize the system time, thus saving board space.

One might end up using an SBC in a situation where no internet connection is available, or where the delay before online time synchronization is unacceptable, or any of a myriad of other reasons. In this case, one may want to add an RTC peripheral to the board and configure the OS to make use of it.

Adding an RTC

One can cheaply get RTCs as a ready-to-use module, often based around the DS1307 chip. This is a 5V module, which connects to the SBC (or MCU) via the I2C bus:

This image is of a small DS1307-based RTC module. As one can see, it has the RTC chip, a crystal, and an MCU. The last of these is used to communicate with the host system, regardless of whether it is an SoC or MCU-based board. All that one requires is the ability to provide the desired voltage (and current) the RTC module operates on, along with an I2C bus.

After connecting the RTC module to the SBC board, the next goal is to have the OS also use it. For this, we must make sure that the I2C kernel module is loaded so that we can use I2C devices.

Linux distributions for SBCs, such as Raspbian and Armbian, usually come with drivers for a number of RTC modules. This allows us to relatively quickly set up the RTC module and integrate it with the OS. With the module we looked at earlier, we require the I2C and DS1307 kernel modules. For a Raspbian OS on a first-generation Raspberry Pi SBC, these modules would be called `i2c-dev`, `2cbcm2708`, and `rtc-ds1307`.

First, you have to enable these modules so that they are loaded when the system starts. For Raspbian Linux, one can edit the `/etc/modules` file to do so, as well as other configuration tools made available for this platform. After a reboot, we should be able to detect the RTC device on the I2C bus using an I2C scanner tool.

With the RTC device working, we can remove the fake-hwclock package on Raspbian. This is a simple module that fakes an RTC, but merely stores the current time in a file before the system is shut down so that on the next boot the filesystem dates and similar will be consistent due to resuming from that stored date and time, without any new files one creates suddenly being *older* than the existing files.

Instead, we'll be using the hwclock utility, which will use any real RTC to synchronize the system time with. This requires one to modify the way the OS starts, with the location of the RTC module passed as boot parameters in the following form:

```
rtc.i2c=ds1307,1,0x68
```

This will initialize an RTC (`/dev/rtc0`) device on the I2C bus, with address 0x68.

Custom drivers

The exact format and integration of drivers (kernel modules) with the OS kernel differs for each OS and thus would be impossible to fully cover here. We will, however, look at how the driver for the RTC module we used earlier is implemented for Linux.

In addition, we will look at how to use an I2C peripheral from user space later in this chapter, in the club room monitoring example. Using a user space-based driver (library) is often a good alternative to implementing it as a kernel module.

The RTC functionality is integrated into the Linux kernel, with the code for it found in the `/drivers/rtc` folder (on GitHub,
at `https://github.com/torvalds/linux/tree/master/drivers/rtc`).

The `rtc-ds1307.c` file contains two functions we need to read and set the RTC, respectively: `ds1307_get_time()` and `ds1307_set_time()`. The basic functionality of these functions is very similar to what we'll be using in the club room monitoring example later in this chapter, where we simply integrate I2C device support into our application.

A major advantage of communicating with I2C, SPI, and other such peripherals from user space is that we are not limited by the compile environment supported by the OS kernel. Taking the Linux kernel as an example, it is written mostly in C with some assembly. Its APIs are C-style APIs and thus we would have to use a distinctly C-style coding approach to writing our kernel modules.

Obviously, this would negate most of the advantages, not to mention the point, of attempting to write these modules in C++ to begin with. When moving our module code to user space and using it either as part of an application or as a shared library, we have no such limitations and can freely use any and all C++ concepts and functionality.

For completeness' sake, the basic template for a Linux kernel module looks as follows:

```
#include <linux/module.h>       // Needed by all modules
#include <linux/kernel.h>       // Needed for KERN_INFO

int init_module() {
        printk(KERN_INFO "Hello world.n");

        return 0;
}

void cleanup_module() {
        printk(KERN_INFO "Goodbye world.n");
}
```

This is the requisite Hello World example, written in C++-style.

One final consideration when considering kernel- and user space-based driver modules is that of context switches. From an efficiency point of view, kernel modules are faster and have lower latency because the CPU does not have to switch from a user to kernel space context and back repeatedly to communicate with a device and pass messages from it back to the code communicating with it.

For high bandwidth devices (such as storage and capturing), this could make the difference between a smoothly functioning system and one that severely lags and struggles to perform its tasks.

However, when considering the club room monitoring example in this chapter and its occasional use of an I2C device, it should be obvious that a kernel module would be severe overkill without any tangible benefits.

Resource limitations

Even though SBCs and SoCs tend to be fairly powerful, they are still no direct comparison to a modern desktop system or server. They have distinct limits in terms of RAM, storage size, and lack of expansion options.

With wildly varying amounts of (permanently installed) RAM, you have to consider the memory needs of the applications one wishes to run on the system before even considering the relatively sluggish CPU performance.

As SBCs tend to not have any, or significant amounts of, storage with a high endurance rate (meaning it can be written to often without limited write cycles to take into account), they generally do not have swap space and keep everything in the available RAM. Without the fallback of swap, any memory leaks and excessive memory usage will rapidly lead to a non-functioning or constantly restarting system.

Even though CPU performance on SBCs has increased significantly over the years for commonly available models, it is generally still advisable to use a cross-compiler to produce code for the SBC on a fast desktop system or server.

More on development issues and solutions will be covered in Chapter 6, *Testing OS-Based Applications*, and Appendix, *Best Practices*.

Example – club room monitoring

In this section, we will be looking at a practical implementation of an SBC-based solution that performs the following functionality for a club room:

- Monitors the status of the club door's lock
- Monitors the club status switch
- Sends status change notifications over MQTT
- Provides a REST API for the current club status
- Controls status lights
- Controls the power in the club room

The basic use case here is that we have a club room for which we want to be able to monitor the status of its lock, and have a switch inside the club to regulate whether the non-permanent power outlets in the club are powered on or not. Turning the club status switch to *on* would provide power to those outlets. We also want to send out a notification over MQTT so that other devices in the club room or elsewhere can update their status.

MQTT is a simple, binary publish/subscribe protocol on top of TCP/IP. It offers a lightweight communication protocol, suitable for resource-restricted applications such as sensor networks. Each MQTT client communicates with a central server: the MQTT broker.

Hardware

The block diagram of the `clubstatus` system looks as follows:

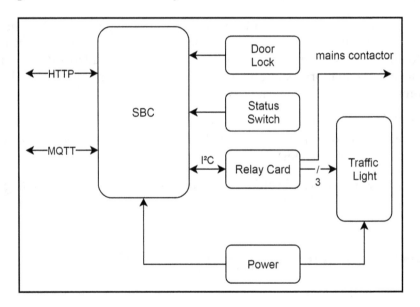

For the SBC platform, we use a Raspberry Pi, either the Raspberry Pi B+ model or a newer member of the B-series, such as the Raspberry Pi 3 Model B:

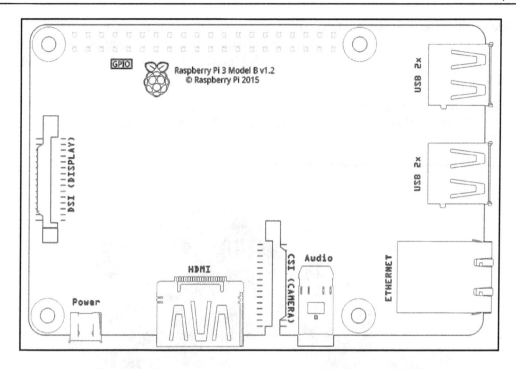

The main features we are looking for in the SBC system are an Ethernet connection and, of course, the Raspberry Pi-compatible **general-purpose input/output** (**GPIO**) header.

With this board, we'll use a standard Raspbian OS installation on the µSD card. No special configuration is needed beyond this. The primary reason for choosing the B+ model or similar is that these have a standard mounting hole pattern.

Relays

To control the status lights and the non-permanent power outlets in the room, we use a number of relays, in this case four relays:

Relay	Function
0	Power status of non-permanent outlets
1	Green status light
2	Yellow status light
3	Red status light

The idea here is that the power status relay is connected to a switch that controls the mains power to outlets that are not powered when the club status is off. The status lights indicate the current club status. The next section provides the details on the implementation of this concept.

To simplify the design, we will use a ready-made relay board containing four relays, which are driven by an NXP PCAL9535A I/O port chip (GPIO expander) connected to the I2C bus of the Raspberry Pi SBC:

This particular board is the Seeed Studio Raspberry Pi Relay Board v1.0:
`http://wiki.seeedstudio.com/Raspberry_Pi_Relay_Board_v1.0/`. It offers the four relays we require, allowing us to switch lights and switches up to 30 VDC (direct current) or 250 VAC (alternating current). This allows one to connect practically any type of lighting and further relays and kin.

The connection with the SBC is made by stacking the relay board on top of the SBC using its GPIO header, which allows us to add further boards on top of the relay board. This allows us to add the debounce functionality to the system, as indicated in the wiring plan diagram.

Debounce

The debounce board has the debouncing of switch signals as a requirement, as well as providing the Raspberry Pi board with power. The theory and reason behind the debouncing of mechanical switches is that the signal provided by those switches is not clean, meaning that they don't immediately switch from open to closed. They will briefly close (make contact) before the springiness of the metal contacts causes them to open again and rapidly move between these two states, before finally settling into its final position, as we can see in the following diagram from an oscilloscope connected to a simple switch:

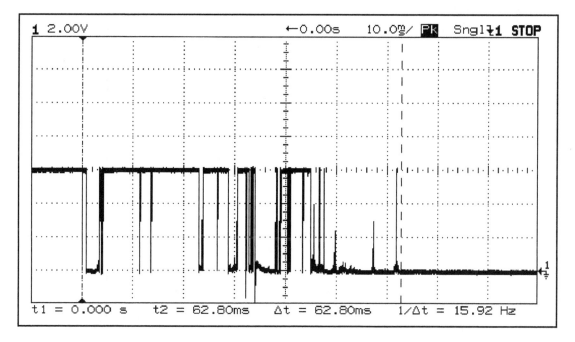

The result of this property is that the signal that arrives at the SBC's GPIO pins will rapidly change for a number of milliseconds (or worse). Performing any kind of action based upon these switch input changes would therefore lead to immense problems, as one cannot easily distinguish between a desired switch change and the rapid bouncing of the switch contacts during this change.

It is possible to debounce a switch either in hardware or software. The latter solution involves the starting of a timer when the state of the switch first changes. The assumption behind this is that after a certain time (in milliseconds) has expired, the switch is in a stable state and can be safely read out. This approach has disadvantages in that it puts an extra burden on the system by taking up one or more timers, or pausing the program's execution. Also, using interrupts on the input for the switch requires one to disable interrupts while the timer is running, adding further complexity to the code.

Debouncing in hardware can be done using discrete components, or using an SR latch (consisting of two NAND gates). For this application, we will use the following circuit, which works well with the most commonly used SPST (single-pole, single-throw) type of switch:

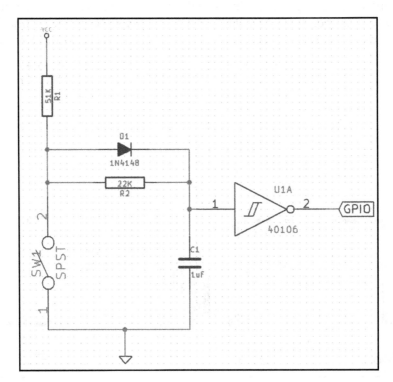

The concept behind this circuit is that when the switch is open, the capacitor is charged via R1 (and D1), causing the input on the inverting Schmitt trigger circuit (U1) to go high, resulting in the GPIO pin of the SBC connected to the output of U1 to read low. When the switch closes, the capacitor is discharged to the ground over R2.

Both the charging and discharging will take a certain amount of time, which adds latency before a change is registered on the input of U1. The charging and discharging rates are determined by the values of R1 and R2, the formulas for which are as follows:

- Charging: $V(t) = V_S(1 - e^{-(t/RC)})$
- Discharging: $V(t) = V_S e^{-(t/RC)}$

Here, $V(t)$ is the voltage at time t (in seconds). V_s is the source voltage and t is the time in seconds after the source voltage has been applied. R is the circuit resistance in Ohm and C the capacitance in farads. Finally, e is a mathematical constant with the value of 2.71828 (approximately), also known as Euler's number.

For the charging and discharging of capacitors, the RC time constant, tau (τ), is used, which is defined as follows:

$\tau = RC$

This defines the time it takes for the capacitor to be charged up to 63.2% (1τ), then 86% (2τ). The discharging of a capacitor for 1τ from fully charged will reduce its charge to 37%, and 13.5% after 2τ. One of the things one notices here is that a capacitor is never fully charged or discharged; the process of charging or discharging just slows down to the point where it becomes almost imperceptible.

With the values that we used for our debounce circuit, we get the following charge time constant for charging:

$0.051 = 51000 \cdot 0.000001$

The discharge time is as follows:

$0.022 = 22000 \cdot 0.000001$

This corresponds to 51 and 22 microseconds, respectively.

Like any Schmitt trigger, it has so-called hysteresis, meaning that it has dual thresholds. This effectively adds a dead zone in the output response above and below, which the output will not change:

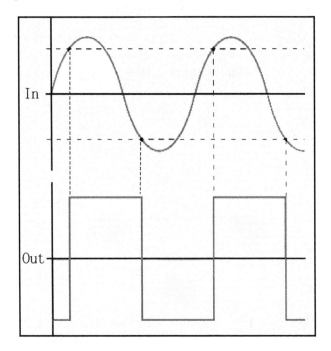

The hysteresis from a Schmitt trigger is usually used to remove noise from an incoming signal by setting explicit trigger levels. Even though the RC circuit we are already using should filter out practically all noises, adding a Schmitt trigger adds that little bit more insurance without any negative repercussions.

 When available, it is also possible to use the hysteresis functionality of an SBC's GPIO pins. For this project and the chosen debounce circuit, we also want the inverting property of the chip so that we get the expected high/low response for the connected switch instead of having to invert the meaning in software.

Debounce HAT

Using the information and debounce circuit from the previous section, a prototype board is assembled:

This prototype implements two debounce channels for the two switches that are required by the project. It also adds a screw terminal to connect the SBC power connection to. This allows one to power the SBC via the 5V header pins instead of having to use the micro-USB connector of the Raspberry Pi. For integration purposes, it's usually easier to just run the wires directly from the power supply into a screw terminal or similar than to bodge on a micro-USB plug.

This prototype is, of course, not a proper HAT, as defined by the Raspberry Pi Foundation's rules. These require the following features:

- It has a valid EEPROM containing vendor information, GPIO map, and device information connected to the `ID_SC` and `ID_SD` I2C bus pins on the Raspberry Pi SBC
- It has the modern 40-pin (female) GPIO connector, also spacing the HAT from the SBC by at least 8 millimeters
- It follows the mechanical specification
- If providing power to the SBC via the 5V pins, the HAT has to be able to provide at least 1.3 amperes continuously

With the required I2C EEPROM (CAT24C32) and other features added, we can see what a full version using the six channels offered by the inverting hex Schmitt trigger IC (40106) looks like:

The files for this KiCad project can be found at the author's GitHub account at `https://github.com/MayaPosch/DebounceHat`. With the extended number of channels, it would be relatively easy to integrate further switches, relays, and other elements into the system, possibly monitoring things like windows and such with various sensors that output a high/low signal.

Power

For our project, the required voltages we need are 5V for the Raspberry Pi board and a second voltage for the lights that we switch on and off via the relays. The power supply we pick has to be able to provide sufficient power to the SBC and the lights. For the former, 1-2 A should suffice, with the latter depending on the lights being used and their power requirements.

Implementation

The monitoring service will be implemented as a basic `systemd` service, meaning that it will be started by the operating system when the system starts, and the service can be monitored and restarted using all the regular systemd tools.

We will have the following dependencies:

- POCO
- WiringPi
- libmosquittopp (and libmosquitto)

The libmosquitto dependency (`https://mosquitto.org/man/libmosquitto-3.html`) is used to add MQTT support. The libmosquittopp dependency is a wrapper around the C-based API to provide a class-based interface, which makes integration into C++ projects easier.

The POCO framework (`https://pocoproject.org/`) is a highly portable set of C++ APIs, which provides everything from network-related functions (including HTTP) to all common low-level functions. In this project, its HTTP server will be used, along with its support for handling configuration files.

Finally, WiringPi (`http://wiringpi.com/`) is the de facto standard header for accessing and using the GPIO header features on the Raspberry Pi and compatible systems. It implements APIs to communicate with I2C devices and UARTs, and uses PWM and digital pins. In this project, it allows us to communicate with the relay board and the debounce board.

 The current version of this code can also be found at the author's GitHub account: `https://github.com/MayaPosch/ClubStatusService`.

We will start with the main file:

```
#include "listener.h"

#include <iostream>
#include <string>

using namespace std;

#include <Poco/Util/IniFileConfiguration.h>
#include <Poco/AutoPtr.h>
#include <Poco/Net/HTTPServer.h>

using namespace Poco::Util;
using namespace Poco;
using namespace Poco::Net;

#include "httprequestfactory.h"
#include "club.h"
```

Here, we include some basic STL functionality, along with the HTTP server and `ini` file support from POCO. The listener header is for our MQTT class, with the `httprequestfactory` and club headers being for the HTTP server and the main monitoring logic, respectively:

```
int main(int argc, char* argv[]) {
        Club::log(LOG_INFO, "Starting ClubStatus server...");
        int rc;
        mosqpp::lib_init();

        Club::log(LOG_INFO, "Initialised C++ Mosquitto library.");

        string configFile;
        if (argc > 1) { configFile = argv[1]; }
        else { configFile = "config.ini"; }

        AutoPtr<IniFileConfiguration> config;
        try {
                config = new IniFileConfiguration(configFile);
        }
        catch (Poco::IOException &e) {
                Club::log(LOG_FATAL, "Main: I/O exception when opening
configuration file: " + configFile + ". Aborting...");
                return 1;
        }

        string mqtt_host = config->getString("MQTT.host", "localhost");
        int mqtt_port = config->getInt("MQTT.port", 1883);
```

```
            string mqtt_user = config->getString("MQTT.user", "");
            string mqtt_pass = config->getString("MQTT.pass", "");
            string mqtt_topic = config->getString("MQTT.clubStatusTopic",
"/public/clubstatus");
            bool relayactive = config->getBool("Relay.active", true);
            uint8_t relayaddress = config->getInt("Relay.address", 0x20);
```

In this section, we initialize the MQTT library (libmosquittopp) and try to open the configuration file, using the default path and name if nothing is specified in the command-line parameters.

POCO's IniFileConfiguration class is used to open and read in the configuration file, throwing an exception if it cannot be found or opened. POCO's AutoPtr is equivalent to C++11's unique_ptr, allowing us to create a new heap-based instance without having to worry about disposing of it later.

Next, we read out the values that we are interested in for the MQTT and relay board functionality, specifying defaults where it makes sense to do so:

```
Listener listener("ClubStatus", mqtt_host, mqtt_port, mqtt_user,
mqtt_pass);

    Club::log(LOG_INFO, "Created listener, entering loop...");

    UInt16 port = config->getInt("HTTP.port", 80);
    HTTPServerParams* params = new HTTPServerParams;
    params->setMaxQueued(100);
    params->setMaxThreads(10);
    HTTPServer httpd(new RequestHandlerFactory, port, params);
    try {
            httpd.start();
    }
    catch (Poco::IOException &e) {
            Club::log(LOG_FATAL, "I/O Exception on HTTP server: port already
in use?");
            return 1;
    }
    catch (...) {
            Club::log(LOG_FATAL, "Exception thrown for HTTP server start.
Aborting.");
            return 1;
    }
```

In this section, we start the MQTT class, providing it with the parameters it needs to connect to the MQTT broker. Next, the HTTP server's configuration details are read out and a new HTTPServer instance is created.

The server instance is configured with the provided port and some limits for the maximum number of threads the HTTP server is allowed to use, as well as for the maximum queued connections it can keep. These parameters are useful to optimize system performance and fit code like this into systems with fewer resources to spare.

New client connections are handled by the custom `RequestHandlerFactory` class, which we will look at later:

```
Club::mqtt = &listener;
Club::start(relayactive, relayaddress, mqtt_topic);

while(1) {
        rc = listener.loop();
        if (rc){
                Club::log(LOG_ERROR, "Disconnected. Trying to
                reconnect...");
                listener.reconnect();
        }
}

mosqpp::lib_cleanup();
httpd.stop();
Club::stop();

return 0;
}
```

Finally, we assign a reference to the Listener instance we created to the static `Club` class's `mqtt` member. This will allow the `Listener` object to be used more easily later on, as we will see.

With calling `start()` on `Club`, the monitoring and configuring of the connected hardware will be handled and we are done with that aspect in the main function.

Finally, we enter a loop for the MQTT class, ensuring that it remains connected to the MQTT broker. Upon leaving the loop, we will clean up resources and stop the HTTP server and others. However, since we are in an infinite loop here, this code will not be reached with this implementation.

 Since this implementation would be run as a service that runs 24/7, a way to terminate the service cleanly is not an absolute requirement. A relatively easy way to do this would be to add a signal handler that would interrupt the loop once triggered. For simplicity's sake, this has been left out of this project.

Listener

The class declaration for the `Listener` class looks like this:

```
class Listener : public mosqpp::mosquittopp {
        //

  public:
        Listener(string clientId, string host, int port, string user,
string pass);
        ~Listener();

        void on_connect(int rc);
        void on_message(const struct mosquitto_message* message);
        void on_subscribe(int mid, int qos_count, const int*
granted_qos);

        void sendMessage(string topic, string& message);
        void sendMessage(string& topic, char* message, int msgLength);
  };
```

This class provides a simple API to connect to an MQTT broker and send messages to said broker. We inherit from the `mosquittopp` class, re-implementing a number of callback methods to handle the events of connecting newly received messages and completed subscriptions to MQTT topics.

Next, let's have a look at the implementation:

```
#include "listener.h"

#include <iostream>

using namespace std;
Listener::Listener(string clientId, string host, int port, string user,
string pass) : mosquittopp(clientId.c_str()) {
        int keepalive = 60;
        username_pw_set(user.c_str(), pass.c_str());
        connect(host.c_str(), port, keepalive);
}


Listener::~Listener() {
        //
}
```

In the constructor, we assign the unique MQTT client identification string using the mosquittopp class's constructor. We use a default value for the keep alive setting of 60 seconds, meaning the time for which we will keep a connection open to the MQTT broker without any side sending a control or other message.

After setting a username and password, we connect to the MQTT broker:

```
void Listener::on_connect(int rc) {
    cout << "Connected. Subscribing to topics...n";

        if (rc == 0) {
            // Subscribe to desired topics.
            string topic = "/club/status";
            subscribe(0, topic.c_str(), 1);
        }
        else {
            cerr << "Connection failed. Aborting subscribing.n";
        }
    }
```

This callback function is called whenever a connection attempt has been made with the MQTT broker. We check the value of `rc` and if the value is zero—indicating success—we start subscribing to any desired topics. Here, we subscribe to just one topic: /club/status. If any other MQTT clients send a message to this topic, we will receive it in the following callback function:

```
void Listener::on_message(const struct mosquitto_message* message) {
            string topic = message->topic;
            string payload = string((const char*) message->payload,
    message->payloadlen);

        if (topic == "/club/status") {
            string topic = "/club/status/response";
            char payload[] = { 0x01 };
            publish(0, topic.c_str(), 1, payload, 1); // QoS 1.
        }
    }
```

In this callback function, we receive a struct with the MQTT topic and payload. We then compare the topic to the topic strings we subscribed to, which in this case is just the /club/status topic. Upon receiving a message for this topic, we publish a new MQTT message with a topic and payload. The last parameter is the **quality of service (QoS)** value, with in this case setting is the *deliver at least once* flag. This guarantees that at least one other MQTT client will receive our message.

The MQTT payload is always a binary, that is, 1 in this example. To make it reflect the status of the club room (opened or closed), we would have to integrate the response from the static `Club` class, which we will be looking at in the next section.

First, we look at the remaining functions for the `Listener` class:

```
void Listener::on_subscribe(int mid, int qos_count, const int*
granted_qos) {
        //
}


void Listener::sendMessage(string topic, string &message) {
        publish(0, topic.c_str(), message.length(), message.c_str(),
true);
}


void Listener::sendMessage(string &topic, char* message, int msgLength) {
        publish(0, topic.c_str(), msgLength, message, true);
}
```

The callback function for a new subscription is left empty here, but could be used to add logging or such functionality. Furthermore, we have an overloaded `sendMessage()` function, which allows other parts of the application to also publish MQTT messages.

The main reason to have these two different functions is that sometimes it's easier to use a `char*` array to send, for example, an array of 8-bit integers as part of a binary protocol, whereas other times an STL string is more convenient. This way, we get the best of both worlds, without having to convert one or the other whenever we wish to send an MQTT message anywhere in our code.

The first parameter to `publish()` is the message ID, which is a custom integer we can assign ourselves. Here, we leave it at zero. We also make use of the *retain* flag (last parameter), setting it to true. This implies that whenever a new MQTT client subscribes to the topic we published a retained message on, this client will always receive the last message that was published on that particular topic.

Since we will be publishing the status of the club rooms on an MQTT topic, it is desirable that the last status message is retained by the MQTT broker so that any client that uses this information will immediately receive the current status the moment it connects to the broker, instead of having to wait for the next status update.

Club

The club header declares the classes that form the core of the project, and is responsible for dealing with the inputs from the switches, controlling the relays, and updating the status of the club room:

```
#include <wiringPi.h>
 #include <wiringPiI2C.h>
```

The first thing of note in this header file are the includes. They add the basic WiringPi GPIO functionality to our code, as well as those for I2C usage. Further WiringPi one could include for other projects requiring such functionality would be SPI, UART (serial), software PWM, Raspberry Pi (Broadcom SoC) specific functionality, and others:

```
enum Log_level {
    LOG_FATAL = 1,
    LOG_ERROR = 2,
    LOG_WARNING = 3,
    LOG_INFO = 4,
    LOG_DEBUG = 5
};
```

We define the different log levels we will be using as an `enum`:

```
class Listener;
```

We forward declare the `Listener` class, as we will be using it in the implementation for these classes, but don't want to include the entire header for it yet:

```
class ClubUpdater : public Runnable {
        TimerCallback<ClubUpdater>* cb;
        uint8_t regDir0;
        uint8_t regOut0;
        int i2cHandle;
        Timer* timer;
        Mutex mutex;
        Mutex timerMutex;
        Condition timerCnd;
        bool powerTimerActive;
        bool powerTimerStarted;

    public:
        void run();
        void updateStatus();
        void writeRelayOutputs();
        void setPowerState(Timer &t);
};
```

The `ClubUpdater` class is responsible for configuring the I2C-based GPIO expander, which controls the relays, as well as handling any updates to the club status. A `Timer` instance from the POCO framework is used to add a delay to the power status relay, as we will see when we look at the implementation.

This class inherits from the POCO `Runnable` class, which is the base class that's expected by the POCO `Thread` class, which is a wrapper around native threads.

The two `uint8_t` member variables mirror two registers on the I2C GPIO expander device, allowing us to set the direction and value of the output pins on the device, which effectively controls the attached relays:

```
class Club {
        static Thread updateThread;
        static ClubUpdater updater;

        static void lockISRCallback();
        static void statusISRCallback();

 public:
        static bool clubOff;
        static bool clubLocked;
        static bool powerOn;
        static Listener* mqtt;
        static bool relayActive;
        static uint8_t relayAddress;
        static string mqttTopic;       // Topic we publish status updates
on.

        static Condition clubCnd;
        static Mutex clubCndMutex;
        static Mutex logMutex;
        static bool clubChanged ;
        static bool running;
        static bool clubIsClosed;
        static bool firstRun;
        static bool lockChanged;
        static bool statusChanged;
        static bool previousLockValue;
        static bool previousStatusValue;

        static bool start(bool relayactive, uint8_t relayaddress, string
topic);
        static void stop();
        static void setRelay();
        static void log(Log_level level, string msg);
 };
```

The `Club` class can be regarded as the input side of the system, setting up and handling the ISRs (interrupt handlers), as well as acting as the central (static) class with all of the variables pertaining to the club status, such as the status of the lock switch, status switch, and status of the power system (club open or closed).

This class is made fully static so that it can be used freely by different parts of the program to inquire about the room status.

Moving on, here is the implementation:

```
#include "club.h"

#include <iostream>

using namespace std;


#include <Poco/NumberFormatter.h>

using namespace Poco;


#include "listener.h"
```

Here, we include the `Listener` header so that we can use it. We also include the POCO `NumberFormatter` class to allow us to format integer values for logging purposes:

```
#define REG_INPUT_PORT0                  0x00
#define REG_INPUT_PORT1                  0x01
#define REG_OUTPUT_PORT0                 0x02
#define REG_OUTPUT_PORT1                 0x03
#define REG_POL_INV_PORT0                0x04
#define REG_POL_INV_PORT1                0x05
#define REG_CONF_PORT0                   0x06
#define REG_CONG_PORT1                   0x07
#define REG_OUT_DRV_STRENGTH_PORT0_L 0x40
#define REG_OUT_DRV_STRENGTH_PORT0_H 0x41
#define REG_OUT_DRV_STRENGTH_PORT1_L 0x42
#define REG_OUT_DRV_STRENGTH_PORT1_H 0x43
#define REG_INPUT_LATCH_PORT0            0x44
#define REG_INPUT_LATCH_PORT1            0x45
#define REG_PUD_EN_PORT0                 0x46
#define REG_PUD_EN_PORT1                 0x47
#define REG_PUD_SEL_PORT0                0x48
#define REG_PUD_SEL_PORT1                0x49
#define REG_INT_MASK_PORT0               0x4A
#define REG_INT_MASK_PORT1               0x4B
```

```
#define REG_INT_STATUS_PORT0          0x4C
#define REG_INT_STATUS_PORT1          0x4D
#define REG_OUTPUT_PORT_CONF          0x4F
```

Next, we define all of the registers of the target GPIO expander device, the NXP PCAL9535A. Even though we only use two of these registers, it's generally a good practice to add the full list to simplify later expansion of the code. A separate header can be used as well to allow one to easily use different GPIO expanders without significant changes to your code, or any at all:

```
#define RELAY_POWER 0
#define RELAY_GREEN 1
#define RELAY_YELLOW 2
#define RELAY_RED 3
```

Here, we define which functionality is connected to which relay, corresponding to a specific output pin of the GPIO expander chip. Since we have four relays, four pins are used. These are connected to the first bank (of two in total) of eight pins on the chip.

Naturally, it is important that these definitions match up with what is physically hooked up to those relays. Depending on the use case, one could make this configurable as well:

```
bool Club::clubOff;
bool Club::clubLocked;
bool Club::powerOn;
Thread Club::updateThread;
ClubUpdater Club::updater;
bool Club::relayActive;
uint8_t Club::relayAddress;
string Club::mqttTopic;
Listener* Club::mqtt = 0;

Condition Club::clubCnd;
Mutex Club::clubCndMutex;
Mutex Club::logMutex;
bool Club::clubChanged = false;
bool Club::running = false;
bool Club::clubIsClosed = true;
bool Club::firstRun = true;
bool Club::lockChanged = false;
bool Club::statusChanged = false;
bool Club::previousLockValue = false;
bool Club::previousStatusValue = false;
```

As `Club` is a fully static class, we initialize all of its member variables before we move into the `ClubUpdater` class's implementation:

```
void ClubUpdater::run() {
    regDir0 = 0x00;
    regOut0 = 0x00;
    Club::powerOn = false;
    powerTimerActive = false;
    powerTimerStarted = false;
    cb = new TimerCallback<ClubUpdater>(*this,
&ClubUpdater::setPowerState);
    timer = new Timer(10 * 1000, 0);
```

When we start an instance of this class, its `run()` function gets called. Here, we set a number of defaults. The direction and output register variables are initially set to zero. The club room power status is set to false, and the power timer-related Booleans are set to false, as the power timer is not active yet. This timer is used to set a delay before the power is turned on or off, as we will see in more detail in a moment.

By default, the delay on this timer is ten seconds. This can, of course, also be made configurable:

```
if (Club::relayActive) {
    Club::log(LOG_INFO, "ClubUpdater: Starting i2c relay device.");
    i2cHandle = wiringPiI2CSetup(Club::relayAddress);
    if (i2cHandle == -1) {
        Club::log(LOG_FATAL, string("ClubUpdater: error starting
        i2c relay device."));
        return;
    }

    wiringPiI2CWriteReg8(i2cHandle, REG_CONF_PORT0, 0x00);
    wiringPiI2CWriteReg8(i2cHandle, REG_OUTPUT_PORT0, 0x00);

    Club::log(LOG_INFO, "ClubUpdater: Finished configuring the i2c
    relay device's registers.");
}
```

Next, we set up the I2C GPIO expander. This requires the I2C device address, which we passed to the `Club` class earlier on. What this setup function does is ensure that there is an active I2C device at this address on the I2C bus. After this, it should be ready to communicate with. It is also possible to skip this step via setting the relayActive variable to false. This is done by setting the appropriate value in the configuration file, which is useful when running integration tests on a system without an I2C bus or connected device.

With the setup complete, we write the initial values of the direction and output registers for the first bank. Both are written with null bytes so that all eight pins they control are set to both output mode and to a binary zero (low) state. This way, all relays connected to the first four pins are initially off:

```
updateStatus();

Club::log(LOG_INFO, "ClubUpdater: Initial status update
complete.");
Club::log(LOG_INFO, "ClubUpdater: Entering waiting condition.");

while (Club::running) {
        Club::clubCndMutex.lock();
        if (!Club::clubCnd.tryWait(Club::clubCndMutex, 60 * 1000))
{.
                Club::clubCndMutex.unlock();
                if (!Club::clubChanged) { continue; }
        }
        else {
                Club::clubCndMutex.unlock();
        }

        updateStatus();
    }
}
```

After completing these configuration steps, we run the first update of the club room status, using the same function that will also be called later on when the inputs change. This results in all of the inputs being checked and the outputs being set to a corresponding status.

Finally, we enter a waiting loop. This loop is controlled by the `Club::running` Boolean variable, allowing us to break out of it via a signal handler or similar. The actual waiting is performed using a condition variable, which we wait for here until either a time-out occurs on the one-minute wait (after which, we return to waiting after a quick check), or we get signaled by one of the interrupts that we will set later on for the inputs.

Moving on, we look at the function that's used to update the status of the outputs:

```
void ClubUpdater::updateStatus() {
    Club::clubChanged = false;

    if (Club::lockChanged) {
            string state = (Club::clubLocked) ? "locked" : "unlocked";
            Club::log(LOG_INFO, string("ClubUpdater: lock status changed to
") + state);
```

```
            Club::lockChanged = false;

        if (Club::clubLocked == Club::previousLockValue) {
                Club::log(LOG_WARNING, string("ClubUpdater: lock interrupt
triggered, but value hasn't changed. Aborting."));
                return;
        }

        Club::previousLockValue = Club::clubLocked;
    }
    else if (Club::statusChanged) {
        string state = (Club::clubOff) ? "off" : "on";
        Club::log(LOG_INFO, string("ClubUpdater: status switch status
changed to ") + state);
        Club::statusChanged = false;

        if (Club::clubOff == Club::previousStatusValue) {
                Club::log(LOG_WARNING, string("ClubUpdater: status
interrupt triggered, but value hasn't changed. Aborting."));
                return;
        }

        Club::previousStatusValue = Club::clubOff;
    }
    else if (Club::firstRun) {
        Club::log(LOG_INFO, string("ClubUpdater: starting initial update
run."));
        Club::firstRun = false;
    }
    else {
        Club::log(LOG_ERROR, string("ClubUpdater: update triggered, but
no change detected. Aborting."));
        return;
    }
```

The first thing we do when we enter this update function is to ensure that the
Club::clubChanged Boolean is set to false so that it can be set again by one of the
interrupt handlers.

After this, we check what has changed exactly on the inputs. If the lock switch got
triggered, its Boolean variable will have been set to true, or the variable for the status
switch will likely have been triggered. If this is the case, we reset the variable and compare
the newly read value with the last known value for that input.

As a sanity check, we ignore the triggering if the value hasn't changed. This could happen if the interrupt got triggered due to noise, such as when the signal wire for a switch runs near power lines. Any fluctuation in the latter would induce a surge in the former, which can trigger the GPIO pin's interrupt. This is one obvious example of both the reality of dealing with a non-ideal physical world and a showcase for the importance of both the hardware and software in how they affect the reliability of a system.

In addition to this check, we log the event using our central logger, and update the buffered input value for use in the next run.

The last two cases in the if/else statement deal with the initial run, as well as a default handler. When we initially run this function the way we saw earlier, no interrupt will have been triggered, so obviously we have to add a third situation to the first two for the status and lock switches:

```
if (Club::clubIsClosed && !Club::clubOff) {
        Club::clubIsClosed = false;

        Club::log(LOG_INFO, string("ClubUpdater: Opening club."));

        Club::powerOn = true;
        try {
                if (!powerTimerStarted) {
                        timer->start(*cb);
                        powerTimerStarted = true;
                }
                else {
                        timer->stop();
                        timer->start(*cb);
                }
        }
        catch (Poco::IllegalStateException &e) {
                Club::log(LOG_ERROR, "ClubUpdater: IllegalStateException on
timer start: " + e.message());
                return;
        }
        catch (...) {
                Club::log(LOG_ERROR, "ClubUpdater: Unknown exception on
timer start.");
                return;
        }

        powerTimerActive = true;

        Club::log(LOG_INFO, "ClubUpdater: Started power timer...");

        char msg = { '1' };
```

```
            Club::mqtt->sendMessage(Club::mqttTopic, &msg, 1);

            Club::log(LOG_DEBUG, "ClubUpdater: Sent MQTT message.");
    }
    else if (!Club::clubIsClosed && Club::clubOff) {
            Club::clubIsClosed = true;

            Club::log(LOG_INFO, string("ClubUpdater: Closing club."));

            Club::powerOn = false;

            try {
                    if (!powerTimerStarted) {
                            timer->start(*cb);
                            powerTimerStarted = true;
                    }
                    else {
                            timer->stop();
                            timer->start(*cb);
                    }
            }
            catch (Poco::IllegalStateException &e) {
                    Club::log(LOG_ERROR, "ClubUpdater: IllegalStateException on
timer start: " + e.message());
                    return;
            }
            catch (...) {
                    Club::log(LOG_ERROR, "ClubUpdater: Unknown exception on
timer start.");
                    return;
            }

            powerTimerActive = true;

            Club::log(LOG_INFO, "ClubUpdater: Started power timer...");

            char msg = { '0' };
            Club::mqtt->sendMessage(Club::mqttTopic, &msg, 1);

            Club::log(LOG_DEBUG, "ClubUpdater: Sent MQTT message.");
    }
```

Next, we check whether we have to change the status of the club room from closed to open, or the other way around. This is determined by checking whether the club status (`Club::clubOff`) Boolean has changed relative to the `Club::clubIsClosed` Boolean, which stores the last known status.

Essentially, if the status switch is changed from on to off or the other way around, this will be detected and a change to the new status will be started. This means that a power timer will be started, which will turn the non-permanent power in the club room on or off after the preset delay.

The POCO `Timer` class requires that we first stop the timer before starting it if it has been started previously. This requires us to add one additional check.

In addition, we also use our reference to the MQTT client class to send a message to the MQTT broker with the updated club room status, here as either an ASCII 1 or 0. This message can be used to trigger other systems, which could update an online status for the club room, or be put to even more creative uses.

Naturally, the exact payload of the message could be made configurable.

In the next section, we will update the colors on the status light, taking into account the state of power in the room. For this, we use the following table:

Color	Status switch	Lock switch	Power status
Green	On	Unlocked	On
Yellow	Off	Unlocked	Off
Red	Off	Locked	Off
Yellow and red	On	Locked	On

Here is the implementation:

```
    if (Club::clubOff) {
        Club::log(LOG_INFO, string("ClubUpdater: New lights, clubstatus
off."));

        mutex.lock();
        string state = (Club::powerOn) ? "on" : "off";
        if (powerTimerActive) {
            Club::log(LOG_DEBUG, string("ClubUpdater: Power timer
active, inverting power state from: ") + state);
            regOut0 = !Club::powerOn;
        }
        else {
            Club::log(LOG_DEBUG, string("ClubUpdater: Power timer not
active, using current power state: ") + state);
            regOut0 = Club::powerOn;
        }

        if (Club::clubLocked) {
            Club::log(LOG_INFO, string("ClubUpdater: Red on."));
```

```
                    regOut0 |= (1UL << RELAY_RED);
            }
            else {
                    Club::log(LOG_INFO, string("ClubUpdater: Yellow on."));
                    regOut0 |= (1UL << RELAY_YELLOW);
            }

            Club::log(LOG_DEBUG, "ClubUpdater: Changing output register to:
    0x" + NumberFormatter::formatHex(regOut0));

            writeRelayOutputs();
            mutex.unlock();
    }
```

We first check the state of the club room power, which tells us what value to use for the first bit of the output register. If the power timer is active, we have to invert the power state, as we want to write the current power state, not the future state that is stored in the power state Boolean.

If the club room's status switch is in the off position, then the state of the lock switch determines the final color. With the club room locked, we trigger the red relay, otherwise we trigger the yellow one. The latter would indicate the intermediate state, where the club room is off but not yet locked.

The use of a mutex here is to ensure that the writing of the I2C device's output register—as well as updating the local register variable—is done in a synchronized manner:

```
    else {
                    Club::log(LOG_INFO, string("ClubUpdater: New lights,
    clubstatus on."));

                    mutex.lock();
                    string state = (Club::powerOn) ? "on" : "off";
                    if (powerTimerActive) {
                            Club::log(LOG_DEBUG, string("ClubUpdater: Power timer
    active,    inverting power state from: ") + state);
                            regOut0 = !Club::powerOn; // Take the inverse of what
    the timer    callback will set.
                    }
                    else {
                            Club::log(LOG_DEBUG, string("ClubUpdater: Power timer
    not active,    using current power state: ") + state);
                            regOut0 = Club::powerOn; // Use the current power
    state value.
                    }

                    if (Club::clubLocked) {
```

```
                            Club::log(LOG_INFO, string("ClubUpdater: Yellow & Red
on."));

                            regOut0 |= (1UL << RELAY_YELLOW);
                            regOut0 |= (1UL << RELAY_RED);
                    }
                    else {
                            Club::log(LOG_INFO, string("ClubUpdater: Green
on."));

                            regOut0 |= (1UL << RELAY_GREEN);
                    }

                    Club::log(LOG_DEBUG, "ClubUpdater: Changing output register
to: 0x" +    NumberFormatter::formatHex(regOut0));

                    writeRelayOutputs();
                    mutex.unlock();
            }
    }
```

If the club room's status switch is set to on, we get two other color options, with green being the usual one, which sees both the club room unlocked and the status switch enabled. If, however, the latter is on but the room is locked, we would get yellow and red.

After finishing the new contents of the output register, we always use the `writeRelayOutputs()` function to write our local version to the remote device, thus triggering the new relay state:

```
void ClubUpdater::writeRelayOutputs() {
    wiringPiI2CWriteReg8(i2cHandle, REG_OUTPUT_PORT0, regOut0);

    Club::log(LOG_DEBUG, "ClubUpdater: Finished writing relay outputs with:
0x"
                    + NumberFormatter::formatHex(regOut0));
}
```

This function is very simple, and uses WiringPi's I2C API to write a single 8-bit value to the connected device's output register. We also log the written value here:

```
    void ClubUpdater::setPowerState(Timer &t) {
            Club::log(LOG_INFO, string("ClubUpdater: setPowerState
called."));

            mutex.lock();
            if (Club::powerOn) { regOut0 |= (1UL << RELAY_POWER); }
            else { regOut0 &= ~(1UL << RELAY_POWER); }

            Club::log(LOG_DEBUG, "ClubUpdater: Writing relay with: 0x" +
```

```
            NumberFormatter::formatHex(regOut0));

                writeRelayOutputs();

                powerTimerActive = false;
                mutex.unlock();
    }
```

In this function, we set the club room power state to whatever value its Boolean variable contains. We use the same mutex as we used when updating the club room status colors. However, we do not create the contents of the output register from scratch here, instead opting to toggle the first bit in its variable.

After toggling this bit, we write to the remote device as usual, which will cause the power in the club room to toggle state.

Next, we look at the static `Club` class, starting with the first function we call to initialize it:

```
    bool Club::start(bool relayactive, uint8_t relayaddress, string topic) {
            Club::log(LOG_INFO, "Club: starting up...");

            relayActive = relayactive;
            relayAddress = relayaddress;
            mqttTopic = topic;

            wiringPiSetup();

            Club::log(LOG_INFO,  "Club: Finished wiringPi setup.");

            pinMode(0, INPUT);
            pinMode(7, INPUT);
            pullUpDnControl(0, PUD_DOWN);
            pullUpDnControl(7, PUD_DOWN);
            clubLocked = digitalRead(0);
            clubOff = !digitalRead(7);

            previousLockValue = clubLocked;
            previousStatusValue = clubOff;

            Club::log(LOG_INFO, "Club: Finished configuring pins.");

            wiringPiISR(0, INT_EDGE_BOTH, &lockISRCallback);
            wiringPiISR(7, INT_EDGE_BOTH, &statusISRCallback);

            Club::log(LOG_INFO, "Club: Configured interrupts.");

            running = true;
```

```
        updateThread.start(updater);

        Club::log(LOG_INFO, "Club: Started update thread.");

        return true;
}
```

With this function, we start the entire club monitoring system, as we saw earlier in the application entry point. It accepts a few parameters, allowing us to turn the relay functionality on or off, the relay's I2C address (if using a relay), and the MQTT topic on which to publish changes to the club room status.

After setting the values for member variables using those parameters, we initialize the WiringPi framework. There are a number of different initialization functions offered by WiringPi, which basically differ in how one can access the GPIO pins.

The `wiringPiSetup()` function we use here is generally the most convenient one to use, as it will use virtual pin numbers that map to the underlying Broadcom SoC pins. The main advantage of the WiringPi numbering is that it remains constant between different revisions of the Raspberry Pi SBCs.

With the use of either Broadcom (BCM) numbers or the physical position of the pins in the header on the SBC's circuit board, we risk that this changes between board revisions, but the WiringPi numbering scheme can compensate for this.

For our purposes, we use the following pins on the SBC:

	Lock switch	**Status switch**
BCM	17	4
Physical position	11	7
WiringPi	0	7

After initializing the WiringPi library, we set the desired pin mode, making both of our pins into inputs. We then enable a pull-down on each of these pins. This enables a built-in pull-down resistor in the SoC, which will always try to pull the input signal low (referenced to ground). Whether or not one needs a pull-down or pull-up resistor enabled for an input (or output) pin depends on the circumstances, especially the connected circuit.

It's important to look at the behavior of the connected circuit; if the connected circuit has a tendency to "float" the value on the line, this would cause undesirable behavior on the input pin, with the value randomly changing. By pulling the line either low or high, we can be certain that what we read on the pin is not just noise.

With the mode set on each of our pins, we read out the values on them for the first time, which allows us to run the update function from the `ClubUpdater` class with the current values in a moment. Before we do that, however, we first register our interrupt methods for both pins.

An interrupt handler is little more than a callback that gets called whenever the specified event occurs on the specified pin. The WiringPi ISR function accepts the pin number, the type of event, and a reference to the handler function we wish to use. For the event type we picked here, we will have our interrupt handler triggered every time the value on the input pin goes from high to low, or the other way around. This means that it will be triggered when the connected switch goes from on to off, or off to on.

Finally, we started the update thread by using the `ClubUpdater` class instance and pushing it into its own thread:

```
void Club::stop() {
        running = false;
}
```

Calling this function will allow the loop in the `run()` function of `ClubUpdater` to end, which will terminate the thread it runs in, allowing the rest of the application to safely shut down as well:

```
void Club::lockISRCallback() {
        clubLocked = digitalRead(0);
        lockChanged = true;

        clubChanged = true;
        clubCnd.signal();
}


void Club::statusISRCallback() {
        clubOff = !digitalRead(7);
        statusChanged = true;

        clubChanged = true;
        clubCnd.signal();
}
```

Both of our interrupt handlers are pretty simple. When the OS receives the interrupt, it triggers the respective handler, which results in them reading the current value of the input pin, inverting the value as needed. The `statusChanged` or `lockChanged` variable is set to true to indicate to the update function which of the interrupts got triggered.

We do the same for the `clubChanged` Boolean variable before signaling the condition variable on which the `run` loop of `ClubUpdate` is waiting.

The last part of this class is the logging function:

```
void Club::log(Log_level level, string msg) {
    logMutex.lock();
    switch (level) {
        case LOG_FATAL: {
                cerr << "FATAL:t" << msg << endl;
                string message = string("ClubStatus FATAL: ") + msg;
                if (mqtt) {
                        mqtt->sendMessage("/log/fatal", message);
                }

                break;
        }
        case LOG_ERROR: {
                cerr << "ERROR:t" << msg << endl;
                string message = string("ClubStatus ERROR: ") + msg;
                if (mqtt) {
                        mqtt->sendMessage("/log/error", message);
                }

                break;
        }
        case LOG_WARNING: {
                cerr << "WARNING:t" << msg << endl;
                string message = string("ClubStatus WARNING: ") + msg;
                if (mqtt) {
                        mqtt->sendMessage("/log/warning", message);
                }

                break;
        }
        case LOG_INFO: {
                cout << "INFO: t" << msg << endl;
                string message = string("ClubStatus INFO: ") + msg;
                if (mqtt) {
                        mqtt->sendMessage("/log/info", message);
                }
```

```
                    break;
            }
        case LOG_DEBUG: {
                cout << "DEBUG:t" << msg << endl;
                string message = string("ClubStatus DEBUG: ") + msg;
                if (mqtt) {
                        mqtt->sendMessage("/log/debug", message);
                }

                break;
        }
        default:
                break;
    }

    logMutex.unlock();
}
```

We use another mutex here to synchronize the log outputs in the system log (or console) and to prevent concurrent access to the MQTT class when different parts of the application call this function simultaneously. As we will see in a moment, this logging function is used in other classes as well.

With this logging function, we can log both locally (system log) and remotely using MQTT.

HTTP request handler

Whenever POCO's HTTP server receives a new client connection, it uses a new instance of our `RequestHandlerFactory` class to get a handler for the specific request. Because it's such a simple class, it's fully implemented in the header:

```
#include <Poco/Net/HTTPRequestHandlerFactory.h>
#include <Poco/Net/HTTPServerRequest.h>

using namespace Poco::Net;

#include "statushandler.h"
#include "datahandler.h"


class RequestHandlerFactory: public HTTPRequestHandlerFactory {
public:
        RequestHandlerFactory() {}
        HTTPRequestHandler* createRequestHandler(const HTTPServerRequest&
request) {
                if (request.getURI().compare(0, 12, "/clubstatus/") == 0) {
```

```
                    return new StatusHandler();
          }
          else { return new DataHandler(); }
       }
    };
```

Our class doesn't do a whole lot more than compare the URL that the HTTP server was provided to determine which type of handler to instantiate and return. Here, we can see that if the URL string starts with `/clubstatus`, we return the status handler, which implements the REST API.

The default handler is a simple file server, which attempts to interpret the request as a filename, as we will see in a moment.

Status handler

This handler implements a simple REST API, returning a JSON structure containing the current club status. This can be used by an external application to show real-time information on the system, which is useful for a dashboard or website.

Due to its simplicity, this class is also fully implemented in its header:

```
#include <Poco/Net/HTTPRequestHandler.h>
#include <Poco/Net/HTTPServerResponse.h>
#include <Poco/Net/HTTPServerRequest.h>
#include <Poco/URI.h>

using namespace Poco;
using namespace Poco::Net;

#include "club.h"


class StatusHandler: public HTTPRequestHandler {
public:
        void handleRequest(HTTPServerRequest& request,
HTTPServerResponse& response)  {
                Club::log(LOG_INFO, "StatusHandler: Request from " +
request.clientAddress().toString());

                URI uri(request.getURI());
                vector<string> parts;
                uri.getPathSegments(parts);

                response.setContentType("application/json");
                response.setChunkedTransferEncoding(true);
```

```
                        if (parts.size() == 1) {
                                ostream& ostr = response.send();
                                ostr << "{ "clubstatus": " << !Club::clubOff << ",";
                                ostr << ""lock": " << Club::clubLocked << ",";
                                ostr << ""power": " << Club::powerOn << "";
                                ostr << "}";
                        }
                        else {
                                response.setStatus(HTTPResponse::HTTP_BAD_REQUEST);
                                ostream& ostr = response.send();
                                ostr << "{ "error": "Invalid request." }";
                        }
                }
        };
```

We use the central logger function from the `Club` class here to register details on incoming requests. Here, we just log the IP address of the client, but one could use the POCO `HTTPServerRequest` class's API to request even more detailed information.

Next, the URI is obtained from the request and we split the path section of the URL into a vector instance. After setting the content type and a transfer encoding setting on the response object, we check that we did indeed get the expected REST API call, at which point we compose the JSON string, obtain the club room status information from the `Club` class, and return this.

In the JSON object, we include information about the club room's status in general, inverting its Boolean variable, as well as the status of the lock and the power status, with a 1, indicating that the lock is closed or the power is on, respectively.

If the URL path had further segments, it would be an unrecognized API call, which would lead us to return an HTTP 400 (Bad Request) error instead.

Data handler

The data handler is called whenever no REST API call is recognized by the request handler factory. It tries to find the specified file, read it from disk, and return it, along with the proper HTTP headers. This class is also implemented in its header:

```
#include <Poco/Net/HTTPRequestHandler.h>
#include <Poco/Net/HTTPServerResponse.h>
#include <Poco/Net/HTTPServerRequest.h>
#include <Poco/URI.h>
#include <Poco/File.h>

using namespace Poco::Net;
```

```
using namespace Poco;


class DataHandler: public HTTPRequestHandler {
public:
    void handleRequest(HTTPServerRequest& request, HTTPServerResponse&
response) {
        Club::log(LOG_INFO, "DataHandler: Request from " +
request.clientAddress().toString());

        // Get the path and check for any endpoints to filter on.
        URI uri(request.getURI());
        string path = uri.getPath();

        string fileroot = "htdocs";
        if (path.empty() || path == "/") { path = "/index.html"; }

        File file(fileroot + path);

        Club::log(LOG_INFO, "DataHandler: Request for " + file.path());
```

We make the assumption here that any files to be served can be found in a subfolder of the folder in which this service is running. The filename (and path) is obtained from the request URL. If the path was empty, we assign it a default index file to be served instead:

```
        if (!file.exists() || file.isDirectory()) {
            response.setStatus(HTTPResponse::HTTP_NOT_FOUND);
            ostream& ostr = response.send();
            ostr << "File Not Found.";
            return;
        }

        string::size_type idx = path.rfind('.');
        string ext = "";
        if (idx != std::string::npos) {
            ext = path.substr(idx + 1);
        }

        string mime = "text/plain";
        if (ext == "html") { mime = "text/html"; }
        if (ext == "css") { mime = "text/css"; }
        else if (ext == "js") { mime = "application/javascript"; }
        else if (ext == "zip") { mime = "application/zip"; }
        else if (ext == "json") { mime = "application/json"; }
        else if (ext == "png") { mime = "image/png"; }
        else if (ext == "jpeg" || ext == "jpg") { mime = "image/jpeg"; }
        else if (ext == "gif") { mime = "image/gif"; }
        else if (ext == "svg") { mime = "image/svg"; }
```

We first check that the resulting file path is valid and that it is a regular file, not a directory. If this check fails, we return an HTTP 404 File Not Found error.

After passing this check, we try to obtain the file extension from the file path to try and determine a specific MIME type for the file. If this fails, we use a default MIME type for plain text:

```
        try {
                response.sendFile(file.path(), mime);
        }
        catch (FileNotFoundException &e) {
                Club::log(LOG_ERROR, "DataHandler: File not found
exception    triggered...");
                cerr << e.displayText() << endl;

                response.setStatus(HTTPResponse::HTTP_NOT_FOUND);
                ostream& ostr = response.send();
                ostr << "File Not Found.";
                return;
        }
        catch (OpenFileException &e) {
                Club::log(LOG_ERROR, "DataHandler: Open file
exception triggered: " +    e.displayText());

response.setStatus(HTTPResponse::HTTP_INTERNAL_SERVER_ERROR);
                ostream& ostr = response.send();
                ostr << "Internal Server Error. Couldn't open file.";
                return;
        }
    }
};
```

As the final step, we use the response object's `sendFile()` method to send the file to the client, along with the MIME type we determined earlier.

We also handle the two exceptions this method can throw. The first one occurs when the file cannot be found for some reason. This results in us returning another HTTP 404 error.

If the file cannot be opened for some reason, we return an HTTP 500 Internal Server Error instead, along with the text from the exception.

Service configuration

With the Raspbian Linux distribution for Raspberry Pi SBCs, system services are usually managed with `systemd`. This uses a simple configuration file, with our club monitoring service using something like the following:

```
[Unit]
Description=ClubStatus monitoring & control

[Service]
ExecStart=/home/user/clubstatus/clubstatus /home/user/clubstatus/config.ini
User=user
WorkingDirectory=/home/user/clubstatus
Restart=always
RestartSec=5

[Install]
WantedBy=multi-user.target
```

This service configuration specifies the name of the service, with the service being started from the "`user`" user account's folder, and the configuration file for the service being found in the same folder. We set the working directory for the service, also enabling the automatic restarting of the service after five seconds if it were to fail for whatever reason.

Finally, the service will be started after the system has started to the point where a user can log in to the system. This way, we are sure that networking and other functionality has been started already. If one starts a system service too soon, it could fail due to missing functionality on account of things not having been initialized yet.

Next, here is the INI file configuration file:

```
[MQTT]
; URL and port of the MQTT server.
host = localhost
port = 1883

; Authentication
user = user
pass = password

; The topic status on which changes will be published.
clubStatusTopic = /my/topic

[HTTP]
port = 8080
```

```
[Relay]
; Whether an i2c relay board is connected. 0 (false) or 1 (true).
active = 0
; i2c address, in decimal or hexadecimal.
address = 0x20
```

The configuration file is divided into three sections, MQTT, HTTP, and Relay, with each section containing the relevant variables.

For MQTT, we have the expected options for connecting to the MQTT broker, including password-based authentication. We also specify the topic regarding which club status updates will be published here.

The HTTP section just contains the port we will be listening on, with the server listening on all interfaces by default. If necessary, one could make the network interface a used configurable as well by making this property configurable before starting the HTTP server.

Finally, the Relay section allows us to turn the relay board feature on or off, as well as configure the I2C device address if we are making use of this feature.

Permissions

Since both the GPIO and I2C are treated as common Linux devices, they come with their own set of permissions. Assuming one wishes to avoid running the service as root, we need to add an account that runs the service to both the gpio and i2c user groups:

```
sudo usermod -a -G gpio user
sudo usermod -a -G i2c user
```

After this, we need to restart the system (or log out and in again) for the changes to take effect. We should now be able to run the service without any issues.

Final results

With the application and systemd service configured and installed on the target SBC, it will automatically start and configure itself. To complete the system, you could install it along with a suitable power supply into an enclosure, into which you would run the signal wires from the switches, the network cable, and so on.

One implementation of this system was installed at the Entropia hackerspace in Karlsruhe, Germany. This setup uses a real traffic light (legally obtained) outside the club door with 12 volt LED lights for status indication. The SBC, relay board, debounce board, and power supply (5V and 12V MeanWell industrial PSU) are all integrated into a single, laser-cut wooden enclosure:

However, you are free to integrate the components any way you wish. The main thing to consider here is that the electronics are all safely protected from harm and accidental contact as the relay board could be switching mains voltage, along with possibly the mains voltage line for the power supply.

Example – basic media player

Another basic example of an SBC-based embedded system is a media player. This can involve both audio and audio-visual (AV) media formats. The difference between an SBC-based system being used to play back media with regular keyboard and mouse input, and an embedded SBC-based media player, is that in the latter's case the system can only ever be used for that purpose, with the software and user interface (physical- and software-wise) both optimized for media player use.

To this end, a software-based frontend has to be developed, along with a physical interface peripheral, using which the media player can be controlled. This could be something as simple as a series of switches connected to the GPIO pins, with a regular HDMI display for output. Alternatively, one could use a touch screen, although this would require a more complex driver setup.

Since our media player system stores media files locally, we want to use an SBC that supports external storage beyond the SD card. Some SBCs come with a SATA connection, allowing us to connect a hard disk drive (HDD) of capacities far exceeding those of SD cards. Even if we stick to compact 2.5" HDDs, which are roughly the same size as many popular SBCs, we can easily and fairly cheaply get multiple terabytes worth of storage.

Beyond the storage requirement, we also need to have a digital video output, and we want to either use the GPIO or the USB side for the user interface buttons.

A very suitable board for this purpose is the LeMaker Banana Pro, which comes with the H3 ARM SoC, hardware SATA, and Gigabit Ethernet support, as well as a full-sized HDMI output with 4k video decoding support:

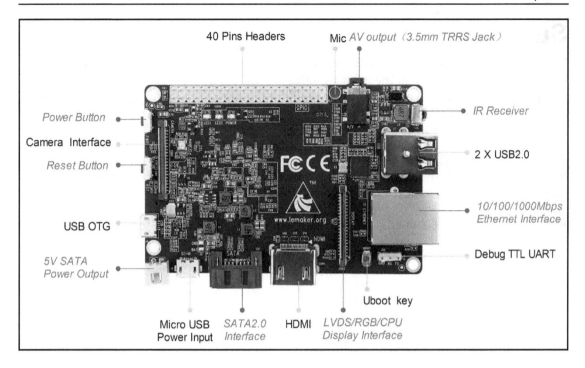

After going through the basics of installing Armbian or similar OSes on the SBC, we can set up a media player application on the system, having it start together with the OS and configuring it to both load a playlist and to listen to events on a number of GPIO pins. These GPIO pins would be connected to a number of control switches, allowing us to scroll through the playlist and start, pause, and stop playlist items.

Other interaction methods are possible, such as an infrared or radio-based remote control, each of which come with their own advantages and disadvantages.

We will be working through the creation of this media player system and turning it into an infotainment system in the following chapters:

- Chapter 6, *Testing OS-Based Applications*
- Chapter 8, *Example - Linux-Based Infotainment System*
- Chapter 11, *Developing Embedded Systems with Qt*

Summary

In this chapter, we looked at OS-based embedded systems, exploring the many operating systems available to us, with the most significant differences, especially those of real-time operating systems. We also saw how one would integrate an RTC peripheral into an SBC-based Linux system and explored user space- and kernel space-based driver modules, along with their advantages and disadvantages.

Along with the example project in this chapter, the reader should now have a good idea of how to translate a set of requirements into a functioning OS-based embedded system. The reader will know how to add external peripherals and use them from the OS.

In the next chapter, we will be looking at developing for resource-restricted embedded systems, including 8-bit MCUs and their larger brethren.

4

Resource-Restricted Embedded Systems

Using a smaller embedded system such as a microcontroller (MCU) means having small amounts of RAM, CPU power, and storage. This chapter deals with planning for and making efficient use of limited resources taking into account the wide range of currently available MCUs and **System-on-Chip** (**SoC**) solutions. We will be considering the following aspects

- Selecting the right MCU for a project
- Concurrency and memory management
- Adding sensors, actuators, and network access
- Bare-metal development versus real-time OSes

The big picture for small systems

When first confronted with a new project that requires the use of at least one type of MCU, it can seem like an overwhelming task to. As we saw in Chapter 1, *What are Embedded Systems?*, there is a large number of MCUs to choose from, even if we limit ourselves to just those that have been released recently.

It may seem obvious to start by asking how many bits one needs, as in selecting between 8-bit, 16-bit, and 32-bit MCUs, or something as easy to quantify as clock speed, but these metrics are sometimes misleading and often don't lend themselves well to narrowing down the product selection. As it turns out, the parent categories are availability of sufficient I/O and the integrated peripherals to make the hardware happen in a lean and reliable way, as well as processing power tailored to the requirements faced at design-time and predicted to emerge throughout the product life-time.

So in more detail we need to answer questions like these:

- **Peripherals**: Which peripherals are needed to interact with the rest of the system?
- **CPU**: What level of CPU power is needed to run the application code?
- **Floating point**: Do we need hardware floating point support?
- **ROM**: How much ROM do we need to store the code?
- **RAM**: How much RAM is required to run the code?
- **Power and thermals**: What are the electrical power and thermal limitations?

Each MCU family has its own strengths and weaknesses, though one of the most important factors to pick one MCU family over another the quality of its development tools. For hobby and other noncommercial projects, one would primarily consider the strength of the community and the available free development tools, while in the context of commercial projects one would also look at the support one could expect from the MCU manufacturer and possible third parties.

A key aspect of embedded development is in-system programming and debugging. Since programming and debugging are intertwined, we'll be looking at the corresponding interface options later to be able to identify what satisfies our requirements and constraints.

A popular and powerful debugging interface has become synonymous to the underlying Joint Test Action Group (JTAG) IEEE standard 1149.1 and easily recognized by signals frequently labeled TDI, TDO, TCK, TMS and TRST, defining the aptly-named Test Action Port (TAP). The larger standard has since been expanded up to 1149.8 and not all versions apply to digital logic, so we'll limit our scope to 1149.1 and a reduced pin count version described under 1149.7. For now we just require that at least one of the full-featured JTAG, SWD and UPDI interfaces be supported.

Debugging MCU-based systems along with on-chip debugging, using both command-line tools and IDEs, is something that we will take an in-depth look at in Chapter 7, *Testing Resource-Limited Platforms.*

Finally, if we are going to be making products containing the chosen MCU for an active production phase of a few years, it's vital that we ensure the MCU availability (or that of compatible replacements) for at least that period. Reputable manufacturers provide product life cycle information as part of their supply chain management, with discontinuation notices being sent 1 to 2 years in advance, and recommendations for lifetime buys.

For many applications, it is hard to ignore the wide availability of cheap, powerful, and easy-to-use Arduino compatible boards, especially the popular ones designed around the AVR family of MCUs. Among these, the ATmega MCUs—the mega168/328, and in particular the mega1280/2560 variants—provide significant amounts of processing power, ROM, and RAM for both high-level functionality and the handling of data for input, control, and telemetry, as well as a differentiated but rich sets of peripherals and GPIO.

All of these aspects make prototyping exceedingly simple before even committing to a more definitive variant with lower specifications and (hopefully) better BOM cost. As an example, the ATmega2560 "MEGA" board is shown as follows, and we will look at other boards in more detail later in this chapter as we work through a number of examples on how to develop for the AVR platform.

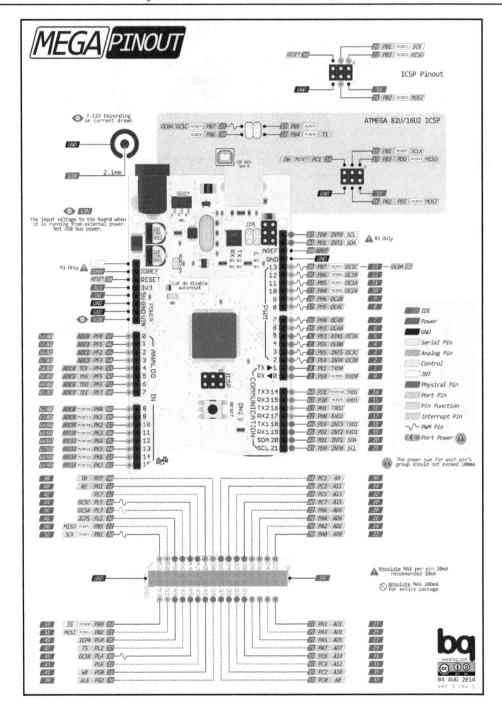

Generally, one would pick a number of MCUs that might work for the project, get the development boards, hook them up to the rest of the projected system components (often on their own development or breakout boards), and start developing the software for the MCU that will make everything work together.

As more and more parts of the system become finalized, the number of development boards and bread-boarded components will dwindle until one reaches the point where one starts working on the final **printed circuit board** (**PCB**) layout. This will go through a number of iterations as well, as issues get ironed out, last-minute features are added, and the system as a whole is tested and optimized.

MCUs in such systems work on a physical level with the hardware, thus it is often a requirement to specify both hardware and software in tandem, if only because the software is so reliant on the hardware functionality. A common theme encountered in the industry is hardware modularity, either as small add-on PCBs with minimum added complexity, adding sensor or communication interfaces to devices such as temperature controllers and variable-frequency drives, or as full-fledged DIN rail modules connected to a common serial bus.

Example – Machine controller for a laser cutter

One of the fastest and most accurate ways to cut a wide range of materials is using a high-power laser. With the price of carbon dioxide (CO_2) having dropped sharply over the years, this has led to widespread use of affordable (cheap) laser cutters as shown in the following image:

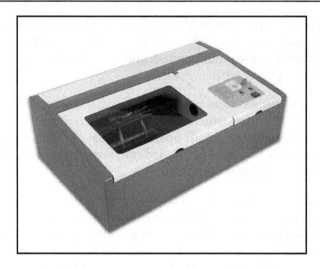

While it's perfectly possible to operate a laser cutter with nothing more than just a basic enclosure and the stepper motion control board that move the head across the machin bed, from a usability and safety point of view, this is not desirable. Still, many of the cheap laser cutters one can purchase online, however, do not come with any safety or usability features whatsoever.

Functional specification

To complete the product, we need to add a control system that uses sensors and actuators to monitor and control the state of the machine, ensuring that it is always in a safe state and shutting down the laser beam if necessary. This means protecting access to each of the following three sections:

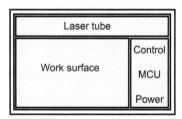

The cutting beam is usually generated by a CO_2 laser, a type of gas laser that was invented in 1964. The application of a high voltage causes current flow and thereby excitement of the gas molecules in the bore that make up the gain medium, ultimately resulting in the formation of a coherent beam of **long-wavelength infrared** (**LWIR**) or IR-C, light at a wavelength of 9.4 or 10.6 μm.

One characteristic of LWIR is that it is strongly absorbed by a large number of materials, so that it can be used for engraving, cutting, and even surgery on tissues as the water in biological tissues efficiently absorbs the laser beam. This also makes it obvious why even brief exposure of one's skin to a CO_2 laser's beam is extremely dangerous.

To achieve safe operation, exposure to laser light must be inhibited by locking the enclosure during normal operation, deactivating the laser power supply, and closing a beam shutter or preferably a combination of these measures when any of the interlocks is opened or any other safety condition is no longer satisfied.

For example, temperature limits have to be upheld: most CO_2 lasers comprise of water-cooled gas discharge tube, which can quickly crack or bend in case of a cooling fault. What's more, the cutting process creates irritating or toxic fumes that need to be continuously removed from the enclosure so as not to contaminate the optics and exit into the environment when the lid is opened.

These requirements necessitate that we monitor cooling water flow and temperature, air flow for the exhaust, and the air flow resistance (pressure drop over mass flow) of over the exhaust filter.

Finally, we also want to make it convenient to use the laser cutter and avoid having to "bring your own device" to process the design in a machine-specific way, then convert it and upload it to the stepper motion controller board via USB. Instead, we want to load the design project from an SD card or USB stick and use a simple LCD and buttons to set options.

The design requirements

With the earlier requirements in mind, we can formulate a list of features needed for the control system:

- Operator safety:
    - Interlock switches on access panels (closed with the panel closed)
    - Locking mechanism (mechanically locking access panel; redundant)
    - Emergency stop

- Laser cooling:
    - Pump relay
    - Temperature sensor in water tank (cooling capacity, inlet temperature)
    - Temperature sensor on valve cooling exhaust (mantle temperature)
    - Flow sensor (water flow speed; redundant)
- Air exhaust:
    - Fan relay
    - Air filter status (differential pressure sensor)
    - Fan speed (RPM)
- Laser module:
    - Laser power relay
    - Beam shutter (redundant)
- User interface
    - Alert indicators for:
        - Panel interlock
        - Air filter condition
        - Fan status
        - Pump status
        - Water temperature
    - Indicator LEDs for:
        - Standby
        - Starting
        - Operation
        - Emergency stop
        - Cool down
- Communication:
    - USB communication with stepper board (UART)
    - Motion control: generate stepper motor instructions
    - Read files from SD card/USB stick
    - Accept files over Ethernet/Wi-Fi
    - NFC reader to identify users

Implementation-related choices

As pointed out at the beginning of this chapter, mid-range MCUs are currently capable of providing the resources to satisfy most, if not all of our design requirements. So one of the tough questions is what we'll be spending our money on: hardware components or software development? Imponderabilities aside, we'll now take a closer look at three candidate solutions:

- A single mid-range AVR MCU board (ATmega2560)
- A higher-end Cortex-M3 MCU board (SAM3X8E)
- A tandem of mid-range MCU board and an SBC with OS

We're pretty close to meeting hte design requirements with just an Arduino Mega (ATmega2560), as the first five sections require little in terms of CPU speed, just a number of digital input and output pins and a few analog ones depending on the exact sensors we'll be using or at most a peripheral interface to make use of (for example, for MEMS pressure sensors).

The challenge starts with motion control feature under communications in the previous feature list, where we suddenly have to convert a **vector graphics file** (**.svg**) to a series of stepper commands. This is a compound problem of data transfer, file parsing, path generation, and what is known in the robotic world as inverse kinematics. USB communications can also be problematic for our 8-bit MCU, mostly because of peak processor loads coinciding with timeouts for USB endpoint communication or UART RX buffer register handling.

The key is knowing when to change gears. Motion control is time critical as it's tied to the inertia of the physical world. Additionally, we're constrained by the processing and bandwidth resources of our controller to make control and data transfers, buffering, and ultimately the processing and output generation itself happen. As a general pattern, more capable internal or external peripherals can relax timing requirements by handling events and memory transactions themselves, reducing context switching and processing overhead. Here's an incomplete list of such considerations:

- Simple UART requires collecting every byte upon RX Complete (RXC). Failure to do so results in data loss, as indicated by the DOR flag. A few controllers such as ATmega8u2 through ATmega32u4 provide native hardware flow control via RTS/CTS lines, which can prevent USB-UART converters such as PL2303 and FT232 from sending, forcing them to do the buffering instead until UDR is conveniently emptied again.

- Dedicated USB host peripherals such as the MAX3421 are connected via SPI and effectively remove USB timing requirements for mass storage integration.
- UART aside, network communication peripherals are inherently buffered in software due to the complexity of the layer stack. For Ethernet, the W5500 is an attractive solution.
- It sometimes makes sense to add another smaller MCU that independently handles I/O and pattern generation while implementing an interface of our choice – e.g. serial or parallel. This is already the case with some Arduino boards featuring an ATmega16u2 for USB serial conversion.

The NFC reader feature requirement calls for **Near-Field Communication** (**NFC**, a subset of RFID) to prevent unauthorized use of the laser cutter, which would add the biggest burden of all. Not due to the communicating with the NFC reader itself, but due to the increase in code size and CPU requirements to handle cryptography with certificates depending on the security level chosen. We would also need a secure place to store the certificates which usually bumps up MCU specs.

Now we are at the point where we consider the more advanced options. The simpler ATmega2560 remains a great fit with its large amount of GPIO and can read SD cards over SPI along with communicating with an external integrated ethernet chip. However, the computationally or memory intensive tasks in motion control and NFC reader feature list would likely overburden the MCU or lead to convoluted "optimized" solutions with inferior maintainability if one were to try.

Upgrading the MCU to an ARM Cortex-M3 such as found on the Arduino Due development board, would likely resolve all those bottlenecks. It would preserve the large number of GPIO we got accustomed to on the ATmega2560, while increasing CPU performance significantly. The stepper drive patterns can be generated on the MCU, which also presents with native USB support, along with other advanced peripherals (USART, SPI and I2C and HSMCI, which also have DMA).

A basic NFC tag reader could be connected via a UART, SPI, or I2C, and this design choice would lead to a system as shown:

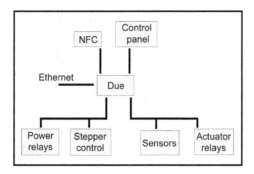

The third embodiment involving an SBC would again make use of the ATmega2560 and add a low-powered SBC running an OS. This SBC would handle any CPU-intensive tasks, Ethernet and Wi-Fi connectivity, USB (host) tasks, and so on. It would communicate with the ATmega side via a UART, possibly adding a digital isolator or level shifter in between the boards to accommodate the 3.3V (SBC) and 5V TTL (Atmega) logic levels.

Choosing the SBC + MCU solution would substantially change the software challenges but only slightly reorganize our system on the hardware side. This would look as follows:

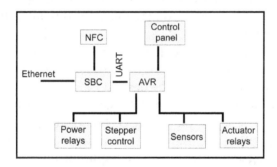

As with most development processes, there are only a few absolute answers, and many solutions pass functional requirements as *good enough* after trade-offs between power usage, complexity, and maintenance requirements affecting the final design choice.

In this particular example, one could choose either the higher-end single or dual-board solution, and it would most likely entail the same amount of effort to satisfy the requirements. One of the main differences would be that the OS-based solution adds the need to perform frequent OS updates, on account of it being a network-connected system running a full-blown OS whereas embedded ethernet controllers with offloaded hardwired TCP/IP stack and memories tend to be more robust and proven.

The Cortex-M3-based option (or the even faster Cortex-M4) would feature just our own code, and thus would be unlikely to have any common security issues that could be easily targeted. We wouldn't be off the hook for maintenance, but our code would be small enough to validate and read through in its entirety, with the only letdown that the Arduino Due design fails to break out the pins for RMII to hook up an external Ethernet PHY, discouraging the use of its internal Ethernet MAC.

Running down the checklist we put together at the beginning of this chapter, but this time with the ATmega2560 + SBC and application in mind, gives us the following distribution of duties:

- **Peripherals**: The MCU side will mostly need GPIO, some analog (ADC) inputs, Ethernet, USB, along with SPI and/or I2C.
- **CPU**: The required MCU performance is time-critical but minor, except for when we need to do the processing of the vector path elements into stepper instructions. The SBC side can be sophisticated as long as enough commands can be queued for MCU-side execution and time-critical interaction is avoided.
- **Floating point**: The stepper instruction conversion algorithm on an MCU executes substantially faster if we have hardware floating point support. The length and time scales involved may make fixed point arithmetic feasible, relaxing this requirement.
- **ROM**: The entire MCU code will likely fit into a few kilobytes since it's not very complex. The SBC code will be larger by orders of magnitude just by invoking high-level libraries to provide the desired functionality but this will be more than offset by the similarly scaled mass storage and processing capabilities.
- **RAM**: A few KB of SRAM on the MCU should suffice. The stepper instruction conversion algorithm may require modifications to fit into the SRAM limitations with its buffering and processing data requirements. In a worst-case scenario, buffers can be downsized.
- **Power and thermals**: In the light of the laser cutter system's power needs and cooling system, we have got no significant power or thermal limitations. The section containing the control system also houses the main power supply and is already equipped with an appropriately sized cooling fan.

It's important to note at this point that although we realized the complexity and requirements of the task at hand sufficiently to draw conclusions leading us to a selection of hardware components, the aspects of how to achieve them in detail are still left to the software developer.

For example, we could define our own data structures and formats and implement the machine-specific path generation and motion control ourselves, or adopt a (RS-274) G-code intermediate format which has been well-established in numerical control applications for several decades, and that lends itself well to generating motion control commands. G-code and has also found widespread acceptance in the diy hardware community, expecially for FDM 3D printing.

One noteworthy mature open source implementation of G-code based motion control is GRBL, introduced as:

> *Grbl is a free, open source, high performance software for controlling the motion of machines that move, that make things, or that make things move, and will run on a straight Arduino. If the maker movement was an industry, Grbl would be the industry standard.*
> *--https://github.com/gnea/grbl*

Most likely we'll have to add halt and emergency stop features for different violations of our safety checks. While temperature excursions or a clogged filter would preferably just halt the laser cutter and permit resuming the job with the issues resolved, an interlock tripped by opening the enclosure must result in immediate shutdown of the laser, even without finishing the last command for a path segment and motion.

The choice to modularize the motion control task and produce G-code for it has benefits beyond the availability of proven implementations, allowing us to easily add usability features like manual control for setup and calibration as well as testability using previously generated, human-readable codes on the machine side just as inspection on the output of our file interpretation and path generation algorithms.

With the list of requirements, the initial design completed, and a deepened understanding of how we are going to achieve our goals, the next step would be to obtain a development board (or boards) with the chosen MCU and/or SoC, along with any peripherals so that one can get started on developing the firmware and integrating the system.

While the full implementation of the machine control system as described in this example is beyond the scope of this book, an in-depth understanding of the development for both microcontroller and SBC target varieties will be strived for in the remainder of this chapter and Chapter 6, *Testing OS-Based Applications*, Chapter 8, *Example - Linux-Based Infotainment System*, and Chapter 11, *Developing for Hybrid SoC/FPGA Systems*, respectively.

Embedded IDEs and frameworks

While the application development for SoCs tends to be quite similar to desktop and server environments, as we saw in the previous chapter, MCU development requires a far more intimate knowledge of the hardware that one is developing for, sometimes down to the exact bits to set in a particular register.

There exist some frameworks that seek to abstract away such details for particular MCU series, so that one can develop for a common API without having to worry about how it is implemented on a specific MCU. Of these, the Arduino framework is the most well-known outside of industrial applications, though there are also a number of commercial frameworks that are certified for production use.

Frameworks such as the **Advanced Software Framework** (**ASF**) for AVR and SAM MCUs can be used with a variety of IDEs, including Atmel Studio, Keil µVision, and IAR Embedded Workbench.

A non-exhaustive list of popular embedded IDEs follows:

Name	Company	License	Platforms	Notes
Atmel Studio	Microchip	Proprietary	AVR, SAM (ARM Cortex-M).	Originally developed by Atmel before being bought by Microchip.
µVision	Keil (ARM)	Proprietary	ARM Cortex-M, 166, 8051, 251.	Part of the **Microcontroller Development Kit** (**MDK**) toolchain.
Embedded Workbench	IAR	Proprietary	ARM Cortex-M, 8051, MSP430, AVR, Coldfire, STM8, H8, SuperH, etc.	Separate IDE for each MCU architecture.
MPLAB X	Microchip	Proprietary	PIC, AVR.	Uses the Java-based NetBeans IDE as foundation.
Arduino	Arduino	GPLv2	Some AVR and SAM MCUs (extendable).	Java-based IDE. Only supports its own C dialect language.

The main goal of an IDE is to integrate the entire workflow into a single application, from writing the initial code to programming the MCU memory with the compiled code and debugging the application while it runs on the platform.

Whether to use a full IDE is a matter of preference, however. All of the essential features are still there when using a basic editor and the tools from the command line, although frameworks such as the ASF are written to deeply integrate with IDEs.

One of the main advantages of the popular Arduino framework is that it has more or less standardized an API for various MCU peripherals and other functionality that is supported across an ever-growing number of MCU architectures. Coupled with the open source nature of the framework, it makes for an attractive target for a new project. This is particularly attractive when it comes to prototyping, courtesy of a large number of libraries and drivers written for this API.

Unfortunately, the Arduino IDE is unfortunately focused purely on a stripped-down dialect of the C programming language, despite its core libraries making widespread use of C++. Still this enables us to integrate just the libraries into our own embedded C++ projects, as we will see later in this chapter.

Programming MCUs

After we have compiled our code for the target MCU, the binary image needs to be written to a controller memory prior to execution and debugging. In this section we will look at the varied ways in which this can be accomplished. These days only factory-side programming is done with test sockets, or better yet at the wafer level before a known good die is bonded to a leadframe and encapsulated. Surface-mount parts already rule out easy removal of an MCU for (repeated) programming.

A number of (frequently vendor-specific) options for in-circuit programming exist, distinguished by the peripherals they use and the memories they affect.

So a pristine MCU often needs to be programmed using an external programming adapter. These generally work by setting the pins of the MCU so that it enters programming mode, after which the MCU accepts the data stream containing the new ROM image.

Another option that is commonly used is to add a boot loader to the first section of the ROM, which allows the MCU to program itself. This works by having the boot loader check on startup whether it should switch to programming mode or continue loading the actual program, placed right after the boot loader section.

Memory programming and device debugging

External programming adapters often utilize dedicated interfaces and associated protocols which permit programming and debugging of the target device. Protocols with which one can program an MCU include the following:

Name	Pins	Features	Description
SPI (ISP)	4	program	**Serial Peripheral Interface** (**SPI**), used with older AVR MCUs to access its Serial Programmer mode (**In-circuit Serial Programming (ISP)**).
JTAG	5	program debug boundary	Dedicated, industry-standard on-chip interface for programming and debugging support. Supported on AVR ATxmega devices.
UPDI	1	program debug	The **Unified Programming and Debug Interface** (**UDPI**) used with newer AVR MCUs, including ATtiny devices. It's a single-wire interface that's the successor to the two-wire PDI found on ATxmega devices.
HVPP/ HVSP	17/ 5	program	High Voltage Parallel Programming / High Voltage Serial Programming. AVR programming mode using 12V on the reset pin and direct access to 8+ pins. Ignores any internal fuse setting or other configuration option. Mostly used for in-factory programming and for recovery.
TPI	3	program	Tiny Programming Interface, used with some ATtiny AVR devices. These devices also lack the number of pins for HVPP or HVSP.
SWD	3	program debug boundary	Serial Wire Debug. Similar to reduced pin count JTAG with two lines, but uses ARM Debug Interface features, allowing a connected debugger to become a bus master with access to the MCU's memory and peripherals.

ARM MCUs generally provide JTAG as their primary means of programming and debugging. On 8-bit MCUs, JTAG is far less common, which is mostly due to the complexity of its requirements.

AVR MCUs tend to offer In-System Programming (ISP) via SPI in addition to high voltage programming modes. Entering programming mode requires that the reset pin be held low during programming and verification and released and strobed at the end of the programming cycle.

One requirement for ISP is that the relevant (SPIEN fuse bit) in the MCU is set to enable the in-system programming interface. Without this bit set, the device won't respond on the SPI lines. Without JTAG available and enabled via the JTAGEN fuse bit, only HVPP or HVSP are available to recover and reprogram the chip. In the latter case, the unusual set of pins and the 12V supply voltage do not necessarily integrate well into the board circuitry.

The physical connections required for most serial programming interfaces are fairly simple, even when the MCU has already been integrated into a circuit as shown in the following diagram:

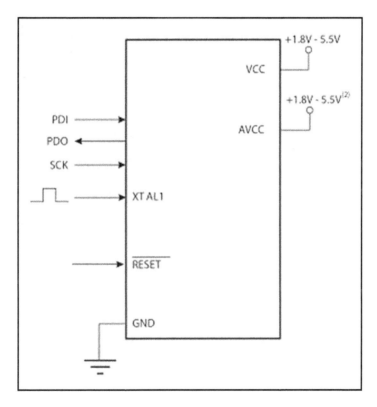

Here, the external oscillator is optional if an internal one exists. The **PDI**, **PDO**, and **SCK** lines correspond to their respective SPI lines. The Reset line is held active (low) during programming. After connecting to the MCU in this manner, we are free to write to its flash memory, EEPROM, and configuration fuses.

On newer AVR devices, we find the **Unified Programming and Debug Interface (UPDI)**, which uses just a single wire (in addition to the power and ground lines) to connect to the target MCU to provide both programming and debug support.

This interface simplifies the previous connection diagram to the following:

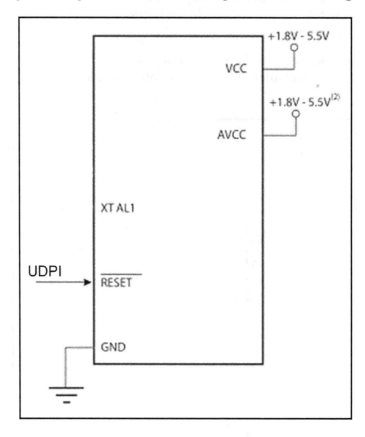

This favorably compares to JTAG (IEEE 1149.1) on the ATxmega (when enabled) as follows:

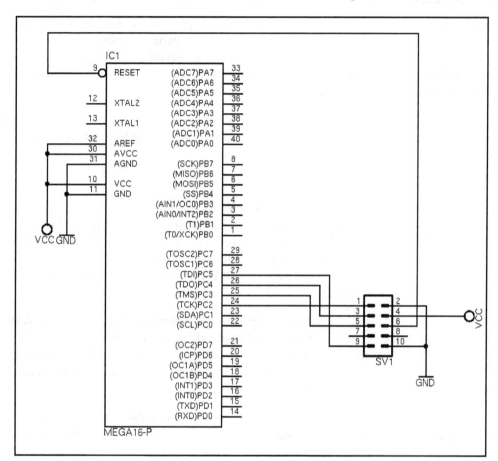

Thereduced pin count JTAG standard (IEEE 1149) implemented on the ATxmega requires only one clock TCKC, one data wire TMSC and is aptly called Compact JTAG. Of these interfaces, UPDI still requires the fewest connections with the target device. Apart from that, both support similar features for AVR MCUs.

For other systems using JTAG for programming and debugging, no standard connection exists. Each manufacturer uses their own preferred connector, ranging from 2 x 5 pins (Altera, AVR) to 2 x 10 pins (ARM), or a single 8-pin connector (Lattice).

With JTAG being more a protocol standard rather than a physical specification, one should consult the documentation for one's target platform for the specific details.

Boot loader

The boot loader has been introduced as a small extra application that uses an existing interface (for example, UART or Ethernet) to provide self-programming capabilities. On the AVR, a boot loader section of 256 bytes to 4 KB can be reserved in its flash. This code can perform any number of user-defined tasks, from setting up a serial link with a remote system, to booting from a remote image over Ethernet using PXE.

At its core, an AVR boot loader is no different from any other AVR application, except that when compiling it one extra linker flag is added to set the starting byte address for the boot loader:

```
--section-start=.text=0x1800
```

Replace this address with a similar one for the specific MCU that you're using (for AVR depending on the BOOTSZ flags set and controller used, see datasheet table about Boot Size Configuration: Boot Reset Address, where, for example, the boot reset address is 0xC00 is in words and the section start is defined in bytes). This ensures that the boot loader code will be written to the proper location in the MCU's ROM. Writing the boot loader code to the ROM is almost always done via ISP.

AVR MCUs divide the flash ROM into two sections: the **no-read-while-write** (**NRWW**) (for most, if not all application memory space) and **read-while-write** (**RWW**) sections. In brief, this means that the RWW section can be safely erased and rewritten without affecting the CPU's operation. This is why the boot loader resides in the NRWW section and also why it's not easy to have the boot loader update itself.

Another important detail is that the boot loader can also not update the fuses that set various flags in the MCU. To change these, one has to externally program the device.

After programming the MCU with a boot loader, one would generally set the flags in the MCU that let the processor know that a boot loader has been installed. In the case of AVR, these flags are BOOTSZ and BOOTRST.

Memory management

The storage and memory system of microcontrollers consists out of multiple components. There is a section of **read-only-memory** (**ROM**) that is only written to once when the chip is programmed, but which cannot normally be altered by the MCU itself, as we saw in the previous section.

The MCU may also have a bit of persistent storage, in the form of EEPROM or equivalent. Finally, there are CPU registers and the **random-access memory (RAM)**. This results in the following exemplary memory layout:

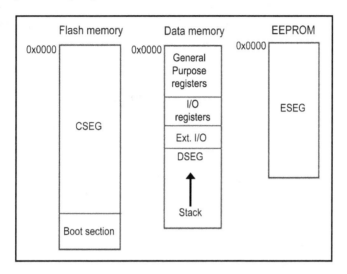

The use of a modified Harvard architecture (split program and data memory at some architectural level, generally with the data buses) is common with MCUs. With the AVR architecture, for example, the program memory is found in the ROM, which for the ATmega2560 is connected using its own bus with the CPU core, as one can seen on the block diagram for this MCU, which we looked at previously in Chapter 1, *What Are Embedded Systems?*

A major advantage of having separate buses for these memory spaces is that one can address each of them separately, which makes better use of the limited addressing space available to an 8-bit processor (1 and 2 byte wide address). It also allows for concurrent accesses while the CPU is busy with the other memory space, further optimizing the available resources.

For the data memory in the SRAM, we are then free to use it as we want. Here, we do need at least a stack to be able to run a program. Depending on how much SRAM is left in the MCU, we can then also add a heap. Applications of moderate complexity can be realized with only stack and statically allocated memory though, not involving higher-level language features that produce code with heap allocations.

Stack and heap

Whether one needs to initialize the stack on the MCU that one is programming for depends on how low-level one wishes to go. When using the C-runtime (on AVR: `avr-libc`), the runtime will handle initializing the stack and other details by letting the linker place naked code into init sections, for example specified by:

```
__attribute__ ((naked, used, section (".init3")))
```

Preceding the execution of any of our own application code.

The standard RAM layout on AVR is to start with the `.data` variables at the beginning of the RAM, followed by `.bss`. The stack is started from the opposite site of the RAM, growing towards the beginning. There will be room left between the end of the `.bss` section and the end of the stack illustrated as follows:

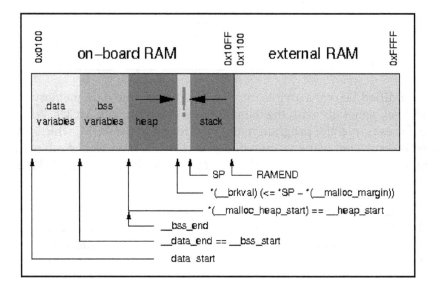

Since the stack grows depending on the depth of the function calls in the application being run, it is hard to say how much space is available. Some MCUs allow one to use external RAM as well, which would be a possible location for the heap as follows:

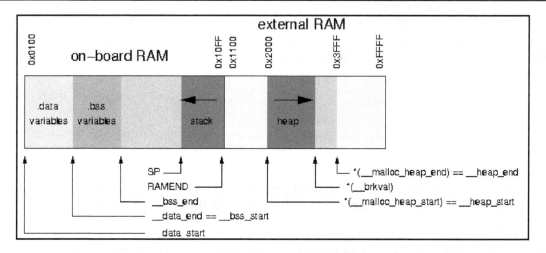

The AVR Libc library implements a `malloc()` memory allocator routine, optimized for the AVR architecture. Using it, one can implement one's own `new` and `delete` functionality as well—if one so desires—since the AVR toolchain does not implement either.

In order to use external memory with an AVR MCU for heap storage, one would have to make sure that the external memory has been initialized, after which the address space becomes available to `malloc()`. The start and end of the heap space is hereby defined by these global variables:

```
char * __malloc_heap_start
char * __malloc_heap_end
```

The AVR documentation has the following advice regarding adjusting the heap:

> *If the heap is going to be moved to external RAM,* `__malloc_heap_end` *must be adjusted accordingly. This can either be done at runtime, by writing directly to this variable, or it can be done automatically at link-time, by adjusting the value of the symbol* `__heap_end`.

Interrupts, ESP8266 IRAM_ATTR

On a desktop PC or server the entire application binary would be loaded into RAM. On MCUs though it is common to leave as many of the program instructions in the ROM as possible until they are needed. This means that most of our application's instructions cannot be executed immediately, but first have to be fetched from ROM before the CPU of our MCU can fetch them via the instruction bus to be executed.

On the AVR, each possible interrupt is defined in a vector table, which is stored in ROM. This offers either default handlers for each interrupt type, or the user-defined version. To mark an interrupt routine, one either uses the `__attribute__((signal))` attribute, or uses the `ISR()` macro:

```
#include <avr/interrupt.h>

ISR(ADC_vect) {
        // user code
}
```

This macro handles the details of registering an interrupt. One just has to specify the name and define a function for the interrupt handler. This will then get called via the interrupt vector table.

With the ESP8266 (and its successor, the ESP32) we can mark the interrupt handler function with a special attribute, `IRAM_ATTR`. Unlike the AVR, the ESP8266 MCU does not have built-in ROM, but has to use its SPI peripheral to load any instructions into RAM, which is obviously quite slow.

An example of using this attribute with an interrupt handler looks as follows:

```
void IRAM_ATTR MotionModule::interruptHandler() {
        int val = digitalRead(pin);
        if (val == HIGH) { motion = true; }
        else { motion = false; }
}
```

Here, we have an interrupt handler that is connected to the signal from a motion detector, connected to an input pin. As with any well-written interrupt handler, it is quite simple and meant to be quickly executed before returning to the normal flow of the application.

Having this handler in ROM would mean that the routine would not respond near-instantly to the motion sensor's output changing. Worse, it would cause the handler to take much longer to finish, which would consequently delay the execution of the rest of the application code.

By marking it with `IRAM_ATTR`, we can avoid this problem, since the entire handler will already be in RAM when it's needed, instead of the whole system stalling as it waits for the SPI bus to return the requested data before it can continue.

> Note that, tempting as it may seem, this kind of attribute should be used sparingly, as most MCUs have much more ROM than RAM. In the case of ESP8266, there are 64kB RAM for code execution complemented by possibly megabytes of external Flash ROM.

When compiling our code, the compiler will put instructions marked with this attribute into a special section, so that the MCU knows to load it into RAM.

Concurrency

With a few exceptions, MCUs are single-core systems. Multitasking is not something that is generally done; instead, there's a single thread of execution with timers and interrupts adding asynchronous methods of operation.

Atomic operations are generally supported by compilers and AVR is no exception. The need for atomic blocks of instructions can be seen in the following cases. Keep in mind that while a few exceptions exist (MOVW to copy a register pair and indirect addressing via X, Y, Z pointers), instructions on an 8 bit architecture generally only affect 8 bit values.

- A 16 bit variable is byte-wise read in the main function and updated in an ISR.
- A 32 bit variable is read, modified and subsequently stored back in either main function or ISR while the other routine could try to access it.
- The execution of a block of code is time-critical (bitbanging I/O, disabling JTAG).

A basic example for the first case is given in the AVR libc documentation:

```
#include <cinttypes>
#include <avr/interrupt.h>
#include <avr/io.h>
#include <util/atomic.h>

volatile uint16_t ctr;

ISR(TIMER1_OVF_vect) {
    ctr--;
}

int main() {
        ctr = 0x200;
        start_timer();
        sei();
        uint16_t ctr_copy;
        do {
```

```
                    ATOMIC_BLOCK(ATOMIC_FORCEON)
                    {
                            ctr_copy = ctr;
                    }
            }
            while (ctr_copy != 0);

            return 0;
    }
```

In this code, a 16-bit integer is being changed in the interrupt handler, while the main routine is copying its value into a local variable. We call `sei()` (SEt global Interrupt flag) to ensure that the interrupt register is in a known state. The `volatile` keyword hints to the compiler that this variable and how it's accessed should not be optimized in any way.

Because we included the AVR atomic header, we can use the `ATOMIC_BLOCK` macro, along with the `ATOMIC_FORCEON` macro. What this does is create a code section that is guaranteed to be executed atomically, without any interference from interrupt handlers and the like. The parameter we pass to `ATOMIC_BLOCK` forces the global interrupt status flag into an **enabled** state.

Since we set this flag to the same state before we started the atomic block, we do not need to save the previous value of this flag, which saves resources.

As noted earlier, MCUs tend to be single-core systems, with limited multitasking and multithreading capabilities. For proper multithreading and multitasking, one would need to do context switches, whereby not only the stack pointer of the running task is saved, but also the state of all registers and related.

This means that while it would be possible to run multiple threads and tasks on a single MCU, in the case of 8-bit MCUs such as the AVR and PIC (8-bit range), the effort would most likely not be worth it, and would require a significant amount of labor.

On more powerful MCUs (like the ESP8255 and ARM Cortex-M), one could run **real-time OSes (RTOSes)**, which implement exactly such context switching, without having to do all of the heavy lifting. We will look at RTOSes later in this chapter.

AVR development with Nodate

Microchip provides a binary version of the GCC toolchain for AVR development. At the time of writing, the most recent release of AVR-GCC is 3.6.1, containing GCC version 5.4.0. This implies full support for C++14 and limited support for C++17.

Using this toolchain is pretty easy. One can simply download it from the Microchip website, extract it to a suitable folder, and add the folder containing the GCC executable files to the system path. After this, it can be used to compile AVR applications. Some platforms will have the AVR toolchain available via a package manager as well, which makes the process even easier.

One thing that one may notice after installing this GCC toolchain is that there is no C++ STL available. As a result, one is limited to just the C++ language features supported by GCC. As the Microchip AVR FAQ notes:

- Obviously, none of the C++ related standard functions, classes, and template classes are available.
- The operators new and delete are not implemented; attempting to use them will cause the linker to complain about undefined external references. (This could perhaps be fixed.)
- Some of the supplied include files are not C++ safe, that is, they need to be wrapped into extern"C" { . . . }. (This could certainly be fixed, too.)
- Exceptions are not supported. Since exceptions are enabled by default in the C++ frontend, they explicitly need to be turned off using -fno-exceptions in the compiler options. Failing this, the linker will complain about an undefined external reference to __gxx_personality_sj0.

With the lack of a Libstdc++ implementation that would contain the STL features, we can only add such functionality by using a third-party implementation. These include versions that provide essentially the full STL, as well as lightweight re-implementations that do not follow the standard STL API. An example of the latter is the Arduino AVR core, which provides classes such as String and Vector, which are similar to their STL equivalents albeit with some limitations and differences.

An upcoming alternative to the Microchip AVR GCC toolchain is LLVM, a compiler framework to which experimental support for AVR as been recently added, and which at some point in the future should allow producing binaries for AVR MCUs, all the while providing full STL functionality via its Clang frontend (C/C++ support).

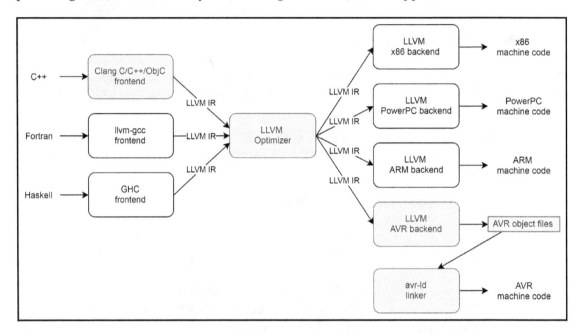

Consider this an abstract snapshot of LLVM development—all the while illustrating the general concept of LLVM and its emphasis on Intermediate Representation.

 Unfortunately the PIC range of MCUs, despite also being owned by Microchip and resembling AVR in many ways, does at this point not have a C++ compiler available for it from Microchip until one moves up to the PIC32 (MIPS-based) range of MCUs.

Enter Nodate

You could at this point opt to use one of the IDEs we discussed previously in this chapter, but that wouldn't be nearly as educational for AVR development itself. For this reason, we will look at a simple application developed for an ATmega2560 board that uses a modified version of the Arduino AVR core, called Nodate (`https://github.com/MayaPosch/Nodate`). This framework restructures the original core to allow it to be used as a regular C++ library instead of only with the Arduino C-dialect parser and frontend.

Installing Nodate is pretty easy: simply download to a suitable location on one's system and have the NODATE_HOME system variable point to the root folder of the Nodate installation. After this, we can take one of the example applications as a basis for a new project.

Example – CMOS IC Tester

Here, we will look at a more full-featured example project, implementing an **integrated circuit** (IC) tester for 5V logic chips. In addition to probing chips with its GPIO pins, this project also reads a chip description and test program (in the form of a logic table) from an SD card over SPI. User control is added in the form of a serial-based command-line interface.

First, we look at the Makefile for this Nodate project, as found in the root of the project:

```
ARCH ?= avr

# Board preset.
BOARD ?= arduino_mega_2560

# Set the name of the output (ELF & Hex) file.
OUTPUT := sdinfo

# Add files to include for compilation to these variables.
APP_CPP_FILES = $(wildcard src/*.cpp)
APP_C_FILES = $(wildcard src/*.c)


#
# --- End of user-editable variables --- #
#

# Nodate includes. Requires that the NODATE_HOME environment variable has
been set.
APPFOLDER=$(CURDIR)
export

all:
    $(MAKE) -C $(NODATE_HOME)

flash:
    $(MAKE) -C $(NODATE_HOME) flash

clean:
    $(MAKE) -C $(NODATE_HOME) clean
```

The first item we specify is the architecture we are targeting, since Nodate can be used to target other MCU types as well. Here, we specify AVR as the architecture.

Next, we use the preset for the Arduino Mega 2560 development board. Inside Nodate, we have a number of presets like these, which define a number of details about the board. For the Arduino Mega 2560, we get the following presets:

```
MCU := atmega2560
PROGRAMMER := wiring
VARIANT := mega # "Arduino Mega" board type
```

If no board preset is defined, one has to define those variables in the project's Makefile and pick an existing value for each variable, each of which is defined as its own Makefile within the Nodate AVR subfolders. Alternatively, one can add one's own MCU, programmer, and (pin) variant file to Nodate, along with a new board preset, and use that.

With the makefile complete it is time to implement the main function:

```
#include <wiring.h>
 #include <SPI.h>
 #include <SD.h>


 #include "serialcomm.h"
```

The wiring header provides access to all GPIO-related functionality. Furthermore, we include headers for the SPI bus, the SD card reader device, and a custom class that wraps the serial interface, as we will see in more detail in a moment:

```
int main () {
    init();
    initVariant();

    Serial.begin(9600);

    SPI.begin();
```

Upon entering the main function, we initialize the GPIO functionality with a call to `init()`. The next call loads the pin configuration for the particular board we are targeting (the VARIANT variable on the top or in the board preset Makefile).

After this, we start the first serial port with a speed of 9,600 baud, followed by the SPI bus, and finally the output of a welcome message, as follows:

```
    Serial.println("Initializing SD card...");

    if (!SD.begin(53)) {
```

```
            Serial.println("Initialization failed!");
            while (1);
    }

    Serial.println("initialization done.");

    Serial.println("Commands: index, chip");
    Serial.print("> ");
```

An SD card is expected to be attached to the Mega board at this point, containing a list of available chips we can test. Here, pin 53 is the hardware SPI chip-select pin that is conveniently located next to the rest of the SPI pins on the board.

Assuming the board is hooked up properly and the card can be read without issues, we are presented with a command-line prompt on the console screen:

```
            while (1) {
                String cmd;
                while (!SerialComm::readLine(cmd)) { }

                if (cmd == "index") { readIndex(); }
                else if (cmd == "chip") { readChipConfig(); }
                else { Serial.println("Unknown command."); }

                Serial.print("> ");
            }

            return 0;
    }
```

This loop simply waits for input to arrive on the serial input, after which it will attempt to execute the received command. The function we call for reading from the serial input is blocking, returning only if it has either received a newline (user pressed *Enter*), or its internal buffer size was exceeded without receiving a newline. In the latter case, we simply dismiss the input and try to read from the serial input once more. This concludes the main() implementation.

Let's now look at the header of the SerialComm class:

```
    #include <HardwareSerial.h>        // UART.


    static const int CHARBUFFERSIZE 64


    class SerialComm {
            static char charbuff[CHARBUFFERSIZE];
```

```
public:
        static bool readLine(String &str);
};
```

We include the header for the hardware serial connection support. This gives us access to the underlying UART peripheral. The class itself is purely static, defining the maximum size of the character buffer, and the function to read a line from the serial input.

Next is its implementation:

```
#include "serialcomm.h"

char SerialComm::charbuff[CHARBUFFERSIZE];


bool SerialComm::readLine(String &str) {
        int index = 0;

        while (1) {
                while (Serial.available() == 0) { }

                char rc = Serial.read();
                Serial.print(rc);

                if (rc == '\n') {
                        charbuff[index] = 0;
                        str = charbuff;
                        return true;
                }

                if (rc >= 0x20 || rc == ' ') {
                        charbuff[index++] = rc;
                        if (index > CHARBUFFERSIZE) {
                                return false;
                        }
                }
        }

        return false;
}
```

In the `while` loop, we first enter a loop that runs while there are no characters to be read in the serial input buffer. This makes it a blocking read.

Since we want to be able to see what we're typing, in the next section we echo back any character we have read. After this, we check whether we have received a newline character. If we did, we add a terminating null byte to the local buffer and read it into the String instance we were provided a reference to, after which we return true.

A possible improvement one could implement here is that of a backspace feature, where the user could delete characters in the read buffer by using the backspace key. For this, one would have to add a case for the backspace control character (ASCII 0x8), which would delete the last character from the buffer, and optionally also have the remote terminal delete its last visible character.

With no newline found yet, we continue to the next section. Here, we check whether we have received a valid character considered as ASCII 0x20, or a space. If we did, we continue to add the new character to the buffer and finally check whether we have reached the end of the read buffer. If we did not, we return false to indicate that the buffer is full yet no newline has been found.

Next are the handler functions `readIndex()` and `readChipConfig()` for the `index` and `chip` commands, respectively:

```
void readIndex() {
        File sdFile = SD.open("chips.idx");
        if (!sdFile) {
            Serial.println("Failed to open IC index file.");
            Serial.println("Please check SD card and try again.");
            while(1);
        }

        Serial.println("Available chips:");
        while (sdFile.available()) {
            Serial.write(sdFile.read());
        }

        sdFile.close();
}
```

This function makes heavy use of the `SD` and associated `File` classes from the Arduino SD card library. Essentially, we open the chips index file on the SD card, ensure we got a valid file handle, then proceed to read out and print each line in the file. This file is a simple line-based text-file, with one chip name per line.

At the end of the handler code, we're done reading from SD and the file handle can be closed with `sdFile.close()`. The same applies to the slightly more lengthy upcoming `readChipHandler()` implementation.

Usage

As an example, when we run the test with a simple HEF4001 IC (4000 CMOS series Quad 2-Input OR Gate) hooked up, we have to add a file to the SD card which contains the test description and control data for this IC. The `4001.ic` test file is shown here as it lends itself to following along the code that parses it and performs the corresponding tests.

```
HEF4001B
Quad 2-input NOR gate.
A1-A2: 22-27, Vss: GND, 3A-4B: 28-33, Vdd: 5V
22:0,23:0=24:1
22:0,23:1=24:0
22:1,23:0=24:0
22:1,23:1=24:0
26:0,27:0=25:1
26:0,27:1=25:0
26:1,27:0=25:0
26:1,27:1=25:0
28:0,29:0=30:1
28:0,29:1=30:0
28:1,29:0=30:0
28:1,29:1=30:0
33:0,32:0=31:1
33:0,32:1=31:0
33:1,32:0=31:0
33:1,32:1=31:0
```

The first three lines are printed verbatim as we saw earlier, with the remaining lines specifying individual test scenarios. These tests are lines and use the following format:

```
<pin>:<value>,[..,]<pin>:<value>=<pin>:<value>
```

We write this file as `4001.ic` along with an updated `index.idx` file (containing the '4001' entry on a new line) to the SD card. to support more ICs we would simply repeat this pattern with their respective test sequences and list them in the index file.Finally there is the handler for the chip configuration, which also starts the testing procedure:

```
void readChipConfig() {
        Serial.println("Chip name?");
        Serial.print("> ");
        String chip;
        while (!SerialComm::readLine(chip)) { }
```

We start by asking the user for the name of the IC, as printed out earlier by the `index` command:

```
File sdFile = SD.open(chip + ".ic");
if (!sdFile) {
        Serial.println("Failed to open IC file.");
        Serial.println("Please check SD card and try again.");
        return;
}

String name = sdFile.readStringUntil('\n');
String desc = sdFile.readStringUntil('\n');
```

We attempt to open the file with the IC details, continuing with reading out the file contents, starting with the name and description of the IC that we are testing:

```
Serial.println("Found IC:");
Serial.println("Name: " + name);
Serial.println("Description: " + desc);

String pins = sdFile.readStringUntil('\n');
Serial.println(pins);
```

After displaying the name and description of this IC, we read out the line that contains the instructions on how to connect the IC to the headers of our Mega board:

```
Serial.println("Type 'start' and press <enter> to start test.");
Serial.print("> ");
String conf;
while (!SerialComm::readLine(conf)) { }
if (conf != "start") {
        Serial.println("Aborting test.");
        return;
}
```

Here, we ask the user for confirmation on whether to start testing the IC. Any command beyond `start` will abort the test and return to the central command loop.

Upon receiving `start` as a command, the testing begins:

```
int result_pin, result_val;
while (sdFile.available()) {
        // Read line, format:
        // <pin>:<value>, [..,]<pin>:<value>=<pin>:<value>
        pins = sdFile.readStringUntil('=');
        result_pin = sdFile.readStringUntil(':').toInt();
        result_val = sdFile.readStringUntil('\n').toInt();
        Serial.print("Result pin: ");
```

```
Serial.print(result_pin);
Serial.print(", expecting: ");
Serial.println(result_val);
Serial.print("\n");

pinMode(result_pin, INPUT);
```

As the first step, we read out the next line in the IC file, which should contain the first test. The first section contains the input pin settings, with the section after the equal sign containing the IC's output pin and its expected value for this test.

We print out the board header number that the result pin is connected to and the expected value. Next, we set the result pin to be an input pin so that we can read it out after the test has finished:

```
int pin;
bool val;
int idx = 0;
unsigned int pos = 0;
while ((idx = pins.indexOf(':', pos)) > 0) {
        int pin = pins.substring(pos, idx).toInt();
        pos = idx + 1; // Move to character beyond the double
colon.

        bool val = false
        if ((idx = pins.indexOf(",", pos)) > 0) {
                val = pins.substring(pos, idx).toInt();
                pos = idx + 1;
        }
        else {
                val = pins.substring(pos).toInt();
        }

        Serial.print("Setting pin ");
        Serial.print(pin);
        Serial.print(" to ");
        Serial.println(val);
        Serial.print("\n");
        pinMode(pin, OUTPUT);
        digitalWrite(pin, val);
}
```

For the actual test, we use the first String we read out from the file for this test, parsing it to get the values for the input pins. For each pin, we first get its number, then get the value (0 or 1).

We echo these pin numbers and values to the serial output, before setting the pin mode for these pins to output mode and then writing the test value to each of them, as follows:

```
        delay(10);

        int res_val = digitalRead(result_pin);
        if (res_val != result_val) {
                Serial.print("Error: got value ");
                Serial.print(res_val);
                Serial.println(" on the output.");
                Serial.print("\n");
        }
        else {
                Serial.println("Pass.");
        }
    }

    sdFile.close();
}
```

After leaving the inner loop, all of the input values will have been set. We just have to wait briefly to ensure that the IC has had time to settle on its new output values before we attempt to read out the result value on its output pin.

IC validation is a simple read on the result pin, after which we compare the value we received with the expected value. The result of this comparison is then printed to the serial output.

With the test complete, we close the IC file and return to the central command loop to await the next instructions.

After flashing the program to the Mega board and connecting with it on its serial port, we get the following result:

```
Initializing SD card...
initialization done.
Commands: index, chip
> index
```

After starting up, we get the message that the SD card was found and successfully initialized. We can now read from the SD card. We also see the available commands.

Next, we specify the `index` command to get an overview of the available ICs we can test:

```
Available chips:
4001
> chip
Chip name?
> 4001
Found IC:
Name: HEF4001B
Description: Quad 2-input NOR gate.
A1-A2: 22-27, Vss: GND, 3A-4B: 28-33, Vdd: 5V
Type 'start' and press <enter> to start test.
> start
```

With just one IC available to test, we specify the `chip` command to enter the IC entry menu, after which we enter the IC's specifier.

This loads the file we put on the SD card and prints the first three lines. It then waits to give us time to hook up the chip, following the header numbers on the Mega board and the pin designations for the IC as provided by its datasheet.

After checking that we didn't get any of our wires crossed, we type `start` and confirm. This starts the test:

```
Result pin: 24, expecting: 1
Setting pin 22 to 0
Setting pin 23 to 0
Pass.
Result pin: 24, expecting: 0
Setting pin 22 to 0
Setting pin 23 to 1
Pass.
Result pin: 24, expecting: 0
Setting pin 22 to 1
Setting pin 23 to 0
[...]
Result pin: 31, expecting: 0
Setting pin 33 to 1
Setting pin 32 to 0
Pass.
Result pin: 31, expecting: 0
Setting pin 33 to 1
Setting pin 32 to 1
Pass.
>
```

For each of the four identical OR gates in the chip, we run through the same truth table, testing each input combination. This specific IC passed with flying colors and can be safely used in a project.

This kind of testing device would be useful for testing any kind of 5V-level IC, including 74 and 4000 logic chips. It would also be possible to adapt the design to use the PWM, ADC, and other pins to test ICs that aren't strictly digital in their inputs and outputs.

ESP8266 development with Sming

For ESP8266-based development, no official development tools exist from its creator (Espressif) beyond a bare-metal and RTOS-based SDK. Open source projects including Arduino then provide a more developer-friendly framework to develop applications with. The C++ alternative to Arduino on ESP8266 is Sming (`https://github.com/SmingHub/Sming`), which is an Arduino-compatible framework, similar to Nodate for AVR, which we looked at in the previous section.

In the next chapter (`Chapter 5`, *Example - Soil Humidity Monitor with Wi-Fi*) we will take an in-depth look at developing with this framework on the ESP8266.

ARM MCU development

Developing for ARM MCU platforms isn't significantly different from developing for AVR MCUs, except that C++ is far better supported, and there exists a wide range of toolchains to choose from, as we saw at the beginning of this chapter with just the list of popular IDEs. The list of available RTOSes for Cortex-M is much larger than for AVR or ESP8266 as well.

Using a free and open source compiler including GCC and LLVM to target a wide range of ARM MCU architectures (Cortex-M-based and similar) is where developing for ARM MCUs offers a lot of freedom, along with easy access to the full C++ STL (though one might want to hold off on exceptions).

When doing bare-metal development for Cortex-M MCUs, one may have to add this linker flag to provide basic stubs for some functionality that is normally provided by the OS:

```
-specs=nosys.specs
```

One thing that makes ARM MCUs less attractive is that there are far fewer *standard* boards and MCUs, such as with what one sees with AVR in the form of the Arduino boards. Although the Arduino foundation at one point made the Arduino Due board based around a SAM3X8E Cortex-M3 MCU, this board uses the same form factor and roughly same pin layout (just being 3.3V I/O-based instead of 5V) as the ATmega2560-based Arduino Mega board.

Because of this design choice a lot of the functionality of the MCU has not been broken out and is inaccessible unless one is very handy with a soldering iron and thin wires. This functionality includes the Ethernet connection, tens of GPIO (digital) pins, and so on. This same lack of breaking out all pins also happens with the Arduino Mega (ATmega2560) board, but on this Cortex-M MCU it becomes even more noticeable.

The result of this is that as a development and prototyping board, there aren't any obvious generic picks. One might be tempted to just use the relatively cheap and plentiful prototyping boards like those provided by STMicroelectronics for their range of Cortex-M-based MCUs.

RTOS usage

With the limited resources available on the average MCU, and the generally fairly straightforward process loop in the applications that run on them, it is hard to make a case for using an RTOS on these MCUs. It's not until one has to do complicated resource and task management that it becomes attractive to use an RTOS in order to save development time.

The benefit of using an RTOS thus lies mostly in preventing one from having to reinvent the wheel. This is however something that has to be decided on a case-by-case basis. For most projects, having to integrate an RTOS into the development toolchain is more likely than an unrealistic idea that would add more to the workload than it would lighten it.

For projects where one is, for example, trying to balance CPU time and system resources between different communication and storage interfaces, as well as a user interface, the use of an RTOS might make a lot of sense, however.

As we saw in this chapter, a lot of embedded development uses a simple loop (super-loop) along with a number of interrupts to handle real-time tasks. When sharing data between an interrupt function and the super-loop, it is the responsibility of the developer to ensure that it is done safely.

Here, an RTOS would offer a scheduler and even the ability to run tasks (processes) that are isolated from each other (especially on MCUs that have a **Memory Management Unit (MMU)**). On a multi-core MCU, an RTOS easily allows one to make effective use of all cores without having to do one's own scheduling.

As with all things, the use of an RTOS isn't just a collection of advantages. Even ignoring the increase in ROM and RAM space requirements that will likely result from adding an RTOS to one's project, it will also fundamentally change some system interactions and may (paradoxically) result in interrupt latency increasing.

This is why, although the name has *real-time* in it, it is very hard to get more real-time than to use a simple execution loop and a handful of interrupts. The benefit of an RTOS, thus, is absolutely something about which no blanket statements can be made, especially when a support library or framework for bare-metal programming (such as the Arduino-compatible ones addressed in this chapter) is already available to make prototyping and developing for production as simple as tying a number of existing libraries together.

Summary

In this chapter, we took a look at how to select the right MCU for a new project, as well as how to add peripherals and deal with Ethernet and serial interface requirements in a project. We considered how memory is laid out in a variety of MCUs and how to deal with the stack and heap. Finally, we looked at an example AVR project, how to develop for other MCU architectures, and whether to use an RTOS.

At this point, the reader is expected to be able to argue why they would pick one MCU over another, based on a set of project requirements. They should be capable of implementing simple projects using the UART and other peripherals, and understand proper memory management as well as the use of interrupts.

In the next chapter, we will take a good look at how to develop for the ESP8266, in the form of an embedded project that will keep track of soil moisture levels and control a watering pump when needed.

5
Example - Soil Humidity Monitor with Wi-Fi

Keeping indoor plants alive is no small feat. The example project in this chapter will show you how to create a Wi-Fi-enabled soil humidity monitor with actuator options for a pump or similar, like a valve and gravity-fed water tank. Using the built-in web server, we will be able to use its browser-based UI for monitoring the plant health and control system features, or integrate it into a larger system using its HTTP-based REST API.

The topics covered in this chapter are as follows:

- Programming an ESP8266 microcontroller
- Connecting sensors and actuators to an ESP8266
- Implementing an HTTP server on this platform
- Developing a web-based UI for monitoring and control
- Integrating the project into a larger network

Keeping plants happy

To keep plants alive, you need a number of things:

- Nutrients
- Light
- Water

Of these, the first two are usually handled by nutrient-rich soil and putting the plant in a well-lit place, respectively. The main issue with keeping plants alive after satisfying those two points is usually the third point, as this has to be handled on a daily basis.

Here, it's not just a simple matter of keeping the water topped up, but instead of staying within the range where the soil has enough but not too much water. The presence of too much water in the soil affects how much oxygen the plant can absorb via its roots. As a result, with too much water in the soil, the plant will wither and die.

On the other hand, too little water means that the plant cannot take up enough water to compensate for the water that is being evaporated through its leaves, nor can it get the nutrients into its roots. In this case, the plant will also wither and die.

When manually watering plants, we tend to use rough estimates of when the plant will likely need more water, along with a superficial testing of the humidity of the top soil, using our fingers. This tells us little about how much water is actually present around the roots of the plant, far below the upper layer of soil.

To measure the humidity of the soil with more precision, we can use a number of methods:

Type	Principle	Notes
Gypsum block	Resistance——	Water is absorbed by the gypsum, dissolving some of it, which allows a current to flow between two electrodes. The resistance value indicates soil moisture tension.
Tensiometer	Vacuum	A hollow tube has a vacuum meter on one end and a porous tip at the other, allowing water to enter and leave freely. Water getting sucked out of the tube by the soil increases the vacuum sensor readings, indicating that it's harder to extract moisture from the soil for plants (moisture tension).
Capacitance probe	**Frequency Domain Reflectometry (FDR)**	Uses the dielectric constant between two metal electrodes (in the soil) in an oscillator circuit to measure changes to this constant due to changing moisture levels. Indicates moisture content.
Microwave sensor	**Time Domain Reflectometry (TDR)**	Measures the time required for a microwave signal to travel to the end of the parallel probes and back, which differs depending on the dielectric constant of the soil. Measures moisture content.
ThetaProbe	RF amplitude impedance	A 100 MHz sine wave radio signal is sent among four probes enclosing a soil cylinder. The change in the impedance of the sine wave is used to calculate the water in the soil.

Resistance probe	Resistance	This is similar to the gypsum block, except with just the electrodes. Thus, this only measures water presence (and its conductivity) instead of soil moisture tension.

All of these sensor types come with their own sets of advantages of disadvantages. In the case of the gypsum block and tensiometer, there is a significant amount of maintenance, as the former relies on there being enough of the gypsum remaining to dissolve and not throw off the calibration, whereas in the latter case, it is imperative that the airtight seal remains so as not to let air into the tube. Any gap in this seal would immediately render the vacuum sensor useless.

Another big point is that of cost. While FDR- and TDR-based probes may be quite accurate, they also tend to be very expensive. This usually leads people who just want to experiment with soil moisture sensors to pick either the resistance or capacitance-based sensors. Here, the main disadvantage of the former sensor type becomes obvious in a month or less of usage: corrosion.

With two electrodes suspended in a solution containing ions and a current being applied to one of the electrodes, simple chemistry results in one of the electrodes rapidly corroding (losing material), until it is no longer functional. This also pollutes the soil with metal molecules. The use of an **alternating current** (**AC**) instead of a direct current on a single electrode can reduce the corrosive effect somewhat, but it remains an issue.

Among cheap and still accurate soil moisture sensors, only the capacitance probe ticks all of the boxes. Its accuracy is decent enough for sensible measurements and comparisons (after calibration), it is unaffected by the moisture in the soil, and it does not affect the soil in any manner either.

To actually get water to the plant, we need to have a way to get just the right amount to it. Here, it's mostly the scale of the system that determines the choice of water delivery. For watering an entire field, we could use an impeller-based pump, capable of delivering many liters of water per minute.

For a single plant, we would need to be able to deliver in the order of a few hundred milliliters per minute at most. Here, something such as a peristaltic pump would be pretty much ideal. This is the kind of pump you would also use in laboratories and medical applications where you have to provide a small amount of fluid with high accuracy.

Our solution

To keep things simple, we will just be building something that can take care of a single plant. This will provide us with the most flexibility in terms of placement, as we would just have a single system next to each plant, no matter whether it's on a windowsill, table, or terrace somewhere.

In addition to measuring the soil moisture level, we would also want to be able to have the system automatically water the plant at set trigger levels and for us to be able to monitor this process. This requires some kind of network access, preferably wireless so that we don't have to run any more cables than the power connector.

This makes the ESP8266 MCU very attractive, with the NodeMCU development board an attractive target for developing and debugging the system. We'd hook up a soil moisture sensor to it, along with a peristaltic pump.

By connecting to the ESP8266 system's IP address using a web browser, we would see the current status of the system, with the soil humidity level and optionally much more. Configuring the system and more would be done over the commonly used, compact binary MQTT protocol, with the system also publishing the current system status so that we can read it into a database for display and analysis.

This way, we can also write a backend service later on that combines many of such nodes into a coherent system with central control and management. This is something that we will actually look at in great detail in `Chapter 9`, *Example - Building Monitoring and Control*.

The hardware

Our ideal solution would have the most accurate sensor, without breaking the bank. This means that we pretty much have to use a capacitance sensor, as we saw earlier in this chapter. These sensors can be obtained as capacitive soil moisture sensors for little more than a few euros or dollars for a simple 555 timer IC-based design such as these:

You would simply stick these into the soil up to the point where the circuitry begins, then connect it with a power source as well as the connection to the analog to digital converter of the MCU.

Most peristaltic pumps one can purchase require 12V. This means that we need to either have a power supply that can provide both 5V and 12V, or use a so-called boost converter to convert the 5V to 12V. Either way, we would also need to have some method to turn the pump on or off. With the boost converter, we can use its *enable* pin to turn its output on or off using a GPIO pin on our MCU.

For prototyping, we can use one of these common 5V to 12V boost converter modules that use an ME2149 step-up switching regulator:

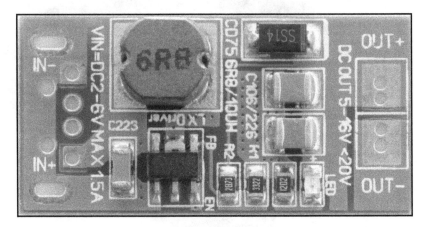

These do not have the enable pin broken out in any way, but we can easily solder on a wire to the pin in question:

This boost-converter module's outputs are then connected to the peristaltic pump:

Here, we need to get some tubing of the right diameter to connect it to the water reservoir and the plant. The pump itself will rotate either direction. As it consists of essentially a set of rollers on the section of internal tubing, which push the liquid inside one way, either side of the pump can be the input or output.

Be sure to test the flow direction beforehand with two containers and some water, and mark the direction on the pump casing, along with the positive and negative terminal connections used.

In addition to these components, we also want to have an RGB LED connected for some signaling and just for looks. For this, we will use the **APA102** RGB LED module, which connects to the ESP8266 over the SPI bus:

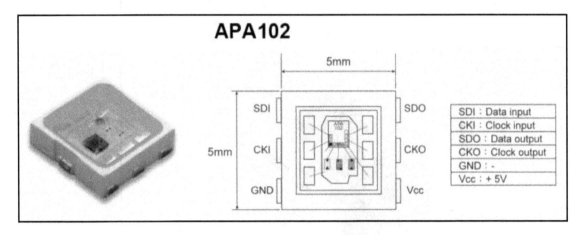

We can use a single power supply that can be provide 5V with 1A or more, as well as cope with the sudden power draw from the boost converter every time that the pump is activated.

The whole system would look like this:

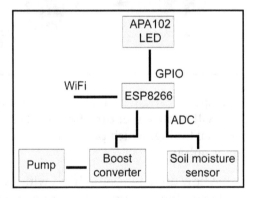

The firmware

For this project, we will be implementing a module for the same firmware that we will be using in `Chapter 9`, *Example - Building Monitoring and Control*. Therefore, this chapter will only cover the parts that are unique to this plant-watering module.

Before we can start with the firmware itself, we first have to set up the development environment. This involves the installation of the ESP8266 SDK and the Sming framework.

Setting up Sming

The Sming-based ESP8266 development environment can be used on Linux, Windows, and macOS. You want to preferably use the development branch of Sming, however, which is where using it on Linux (or in a Linux VM, or Windows 10's **Windows Subsystem for Linux (WSL)**) is the easiest way, and definitely recommended. On Linux installing in the `/opt` folder is recommended for consistency with the Sming quick start guide.

This quick start guide for Linux can be found at
`https://github.com/SmingHub/Sming/wiki/Linux-Quickstart`.

On Linux, we can use the Open SDK for ESP8266, which takes the official Espressif (non-RTOS) SDK, and replaces all the non-open components it can with open source alternatives. This can be installed using this code:

```
git clone --recursive https://github.com/pfalcon/esp-open-sdk.git
cd esp-open-sdk
make VENDOR_SDK=1.5.4 STANDALONE=y
```

This will get the current source for the Open SDK and compile it, targeting version 1.5.4 of the official SDK. While a 2.0 version of the SDK already exists, some compatibility issues within the Sming framework can remain. Using the 1.5.4 version offers pretty much the same experience while using well-tested code. This will of course change over time, so be sure to check the official Sming documentation for updated instructions.

The `STANDALONE` option means that the SDK will be built as a standalone installation of the SDK and the toolchain, without further dependencies. This is the desired option for use with Sming.

Installing `Sming` is as easy as this:

```
git clone https://github.com/SmingHub/Sming.git
cd Sming
make
```

This will build the Sming framework. If we are adding new libraries to Sming in its `Libraries` folder, we have to execute the last step again to have a new Sming shared library instance to be built and installed.

 For this project, copy the folders in the `libs` folder of the software project for this chapter to the `Sming/Sming/Libraries` folder prior to compiling Sming, or the project code will not compile.

We can also compile Sming with SSL support. This requires us to compile it with the `ENABLE_SSL=1` parameter to Make. This will enable the axTLS-based encryption support throughout the Sming library as it is compiled.

With these steps complete, we just have to install `esptool.py` and `esptool2`. While in the `/opt` folder, execute these commands to obtain esptool:

```
wget https://github.com/themadinventor/esptool/archive/master.zip
unzip master.zip
mv esptool-master esp-open-sdk/esptool
```

`Esptool.py` is a Python script that allows us to communicate with the SPI ROM that is part of each ESP8266 module. It is the way we will flash the MCU's ROM with our code. This tool is automatically used by Sming:

```
cd $ESP_HOME
git clone https://github.com/raburton/esptool2
cd esptool2
make
```

The `esptool2` utility is an alternative to the set of scripts in the official SDK that turn the linker output into a ROM format that we can write to the ESP8266. It is called by Sming when we are compiling our application.

Finally, assuming that we installed the SDK and Sming under `/opt`, we can add the following global variables and addition to the system `PATH` variable:

```
export ESP_HOME=/opt/esp-open-sdk
export SMING_HOME=/opt/Sming/Sming
export PATH=$PATH:$ESP_HOME/esptool2
export PATH=$PATH:$ESP_HOME/xtensa-lx106-elf/bin
```

The last line adds the toolchain's binaries to the path, which we will need when debugging ESP8266 applications, as will see in Chapter 7, *Testing Resource-Restricted Platforms*. At this point, we can develop with Sming and create ROM images that we can write to the MCU.

Plant module code

In this section, we will look at the basic source code for this project, starting with the core module, OtaCore, and continuing with the BaseModule class, which all firmware modules register with. Finally, we look at the PlantModule class itself, which contains the business logic for the project requirements that we discussed in this chapter.

Also of note is that for this project we enabled both the rBoot bootmanager and the rBoot Big Flash options in the project Makefile. What this does is create four 1 MB blocks in the 4 MB of ROM that we have available on our ESP8266 module (which is all ESP-12E/F modules), of which two are used for firmware images and the remaining two for file storage (using the SPIFFS filesystem).

The rBoot bootloader is then written to the beginning of the ROM, so that it will be loaded first on each boot. Of the firmware slots, only one is active at any given time. A handy feature of this setup is that it allows us to easily perform **over-the-air** (**OTA**) updates, by writing the new firmware image to the inactive firmware slot, changing the active slot, and restarting the MCU. If rBoot fails to boot from the new firmware image, it will fall back on the other firmware slot, which is our known working firmware that we performed the OTA update from.

Makefile-user.mk

In the root of the project folder, we find this Makefile. It contains a number of settings that we may want to set to suit our purposes:

Name	Description
COM_PORT	If we always connect the board to the same serial port, we can hardcode it here to save ourselves some typing.
SPI_MODE	This sets the SPI mode used while flashing the firmware images to the SPI ROM. With dio only two data lines (SD_D0, D1) or four (SD_D0-3). Not all SPI ROMs have all four data lines connected. The qio mode is faster, but dio should always work.
RBOOT_ENABLED	When set to 1, this enables rBoot bootloader support. We want this enabled.
RBOOT_BIG_FLASH	With 4 MB of ROM available, we wish to use all of this. Enable this as well.
RBOOT_TWO_ROMS	This option can be used if we wish to place two firmware images in a single 1 MB ROM chip instead. This applies to some ESP8266 modules and derivatives.

SPI_SIZE	Here, we set the size of the SPI ROM chip, which should be 4M for this project.
SPIFF_FILES	The location of the folder containing the files that will be put on the SPIFFS ROM image that will be written to the MCU.
SPIFFS_SIZE	The size of the SPIFFS ROM image to create. Here, 64 KB is standard, but we could use up to 1 MB if we needed to when using a 4 MB ROM with the RBOOT_BIG_FLASH option enabled.
WIFI_SSID	The SSID of the Wi-Fi network that we wish to connect to.
WIFI_PWD	The password for the Wi-Fi network.
MQTT_HOST	The URL or IP address of the MQTT server (broker) to use.
ENABLE_SSL	Enable this with SSL support compiled into Sming to make the firmware use TLS-encrypted connections with the MQTT broker.
MQTT_PORT	The port of the MQTT broker. This depends on whether SSL is enabled.
USE_MQTT_PASSWORD	Set to true if you wish to connect to the MQTT broker with a username and password.
MQTT_USERNAME	The MQTT broker username, if required.
MQTT_PWD	The MQTT broker password, if required.
MQTT_PREFIX	A prefix you can optionally add in front of each MQTT topic used by the firmware, if necessary. It has to end with a slash if not left empty.
OTA_URL	The hardcoded URL that will be used by the firmware whenever an OTA update is requested.

Of these, the Wi-Fi, MQTT, and OTA settings are essential, as they will allow the application to connect to the network and MQTT broker, as well as receive firmware updates without having to flash the MCU over its serial interface.

Main

The main source file and with it the application entry point is pretty uneventful:

```
#include "ota_core.h"
void onInit() {
    //
}
void init() {
        OtaCore::init(onInit);
  }
```

With the OtaCore class containing the main application logic, we merely call its static initialization function while providing a callback function if we wish to execute any further logic after the core class has finished setting up the network, MQTT, and other functionality.

OtaCore

In this class, we set up all of the basic network functionality for the specific feature modules, in addition to providing utility functions for logging and MQTT functionality. This class also contains the main command processor for commands received over MQTT:

```
#include <user_config.h>
#include <SmingCore/SmingCore.h>
```

These two includes are required to make use of the Sming framework. With them, we include the main headers of the SDK (user_config.h) and those of Sming (SmingCore.h). This also defines a number of preprocessor statements, such as to use the open source **Light-Weight IP stack** (**LWIP**) and to deal with some issues in the official SDK.

Also of note is the esp_cplusplus.h header, which is indirectly included this way. Its source file implements the new and delete functions, as well as a few handlers for class-related functionality, such as vtables when using virtual classes. This enables compatibility with the STL:

```
enum {
        LOG_ERROR = 0,
        LOG_WARNING,
        LOG_INFO,
        LOG_DEBUG,
        LOG_TRACE,
        LOG_XTRACE
};


enum ESP8266_pins {
        ESP8266_gpio00 = 0x00001,      // Flash
        ESP8266_gpio01 = 0x00002,      // TXD 0
        ESP8266_gpio02 = 0x00004,      // TXD 1
        ESP8266_gpio03 = 0x00008,      // RXD 0
        ESP8266_gpio04 = 0x00010,      //
        ESP8266_gpio05 = 0x00020,      //
        ESP8266_gpio09 = 0x00040,      // SDD2 (QDIO Flash)
        ESP8266_gpio10 = 0x00080,      // SDD3 (QDIO Flash)
        ESP8266_gpio12 = 0x00100,      // HMISO (SDO)
        ESP8266_gpio13 = 0x00200,      // HMOSI (SDI)
```

```
            ESP8266_gpio14 = 0x00400,      // SCK
            ESP8266_gpio15 = 0x00800,      // HCS
            ESP8266_gpio16 = 0x01000,      // User, Wake
            ESP8266_mosi = 0x02000,
            ESP8266_miso = 0x04000,
            ESP8266_sclk = 0x08000,
            ESP8266_cs = 0x10000
    };
```

These two enumerations define the logging levels, and the individual GPIO and other pins of the ESP8266 that we may want to use. The values for the ESP8266 pin enumeration correspond to positions in a bitmask:

```
#define SCL_PIN 5
#define SDA_PIN 4
```

Here, we define the fixed pins for the I2C bus. These correspond to GPIO 4 and 5, also known as **D1** and **D2** on NodeMCU boards. The main reason for having these pins predefined is that they are two of the few *safe* pins on the ESP8266.

Many pins of the ESP8266 will change levels during startup before settling, which can cause unwanted behavior with any connected peripherals.

```
typedef void (*topicCallback)(String);
typedef void (*onInitCallback)();
```

We define two function pointers, one to be used by feature modules when they wish to register an MQTT topic, along with a callback function. The other is the callback we saw in the main function.

```
class OtaCore {
        static Timer procTimer;
        static rBootHttpUpdate* otaUpdater;
        static MqttClient* mqtt;
        static String MAC;
        static HashMap<String, topicCallback>* topicCallbacks;
        static HardwareSerial Serial1;
        static String location;
        static String version;
        static int sclPin;
        static int sdaPin;
        static bool i2c_active;
        static bool spi_active;
        static uint32 esp8266_pins;

        static void otaUpdate();
        static void otaUpdate_CallBack(rBootHttpUpdate& update, bool
```

```
result);
        static void startMqttClient();
        static void checkMQTTDisconnect(TcpClient& client, bool flag);
        static void connectOk(IPAddress ip, IPAddress mask, IPAddress
gateway);
        static void connectFail(String ssid, uint8_t ssidLength, uint8_t
*bssid,    uint8_t reason);
        static void onMqttReceived(String topic, String message);
        static void updateModules(uint32 input);
        static bool mapGpioToBit(int pin, ESP8266_pins &addr);

public:
        static bool init(onInitCallback cb);
        static bool registerTopic(String topic, topicCallback cb);
        static bool deregisterTopic(String topic);
        static bool publish(String topic, String message, int qos = 1);
        static void log(int level, String msg);
        static String getMAC() { return OtaCore::MAC; }
        static String getLocation() { return OtaCore::location; }
        static bool starti2c();
        static bool startSPI();
        static bool claimPin(ESP8266_pins pin);
        static bool claimPin(int pin);
        static bool releasePin(ESP8266_pins pin);
        static bool releasePin(int pin);
};
```

The class declaration itself gives a good overview of the functionality provided by this class. The first thing we notice is that it is completely static. This ensures that this class's functionality is immediately initialized when the firmware starts, and that it can be accessed globally without having to worry about specific instances.

We can also see the first use of the uint32 type, which along with other integer types is defined similar to those in the cstdint header.

Moving on, here is the implementation:

```
#include <ota_core.h>

#include "base_module.h"

#define SPI_SCLK 14
#define SPI_MOSI 13
#define SPI_MISO 12
#define SPI_CS 15
```

```
Timer OtaCore::procTimer;
rBootHttpUpdate* OtaCore::otaUpdater = 0;
MqttClient* OtaCore::mqtt = 0;
String OtaCore::MAC;
HashMap<String, topicCallback>* OtaCore::topicCallbacks = new
HashMap<String, topicCallback>();
HardwareSerial OtaCore::Serial1(UART_ID_1); // UART 0 is 'Serial'.
String OtaCore::location;
String OtaCore::version = VERSION;
int OtaCore::sclPin = SCL_PIN; // default.
int OtaCore::sdaPin = SDA_PIN; // default.
bool OtaCore::i2c_active = false;
bool OtaCore::spi_active = false;
uint32 OtaCore::esp8266_pins = 0x0;
```

We include the `BaseModule` class's header here, so that we can call its own initialization function later on after we have finished setting up the basic functionality. The static class members are also initialized here, with a number of default values assigned where relevant.

Of note here is the initializing of a second serial interface object in addition to the default Serial object instance. These correspond to the first (UART0, Serial) and second (UART1, Serial1) UART on the ESP8266.

With older versions of Sming, the SPIFFS-related file functions had trouble with binary data (due to internally assuming null-terminated strings), which is why the following alternative functions were added. Their naming is a slightly inverted version from the original function name to prevent naming collisions.

Since TLS certificates and other binary data files stored on SPIFFS have to be able to be written and read for the firmware to function correctly, this was a necessary compromise.

```
String getFileContent(const String fileName) {
        file_t file = fileOpen(fileName.c_str(), eFO_ReadOnly);

        fileSeek(file, 0, eSO_FileEnd);
        int size = fileTell(file);
        if (size <= 0)    {
                fileClose(file);
                return "";
        }

        fileSeek(file, 0, eSO_FileStart);
        char* buffer = new char[size + 1];
        buffer[size] = 0;
        fileRead(file, buffer, size);
        fileClose(file);
        String res(buffer, size);
```

```
                delete[] buffer;
                return res;
        }
```

This function reads the entire contents of the specified file into a String instance that is returned.

```
        void setFileContent(const String &fileName, const String &content) {
                file_t file = fileOpen(fileName.c_str(),
        eFO_CreateNewAlways | eFO_WriteOnly);
                fileWrite(file, content.c_str(), content.length());
                fileClose(file);
        }
```

This function replaces the existing content in a file with the new data in the provided String instance.

```
        bool readIntoFileBuffer(const String filename, char* &buffer, unsigned int
        &size) {
                file_t file = fileOpen(filename.c_str(), eFO_ReadOnly);

                fileSeek(file, 0, eSO_FileEnd);
                size = fileTell(file);
                if (size == 0)      {
                        fileClose(file);
                        return true;
                }

                fileSeek(file, 0, eSO_FileStart);
                buffer = new char[size + 1];
                buffer[size] = 0;
                fileRead(file, buffer, size);
                fileClose(file);
                return true;
        }
```

This function is similar to getFileContent(), but returns a simple character buffer instead of a String instance. It's mostly used for reading in the certificate data, which is passed into a C-based TLS library (called axTLS), where converting to a String instance would be wasteful with the copying involved, especially where certificates can be a few KB in size.

Next is the initialization function for this class:

```
bool OtaCore::init(onInitCallback cb) {
        Serial.begin(9600);

        Serial1.begin(SERIAL_BAUD_RATE);
        Serial1.systemDebugOutput(true);
```

We first initialize the two UARTs (serial interfaces) in the NodeMCU. Although officially there are two UARTs in the ESP8266, the second one consists only out of a TX output line (GPIO 2, by default). Because of this, we want to keep the first UART free for applications requiring a full serial line, such as some sensors.

The first UART (`Serial`) is thus initialized so that we can later use it with feature modules, while the second UART (`Serial1`) is initialized to the default baud rate of 115,200, along with the system's debug output (WiFi/IP stack, and so on) being directed to this serial output as well. This second serial interface will thus be used solely for logging output.

```
        BaseModule::init();
```

Next, the `BaseModule` static class is initialized as well. This causes all feature modules active in this firmware to be registered, allowing them to be activated later on.

```
        int slot = rboot_get_current_rom();
        u32_t offset;
        if (slot == 0) { offset = 0x100000; }
        else { offset = 0x300000; }
        spiffs_mount_manual(offset, 65536);
```

Automatically mounting the SPIFFS filesystem while using the rBoot bootloader did not work with older releases of Sming, which is why we are doing it manually here. To do this, we get the current firmware slot from rBoot, using which we can pick the proper offset, either at the start of the second megabyte in the ROM, or of the fourth megabyte.

With the offset determined, we use the SPIFFS manual-mounting function with our offset and the size of the SPIFFS section. We are now able to read and write to our storage.

```
        Serial1.printf("\r\nSDK: v%s\r\n", system_get_sdk_version());
        Serial1.printf("Free Heap: %d\r\n", system_get_free_heap_size());
        Serial1.printf("CPU Frequency: %d MHz\r\n", system_get_cpu_freq());
        Serial1.printf("System Chip ID: %x\r\n", system_get_chip_id());
        Serial1.printf("SPI Flash ID: %x\r\n", spi_flash_get_id());
```

Next, we print out a few system details to the serial debug output. This includes the ESP8266 SDK version we compiled against, the current free heap size, CPU frequency, the MCU ID (32-bit ID), and the ID of the SPI ROM chip.

```
mqtt = new MqttClient(MQTT_HOST, MQTT_PORT, onMqttReceived);
```

We create a new MQTT client on the heap, providing the callback that will be called when we receive a new message. The MQTT broker host and port are filled in by the preprocessor from the details we added in the user Makefile for the project.

```
Serial1.printf("\r\nCurrently running rom %d.\r\n", slot);

WifiStation.enable(true);
WifiStation.config(WIFI_SSID, WIFI_PWD);
WifiStation.connect();
WifiAccessPoint.enable(false);


WifiEvents.onStationGotIP(OtaCore::connectOk);
WifiEvents.onStationDisconnect(OtaCore::connectFail);

(*cb)();
}
```

As the final steps in the initialization, we output the current firmware slot that we are running from, then enable the Wi-Fi client while disabling the **wireless access point** (**WAP**) functionality. The WiFi client is told to connect to the WiFi SSID with the credentials that we specified previously in the Makefile.

Finally, we define the handlers for a successful WiFi connection and for a failed connection attempt, before calling the callback function we were provided with as a parameter.

After an OTA update of the firmware, the following callback function will be called:

```
void OtaCore::otaUpdate_CallBack(rBootHttpUpdate& update, bool result) {
        OtaCore::log(LOG_INFO, "In OTA callback...");
        if (result == true) { // success
                uint8 slot = rboot_get_current_rom();
                if (slot == 0) { slot = 1; } else { slot = 0; }

                Serial1.printf("Firmware updated, rebooting to ROM slot
%d...\r\n",
slot);
                OtaCore::log(LOG_INFO, "Firmware updated, restarting...");
                rboot_set_current_rom(slot);
                System.restart();
        }
```

```
        else {
            OtaCore::log(LOG_ERROR, "Firmware update failed.");
        }
    }
```

In this callback, we change the active ROM slot if the OTA update was successful, followed by a reboot of the system. Otherwise, we simply log an error and do not restart.

Next are a few MQTT-related functions:

```
    bool OtaCore::registerTopic(String topic, topicCallback cb) {
        OtaCore::mqtt->subscribe(topic);
        (*topicCallbacks)[topic] = cb;
        return true;
    }

    bool OtaCore::deregisterTopic(String topic) {
        OtaCore::mqtt->unsubscribe(topic);
        if (topicCallbacks->contains(topic)) {
            topicCallbacks->remove(topic);
        }

        return true;
    }
```

These two functions allow feature modules to respectively register and deregister an MQTT topic along with a callback. The MQTT broker is called with a subscription or unsubscribe request and the `HashMap` instance is updated accordingly:

```
    bool OtaCore::publish(String topic, String message, int qos /* = 1 */) {
        OtaCore::mqtt->publishWithQoS(topic, message, qos);
        return true;
    }
```

Any feature modules can publish an MQTT message on any topic using this function. The **Quality of Service (QoS)** parameter determines the publish mode. By default, messages are published in *retain* mode, meaning that the broker will retain the last published message for a particular topic.

The entry point for the OTA update functionality is found in the following function:

```
    void OtaCore::otaUpdate() {
        OtaCore::log(LOG_INFO, "Updating firmware from URL: " +
    String(OTA_URL));

        if (otaUpdater) { delete otaUpdater; }
        otaUpdater = new rBootHttpUpdate();
```

```
rboot_config bootconf = rboot_get_config();
uint8 slot = bootconf.current_rom;
if (slot == 0) { slot = 1; } else { slot = 0; }

otaUpdater->addItem(bootconf.roms[slot], OTA_URL + MAC);

otaUpdater->setCallback(OtaCore::otaUpdate_CallBack);
otaUpdater->start();
}
```

For an OTA update, we need to create a clean `rBootHttpUpdate` instance. We then need to configure this instance with the details of the current firmware slot, for which we obtain the configuration from rBoot and with it the current firmware slot number. This we use to give the number of the other firmware slot to the OTA updater.

Here, we only configure it to update the firmware slot, but we could also update the SPIFFS section for the other firmware slot as well this way. The firmware will be fetched over HTTP from the fixed URL we set before. The ESP8266's MAC address is affixed to the end of it as a unique query string parameter so that the update server knows which firmware image fits this system.

After setting the `callback` function that we looked at earlier, we start the update:

```
void OtaCore::checkMQTTDisconnect(TcpClient& client, bool flag) {
        if (flag == true) { Serial1.println("MQTT Broker disconnected.");
}
        else {
                String tHost = MQTT_HOST;
                Serial1.println("MQTT Broker " + tHost + " unreachable."); }

        procTimer.initializeMs(2 * 1000,
OtaCore::startMqttClient).start();
}
```

Here, we define the MQTT disconnection handler. It is called whenever the connection with the MQTT broker fails so that we can try reconnecting after a two-second delay.

The flag parameter is set to true if we previously were connected, and false if the initial MQTT broker connection failed (no network access, wrong address, and so on).

Next is the function to configure and start the MQTT client:

```
void OtaCore::startMqttClient() {
        procTimer.stop();
        if (!mqtt->setWill("last/will",
"The connection from this device is lost:(",    1, true)) {
                debugf("Unable to set the last will and testament. Most
probably there is not enough memory on the device.");
        }
```

We stop the procTimer timer if it's running in case we were being called from a reconnect timer. Next, we set the **last will and testament** (**LWT**) for this device, which allows us to set a message that the MQTT broker will publish when it loses the connection with the client (us).

Next, we define three different execution paths, only one of which will be compiled, depending on whether we are using TLS (SSL), a username/password login, or anonymous access:

```
#ifdef ENABLE_SSL
        mqtt->connect(MAC, MQTT_USERNAME, MQTT_PWD, true);
        mqtt->addSslOptions(SSL_SERVER_VERIFY_LATER);

    Serial1.printf("Free Heap: %d\r\n", system_get_free_heap_size());

        if (!fileExist("esp8266.client.crt.binary")) {
                Serial1.println("SSL CRT file is missing:
esp8266.client.crt.binary.");
                return;
        }
        else if (!fileExist("esp8266.client.key.binary")) {
                Serial1.println("SSL key file is missing:
esp8266.client.key.binary.");
                return;
        }

        unsigned int crtLength, keyLength;
        char* crtFile;
        char* keyFile;
        readIntoFileBuffer("esp8266.client.crt.binary", crtFile,
crtLength);
        readIntoFileBuffer("esp8266.client.key.binary", keyFile,
keyLength);

        Serial1.printf("keyLength: %d, crtLength: %d.\n", keyLength,
crtLength);
        Serial1.printf("Free Heap: %d\r\n", system_get_free_heap_size());
```

```
            if (crtLength < 1 || keyLength < 1) {
                    Serial1.println("Failed to open certificate and/or key
file.");
                    return;
            }

            mqtt->setSslClientKeyCert((const uint8_t*) keyFile, keyLength,
                                              (const uint8_t*) crtFile,
crtLength, 0, true);
                delete[] keyFile;
                delete[] crtFile;

        Serial1.printf("Free Heap: %d\r\n", system_get_free_heap_size());
```

If we are using TLS certificates, we establish a connection with the MQTT broker, using our `MAC` as client identifier, then enable the SSL option for the connection. The available heap space is printed to the serial logging output for debugging purposes. Usually, at this point, we should have around 25 KB of RAM left, which is sufficient for holding the certificate and key in memory, along with the RX and TX buffers for the TLS handshake if the latter are configured on the SSL endpoint to be an acceptable size using the SSL fragment size option. We will look at this in more detail in `Chapter 9`, *Example - Building Management and Control*.

Next, we read the DER-encoded (binary) certificate and key files from SPIFFS. These files have a fixed name. For each file, we print out the file size, along with the current free heap size. If either file size is zero bytes, we consider the read attempt to have failed and we abort the connection attempt.

Otherwise, we use the key and certificate data with the MQTT connection, which should lead to a successful handshake and establishing an encrypted connection with the MQTT broker.

After deleting the key and certificate file data, we print out the free heap size to allow us to check that the cleanup was successful:

```
#elif defined USE_MQTT_PASSWORD
        mqtt->connect(MAC, MQTT_USERNAME, MQTT_PWD);
```

When using an MQTT username and password to log in to the broker, we just need to call the previous function on the MQTT client instance, providing our MAC as client identifier along with the username and password:

```
#else
        mqtt->connect(MAC);
#endif
```

To connect anonymously, we set up a connection with the broker and pass our MAC as the client identifier:

```
mqtt->setCompleteDelegate(checkMQTTDisconnect);

mqtt->subscribe(MQTT_PREFIX"upgrade");
mqtt->subscribe(MQTT_PREFIX"presence/tell");
mqtt->subscribe(MQTT_PREFIX"presence/ping");
mqtt->subscribe(MQTT_PREFIX"presence/restart/#");
mqtt->subscribe(MQTT_PREFIX"cc/" + MAC);

delay(100);

mqtt->publish(MQTT_PREFIX"cc/config", MAC);
}
```

Here, we first set the MQTT disconnect handler. Then, we subscribe to a number of topics that we wish to respond to. These all relate to management functionality for this firmware, allowing the system to be queried and configured over MQTT.

After subscribing, we briefly (100 ms) wait to give the broker some time to process these subscriptions before we publish on the central notification topic, using our MAC to let any interested clients and servers know that this system just came online.

Next are the WiFi connection handlers:

```
void OtaCore::connectOk(IPAddress ip, IPAddress mask, IPAddress gateway) {
        Serial1.println("I'm CONNECTED. IP: " + ip.toString());

        MAC = WifiStation.getMAC();
        Serial1.printf("MAC: %s.\n", MAC.c_str());

        if (fileExist("location.txt")) {
                location = getFileContent("location.txt");
        }
        else {
                location = MAC;
        }

        if (fileExist("config.txt")) {
                String configStr = getFileContent("config.txt");
                uint32 config;
                configStr.getBytes((unsigned char*) &config,
sizeof(uint32), 0);
                updateModules(config);
        }
```

```
        startMqttClient();
 }
```

This handler is called when we have successfully connected to the configured WiFi network using the provided credentials. After connecting, we keep a copy of our MAC in memory as our unique ID.

This firmware also supports specifying a user-defined string as our location or similar identifier. If one has been defined before, we load it from SPIFFS and use it; otherwise, our location string is simply the MAC.

Similarly, we load the 32-bit bitmask that defines the feature module configuration from SPIFFS if it exists. If not, all feature modules are initially left deactivated. Otherwise, we read the bitmask and pass it to the updateModules() function so that the relevant modules will be activated:

```
void OtaCore::connectFail(String ssid, uint8_t ssidLength,
                                        uint8_t* bssid, uint8_t
reason) {
        Serial1.println("I'm NOT CONNECTED. Need help :(");
        debugf("Disconnected from %s. Reason: %d", ssid.c_str(), reason);

        WDT.alive();

        WifiEvents.onStationGotIP(OtaCore::connectOk);
        WifiEvents.onStationDisconnect(OtaCore::connectFail);
 }
```

If connecting to the Wi-Fi network fails, we log this fact, then tell the MCU's watchdog timer that we are still alive to prevent a soft restart before we attempt to connect again.

This finishes all of the initialization functions. Next up are the functions used during normal activity, starting with the MQTT message handler:

```
void OtaCore::onMqttReceived(String topic, String message) {
        Serial1.print(topic);
        Serial1.print(":\n");
        Serial1.println(message);

        log(LOG_DEBUG, topic + " - " + message);

        if (topic == MQTT_PREFIX"upgrade" && message == MAC) {
                otaUpdate();
        }
        else if (topic == MQTT_PREFIX"presence/tell") {
                mqtt->publish(MQTT_PREFIX"presence/response", MAC);
        }
```

```
        else if (topic == MQTT_PREFIX"presence/ping") {
              mqtt->publish(MQTT_PREFIX"presence/pong", MAC);
        }
        else if (topic == MQTT_PREFIX"presence/restart" && message == MAC)
{
              System.restart();
        }
        else if (topic == MQTT_PREFIX"presence/restart/all") {
              System.restart();
        }
```

We registered this callback when we initially created the MQTT client instance. Every time a topic that we subscribed to receives a new message on the broker, we are notified and this callback receives a string containing the topic and another string containing the actual message (payload).

We can compare the topic with the topics we registered for, and perform the required operation, whether it is to perform an OTA update (if it specifies our MAC), respond to a ping request by returning a pong response with our MAC, or to restart the system.

The next topic is a more generic maintenance one, allowing one to configure active feature modules, set the location string, and request the current status of the system. The payload format consists out of the command string followed by a semicolon, and then the payload string:

```
        else if (topic == MQTT_PREFIX"cc/" + MAC) {
              int chAt = message.indexOf(';');
              String cmd = message.substring(0, chAt);
              ++chAt;

              String msg(((char*) &message[chAt]), (message.length() - chAt));

              log(LOG_DEBUG, msg);

              Serial1.printf("Command: %s, Message: ", cmd.c_str());
              Serial1.println(msg);
```

We start by extracting the command from the payload string using a simple find and substring approach. We then read in the remaining payload string, taking care to read it in as a binary string. For this, we use the remaining string's length and as starting position, the character right after the semicolon.

At this point, we have extracted the command and payload and can see what we have to do:

```
if (cmd == "mod") {
        if (msg.length() != 4) {
                Serial1.printf("Payload size wasn't 4 bytes: %d\n",
msg.length());
                return;
        }

        uint32 input;
        msg.getBytes((unsigned char*) &input, sizeof(uint32), 0);
        String byteStr;
        byteStr = "Received new configuration: ";
        byteStr += input;
        log(LOG_DEBUG, byteStr);
        updateModules(input);
}
```

This command sets which feature modules should be active. Its payload should be an unsigned 32-bit integer forming a bitmask, which we check to make sure that we have received exactly four bytes.

In the bitmask, the bits each match up with a module, which at this point are the following:

Bit position	Value
0x01	THPModule
0x02	CO2Module
0x04	JuraModule
0x08	JuraTermModule
0x10	MotionModule
0x20	PwmModule
0x40	IOModule
0x80	SwitchModule
0x100	PlantModule

Of these, the CO2, Jura, and JuraTerm modules are mutually exclusive, since they all use the first UART (Serial). If two or more of these are still specified in the bitmask, only the first module will be enabled and the others ignored. We will look at these other feature modules in more detail in Chapter 9, *Example - Building Management and Control*.

After we obtain the new configuration bitmask, we send it to the `updateModules()` function:

```
else if (cmd == "loc") {
        if (msg.length() < 1) { return; }
        if (location != msg) {
                location = msg;
                fileSetContent("location.txt", location);
        }
}
```

With this command, we set the new location string, if it is different then the current one, also saving it to the location file in SPIFFS to persist it across a reboot:

```
else if (cmd == "mod_active") {
        uint32 active_mods = BaseModule::activeMods();
        if (active_mods == 0) {
                mqtt->publish(MQTT_PREFIX"cc/response", MAC + ";0");
                return;
        }

        mqtt->publish(MQTT_PREFIX"cc/response", MAC + ";"
+ String((const char*) &active_mods, 4));
        }
        else if (cmd == "version") {
                mqtt->publish(MQTT_PREFIX"cc/response", MAC + ";" +
    version);
        }
        else if (cmd == "upgrade") {
                otaUpdate();
        }
}
```

The last three commands in this section return the current bitmask for the active feature modules, the firmware version, and trigger an OTA upgrade:

```
else {
        if (topicCallbacks->contains(topic)) {
                (*((*topicCallbacks)[topic]))(message);
        }
}
}
```

The last entry in the `if...else` block looks at whether the topic is perhaps found in our list of callbacks for the feature modules. If found, the callback is called with the MQTT message string.

Naturally, this means that only one feature module can register itself to a specific topic. Since each module tends to operate under its own MQTT sub-topic to segregate the message flow, this is generally not a problem:

```
void OtaCore::updateModules(uint32 input) {
        Serial1.printf("Input: %x, Active: %x.\n", input,
BaseModule::activeMods());

        BaseModule::newConfig(input);

        if (BaseModule::activeMods() != input) {
            String content(((char*) &input), 4);
            setFileContent("config.txt", content);
        }
}
```

This function is pretty simple. It mostly serves as a pass-through for the `BaseModule` class, but it also ensures that we keep the configuration file in SPIFFS up to date, writing the new bitmask to it when it has changed.

We absolutely must prevent unnecessary writes to SPIFFs, as the underlying Flash storage has finite write cycles. Limiting write cycles can significantly extend the lifespan of the hardware, as well as reduce overall system load:

```
bool OtaCore::mapGpioToBit(int pin, ESP8266_pins &addr) {
        switch (pin) {
            case 0:
                addr = ESP8266_gpio00;
                break;
            case 1:
                addr = ESP8266_gpio01;
                break;
            case 2:
                addr = ESP8266_gpio02;
                break;
            case 3:
                addr = ESP8266_gpio03;
                break;
            case 4:
                addr = ESP8266_gpio04;
                break;
            case 5:
                addr = ESP8266_gpio05;
                break;
            case 9:
                addr = ESP8266_gpio09;
                break;
```

```
            case 10:
                    addr = ESP8266_gpio10;
                    break;
            case 12:
                    addr = ESP8266_gpio12;
                    break;
            case 13:
                    addr = ESP8266_gpio13;
                    break;
            case 14:
                    addr = ESP8266_gpio14;
                    break;
            case 15:
                    addr = ESP8266_gpio15;
                    break;
            case 16:
                    addr = ESP8266_gpio16;
                    break;
            default:
                    log(LOG_ERROR, "Invalid pin number specified: " +
String(pin));
                    return false;
        };

        return true;
    }
```

This function maps the given GPIO pin number to its position in the internal bitmask. It uses the enumeration we looked at for the header file for this class. With this mapping, we can set the used/unused state of GPIO pins of the ESP8266 module using just a single uint32 value:

```
void OtaCore::log(int level, String msg) {
        String out(lvl);
        out += " - " + msg;

        Serial1.println(out);
        mqtt->publish(MQTT_PREFIX"log/all", OtaCore::MAC + ";" + out);
    }
```

In the logging method, we append the log level to the message string before writing it to the serial output, as well as publishing it on MQTT. Here, we publish on a single topic, but as a refinement you could log on a different topic depending on the specified level.

What makes sense here depends a great deal on what kind of backend you have set up to listen for and process logging output from the ESP8266 systems running this firmware:

```
bool OtaCore::starti2c() {
        if (i2c_active) { return true; }

        if (!claimPin(sdaPin)) { return false; }
        if (!claimPin(sclPin)) { return false; }

        Wire.pins(sdaPin, sclPin);
        pinMode(sclPin, OUTPUT);
        for (int i = 0; i < 8; ++i) {
                digitalWrite(sclPin, HIGH);
                delayMicroseconds(3);
                digitalWrite(sclPin, LOW);
                delayMicroseconds(3);
        }

        pinMode(sclPin, INPUT);

        Wire.begin();
        i2c_active = true;
}
```

This function starts the I2C bus if it hasn't been started already. It tries to register the pins it wishes to use for the I2C bus. If these are available, it will set the clock line (SCL) to output mode and first pulse it eight times to unfreeze any I2C devices on the bus.

After pulsing the clock line like his, we start the I2C bus on the pins and make a note of the active state of this bus.

 Frozen I2C devices can occur if the MCU power cycles when the I2C devices do not, and remain in an indeterminate state. With this pulsing, we make sure that the system won't end up in a non-functional state, requiring manual intervention:

```
bool OtaCore::startSPI() {
    if (spi_active) { return true; }

    if (!claimPin(SPI_SCLK)) { return false; }
    if (!claimPin(SPI_MOSI)) { return false; }
    if (!claimPin(SPI_MISO)) { return false; }
    if (!claimPin(SPI_CS)) { return false; }

    SPI.begin();
    spi_active = true;
}
```

Starting the SPI bus is similar to staring the I2C bus, except without a similar recovery mechanism:

```
bool OtaCore::claimPin(int pin) {
        ESP8266_pins addr;
        if (!mapGpioToBit(pin, addr)) { return false; }

        return claimPin(addr);
}


    bool OtaCore::claimPin(ESP8266_pins pin) {
        if (esp8266_pins & pin) {
            log(LOG_ERROR, "Attempting to claim an already claimed pin:
"
+ String(pin));
            log(LOG_DEBUG, String("Current claimed pins: ") +
String(esp8266_pins));
            return false;
        }

        log(LOG_INFO, "Claiming pin position: " + String(pin));

        esp8266_pins |= pin;

        log(LOG_DEBUG, String("Claimed pin configuration: ") +
String(esp8266_pins));

        return true;
}
```

This overloaded function is used to register a GPIO pin by a feature module before it starts, to ensure that no two modules attempt to use the same pins at the same time. One version accepts a pin number (GPIO) and uses the mapping function we looked at earlier to get the bit address in the `esp8266_pins` bitmask before passing it on to the other version of the function.

In that function, the pin enumeration is used to do a bitwise AND comparison. If the bit has not been set yet, it is toggled and true is returned. Otherwise, the function returns false and the calling module knows that it cannot proceed with its initialization:

```
bool OtaCore::releasePin(int pin) {
        ESP8266_pins addr;
        if (!mapGpioToBit(pin, addr)) { return false; }

        return releasePin(addr);
}
```

```
    bool OtaCore::releasePin(ESP8266_pins pin) {
        if (!(esp8266_pins & pin)) {
            log(LOG_ERROR, "Attempting to release a pin which has not
been set: "
+ String(pin));
            return false;
        }

        esp8266_pins &= ~pin;

        log(LOG_INFO, "Released pin position: " + String(pin));
        log(LOG_DEBUG, String("Claimed pin configuration: ") +
String(esp8266_pins));

        return true;
    }
```

This overloaded function, to release a pin when a feature module is shutting down, works in a similar manner. One uses the mapping function to get the bit address, the other performs a bitwise AND operation to check that the pin has in fact been set, and toggles it to an off position with the bitwise OR assignment operator if it was set.

BaseModule

This class contains the logic for registering and keeping track of which feature modules are currently active or inactive. Its header file looks as follows:

```
#include "ota_core.h"

enum ModuleIndex {
    MOD_IDX_TEMPERATURE_HUMIDITY = 0,
    MOD_IDX_CO2,
    MOD_IDX_JURA,
    MOD_IDX_JURATERM,
    MOD_IDX_MOTION,
    MOD_IDX_PWM,
    MOD_IDX_IO,
    MOD_IDX_SWITCH,
    MOD_IDX_PLANT
};


typedef bool (*modStart)();
typedef bool (*modShutdown)();
```

The inclusion of the `OtaCore` header is to allow us to use the logging feature. Beyond this, we create another enumeration, which maps a specific feature module to a particular bit in the feature module bitmask (`active_mods`).

Finally, function pointers are defined, which are used for respectively starting and shutting down a feature module. These will be defined by the feature modules as they register themselves:

```
#include "thp_module.h"
#include "jura_module.h"
#include "juraterm_module.h"
#include "co2_module.h"
#include "motion_module.h"
#include "pwm_module.h"
#include "io_module.h"
#include "switch_module.h"
#include "plant_module.h"
```

These are the feature modules that currently exist for this firmware as of writing. Since we only need the plant module for this project, we could comment out all header files for the other modules, along with their initialization in the initialization function of this class.

This would not affect the resulting firmware image in any way other than that we cannot enable those modules since they do not exist.

Finally, here is the class declaration itself:

```
class BaseModule {
        struct SubModule {
                modStart start;
                modShutdown shutdown;
                ModuleIndex index;
                uint32 bitmask;
                bool started;
        };

        static SubModule modules[32];
        static uint32 active_mods;
        static bool initialized;
        static uint8 modcount;

public:
        static void init();
        static bool registerModule(ModuleIndex index, modStart start,
modShutdown shutdown);
```

```
            static bool newConfig(uint32 config);
            static uint32 activeMods() { return active_mods; }
};
```

Each feature module is represented internally by a `SubModule` instance, the details of which we can see in a moment in the class definition:

```
#include "base_module.h"

BaseModule::SubModule BaseModule::modules[32];
uint32 BaseModule::active_mods = 0x0;
bool BaseModule::initialized = false;
uint8 BaseModule::modcount = 0;
```

Since this is a static class, we first initialize its class variables. We have an array with space for 32 `SubModule` instances, to fit the full bitmask. Beyond this, no modules are active, so everything is initialized to zero and false:

```
void BaseModule::init() {
    CO2Module::initialize();
    IOModule::initialize();
    JuraModule::initialize();
    JuraTermModule::initialize();
    MotionModule::initialize();
    PlantModule::initialize();
    PwmModule::initialize();
    SwitchModule::initialize();
    THPModule::initialize();
}
```

When we called this function in `OtaCore`, we also triggered the registration of the feature modules defined here. By selectively removing or commenting out modules in this function, we can remove them from the final firmware image. Those modules that are called here will call the following function to register themselves:

```
bool BaseModule::registerModule(ModuleIndex index, modStart start,
modShutdown shutdown) {
        if (!initialized) {
                for (uint8 i = 0; i < 32; i++) {
                        modules[i].start = 0;
                        modules[i].shutdown = 0;
                        modules[i].index = index;
                        modules[i].bitmask = (1 << i);
                        modules[i].started = false;
                }

                initialized = true;
```

```
        }

        if (modules[index].start) {
            return false;
        }

        modules[index].start = start;
        modules[index].shutdown = shutdown;
        ++modcount;

        return true;
    }
```

The first feature module that calls this function will trigger the initialization of the `SubModule` array, setting all of its values to a neutral setting, while also creating the bitmask for this position in the array, which allows us to update the `active_mods` bitmask, as we will see in a moment.

After initializing the array, we check whether this position in the array already has a module registered for it. If it has, we return false. Otherwise, we register the module's function pointers for starting and shutting down, and increase the active module count before returning true:

```
bool BaseModule::newConfig(uint32 config) {
    OtaCore::log(LOG_DEBUG, String("Mod count: ") + String(modcount));
    uint32 new_config = config ^ active_mods;
    if (new_config == 0x0) {
        OtaCore::log(LOG_INFO, "New configuration was 0x0. No
        change.");
        return true;
    }
    OtaCore::log(LOG_INFO, "New configuration: " + new_config);
    for (uint8 i = 0; i < 32; ++i) {
        if (new_config & (1 << i)) {
            OtaCore::log(LOG_DEBUG, String("Toggling module: ") +
            String(i));
            if (modules[i].started) {
                if ((modules[i]).shutdown()) {
                    modules[i].started = false;
                    active_mods ^= modules[i].bitmask;
                }
                else {
                    OtaCore::log(LOG_ERROR, "Failed to shutdown
                    module.");
                    return false;
                }
            }
        }
```

```
            else {
                if ((modules[i].start) && (modules[i]).start()) {
                    modules[i].started = true;
                    active_mods |= modules[i].bitmask;
                }
                else {
                    OtaCore::log(LOG_ERROR, "Failed to start module.");
                    return false;
                }
            }
        }
    }
    return true;
}
```

The input parameter to this function is the bitmask we extracted from the MQTT payload in `OtaCore`. Here, we use a bitwise XOR comparison with the active modules bitmask to obtain a new bitmask indicating any changes to be made. If the result is zero, we know that they're identical and we can return without further action being required.

The `uint32` bitmask we have thus obtained indicates which modules should be toggled on or off. For this, we check each bit of the mask. If it is a `1` (AND operator returns a value that's not zero), we check whether the module at that position in the array exists and has been started yet.

If the module has been started, we attempt to shut it down. If the module's shutdown() function succeeds (returns true), we toggle the bit in the `active_mods` bitmask to update its status. Similarly, if the module has not been started yet, a module has been registered at that location, we attempt to start it, updating the active modules if this succeeds.

We check that a start function callback has been registered to ensure that we do not accidentally call an improperly registered module and crash the system.

PlantModule

At this point, we have had a detailed look at the underlying, supporting code that makes life easy when writing a new module because we don't have to do all of the housekeeping ourselves. The only thing we haven't seen yet is an actual module, or code directly pertaining to this chapter's project.

In this section, we will look at the last part of the puzzle, the `PlantModule` itself:

```cpp
#include "base_module.h"
#include <Libraries/APA102/apa102.h>

#define PLANT_GPIO_PIN 5
#define NUM_APA102 1

class PlantModule {
        static int pin;
        static Timer timer;
        static uint16 humidityTrigger;
        static String publishTopic;
        static HttpServer server;
        static APA102* LED;

        static void onRequest(HttpRequest& request, HttpResponse&
response);

public:
        static bool initialize();
        static bool start();
        static bool shutdown();
        static void readSensor();
        static void commandCallback(String message);
};
```

Of note in this class declaration is the inclusion of the APA102 library header. This is a simple library that allows us to write color and brightness data to APA102 RGB (full-spectrum) LEDs, over the SPI bus.

We also define the pin that we wish to use to trigger the peristaltic pump (GPIO 5) and the number of connected APA102 LED modules (1). You can add multiple APA102 LEDs in series if you want, simply updating the definition to match the count.

Next is the class implementation:

```cpp
#include "plant_module.h"


int PlantModule::pin = PLANT_GPIO_PIN;
Timer PlantModule::timer;
uint16 PlantModule::humidityTrigger = 530;
String PlantModule::publishTopic;
HttpServer PlantModule::server;
APA102* PlantModule::LED = 0;
```

```
enum {
        PLANT_SOIL_MOISTURE = 0x01,
        PLANT_SET_TRIGGER = 0x02,
        PLANT_TRIGGER = 0x04
};
```

In this section, we initialize the static class members, setting the GPIO pin and defining the initial sensor value at which the pump should be triggered. This trigger value should be updated to match your own sensor calibration results.

Finally, we define an enumeration containing the possible commands for this module that can be sent to it over MQTT:

```
bool PlantModule::initialize() {
        BaseModule::registerModule(MOD_IDX_PLANT, PlantModule::start,
PlantModule::shutdown);
}
```

This is the initialization function the `BaseModule` calls on startup. As we can see, it causes this module to register itself with preset values, including its start and shutdown callbacks:

```
bool PlantModule::start() {
        OtaCore::log(LOG_INFO, "Plant Module starting...");

        if (!OtaCore::claimPin(pin)) { return false; }

        publishTopic = MQTT_PREFIX + "plant/response/" +
OtaCore::getLocation();
        OtaCore::registerTopic(MQTT_PREFIX + String("plants/") +
OtaCore::getLocation(), PlantModule::commandCallback);

        pinMode(pin, OUTPUT);

        server.listen(80);
        server.setDefaultHandler(PlantModule::onRequest);

        LED = new APA102(NUM_APA102);
        LED->setBrightness(15);
        LED->clear();
        LED->setAllPixel(0, 255, 0);
        LED->show();

        timer.initializeMs(60000, PlantModule::readSensor).start();
        return true;
}
```

When this module starts, we attempt to claim the pin we wish to use for triggering the pump, as well as register a callback for an MQTT topic so that we can accept commands using the command handler callback. The topic on which we will responses after processing a command is also defined here.

The output pin mode is set, followed by the starting of the HTTP server on port 80, registering a basic handler for client requests. Next, we create a new APA102 class instance and use it to get the connected LED to display green at about half of full brightness.

Finally, we start a timer that will trigger the reading out of the connected soil sensor every minute:

```
bool PlantModule::shutdown() {
        if (!OtaCore::releasePin(pin)) { return false; }

        server.shutdown();

        if (LED) {
            delete LED;
            LED = 0;
        }

        OtaCore::deregisterTopic(MQTT_PREFIX + String("plants/") +
OtaCore::getLocation());

        timer.stop();
        return true;
}
```

When shutting down this module, we release the pin we registered previously, stop the web server, delete the RGB LED class instance (with a check to see that deleting it is necessary), deregister our MQTT topic, and finally stop the sensor timer.

```
void PlantModule::commandCallback(String message) {
        OtaCore::log(LOG_DEBUG, "Plant command: " + message);

        if (message.length() < 1) { return; }
        int index = 0;
        uint8 cmd = *((uint8*) &message[index++]);

        if (cmd == PLANT_SOIL_MOISTURE) {
            readSensor();
        }
        else if (cmd == PLANT_SET_TRIGGER) {
                if (message.length() != 3) { return; }
                uint16 payload = *((uint16*) &message[index]);
                index += 2;
```

```
                    humidityTrigger = payload;
          }
          else if (cmd == PLANT_TRIGGER) {
                    OtaCore::publish(publishTopic, OtaCore::getLocation() + ";"
                                                            +
     String(((char*) &humidityTrigger), 2));
          }
     }
```

This callback is called whenever a message is published on the MQTT topic we registered. In our messages, we expect to find a single byte (uint8) value that defines the command, up to eight distinct commands. For this module, we earlier defined three commands.

These commands are defined as follows:

Command	Meaning	Payload	Return value
0x01	Get soil moisture	-	0xXXXX
0x02	Set trigger level	uint16 (new trigger level)	-
0x04	Get trigger level	-	0xXXXX

Here, every command returns the requested value, if applicable.

After checking that the message string we got has at least one byte in it, we extract the first byte and try to interpret it as a command. If we are setting a new trigger point, we also extract the new value as a uint16 from the message after making sure that we have a properly formed message.

Finally, here is the function in which all of the magic happens that we have been working toward in this project:

```
void PlantModule::readSensor() {
     int16_t val = 0;
     val = analogRead(A0); // calls system_adc_read().

     String response = OtaCore::getLocation() + ";" + val;
     OtaCore::publish(MQTT_PREFIX"nsa/plant/moisture_raw", response);
```

As the first step, we read out the current sensor value from the analog input of the ESP8266 and publish it on the MQTT topic for this:

```
if (val >= humidityTrigger) {
        digitalWrite(pin, HIGH);

        LED->setBrightness(31);
        LED->setAllPixel(0, 0, 255);
        LED->show();

        for (int i = 0; i < 10; ++i) {
                LED->directWrite(0, 0, 255, 25);
                delay(200);
                LED->directWrite(0, 0, 255, 18);
                delay(200);
                LED->directWrite(0, 0, 255, 12);
                delay(200);
                LED->directWrite(0, 0, 255, 5);
                delay(200);
                LED->directWrite(0, 0, 255, 31);
                delay(200);
        }

        digitalWrite(pin, LOW);
    }
}
```

During calibration of one prototype with a soil moisture sensor, it was found that the value for a completely dry sensor (held in the air) was approximately 766, whereas having the same sensor submerged in water got 379 as a value. From this, we can deduce that 60% moisture content should be roughly around a reading of 533, which matches the initial value we set during the static initialization step. The ideal trigger point and target soil moisture level of course depends on the soil type and specific plant.

With this trigger level reached, we set the output pin that is connected to the enable pin of the boost converter to high, causing it to turn on its output, which in turn starts the pump. We wish to let it pump for about ten seconds.

During this time we set the LED color to blue, then during each second we drop its brightness from 100% to nearly off and then back to full brightness again, creating a pulsating effect.

After this, we set the output pin back to low, which disables the pump, and we await the next soil moisture sensor reading:

```
void PlantModule::onRequest(HttpRequest& request, HttpResponse& response) {
        TemplateFileStream* tmpl = new TemplateFileStream("index.html");
        TemplateVariables& vars = tmpl->variables();
        int16_t val = analogRead(A0);
        int8_t perc = 100 - ((val - 379) / 3.87);
        vars["raw_value"] = String(val);
        vars["percentage"] = String(perc);

        response.sendTemplate(tmpl);
}
```

Finally, we see here the request handler for our web server. What it does is read in a template file from SPIFFS (detailed in the next section), gets the list of variables in this template file, and then proceeds to read out the current sensor value.

Using this value, it calculates the current soil moisture percentage and uses both the raw and calculated numbers to fill in the two variables in the template before returning it.

Index.html

For use with the PlantModule's web server, we have to add the following template file to SPIFFS:

```
<!DOCTYPE html>
<html>
<head>
        <title>Plant soil moisture readings</title>
    </head>
    <body>
        Current value: {raw_value}<br>
        Percentage: {percentage}%
</body>
</html>
```

Compiling and flashing

After finishing the code for our application, we can compile it with a single command in the project's root folder:

```
make
```

After this completes, we can find the binaries including the ROM images in the out folder. Since we are using both the rBoot bootloader and SPIFFs, we get three ROM images in total in the firmware folder.

At this point, we can connect an ESP8266 module, either in the form of a NodeMCU board or one of the many alternatives, and note the serial port that it will be connected to. On Windows, this will be something like COM3; on Linux, USB-to-serial adapters usually are registered as /dev/ttyUSB0 or similar.

Unless we have specified the serial port (COM_PORT) in the user Makefile, we have to specify it explicitly when we flash to the ESP8266 module:

```
make flash COM_PORT=/dev/ttyUSB0
```

After executing this command, we should see the output from the esptool.py utility, as it connects to the ESP8266's ROM and starts writing the ROM images to it.

Once this is complete, the MCU will restart and it should boot straight into the new firmware image, where it will await our commands to configure it.

First-time configuration

As noted earlier in this chapter, this firmware is designed to be configured and maintained over MQTT. This requires that an MQTT broker is available. An MQTT broker such as Mosquitto (http://mosquitto.org/) is popular. Since it's a lightweight server, it can be installed on a desktop system, a small SBC, inside a virtual machine, and so on.

In addition the broker and the ESP8266 running the firmware, we also need our own client to interact with the firmware. Since we use binary protocols, our choice there is somewhat limited, as most common MQTT desktop clients assume text-based messages. One approach one can use to publish binary messages is to use the MQTT publish client that comes with Mosquitto and use the **echo** command-line tool's hexadecimal input to send binary data to it as a stream to be published by the client tool

Because of this, the author of this book has developed a new MQTT desktop client (based on C++ and Qt) that is designed around the use and debugging of binary protocols on MQTT: https://github.com/MayaPosch/MQTTCute.

With all three components in place—ESP8266 running the project, the MQTT broker and desktop client—we can have the entire plant monitoring and watering system assembled and send it the command to enable the plant module.

While monitoring the cc/config topic for messages, we should see the ESP8266 report its presence by publishing its `MAC`. We can also get this by hooking up a USB to TTL serial adapter to the serial logging output pin (`D4` on NodeMCU). By looking at the output on our serial console, we will see both the IP address and the `MAC` of the system.

When we compose a new topic of the format `cc/<MAC>`, we can then publish commands to the firmware, for example:

```
log;plant001
```

This would set the location name of the system to `plant001`.

When using the MQTTCute client, we can use echo-style binary input, using hexadecimal input, to activate the plant module:

```
mod;\x00\x01\x00\x00
```

This would send the `mod` command to the firmware, along with a bitmask with the value 0 x 100. After this, the plant module should be activated and running. Since we are persisting both the location string and the configuration, we do not have to repeat this step any more unless we do an OTA update, at which point the new firmware will have an empty SPIFFS filesystem, unless we flash the same SPIFFS image on both SPIFFS slots on the ROM.

 Here, we could expand the OTA code to also download a SPIFFS ROM image in addition to the firmware one, though this might add the complication of possibly overwriting the existing SPIFFS files.

At this point, we should have a working plant-monitoring and -watering system.

Using the system

We can use the measured values and store them in a database by subscribing to the `nsa/plant/moisture_raw` topic. The trigger point can be adjusted by sending a new command to the `plant/<location string>` topic.

The web server on the device can be accessed by taking the IP address, which we can find either by looking at the output on the serial console, as described in the previous section, or by looking at the active IP addresses in your router.

By opening this IP address in the browser, we should see the HTML template filled in with the current values.

Taking it further

You also need to have the following considerations:

- At this point, you can further refine the system by implementing plant-watering profiles to add dry periods or to adjust for certain soil types. You can add new RGB LED modes to make full use of the color choices available.
- The entire hardware could be built into an enclosure, to make it blend into the background, or maybe to make it more visible.
- The web interface could be extended to allow for controlling the trigger point and such from the browser, instead of having to use an MQTT client.
- In addition to the moisture sensor, you could also add a brightness sensor, a temperature sensor, and so on, to measure more aspects that affect the plant's health.
- For bonus points, you could automate the applying of (liquid) fertilizer to the plant.

Complications

One possible complication you may encounter with the ESP8266's ADC is that on the NodeMCU boards, the first reserved (RSV) pin that is right next to the ADC pin is directly connected to the ESP8266 module's ADC input. This can potentially cause issues with electrostatic discharge ESD exposure. Essentially the discharging of a high voltage, but low current, into the MCU. Adding a small capacitor on this RSV pin to ground can help reduce this risk.

One thing that this system obviously cannot help with is to keep your plants pest-free. This means that though the watering may be automated, that doesn't mean that you can just ignore the plants. The regular checking of the plants for any issues, as well as the system for any issues that may be developing (disconnected tubing, things that have fallen over due to cats, and so on) remains an important task.

Summary

In this chapter, we looked at how to take a simple ESP8266-based project from theory and simple requirements to a functioning design with a versatile firmware and a collection of input and output options, using which we can ensure that a connected plant gets just the right amount of water to stay healthy. We also saw how to set up a development environment for the ESP8266.

The reader should now be able to create projects for the ESP8266, program the MCU with new firmware, and have a solid grasp on both the strengths and limitations of this development platform.

In the next chapter, we will be looking at how to test embedded software written for SoCs and other large, embedded platforms.

Section 2: Testing, Monitoring

2

In this section, you will learn the proper workflow for developing for a variety of embedded platforms, including testing strategies and the importance of writing portable code.

The following chapters will be covered in this section:

- Chapter 6, *Testing OS-Based Applications*
- Chapter 7, *Testing Resource-Restricted Platforms*
- Chapter 8, *Example - Linux-Based Infotainment System*
- Chapter 9, *Example - Building Monitoring and Control*

Testing OS-Based Applications

6

Often, an embedded system uses a more or less regular **Operating System (OS)**, which means that, often much, is the same as on our desktop OS in terms of runtime environment and tools, especially when targeting embedded Linux. Yet, differences in terms of performance and access offered by the embedded hardware versus our PC makes it essential to consider where to perform which parts of developing and testing, as well as how to integrate this into our development workflow.

In this chapter, we'll cover the following topics:

- Developing cross-platform code
- Debugging and testing cross-platform code under Linux
- Effectively using cross-compilers
- Creating a build system that supports multiple targets

Avoiding real hardware

One of the biggest advantages of OS-based development on platforms such as embedded Linux is that it's so similar to a regular desktop Linux installation. Especially when running an OS such as a Debian-based Linux distribution (Armbian, Raspbian, and others) on SoCs, we have practically the same tools available, with the entire package manager, compiler collections, and libraries available with a few keystrokes.

This is, however, also its biggest pitfall.

We can write code, copy it over to the SBC, compile it there, run the test, and make changes to the code before repeating the process. Or, we can even write the code on the SBC itself, essentially using it as our sole development platform.

The main reasons why we should never do this are as follows:

- A modern PC is much faster.
- Testing on real hardware should never be done until the final stages of development.
- Automated integration testing is made much harder.

Here, the first point seems fairly obvious. What takes a single or dual-core ARM SoC a good minute to compile will quickly go from start of compilation to linking the objects in ten seconds or less with a relatively modern multi-core, multithreaded processor at 3+ GHz, and a toolchain that supports multi-core compilation.

This means that, instead of waiting half a minute or longer before we can run a new test or start a debugging session, we can do so almost instantly.

The next two points are related. While it may seem advantageous to test on the real hardware, it comes with its own complications. One thing is that this hardware relies on a number of external factors to work properly, including its power supply, any wiring between power sources, peripherals, and signal interfaces. Things such as electromagnetic interference may also cause issues, in terms of signal degradation, as well as interrupts being triggered due to electromagnetic coupling.

An example of electromagnetic coupling became apparent while developing the club status service project of Chapter 3, *Developing for Embedded Linux and Similar Systems*. Here, one of the signal wires for the switches ran alongside 230V AC wiring. Changes in the current on this mains wiring induced pulses in the signal wire, causing false interrupt trigger events.

All of these potential hardware-related issues show that such tests aren't nearly as deterministic as we would wish them to be. The potential result of this is that project development takes much longer than planned, with debugging being complicated due to conflicting and non-deterministic test results.

Another effect of a focus on developing on and for real hardware is that it makes automated testing much harder. The reason for this is that we cannot use any generic build cluster and, for example, Linux VM-based testing environment, as is common with mainstream **Continuous Integration** (CI) services.

Instead of this, we would have to somehow integrate something such as an SBC into the CI system, having it either cross-compile and copy the binary to the SBC for running the test, or compile it on the SBC itself, which gets us back to the first point.

In the next few sections, we'll look at a of approaches to make embedded Linux-based development as painless as possible, starting with cross-compilation.

Cross-compiling for SBCs

The compile process takes the source files, turning them into an intermediate format, after which this format can be used to target a specific CPU architecture. For us, this means that we aren't limited to compiling applications for an SBC on that SBC itself, but we can do so on our development PC.

To do so for an SBC such as the Raspberry Pi (Broadcom Cortex-A-based ARM SoCs), we need to install the `arm-linux-gnueabihf` toolchain, which targets the ARM architecture with hard float (hardware floating point) support, outputting Linux-compatible binaries.

On a Debian-based Linux system, we can install the entire toolchain with the following commands:

```
sudo apt install build-essential
sudo apt install g++-arm-linux-gnueabihf
sudo apt install gdb-multiarch
```

The first command installs the native GCC-based toolchain for the system (if it wasn't already installed), along with any common related tools and utilities, including `make`, `libtool`, `flex`, and others. The second command installs the actual cross-compiler. Finally, the third package is the version of the GDB debugger that supports multiple architectures, which we'll need later on for doing remote debugging on the real hardware, as well as for analyzing core dumps produced when our application crashes.

We can now use the g++ compiler for the target SBC using its full name on the command line:

```
arm-linux-gnueabihf-g++
```

To test whether the toolchain was properly installed, we can execute the following command, which should tell us the compiler details including the version:

```
arm-linux-gnueabihf-g++ -v
```

In addition to this, we may need to link with some shared libraries that exist on the target system. For this, we can copy the entire contents of the /lib and /usr folders and include them as part of the system root for the compiler:

```
mkdir ~/raspberry/sysroot
scp -r pi@Pi-system:/lib ~/raspberry/sysroot
scp -r pi@Pi-system:/usr ~/raspberry/sysroot
```

Here, Pi-system is the IP address or network name of the Raspberry Pi or similar system. After this, we can tell GCC to use these folders instead of the standard paths using the sysroot flag:

```
--sysroot=dir
```

Here dir would be the folder where we copied these folders to, in this example that would be ~/raspberry/sysroot.

Alternatively, we can just copy the header and library files we require and add them as part of the source tree. Whichever approach is the easiest mostly depends on the dependencies of the project in question.

For the club status service project, we require at the very least the headers and libraries for WiringPi, as well as those for the POCO project and its dependencies. We could determine the dependencies we need and copy the required includes and library files that are missing from the toolchain we installed earlier. Unless there's a pressing need to do so, it's far easier to just copy the entire folders from the SBC's OS.

As an alternative to using the sysroot method, we can also explicitly define the paths to the shared libraries that we wish to use while linking our code. This of course comes with its own set of advantages and disadvantages.

Integration test for club status service

In order to test the club status service on a regular desktop Linux (or macOS or Windows) system before we embark on cross-compiling and testing on real hardware, a simple integration test was written, which uses mocks for the GPIO and I2C peripherals.

In the source code for the project covered in Chapter 3, *Developing for Embedded Linux and Similar Systems*, the files for these peripherals are found in the wiring folder of that project.

We start with the `wiringPi.h` header:

```
#include <Poco/Timer.h>
```

```
#define   INPUT               0
#define   OUTPUT                     1
#define   PWM_OUTPUT          2
#define   GPIO_CLOCK          3
#define   SOFT_PWM_OUTPUT           4
#define   SOFT_TONE_OUTPUT    5
#define   PWM_TONE_OUTPUT            6
```

We include a header from the POCO framework to allow us to easily create a timer instance later on. Then, we define all possible pin modes, just as the actual WiringPi header defines:

```
#define   LOW                 0
#define   HIGH                1

#define   PUD_OFF                   0
#define   PUD_DOWN            1
#define   PUD_UP                    2

#define   INT_EDGE_SETUP            0
#define   INT_EDGE_FALLING   1
#define   INT_EDGE_RISING           2
#define   INT_EDGE_BOTH             3
```

These defines define further pin modes, including the digital input levels, the possible states of the pull-ups and pull-downs on the pins, and finally the possible types of interrupts, defining the trigger or triggers for an interrupt:

```
typedef void (*ISRCB)(void);
```

This `typedef` defines the format for an interrupt callback function pointer.

Let's now look at the `WiringTimer` class:

```
class WiringTimer {
    Poco::Timer* wiringTimer;
    Poco::TimerCallback<WiringTimer>* cb;
    uint8_t triggerCnt;

 public:
    ISRCB isrcb_0;
    ISRCB isrcb_7;
    bool isr_0_set;
    bool isr_7_set;
```

```
        WiringTimer();
        ~WiringTimer();
        void start();
        void trigger(Poco::Timer &t);
    };
```

This class is the integral part of the GPIO-side of our mock implementation. Its main purpose is to keep track of which of the two interrupts we're interested in have been registered, and to trigger them at regular intervals using the timer, as we'll see in a moment:

```
    int wiringPiSetup();
    void pinMode(int pin, int mode);
    void pullUpDnControl(int pin, int pud);
    int digitalRead(int pin);
    int wiringPiISR(int pin, int mode, void (*function)(void));
```

Finally, we define the standard WiringPi functions before moving on the implementation:

```
    #include "wiringPi.h"


    #include <fstream>
    #include <memory>


    WiringTimer::WiringTimer() {
        triggerCnt = 0;
        isrcb_0 = 0;
        isrcb_7 = 0;
        isr_0_set = false;
        isr_7_set = false;

        wiringTimer = new Poco::Timer(10 * 1000, 10 * 1000);
        cb = new Poco::TimerCallback<WiringTimer>(*this,
        &WiringTimer::trigger);
    }
```

In the class constructor, we set the default values before creating the timer instance, configuring it to call our callback function every ten seconds, after an initial 10-second delay:

```
    WiringTimer::~WiringTimer() {
        delete wiringTimer;
        delete cb;
    }
```

In the destructor, we delete the timer callback instance:

```
void WiringTimer::start() {
    wiringTimer->start(*cb);
}
```

In this function, we actually start the timer:

```
void WiringTimer::trigger(Poco::Timer &t) {
    if (triggerCnt == 0) {
            char val = 0x00;
            std::ofstream PIN0VAL;
            PIN0VAL.open("pin0val", std::ios_base::binary |
std::ios_base::trunc);
            PIN0VAL.put(val);
            PIN0VAL.close();

            isrcb_0();

            ++triggerCnt;
    }
    else if (triggerCnt == 1) {
            char val = 0x01;
            std::ofstream PIN7VAL;
            PIN7VAL.open("pin7val", std::ios_base::binary |
std::ios_base::trunc);
            PIN7VAL.put(val);
            PIN7VAL.close();

            isrcb_7();

            ++triggerCnt;
    }
    else if (triggerCnt == 2) {
            char val = 0x00;
            std::ofstream PIN7VAL;
            PIN7VAL.open("pin7val", std::ios_base::binary |
std::ios_base::trunc);
            PIN7VAL.put(val);
            PIN7VAL.close();

            isrcb_7();

            ++triggerCnt;
    }
    else if (triggerCnt == 3) {
            char val = 0x01;
            std::ofstream PIN0VAL;
```

```
                    PIN0VAL.open("pin0val", std::ios_base::binary |
        std::ios_base::trunc);
                    PIN0VAL.put(val);
                    PIN0VAL.close();

                    isrcb_0();

                    triggerCnt = 0;
            }
        }
```

This last function in the class is the callback for the timer. The way it functions is that it keeps track of how many times it has been triggered, with it setting the appropriate pin level in the form of a value in a file that we write to disk.

After the initial delay, the first trigger will set the lock switch to `false`, the second the status switch to `true`, the third the status switch back to `false`, and finally the fourth trigger sets the lock switch back to `true`, before resetting the counter and starting over again:

```
namespace Wiring {
    std::unique_ptr<WiringTimer> wt;
    bool initialized = false;
}
```

We add a global namespace in which we have a `unique_ptr` instance for a `WiringTimer` class instance, along with an initialization status indicator.

```
int wiringPiSetup() {
    char val = 0x01;
    std::ofstream PIN0VAL;
    std::ofstream PIN7VAL;
    PIN0VAL.open("pin0val", std::ios_base::binary | std::ios_base::trunc);
    PIN7VAL.open("pin7val", std::ios_base::binary | std::ios_base::trunc);
    PIN0VAL.put(val);
    val = 0x00;
    PIN7VAL.put(val);
    PIN0VAL.close();
    PIN7VAL.close();

    Wiring::wt = std::make_unique<WiringTimer>();
    Wiring::initialized = true;

    return 0;
}
```

The setup function is used to write the default values for the mocked GPIO pin inputs value to disk. We also create the pointer to a `WiringTimer` instance here:

```
void pinMode(int pin, int mode) {
    //

    return;
}

void pullUpDnControl(int pin, int pud) {
    //

    return;
}
```

Because our mocked implementation determines the behavior of the pins, we can ignore any input on these functions. For testing purposes, we could add an assert to validate that these functions have been called at the right times with the appropriate settings:

```
int digitalRead(int pin) {
    if (pin == 0) {
        std::ifstream PIN0VAL;
        PIN0VAL.open("pin0val", std::ios_base::binary);
        int val = PIN0VAL.get();
        PIN0VAL.close();

        return val;
    }
    else if (pin == 7) {
        std::ifstream PIN7VAL;
        PIN7VAL.open("pin7val", std::ios_base::binary);
        int val = PIN7VAL.get();
        PIN7VAL.close();

        return val;
    }

    return 0;
}
```

When reading the value for one of the two mocked pins, we open its respective file and read out its content, which is either the 1 or 0 set by the setup function or by the callback:

```
//This value is then returned to the calling function.


int wiringPiISR(int pin, int mode, void (*function)(void)) {
    if (!Wiring::initialized) {
```

```
        return 1;
    }

    if (pin == 0) {
        Wiring::wt->isrcb_0 = function;
        Wiring::wt->isr_0_set = true;
    }
    else if (pin == 7) {
        Wiring::wt->isrcb_7 = function;
        Wiring::wt->isr_7_set = true;
    }

    if (Wiring::wt->isr_0_set && Wiring::wt->isr_7_set) {
        Wiring::wt->start();
    }

    return 0;
}
```

This function is used to register an interrupt and its associated callback function. After an initial check that the mock has been initialized by the setup function, we then continue to register the interrupt for one of the two specified pins.

Once both pins have had an interrupt set for them, we start the timer, which will in turn start generating events for the interrupt callbacks.

Next is the I2C bus mock:

```
int wiringPiI2CSetup(const int devId);
int wiringPiI2CWriteReg8(int fd, int reg, int data);
```

We just need two functions here: the setup function and the simple one-byte register write function.

The implementation is as follows:

```
#include "wiringPiI2C.h"

#include "../club.h"

#include <Poco/NumberFormatter.h>

using namespace Poco;


int wiringPiI2CSetup(const int devId) {
    Club::log(LOG_INFO, "wiringPiI2CSetup: setting up device ID: 0x"
                +
```

```
NumberFormatter::formatHex(devId));


    return 0;
}
```

In the setup function, we log the requested device ID (I2C bus address) and return a standard device handle. Here, we use the `log()` function from the `Club` class to make the mock integrate into the rest of the code:

```
int wiringPiI2CWriteReg8(int fd, int reg, int data) {
    Club::log(LOG_INFO, "wiringPiI2CWriteReg8: Device handle 0x" +
NumberFormatter::formatHex(fd)
                                    + ", Register 0x" +
NumberFormatter::formatHex(reg)
                                    + " set to: 0x" +
NumberFormatter::formatHex(data));

    return 0;
}
```

Since the code that would call this function wouldn't be expecting a response, beyond a simple acknowledgment that the data has been received, we can just log the received data and further details here. The `NumberFormatter` class from POCO is used here as well for formatting the integer data as hexadecimal values like in the application, for consistency.

We now compile the project and use the following command-line command:

make TEST=1

Running the application (under GDB, to see when new threads are created/destroyed) now gets us the following output:

```
Starting ClubStatus server...
Initialised C++ Mosquitto library.
Created listener, entering loop...
[New Thread 0x7ffff49c9700 (LWP 35462)]
[New Thread 0x7ffff41c8700 (LWP 35463)]
[New Thread 0x7ffff39c7700 (LWP 35464)]
Initialised the HTTP server.
INFO:       Club: starting up...
INFO:       Club: Finished wiringPi setup.
INFO:       Club: Finished configuring pins.
INFO:       Club: Configured interrupts.
[New Thread 0x7ffff31c6700 (LWP 35465)]
INFO:       Club: Started update thread.
Connected. Subscribing to topics...
```

```
    INFO:          ClubUpdater: Starting i2c relay device.
    INFO:          wiringPiI2CSetup: setting up device ID: 0x20
    INFO:          wiringPiI2CWriteReg8: Device handle 0x0, Register 0x6 set to:
0x0
    INFO:          wiringPiI2CWriteReg8: Device handle 0x0, Register 0x2 set to:
0x0
    INFO:          ClubUpdater: Finished configuring the i2c relay device's
registers.
```

At this point, the system has been configured with all interrupts set and the I2C device configured by the application. The timer has started its initial countdown:

```
    INFO:          ClubUpdater: starting initial update run.
    INFO:          ClubUpdater: New lights, clubstatus off.
    DEBUG:         ClubUpdater: Power timer not active, using current power
state: off
    INFO:          ClubUpdater: Red on.
    DEBUG:         ClubUpdater: Changing output register to: 0x8
    INFO:          wiringPiI2CWriteReg8: Device handle 0x0, Register 0x2 set to:
0x8
    DEBUG:         ClubUpdater: Finished writing relay outputs with: 0x8
    INFO:          ClubUpdater: Initial status update complete.
```

The initial status of the GPIO pins has been read out and both switches are found to be in the off position, so we activate the red light on the traffic light indicator by writing its position in the register:

```
    INFO:          ClubUpdater: Entering waiting condition.
    INFO:          ClubUpdater: lock status changed to unlocked
    INFO:          ClubUpdater: New lights, clubstatus off.
    DEBUG:         ClubUpdater: Power timer not active, using current power
state: off
    INFO:          ClubUpdater: Yellow on.
    DEBUG:         ClubUpdater: Changing output register to: 0x4
    INFO:          wiringPiI2CWriteReg8: Device handle 0x0, Register 0x2 set to:
0x4
    DEBUG:         ClubUpdater: Finished writing relay outputs with: 0x4
    INFO:          ClubUpdater: status switch status changed to on
    INFO:          ClubUpdater: Opening club.
    INFO:          ClubUpdater: Started power timer...
    DEBUG:         ClubUpdater: Sent MQTT message.
    INFO:          ClubUpdater: New lights, clubstatus on.
    DEBUG:         ClubUpdater: Power timer active, inverting power state from:
on
    INFO:          ClubUpdater: Green on.
    DEBUG:         ClubUpdater: Changing output register to: 0x2
    INFO:          wiringPiI2CWriteReg8: Device handle 0x0, Register 0x2 set to:
0x2
```

```
DEBUG:        ClubUpdater: Finished writing relay outputs with: 0x2
INFO:         ClubUpdater: status switch status changed to off
INFO:         ClubUpdater: Closing club.
INFO:         ClubUpdater: Started timer.
INFO:         ClubUpdater: Started power timer...
DEBUG:        ClubUpdater: Sent MQTT message.
INFO:         ClubUpdater: New lights, clubstatus off.
DEBUG:        ClubUpdater: Power timer active, inverting power state from:
off
INFO:         ClubUpdater: Yellow on.
DEBUG:        ClubUpdater: Changing output register to: 0x5
INFO:         wiringPiI2CWriteReg8: Device handle 0x0, Register 0x2 set to:
0x5
DEBUG:        ClubUpdater: Finished writing relay outputs with: 0x5
INFO:         ClubUpdater: setPowerState called.
DEBUG:        ClubUpdater: Writing relay with: 0x4
INFO:         wiringPiI2CWriteReg8: Device handle 0x0, Register 0x2 set to:
0x4
DEBUG:        ClubUpdater: Finished writing relay outputs with: 0x4
DEBUG:        ClubUpdater: Written relay outputs.
DEBUG:        ClubUpdater: Finished setPowerState.
INFO:         ClubUpdater: lock status changed to locked
INFO:         ClubUpdater: New lights, clubstatus off.
DEBUG:        ClubUpdater: Power timer not active, using current power
state: off
INFO:         ClubUpdater: Red on.
DEBUG:        ClubUpdater: Changing output register to: 0x8
INFO:         wiringPiI2CWriteReg8: Device handle 0x0, Register 0x2 set to:
0x8
DEBUG:        ClubUpdater: Finished writing relay outputs with: 0x8
```

Next, the timer starts triggering the callback function repeatedly, causing it to go through its different stages. This allows us to ascertain that the basic functioning of the code is correct.

At this point, we can start implementing more complex test cases, conceivably even implementing scriptable test cases using an embedded Lua, Python runtime or similar.

Mock versus hardware

An obvious question to ask when mocking away large sections of code and hardware peripherals is how realistic the resulting mock is. We obviously want to be able to cover as many real-life scenarios as possible with our integration test before we move to testing on the target system.

If we want to know which test cases we wish to cover in our mock, we have to look both at our project requirements (what it should be able to handle), and which situations and inputs can occur in a real-life scenario.

For this, we would analyze the underlying code to see what conditions can occur, and decide on which ones are relevant for us.

In the case of the WiringPi mocks we looked at earlier, a quick glance at the source code for the library's implementation makes it clear just how much we simplified our code compared to the version we would be using on our target system.

Looking at the basic WiringPi setup function, we see that it does the following:

- Determines the exact board model and SoC to get the GPIO layout
- Opens the Linux device for the memory-mapped GPIO pins
- Sets the memory offsets into the GPIO device and uses `mmap()` to map specific peripherals such as PWM, timer, and GPIO into memory

Instead of ignoring calls to `pinMode()`, the implementation does the following:

- Appropriately sets the hardware GPIO direction register in the SoC (for input/output mode)
- Starts PWM, soft PWM, or Tone mode on a pin (as requested); sub-functions set the appropriate registers

This continues with the I2C side, where the setup function implementation looks like this:

```
int wiringPiI2CSetup (const int devId) {
    int rev;
    const char *device;
    rev = piGpioLayout ();
    if (rev == 1) {
        device = "/dev/i2c-0";
    }
    else {
        device = "/dev/i2c-1";
    }
    return wiringPiI2CSetupInterface (device, devId);
}
```

Compared to our mock implementation, the main difference is in that an I2C peripheral is expected to be present on the in-memory filesystem of the OS, and the board revision determines which one we pick.

The last function that gets called tries to open the device, as in Linux and similar OSes every device is simply a file that we can open and get a file handle to, if successful. This file handle is the ID that gets returned when the function returns:

```
int wiringPiI2CSetupInterface (const char *device, int devId) {
    int fd;
    if ((fd = open (device, O_RDWR)) < 0) {
        return wiringPiFailure (WPI_ALMOST, "Unable to open I2C device:
%s\n",
strerror (errno));
    }
    if (ioctl (fd, I2C_SLAVE, devId) < 0) {
        return wiringPiFailure (WPI_ALMOST, "Unable to select I2C device:
%s\n",
strerror (errno));
    }
    return fd;
}
```

After opening the I2C device, the Linux system function, ioctl(), is used to send data to the I2C peripheral, in this case, the address of the I2C slave device that we wish to use. If successful, we get a non-negative response and return the integer that's our file handle.

Writing and reading the I2C bus is also handled using ioctl(), as we can see in the same source file:

```
static inline int i2c_smbus_access (int fd, char rw, uint8_t command, int
size, union i2c_smbus_data *data) {
    struct i2c_smbus_ioctl_data args;

    args.read_write = rw;
    args.command    = command;
    args.size       = size;
    args.data       = data;
    return ioctl(fd, I2C_SMBUS, &args);
}
```

This same inline function is called for every single I2C bus access. With the I2C device that we wish to use already selected, we can simply target the I2C peripheral and have it transmit the payload to the device.

Here, the `i2c_smbus_data` type is a simple union to support various sizes for the return value (when performing a read operation):

```
union i2c_smbus_data {
    uint8_t byte;
    uint16_t word;
    uint8_t block[I2C_SMBUS_BLOCK_MAX + 2];
};
```

Here, we mostly see the benefit of using an abstract API. Without it, we would have peppered our code with low-level calls that would have been much harder to mock away. What we also see is that there are a number of conditions that we should likely be testing as well, such as a missing I2C slave device, read and write errors on the I2C bus that may result in unexpected behavior, as well as unexpected input on GPIO pins, including for interrupt pins as was noted at the beginning of this chapter already.

Although obviously not all scenarios can be planned for, efforts should be made to document all realistic scenarios and incorporate them into the mocked-up implementation, so that they can be enabled at will during integration and regression testing and while debugging.

Testing with Valgrind

Valgrind is the most commonly used collection of open source tools for analyzing and profiling everything from the cache and heap behavior of an application to memory leaks and potential multithreading issues. It works in tandem with the underlying operating system as, depending on the tool used, it has to intercept everything from memory allocations to instructions related to multithreading and related. This is the reason why it is only fully supported under Linux on 64-bit x86_64 architectures.

Using Valgrind on other supported platforms (Linux on x86, PowerPC, ARM, S390, MIPS, and ARM, also Solaris and macOS) is definitely also an option, but the primary development target of the Valgrind project is x86_64/Linux, making it the best platform to do profiling and debugging on, even if other platforms will be targeted later on.

On the Valgrind website at `http://valgrind.org/info/platforms.html`, we can see a full overview of the currently supported platforms.

One very attractive property of Valgrind is that none of its tools require us to alter the source code or resulting binary in any fashion. This makes it very easy to integrate into an existing workflow, including automated testing and integration systems.

On Windows-based system, tools such as Dr. Memory (`http://drmemory.org/`) are available as well, which can handle at least the profiling of memory-related behavior. This particular tool also comes with Dr. Fuzz, a tool that can repeatedly call functions with varying inputs, potentially useful for integration testing.

By using an integration test such as what we looked at in the previous section, we're free to fully analyze the behavior of our code from the comfort of our PC. Since all of Valgrind's tools significantly slow down the execution of our code (10-100 times), being able to do most of the debugging and profiling on a fast system means that we can save a significant amount of time before embarking on testing on the target hardware.

Of the tools we'll likely use the most often, **Memcheck**, **Helgrind**, and **DRD** are useful for detecting memory allocation and multithreading issues. Once our code passes through these three tools, while using an extensive integration test that provides wide coverage of the code, we can move on to profiling and optimizing.

To profile our code, we then use **Callgrind** to see where our code spends the most of the time executing, followed by **Massif** to do profiling of heap allocations. With the information we can glean from this data, we can make changes to the code to streamline common allocation and de-allocation cases. It might also show us where it might make sense to use a cache to reuse resources instead of discarding them from memory.

Finally, we would run another cycle of MemCheck, Helgrind, and DRD to ensure that our changes didn't cause any regressions. Once we're satisfied, we move on to deploying the code on the target system and see how it performs there.

If the target system also runs Linux or other supported OSes, we can use Valgrind on there as well, to check that we didn't miss anything. Depending on the exact platform (OS and CPU architecture), we may run into limitations of the Valgrind port for that platform. These can include errors such as *unhandled instruction*, where the tool hasn't had a CPU instruction implemented and hence Valgrind cannot continue.

By extending the integration test to use the SBC instead of a local process, we can set up a continuous integration system whereby, in addition to the tests on a local process, we also run them on real hardware, taking into account the limitations of the real hardware platform relative to the x86_64-based Linux system used for most of the testing.

Multi-target build system

Cross-compilation and multi-target build systems are among the words that tend to frighten a lot of people, mostly because they evoke images of hugely complicated build scripts that require arcane incantations to perform the desired operation. In this chapter, we'll be looking at a simple Makefile-based build system, based on a build system that has seen use in commercial projects across a range of hardware targets.

The one thing that makes a build system pleasant to use is to be able to get everything set up for compilation with minimal fuss and have a central location from which we can control all relevant aspects of building the project, or parts of it, along with building and running tests.

For this reason, we have a single Makefile at the top of the project, which handles all of the basics, including the determining of which platform we run on. The only simplification we're making here is that we assume a Unix-like environment, with MSYS2 or Cygwin on Windows, and Linux, BSD, and OS X/macOS and others using their native shell environments. We could, however, also adapt it to allow for Microsoft Visual Studio, **Intel Compiler Collection** (**ICC**), and other compilers, so long as they provide the basic tools.

Key to the build system are simple Makefiles, in which we define the specific details of the target platform, for example, for a standard Linux system running on x86_x64 hardware:

```
TARGET_OS = linux
TARGET_ARCH = x86_64

export CC = gcc
export CXX = g++
export CPP = cpp
export AR = ar
export LD = g++
export STRIP = strip
export OBJCOPY = objcopy

PLATFORM_FLAGS = -D__PLATFORM_LINUX__ -D_LARGEFILE64_SOURCE -D __LINUX__
STD_FLAGS = $(PLATFORM_FLAGS) -Og -g3 -Wall -c -fmessage-length=0 -
ffunction-sections -fdata-sections -DPOCO_HAVE_GCC_ATOMICS -
DPOCO_UTIL_NO_XMLCONFIGURATION -DPOCO_HAVE_FD_EPOLL
STD_CFLAGS = $(STD_FLAGS)
STD_CXXFLAGS = -std=c++11 $(STD_FLAGS)
STD_LDFLAGS = -L $(TOP)/build/$(TARGET)/libboost/lib \
                    -L $(TOP)/build/$(TARGET)/poco/lib \
                    -Wl,--gc-sections
STD_INCLUDE = -I. -I $(TOP)/build/$(TARGET)/libboost/include \
                    -I $(TOP)/build/$(TARGET)/poco/include \
```

```
                    -I $(TOP)/extern/boost-1.58.0
STD_LIBDIRS = $(STD_LDFLAGS)
STD_LIBS = -ldl -lrt -lboost_system -lssl -lcrypto -lpthread
```

Here, we can set the names of the command-line tools that we'll be using for compiling, creating archives, stripping debug symbols from binaries, and so on. The build system will use the target OS and architecture to keep the created binaries separate so that we can use the same source tree to create binaries for all target platforms in one run.

We can see how we separate the flags that we'll be passing to the compiler and linker into different categories: platform-specific ones, common (standard) flags, and finally flags specific for the C and C++ compiler. The former is useful when integrating external dependencies that have been integrated into the source tree, yet are written in C. These dependencies we'll find in the extern folder, as we'll see in more detail in a moment.

This kind of file will be heavily customized to fit a specific project, adding the required includes, libraries, and compile flags. For this example file, we can see a project that uses the POCO and Boost libraries, along with OpenSSL, tweaking the POCO library for the target platform.

First, let's look at the top of the configuration file for macOS:

```
TARGET_OS = osx
TARGET_ARCH = x86_64

export CC = clang
export CXX = clang++
export CPP = cpp
export AR = ar
export LD = clang++
export STRIP = strip
export OBJCOPY = objcopy
```

Although the rest of the file is almost the same, here we can see a good example of generalizing what a tool is called. Although Clang supports the same flags as GCC, its tools are called differently. With this approach, we just write the different names once in this file and everything will just work.

This continues with the Linux on ARM target, which is set up as a cross-compilation target:

```
TARGET_OS = linux
TARGET_ARCH = armv7
TOOLCHAIN_NAME = arm-linux-gnueabihf

export CC = $(TOOLCHAIN_NAME)-gcc
export CXX = $(TOOLCHAIN_NAME)-g++
```

```
export AR = $(TOOLCHAIN_NAME)-ar
export LD = $(TOOLCHAIN_NAME)-g++
export STRIP = $(TOOLCHAIN_NAME)-strip
export OBJCOPY = $(TOOLCHAIN_NAME)-objcopy
```

Here, we see the reappearance of the cross-compilation toolchain for ARM Linux platforms, which we looked at earlier in this chapter. To save ourselves typing, we define the basic name once so that it is easy to redefine. This also shows how flexible Makefiles are. With some more creativity, we could create a set of templates that would generalize entire toolchains into a simple Makefile to be included by the main Makefile depending on hints in the platform's Makefile (or other configuration file), making this highly flexible.

Moving on, we'll look at the main Makefile as found in the root of the project:

```
ifndef TARGET
$(error TARGET parameter not provided.)
endif
```

Since we cannot guess what platform the user wants us to target, we require that the target is specified, with the platform name as the value, for example, `linux-x86_x64`:

```
export TOP := $(CURDIR)
export TARGET
```

Later on in the system, we'll need to know which folder we're in on the local filesystem so that we can specify absolute paths. We use the standard Make variable for this and export it as our own environment variable, along with the build target name:

```
UNAME := $(shell uname)
ifeq ($(UNAME), Linux)
export HOST = linux
else
export HOST = win32
export FILE_EXT = .exe
endif
```

Using the (command-line) `uname` command, we can check which OS we're running on, with each OS that supports the command in its shell returning its name, such as `Linux` for Linux and `Darwin` for macOS. On pure Windows (no MSYS2 or Cygwin), the command doesn't exist, which would get us the second part of this `if`/`else` statement.

This statement could be expanded to support more OSes, depending on what the build system requires. In this case, it is only used to determine whether executables we create should have a file extension:

```
ifeq ($(HOST), linux)
export MKDIR    = mkdir -p
export RM               = rm -rf
export CP               = cp -RL
else
export MKDIR    = mkdir -p
export RM               = rm -rf
export CP               = cp -RL
endif
```

In this if/else statement, we can set the appropriate command-line commands for common file operations. Since we're taking the easy way out, we're assuming the use of MSYS2 or similar Bash shell on Windows.

We could take the concept of generalizing further at this point as well, splitting off the OS file CLI tools as its own set of Makefiles, which we can then include as part of OS-specific settings:

```
include Makefile.$(TARGET)

export TARGET_OS
export TARGET_ARCH
export TOOLCHAIN_NAME
```

At this point, we use the target parameter provided to the Makefile to include the appropriate configuration file. After exporting some details from it, we now have a configured build system:

```
all: extern-$(TARGET) core

extern:
    $(MAKE) -C ./extern $(LIBRARY)

extern-$(TARGET):
    $(MAKE) -C ./extern all-$(TARGET)

core:
    $(MAKE) -C ./Core

clean: clean-core clean-extern

clean-extern:
    $(MAKE) -C ./extern clean-$(TARGET)
```

```
clean-core:
    $(MAKE) -C ./Core clean

.PHONY: all clean core extern clean-extern clean-core extern-$(TARGET)
```

From this single Makefile, we can choose to compile the entire project or just the dependencies or the core project. We can also compile a specific external dependency and nothing else.

Finally, we can clean the core project, the dependencies, or both.

This top Makefile is primarily for controlling the underlying Makefiles. The next two Makefiles are found in the `Core` and `extern` folders. Of these, the `Core` Makefile simply directly compiles the project's core:

```
include ../Makefile.$(TARGET)

OUTPUT := CoreProject

INCLUDE = $(STD_INCLUDE)
LIBDIRS = $(STD_LIBDIRS)

include ../version
VERSIONINFO = -D__VERSION="\"$(VERSION)\""
```

As the first step, we include the Makefile configuration for the target platform so that we have access to all of its definitions. These could also have been exported in the main Makefile, but this way we're free to customize the build system even more.

We specify the name of the output binary that we're building, before some small tasks, including opening the `version` file (with Makefile syntax) in the root of the project, which contains the version number of the source we're building from. This is prepared to be passed as a preprocessor definition into the compiler:

```
ifdef RELEASE
TIMESTAMP = $(shell date --date=@`git show -s --format=%ct
$(RELEASE)^{commit}` -u +%Y-%m-%dT%H:%M:%SZ)
else ifdef GITTIME
TIMESTAMP = $(shell date --date=@`git show -s --format=%ct` -u +%Y-%m-
%dT%H:%M:%SZ)
TS_SAFE = _$(shell date --date=@`git show -s --format=%ct` -u +%Y-%m-
%dT%H%M%SZ)
else
TIMESTAMP = $(shell date -u +%Y-%m-%dT%H:%M:%SZ)
TS_SAFE = _$(shell date -u +%Y-%m-%dT%H%M%SZ)
endif
```

This is another section where we rely on having a Bash shell or something compatible around, as we use the date command in order to create a timestamp for the build. The format depends on what parameter was passed to the main Makefile. If we're building a release, we take the timestamp from the Git repository, with the Git commit tag name used to retrieve the commit timestamp for that tag before formatting it.

If `GITTIME` is passed as parameter, the timestamp of the most recent Git commit is used. Otherwise, the current time and date is used (UTC).

This bit of code is intended to solve one of the issues that comes with having lots of test and integration builds: keeping track of which ones were built when and with which revision of the source code. It could be adapted to other file revision systems, as long as it supports similar functionality with the retrieving of specific timestamps.

Of note is the second timestamp we're creating. This is a slightly different formatted version of the timestamp that is affixed to the produced binary, except when we're building in release mode:

```
CFLAGS = $(STD_CFLAGS) $(INCLUDE) $(VERSIONINFO) -
D__TIMESTAMP="\"$(TIMESTAMP)\""
CXXFLAGS = $(STD_CXXFLAGS) $(INCLUDE) $(VERSIONINFO) -
D__TIMESTAMP="\"$(TIMESTAMP)\""

OBJROOT := $(TOP)/build/$(TARGET)/obj
CPP_SOURCES := $(wildcard *.cpp)
CPP_OBJECTS := $(addprefix $(OBJROOT)/,$(CPP_SOURCES:.cpp=.o))
OBJECTS := $(CPP_OBJECTS)
```

Here, we set the flags we wish to pass to the compiler, including the version and timestamp, both being passed as preprocessor definitions.

Finally, the sources in the current project folder are collected and the output folder for the object files is set. As we can see here, we'll be writing the object files to a folder underneath the project root, with further separation by the compile target:

```
.PHONY: all clean

all: makedirs $(CPP_OBJECTS) $(C_OBJECTS)
$(TOP)/build/bin/$(TARGET)/$(OUTPUT)_$(VERSION)_$(TARGET)$(TS_SAFE)
makedirs:
    $(MKDIR) $(TOP)/build/bin/$(TARGET)
    $(MKDIR) $(OBJROOT)
$(OBJROOT)/%.o: %.cpp
    $(CXX) -o $@ $< $(CXXFLAGS)
```

This part is fairly generic for a Makefile. We have the `all` target, along with one to make the folders on the filesystem, if they don't exist yet. Finally, we take in the array of source files in the next target, compiling them as configured and outputting the object file in the appropriate folder:

```
$(TOP)/build/bin/$(TARGET)/$(OUTPUT)_$(VERSION)_$(TARGET)$(TS_SAFE):
$(OBJECTS)
    $(LD) -o $@ $(OBJECTS) $(LIBDIRS) $(LIBS)
    $(CP) $@ $@.debug
ifeq ($(TARGET_OS), osx)
    $(STRIP) -S $@
else
    $(STRIP) -S --strip-unneeded $@
endif
```

After we have created all of the object files from our source files, we want to link them together, which happens in this step. We can also see where the binary will end up: in a `bin` sub-folder of the project's build folder.

The linker is called, and we create a copy of the resulting binary, which we post-fix with `.debug` to indicate that it is the version with all of the debug information. The original binary is then stripped of its debug symbols and other unneeded information, leaving us with a small binary to copy to the remote test system and a larger version with all of the debug information for when we need to analyze core dumps or do remote debugging.

What we also see here is a small hack that got added due to an unsupported command-line flag by Clang's linker, requiring the implementation of a special case. While working on cross-platform compiling and similar tasks, one is likely to run into many of such small details, all of which complicate the writing of a universal build system that simply works:

```
clean:
    $(RM) $(CPP_OBJECTS)
    $(RM) $(C_OBJECTS)
```

As a final step, we allow for the generated object files to be deleted.

The second sub-Makefile in `extern` is also of note, as it controls all of the underlying dependencies:

```
ifndef TARGET
$(error TARGET parameter not provided.)
endif

all: libboost poco

all-linux-%:
```

```
    $(MAKE) libboost poco

all-qnx-%:
    $(MAKE) libboost poco
all-osx-%:
    $(MAKE) libboost poco
all-windows:
    $(MAKE) libboost poco
```

An interesting feature here is the dependency selector based on the target platform. If we have dependencies that shouldn't be compiled for a specific platform, we can skip them here. This feature also allows us to directly instruct this Makefile to compile all dependencies for a specific platform. Here, we allow for the targeting of QNX, Linux, OS X/macOS, and Windows, while ignoring the architecture:

```
libboost:
    cd boost-1.58.0 && $(MAKE)
poco:
    cd poco-1.7.4 && $(MAKE)
```

The actual targets merely call another Makefile at the top of the dependency project, which in turn compiles that dependency and adds it to the build folder, where it can be used by the Core's Makefile.

Of course, we can also directly compile the project from this Makefile using an existing build system, such as here for OpenSSL:

```
openssl:
    $(MKDIR) $(TOP)/build/$(TARGET)/openssl
    $(MKDIR) $(TOP)/build/$(TARGET)/openssl/include
    $(MKDIR) $(TOP)/build/$(TARGET)/openssl/lib
    cd openssl-1.0.2 && ./Configure --
opensssldir="$(TOP)/build/$(TARGET)/openssl" shared
os/compiler:$(TOOLCHAIN_NAME):$(OPENSSL_PARAMS) && \
       $(MAKE) build_libs
    $(CP) openssl-1.0.2/include $(TOP)/build/$(TARGET)/openssl
    $(CP) openssl-1.0.2/libcrypto.a $(TOP)/build/$(TARGET)/openssl/lib/.
    $(CP) openssl-1.0.2/libssl.a $(TOP)/build/$(TARGET)/openssl/lib/.
```

This code works through all of the usual steps of building OpenSSL by hand, before copying the resulting binaries to their target folders.

One issue with cross-platform build systems one may notice is that a common GNU tool such as Autoconf is extremely slow on OSes such as Windows, due to it launching many processes as it runs hundreds of tests. Even on Linux, this process can take a long time, which is very annoying and time consuming when running through the same build process multiple times a day.

The ideal case is having a simple Makefile in which everything is predefined and in a known state so that no library discovery and such are needed. This was one of the motivations behind adding the POCO library source code to one project and having a simple Makefile compile it:

```
include ../../Makefile.$(TARGET)

all: poco-foundation poco-json poco-net poco-util

poco-foundation:
    cd Foundation && $(MAKE)
poco-json:
    cd JSON && $(MAKE)
poco-net:
    cd Net && $(MAKE)
poco-util:
    cd Util && $(MAKE)
clean:
    cd Foundation && $(MAKE) clean
    cd JSON && $(MAKE) clean
    cd Net && $(MAKE) clean
    cd Util && $(MAKE) clean
```

This Makefile then calls the individual Makefile for each module, as in this example:

```
include ../../../Makefile.$(TARGET)

OUTPUT = libPocoNet.a
INCLUDE = $(STD_INCLUDE) -Iinclude
CFLAGS = $(STD_CFLAGS) $(INCLUDE)
OBJROOT = $(TOP)/extern/poco-1.7.4/Net/$(TARGET)
INCLOUT = $(TOP)/build/$(TARGET)/poco
SOURCES := $(wildcard src/*.cpp)
HEADERS := $(addprefix $(INCLOUT)/,$(wildcard include/Poco/Net/*.h))

OBJECTS := $(addprefix $(OBJROOT)/,$(notdir $(SOURCES:.cpp=.o)))

all: makedir $(OBJECTS) $(TOP)/build/$(TARGET)/poco/lib/$(OUTPUT)
$(HEADERS)

$(OBJROOT)/%.o: src/%.cpp
```

```
        $(CC) -c -o $@ $< $(CFLAGS)
makedir:
    $(MKDIR) $(TARGET)
    $(MKDIR) $(TOP)/build/$(TARGET)/poco
    $(MKDIR) $(TOP)/build/$(TARGET)/poco/lib
    $(MKDIR) $(TOP)/build/$(TARGET)/poco/include
    $(MKDIR) $(TOP)/build/$(TARGET)/poco/include/Poco
    $(MKDIR) $(TOP)/build/$(TARGET)/poco/include/Poco/Net
$(INCLOUT)/%.h: %.h
    $(CP) $< $(INCLOUT)/$<

$(TOP)/build/$(TARGET)/poco/lib/$(OUTPUT): $(OBJECTS)
    -rm -f $@
    $(AR) rcs $@ $^
clean:
    $(RM) $(OBJECTS)
```

This Makefile compiles the entire Net module of the library. It's similar in structure to the one for compiling the project core source files. In addition to compiling the object files, it puts them into an archive so that we can link against it later, and copies this archive as well as the header files to their place in the build folder.

The main reason for compiling the library for the project was to allow for specific optimizations and tweaks that wouldn't be available with a precompiled library. By having everything but the basics stripped out of the library's original build system, trying out different settings was made very easy and even worked on Windows.

Remote testing on real hardware

After we have done all of the local testing of our code and are reasonably certain that it should work on the real hardware, we can use the cross-compile build system to create a binary that we can then run on the target system.

At this point, we can simply copy the resulting binary and associated files to the target system and see whether it works. The more scientific way to do this is to use GDB. With the GDB server service installed on the target Linux system, we can connect to it with GDB from our PC, either via the network or a serial connection.

For SBCs running a Debian-based Linux installation, the GDB server can be easily installed:

```
sudo apt install gdbserver
```

Although it is called `gdbserver`, its essential function is that of a remote stub implementation for the debugger, which runs on the host system. This makes `gdbserver` very lightweight and simple to implement for new targets.

After this, we want to make sure that `gdbserver` is running by logging in to the system and starting it in one of a variety of ways. We can do so for TPC connections over the network like this:

```
gdbserver host:2345 <program> <parameters>
```

Or we can attach it to a running process:

```
gdbserver host:2345 --attach <PID>
```

 The `host` part of the first argument refers to the name (or IP address) of the host system that will be connecting. This parameter is currently ignored, meaning that it can also be left empty. The port section has to be a port that is not currently in use on the target system.

Or we can use some kind of serial connection:

```
gdbserver /dev/tty0 <program> <parameters>
gdbserver --attach /dev/tty0 <PID>
```

The moment we launch `gdbserver`, it pauses the execution of the target application if it was already running, allowing us to connect with the debugger from the host system. While on the target system, we can run a binary that has been stripped of its debug symbols; these are required to be present in the binary that we use on the host side:

```
$ gdb-multiarch <program>
(gdb) target remote <IP>:<port>
Remote debugging using <IP>:<port>
```

At this point, debug symbols would be loaded from the binary, along with those from any dependencies (if available). Connecting over a serial connection would look similar, just with the address and port replaced with the serial interface path or name. The `baud` rate of the serial connection (if not the default 9,600 baud) is specified as a parameter to GDB when we're starting:

```
$ gdb-multiarch -baud <baud rate> <program>
```

Once we have told GDB the details of the remote target, we should see the usual GDB command-line interface appear, allowing us to step through, analyze, and debug the program as if it was running locally on our system.

As mentioned earlier in this chapter, we're using `gdb-multiarch` as this version of the GDB debugger supports different architectures, which is useful since we'll likely be running the debugger on an x86_64 system, whereas the SBC is very likely ARM-based, but could also be MIPS or x86 (i686).

In addition to running the application directly with `gdbserver`, we can also start `gdbserver` to just wait for a debugger to connect:

```
gdbserver --multi <host>:<port>
```

Or we can do this:

```
gdbserver --multi <serial port>
```

We would then connect to this remote target like this:

```
$ gdb-multiarch <program>
(gdb) target extended-remote <remote IP>:<port>
(gdb) set remote exec-file <remote file path>
(gdb) run
```

At this point, we should find ourselves at the GDB command-line interface again, with the program binary loaded on both target and host.

A big advantage of this method is that `gdbserver` does not exit when the application that's being debugged exits. In addition, this mode allows us to debug different applications simultaneously on the same target, assuming that the target supports this.

Summary

In this chapter, we looked at how to develop and test embedded, OS-based applications. We learned how to install and use a cross-compilation toolchain, how to do remote debugging using GDB, and how to write a build system that allows us to compile for a wide variety of target systems with minimal effort required to add a new target.

At this point, you are expected to be able to develop and debug an embedded application for a Linux-based SBC or similar, while being able to work in an efficient way.

In the next chapter, we'll be looking at how to develop for and test applications for more constrained, MCU-based platforms.

7
Testing Resource-Restricted Platforms

Developing for MCUs and similar resource-restricted platforms is pretty much exclusively done on regular PCs, except for testing and debugging. The question is when one should be testing on the physical device and when one should be looking at alternative means of testing and debugging code in order to speed up development and debugging efforts.

In this chapter we will cover the following topics:

- Understanding the resource needs of specific code
- Effectively using Linux-based tools to test cross-platform code
- Using remote debugging
- Using cross-compilers
- Creating a platform-independent build system

Reducing wear

Often, during development, there comes that point where one is fixing an issue in a system and have to go through the same tweak-compile-deploy-test cycle, over and over. Here are the main problems that are introduced with this approach:

- **It's not fun**: It's frustrating to have to constantly wait for results without a clear idea of whether it will actually be fixed this time.
- **It's not productive**: You spend a lot of time waiting for results you wouldn't need if you could just analyze the problem better.

- **It wears down the hardware**: After removing and reinserting the same connectors dozens of times, writing and overwriting the same sections of the ROM chip countless times, and power cycling the system hundreds of times, the hardware's lifespan is reduced significantly, along with one's own patience, and new errors are introduced.
- **Fiddling with test hardware isn't fun**: The best-case scenario for any embedded setup is to be able to take the development board, plug in all the peripherals and wiring, flash the ROM with the application, and power it up to see it work. Any deviation from this scenario is frustrating and time-consuming.

Avoiding such cycles during development is therefore essential. The question is how we can most effectively get to a point where we can produce code for something such as an 8-bit MCU or a larger 32-bit ARM MCU without ever touching the hardware until the final stages of testing.

Planning out a design

In `Chapter 4`, *Resource-Restricted Embedded Systems*, we looked at how to pick an appropriate microcontroller for an embedded platform. While designing the firmware for the MCU, it's essential that we consider not only the resource requirements of specific codes, but also the ease of debugging.

An important advantage of using C++ is the abstractions it offers, including the ability to subdivide the code into logical classes, namespaces, and other abstractions that allow us to easily reuse, test, and debug the code. This is a crucial aspect in any design, and an aspect that needs to be implemented fully before one can proceed with actually implementing the design.

Depending on the design, it can be either very easy or frustratingly hard to debug any issue, or anything in between. If there's a clean separation between all the functionality, without leaky APIs or similar problems that could leak internal, private data, creating different versions of fundamental classes for things such as integration and unit testing will be easy.

Simply using classes and the like is no guarantee for a design that is modular. Even with such a design one can still end up passing internal class data between classes, thus breaking modularity. When this happens, i will complicate the overall design as the level of dependencies increases with changes to data structures and data formats potentially causing issues elsewhere in the application and will require creative hacks while writing tests and reimplementing APIs as part of larger integration tests.

In Chapter 4, *Resource-Restricted Embedded Systems*, we looked at how to pick the proper MCU. The points of RAM, ROM, and floating-point usage are obviously down to the design we picked to fit the project. As we covered in Chapter 2, *C++ as an Embedded Language*, it's important to understand what the code we write is compiled into. This understanding allows one to get an intuitive feeling for what the resource cost of a line of code is going to be like without having to step through the generated machine code and create an exact clock cycle count from there.

It should be obvious at this point that before one can pick an MCU, one must have a pretty good idea of the overall design and the resource requirements, so starting off with a solid design is essential.

Platform-independent build systems

Ideally, the project and build system we choose could be used to build the target platform on any desktop platform. Usually, the main consideration here is the availability of the same toolchain and programmer for each development platform. Fortunately, for AVR- and ARM-based MCU platforms, the same GCC-based toolchain is available, so that we do not have to take different toolchains with different naming conventions, flags and settings into account.

The remaining challenge is simply to invoke the toolchain, and subsequently the programmer utility, in a way that doesn't require any knowledge of the underlying OS.

In Chapter 6, *Testing OS-Based Applications*, we looked at a multitarget build system, which could produce binaries for a wide variety of targets with minimal effort for each new target. For an MCU target, there would only be the following two targets:

- The physical MCU target
- The local OS target

Here, the first target is obviously fixed, as we picked out the MCU that we wanted to target. Barring any unpleasant surprises, we will be using this one target for the entire development process. In addition, we will want to preform local testing on our development PC. This is the second target.

Here it would be great if there is a version of the same or similar C++ toolchain on each mainstream desktop OS. Fortunately, we find that GCC is available on just about any platform imaginable, with the Clang C++ frontend of the LLVM toolchain using regular GCC-style flags, providing us with broad compatibility.

Instead of requiring the complexity of a multitarget build system, as we saw in `Chapter 6`, *Testing OS-Based Applications*, we can simplify it so it that just uses GCC, which would allow us to use that toolchain on Linux- and BSD-based OSes, along with Windows (MinGW via MSYS2 or equivalent) and macOS (after installing GCC).

For full compatibility on macOS, the use of GCC is recommended, due to small issues in the Clang implementation. One of these current issues is the `__forceinline` macro attribute being broken, for example, which would break a lot of code that assumes the GCC compiler.

Using cross-compilers

Every compiler toolchain consists of a side (frontend) that takes in the source code and a side that outputs the binary format for the target platform (backend). There's no reason why the backend couldn't work on any other platform than the one it's targeting. In the end, one merely transforms text files into sequences of bytes.

Cross-compiling in this fashion is an essential feature with MCU-oriented development, as compiling directly on those MCUs would be highly inefficient. There is, however, nothing magical about this process. In the case of GCC-based and GCC-compatible toolchains, one would still be interacting with the same interfaces on the toolchain, just with the tools usually prefixed with the target platform name to distinguish them from other toolchains for different targets. Essentially, instead of `g++` one would use `arm-none-eabi-g++`

The resulting binaries would be in the format appropriate for that target platform.

Local and on-chip debugging

In `Chapter 6`, *Testing OS-Based Applications*, we looked at debugging applications using Valgrind and similar tools, as well as GDB and kin. With the OS-based integration tests for MCU-based projects, such as those demonstrated in the *Example – ESP8266 integration test* section, we can use the exact same techniques, profiling and debugging the code without concerning ourselves just yet with the fact that the same code will be running on a much slower and more limited platform during final integration testing on real hardware.

The real challenge comes during that final integration stage, when the firmware—which we have been debugging on our fast desktop system using Valgrind and other highly capable tools—is now running on a paltry 16 MHz ATmega MCU without the ability to quickly launch the code with a Valgrind tool or within a GDB session.

As one will inevitably encounter bugs and issues during this stage, we need to be prepared to deal with this situation. Often, one has to resort to **on-chip debugging** (**OCD**), which can be performed over whichever debugging interface the MCU provides. This can be JTAG, DebugWire or SWD, PDI, or some other type. In Chapter 4, *Resource-Restricted Embedded Systems*, we looked at some of those interfaces in the context of programming these MCUs.

Embedded IDEs will provide the ability to perform OCD right out of the box, connecting with the target hardware, allowing one to set breakpoints, much like one would be used to setting for a local process. Of course, it's also possible to use GDB from the command line to do the same thing, using a program such as OpenOCD (http://openocd.org/), which provides a gdbserver interface for GDB while interfacing with a wide variety of debug interfaces.

Example – ESP8266 integration test

In this example project, we will look at creating an implementation of the Arduino-like APIs of the Sming framework, which we first looked at it in Chapter 5, *Example - Soil Humidity Monitor with Wi-Fi*. The goal of this is to provide a native framework implementation for desktop **operating systems** (**OSes**), allowing the firmware to be compiled to an executable and run locally.

In addition, we want to have simulated sensors and actuators that the firmware can connect to in order to read out environmental data and send data to actuators as part of the BMaC project, which we had a glimpse of in Chapter 5, *Example - Soil Humidity Monitor with WiFi*, and which we will look at in more detail in Chapter 9, *Example - Building Monitoring and Control*. For this, we also need to have a central service that keeps track of such information. This way, we can also have multiple firmware processes running, to simulate entire rooms full of devices.

The reason for this scope of the simulation is due to not having the physical hardware. Without a physical MCU system, we don't have physical sensors, and these sensors would not exist in a physical room. Ergo we have to generate plausible input for the sensors and simulate the effect of any actuators. This does however come with a lot of advantages.

Having this scaling ability is useful in that it allows us to validate the firmware not only as a standalone system, but also as part of the system it would be installed in. In the case of BMaC, this would mean a single node installed in a room of a building, with dozens to hundreds of further nodes installed in the same and other rooms across the building's floors, along with accompanying backend services running on the same network.

With this kind of large-scale simulation ability, one can test not only the basic correctness of the firmware by itself, but also that of the system as a whole, with the different firmware types or even versions running in tandem with the various sensors and actuators (for air-conditioning units, fans, coffee machines, switches, and so on). In addition to this, the backend services would be directing the nodes according to the data being passed to them from the same nodes.

Within the simulated building, one could then configure specific rooms to have particular environmental conditions, run through a working day with people entering, working, and leaving, to determine the effect of different levels of building occupation, outside conditions, and so on. You could also do this with the firmware and backend services that would be used for the final production system. While testing a system this way won't fully eliminate any potential problems, it should at least validate that the software side of the system is functionally correct.

 As embedded systems are by definition part of a larger (hardware-based) system, a full integration test will involve the actual hardware or its equivalent. One could therefore consider this example the software integration test, prior to deploying the firmware to the target hardware in a physical building.

Both the simulation server and the individual firmware processes have their own main function and run independently from each other. This allows us to inspect the functioning of the firmware with as little interference as possible and promotes a clean design. To allow efficient communication between these processes, we use a **remote procedure call** (**RPC**) library, which essentially creates a connection between the firmware and the I2C, SPI, and UART-based devices in the simulated room. The RPC library used with this example is NymphRPC, an RPC library developed by the author. The source for the current version has been included with the source code for this chapter. The current version of the NymphRPC library can be found at its GitHub repository at `https://github.com/MayaPosch/NymphRPC`.

The server

We will first look at the server for this integration test. Its role is to run the RPC server and to maintain the state of each of the sensor and actuator devices, as well as the rooms.

The main file, `simulation.cpp`, sets up the RPC configuration as well as the main loop, as shown in the following code:

```
#include "config.h"
#include "building.h"
```

```
#include "nodes.h"
#include <nymph/nymph.h>
#include <thread>
#include <condition_variable>
#include <mutex>
std::condition_variable gCon;
std::mutex gMutex;
bool gPredicate = false;
void signal_handler(int signal) {
    gPredicate = true;
    gCon.notify_one();
}
void logFunction(int level, string logStr) {
    std::cout << level << " - " << logStr << endl;
}
```

The includes at the top shows us the basic structure and dependencies. We have a custom configuration class, a class defining the building, a static class for the nodes, and finally the multithreading headers (available since C++11) and the NymphRPC RPC header to gain access to its functionality.

A signal handler function is defined to be used with the waiting condition later on, allowing the server to be terminated with a simple control signal. Finally, a logging function is defined for use with the NymphRPC server.

Next, we define the callback functions for the RPC server, as follows:

```
NymphMessage* getNewMac(int session, NymphMessage* msg, void* data) {
    NymphMessage* returnMsg = msg->getReplyMessage();

    std::string mac = Nodes::getMAC();
    Nodes::registerSession(mac, session);

    returnMsg->setResultValue(new NymphString(mac));
    return returnMsg;
}
```

This is the initial function that the clients will call on the server. It will check the global, static `Nodes` class for an available MAC address. This address uniquely identifies a new node instance, the way a device on the network would also be identified by its unique Ethernet MAC address. This is an internal function that will not require modification of the firmware, but shifts the ability to assign MACs to the server, instead of having them hardcoded somewhere. When a new MAC has been assigned, it gets associated with the NymphRPC session ID so that we can later use the MAC to find the appropriate session ID and, with it, the client to call for events generated by simulated devices.

Here, we also see the basic signature of a NymphRPC callback function as used on a server instance. It obviously returns the return message, and it receives as its parameters the session ID associated with the connected client, the message received from this client, and some user-defined data, as shown in the following code:

```
NymphMessage* writeUart(int session, NymphMessage* msg, void* data) {
    NymphMessage* returnMsg = msg->getReplyMessage();

    std::string mac = ((NymphString*) msg->parameters()[0])->getValue();
    std::string bytes = ((NymphString*) msg->parameters()[1])->getValue();
    returnMsg->setResultValue(new NymphBoolean(Nodes::writeUart(mac,
bytes)));
    return returnMsg;
}
```

This callback implements a way to write to the UART interface of a simulated node within the simulation, addressing whichever simulated device is hooked up to it.

To find the node, we use the MAC address and send it, along with the bytes, to be written to the appropriate `Nodes` class function, as shown in the following code:

```
NymphMessage* writeSPI(int session, NymphMessage* msg, void* data) {
    NymphMessage* returnMsg = msg->getReplyMessage();

    std::string mac = ((NymphString*) msg->parameters()[0])->getValue();
    std::string bytes = ((NymphString*) msg->parameters()[1])->getValue();
    returnMsg->setResultValue(new NymphBoolean(Nodes::writeSPI(mac,
bytes)));
    return returnMsg;
}
NymphMessage* readSPI(int session, NymphMessage* msg, void* data) {
    NymphMessage* returnMsg = msg->getReplyMessage();

    std::string mac = ((NymphString*) msg->parameters()[0])->getValue();
    returnMsg->setResultValue(new NymphString(Nodes::readSPI(mac)));
    return returnMsg;
}
```

For the SPI bus, a similar system is used for writing and reading. The MAC identifies the node and either a string is sent to the bus or is received from it. One limitation here is that we assume the presence of only a single SPI device, since there is no way to select a different SPI **chip-select (CS)** line. A separate CS parameter would have to be passed here to enable more than one SPI device. Let's look at the following code:

```
NymphMessage* writeI2C(int session, NymphMessage* msg, void* data) {
    NymphMessage* returnMsg = msg->getReplyMessage();
```

```
    std::string mac = ((NymphString*) msg->parameters()[0])->getValue();
    int i2cAddress = ((NymphSint32*) msg->parameters()[1])->getValue();
    std::string bytes = ((NymphString*) msg->parameters()[2])->getValue();
    returnMsg->setResultValue(new NymphBoolean(Nodes::writeI2C(mac,
i2cAddress, bytes)));
    return returnMsg;
}


NymphMessage* readI2C(int session, NymphMessage* msg, void* data) {
    NymphMessage* returnMsg = msg->getReplyMessage();

    std::string mac = ((NymphString*) msg->parameters()[0])->getValue();
    int i2cAddress = ((NymphSint32*) msg->parameters()[1])->getValue();
    int length = ((NymphSint32*) msg->parameters()[2])->getValue();
    returnMsg->setResultValue(new NymphString(Nodes::readI2C(mac,
i2cAddress, length)));
    return returnMsg;
}
```

For the I2C bus version, we pass the I2C slave device address to allow us to use more than a single I2C device.

Finally, the main function registers the RPC methods, starts the simulation, and then enters a waiting condition, as shown in the following code:

```
int main() {
    Config config;
    config.load("config.cfg");
```

We first get the configuration data for this simulation using the following code. This is all defined in a separate file, that we will load using the special `Config` class, which we will take a more detailed look at in a moment when we look at the configuration parser.

```
    vector<NymphTypes> parameters;
    NymphMethod getNewMacFunction("getNewMac", parameters, NYMPH_STRING);
    getNewMacFunction.setCallback(getNewMac);
    NymphRemoteClient::registerMethod("getNewMac", getNewMacFunction);

    parameters.push_back(NYMPH_STRING);
    NymphMethod serialRxCallback("serialRxCallback", parameters,
NYMPH_NULL);
    serialRxCallback.enableCallback();
    NymphRemoteClient::registerCallback("serialRxCallback",
serialRxCallback);

    // string readI2C(string MAC, int i2cAddress, int length)
    parameters.push_back(NYMPH_SINT32);
```

```
parameters.push_back(NYMPH_SINT32);
NymphMethod readI2CFunction("readI2C", parameters, NYMPH_STRING);
readI2CFunction.setCallback(readI2C);
NymphRemoteClient::registerMethod("readI2C", readI2CFunction);

// bool writeUart(string MAC, string bytes)
parameters.clear();
parameters.push_back(NYMPH_STRING);
parameters.push_back(NYMPH_STRING);
NymphMethod writeUartFunction("writeUart", parameters, NYMPH_BOOL);
writeUartFunction.setCallback(writeUart);
NymphRemoteClient::registerMethod("writeUart", writeUartFunction);

// bool writeSPI(string MAC, string bytes)
NymphMethod writeSPIFunction("writeSPI", parameters, NYMPH_BOOL);
writeSPIFunction.setCallback(writeSPI);
NymphRemoteClient::registerMethod("writeSPI", writeSPIFunction);

// bool writeI2C(string MAC, int i2cAddress, string bytes)
parameters.clear();
parameters.push_back(NYMPH_STRING);
parameters.push_back(NYMPH_SINT32);
parameters.push_back(NYMPH_SINT32);
NymphMethod writeI2CFunction("writeI2C", parameters, NYMPH_BOOL);
writeI2CFunction.setCallback(writeI2C);
NymphRemoteClient::registerMethod("writeI2C", writeI2CFunction);
```

With this code, we register the further methods we wish to provide to the client node processes, allowing these to call the functions we looked at earlier in this source file. In order to register a server-side function with NymphRPC, we have to define the parameter types (in order) and use these to define a new `NymphMethod` instance, which we provide with this parameter type list, the function name, and the return type.

These method instances are then registered with `NymphRemoteClient`, which is the top-level class for the server-side NymphRPC, as shown in the following code:

```
signal(SIGINT, signal_handler);

NymphRemoteClient::start(4004);

Building building(config);

std::unique_lock<std::mutex> lock(gMutex);
while (!gPredicate) {
      gCon.wait(lock);
}
```

```
NymphRemoteClient::shutdown();

Thread::sleep(2000);

return 0;
}
```

Finally, we install the signal handler for SIGINT (*Ctrl + c*) signals. The NymphRPC server is started on port 4004, all interfaces. Next, a `Building` instance is created, providing it with the instance of the configuration we loaded earlier with the configuration parser class.

We then start a loop that checks whether the value of the `gPredicate` global variable has changed to `true`, which will be the case if the signal handler has been triggered, and this Boolean variable has been set to `true`. A condition variable is used to allow us to block the main thread execution as much as possible by having the signal handler notify this condition variable.

By having the condition variable's wait condition inside a loop, we ensure that even if the condition variable's wait condition suffers a spurious wake up, it'll simply go back to waiting to be notified.

Lastly, if the server is requested to terminate, we shut down the NymphRPC server, before giving all active threads an additional two seconds to cleanly terminate. After this, the server shuts down.

Next, let's look at the `config.cfg` file that we loaded for this simulation, as shown in the following code:

```
[Building]
floors=2


[Floor_1]
rooms=1,2

[Floor_2]
rooms=2,3


[Room_1]
; Define the room configuration.
; Sensors and actuators use the format:
; <device_id>:<node_id>
nodes=1
devices=1:1
```

```
[Room_2]
nodes=2

[Room_3]
nodes=3

[Room_4]
nodes=4


[Node_1]
mac=600912760001
sensors=1

[Node_2]
mac=600912760002
sensors=1

[Node_3]
mac=600912760003
sensors=1

[Node_4]
mac=600912760004
sensors=1


[Device_1]
type=i2c
address=0x20
device=bme280

[Device_2]
type=spi
cs_gpio=1

[Device_3]
type=uart
uart=0
baud=9600
device=mh-z19

[Device_4]
type=uart
uart=0
baud=9600
device=jura
```

As we can see, this configuration file uses the standard INI configuration file format. It defines a building with two floors, each with two rooms. Each room has a single node and each node has a BME280 sensor attached to it on the I2C bus.

More devices are defined, but are left unused here.

Let's look at the configuration parser shown in the following code, which parses the preceding format, declared in **config.h**:

```cpp
#include <string>
#include <memory>
#include <sstream>
#include <iostream>
#include <type_traits>

#include <Poco/Util/IniFileConfiguration.h>
#include <Poco/AutoPtr.h>

using Poco::AutoPtr;
using namespace Poco::Util;

class Config {
    AutoPtr<IniFileConfiguration> parser;
public:
    Config();
    bool load(std::string filename);
    template<typename T>
    auto getValue(std::string key, T defaultValue) -> T {
            std::string value;
            try {
                    value = parser->getRawString(key);
            }
            catch (Poco::NotFoundException &e) {
                    return defaultValue;
            }
            // Convert the value to our output type, if possible.
            std::stringstream ss;
            if (value[0] == '0' && value[1] == 'x') {
                    value.erase(0, 2);
                    ss << std::hex << value; // Read as hexadecimal.
            }
            else {
                    ss.str(value);
            }
            T retVal;
            if constexpr (std::is_same<T, std::string>::value) { retVal =
ss.str(); }
            else { ss >> retVal; }
```

```
                  return retVal;
        }
};
```

Here, we see an interesting use of templates, as well as one of their limitations. The type passed to the template is used both for the default parameter and the return type, allowing the template to cast the raw string obtained from the configuration file to the desired type, while also avoiding the issue of incomplete templates by only using the type in the return type of the function.

Due to the limitation of C++, where every function with the same name must have a different set of parameters even if their return value differs, we must use the default value parameter here to circumvent that issue. As most of the time we want to provide a default value for the keys we are trying to read, this isn't much of an issue here.

Finally, we do a bit of type comparison with `std::is_same` to ensure that if the target return type is a string, we copy the string straight out of `stringstream` instead of trying to convert it using formatted output. As we read the values from the INI file using the POCO INI file reader as raw strings, there's no need to do any kind of conversion on this.

Its implementation in `config.cpp` is pretty small, as a result of templates having to be defined in the header file. You can see this in the following code:

```
#include "config.h"

Config::Config() {
    parser = new IniFileConfiguration();
}

bool Config::load(std::string filename) {
    try {
            parser->load(filename);
    }
    catch (...) {
            // An exception has occurred. Return false.
            return false;
    }
    return true;
}
```

We just implement the method here, which actually loads the configuration file from the filename string. In this implementation, we create an instance of the POCO `IniFileConfiguration` class on the assumption that we are trying to parse an INI file. If loading the configuration file fails for whatever reason, we return an error.

In a more fleshed-out version of this parser, we would maybe support different configuration types or even sources, with advanced error handling. For our purposes, the humble INI format more than suffices.

Moving on, the following code shows the `Building` class:

```
#include <vector>
#include <string>

#include "floor.h"


class Building {
    std::vector<Floor> floors;

public:
    Building(Config &cfg);
};
```

Because we haven't added any advanced features to the simulation server, there isn't much to see here yet, nor in its implementation, as shown in the following code:

```
#include "building.h"
#include "floor.h"
Building::Building(Config &config) {
    int floor_count = config.getValue<int>("Building.floors", 0);

    for (int i = 0; i < floor_count; ++i) {
        Floor floor(i + 1, config); // Floor numbering starts at 1.
        floors.push_back(floor);
    }
}
```

Here, we read each floor definition from the file and create a `Floor` instance for it, which we add to an array. The instances also receive a reference to the configuration object.

The `Floor` class is basic as well, for the same reason, as you can see in the following code:

```
#include <vector>
#include <cstdint>

#include "room.h"


class Floor {
    std::vector<Room> rooms;

public:
```

```
    Floor(uint32_t level, Config &config);
};
```

Here's its implementation:

```
#include "floor.h"
#include "utility.h"

#include <string>


Floor::Floor(uint32_t level, Config &config) {
    std::string floor_cat = "Floor_" + std::to_string(level);
    std::string roomsStr = config.getValue<std::string>(floor_cat +
".rooms", 0);


    std::vector<std::string> room_ids;
    split_string(roomsStr, ',', room_ids);
    int room_count = room_ids.size();

    if (room_count > 0) {
        for (int i = 0; i < room_count; ++i) {
            Room room(std::stoi(room_ids.at(i)), config);
            rooms.push_back(room);
        }
    }
}
```

Of note is the way that the central configuration file is being parsed one part at a time by each individual class, with each class instance only caring about the small section that it has been instructed to care about by the ID.

Here, we are only concerned with the rooms that are defined for this floor ID. We extract the IDs for those rooms, then create new class instances for those rooms, saving a copy of each room in a vector. In a more advanced implementation of the simulation server, we could implement floor-wide events here, for example.

The utility header here defines a simple method for splitting strings, as shown in the following code:

```
#include <string>
#include <vector>


void split_string(const std::string& str, char chr,
std::vector<std::string>& vec);
```

Here's its implementation:

```
#include "utility.h"

#include <algorithm>

void split_string(const std::string& str, char chr,
std::vector<std::string>& vec) {
    std::string::const_iterator first = str.cbegin();
    std::string::const_iterator second = std::find(first + 1, str.cend(),
chr);

    while (second != str.cend()) {
        vec.emplace_back(first, second);
        first = second;
        second = std::find(second + 1, str.cend(), chr);
    }

    vec.emplace_back(first, str.cend());
}
```

This function is quite simple, using the provided separator to take a string and separate it into parts defined by said separator, which then get copied into a vector using emplacement.

Next, here's the Room class, as declared in room.h:

```
#include "node.h"
#include "devices/device.h"

#include <vector>
#include <map>
#include <cstdint>


class Room {
    std::map<std::string, Node> nodes;
    std::vector<Device> devices;
    std::shared_ptr<RoomState> state;

public:
    Room(uint32_t type, Config &config);

};
```

Here's its implementation:

```cpp
#include "room.h"

 #include "utility.h"


 Room::Room(uint32_t type, Config &config) {
     std::string room_cat = "Room_" + std::to_string(type);
     std::string nodeStr = config.getValue<std::string>(room_cat + ".nodes",
 "");

     state->setTemperature(24.3);
     state->setHumidity(51.2);
     std::string sensors;
     std::string actuators;
     std::string node_cat;
     if (!nodeStr.empty()) {
         std::vector<std::string> node_ids;
         split_string(nodeStr, ',', node_ids);
         int node_count = node_ids.size();

         for (int i = 0; i < node_count; ++i) {
             Node node(node_ids.at(i), config);
             node_cat = "Node_" + node_ids.at(i);
             nodes.insert(std::map<std::string,
 Node>::value_type(node_ids.at(i), node));
         }

         std::string devicesStr = config.getValue<std::string>(node_cat +
 ".devices", "");
         if (!devicesStr.empty()) {
             std::vector<std::string> device_ids;
             split_string(devicesStr, ':', device_ids);
             int device_count = device_ids.size();

             for (int i = 0; i < device_count; ++i) {
                 std::vector<std::string> device_data;
                 split_string(device_ids.at(i), ':', device_data);
                 if (device_data.size() != 2) {
                     // Incorrect data. Abort.
                     continue;
                 }

                 Device device(device_data[0], config, state);

 nodes.at(device_data[1]).addDevice(std::move(device));
```

```
                        devices.push_back(device);
                }
        }
    }

    }
```

In this class' constructor, we start off by setting the initial conditions of this room, specifically the temperature and humidity values. Next, we read out the nodes and devices for this room ID, creating instances of each. It starts by getting the list of nodes for this room, then for each node we get the list of devices, splitting this string into the individual device IDs.

Each device ID has a device class instantiated for it, with this instance added to the node that uses it. This finishes the basic initialization of the simulation server.

Next, here's the `Device` class:

```cpp
#include "config.h"
#include "types.h"


class Device {
    std::shared_ptr<RoomState> roomState;
    Connection connType;
    std::string device;
    std::string mac;
    int spi_cs;
    int i2c_address;
    int uart_baud;          // UART baud rate.
    int uart_dev;           // UART peripheral (0, 1, etc.)
    Config devConf;
    bool deviceState;
    uint8_t i2c_register;

    void send(std::string data);

public:
    Device() { }
    Device(std::string id, Config &config, std::shared_ptr<RoomState> rs);
    void setMAC(std::string mac);
    Connection connectionType() { return connType; }
    int spiCS() { return spi_cs; }
    int i2cAddress() { return i2c_address; }

    bool write(std::string bytes);
    std::string read();
```

```
    std::string read(int length);
};
```

Here's its definition:

```
#include "device.h"
 #include "nodes.h"


 Device::Device(std::string id, Config &config, std::shared_ptr<RoomState>
rs) :
roomState(rs),
spi_cs(0) {
    std::string cat = "Device_" + id;
    std::string type = config.getValue<std::string>(cat + ".type", "");
    if (type == "spi") {
        connType = CONN_SPI;
        spi_cs = config.getValue<int>(cat + ".cs_gpio", 0);
        device = config.getValue<std::string>(cat + ".device", "");
    }
    else if (type == "i2c") {
        connType == CONN_I2C;
        i2c_address = config.getValue<int>(cat + ".address", 0);
        device = config.getValue<std::string>(cat + ".device", "");
    }
    else if (type == "uart") {
        connType == CONN_UART;
        uart_baud = config.getValue<int>(cat + ".baud", 0);
        uart_dev = config.getValue<int>(cat + ".uart", 0);
        device = config.getValue<std::string>(cat + ".device", "");
    }
    else {
        // Error. Invalid type.
    }

}
```

In the constructor, we read out the information for this specific device using the provided device ID. Depending on the device type, we look for specific keys. These are all stored inside member variables, as shown in the following code:

```
void Device::setMAC(std::string mac) {
    this->mac = mac;
}


// Called when the device (UART-based) wishes to send data.
void Device::send(std::string data) {
```

```
        Nodes::sendUart(mac, data);
    }
```

After a simple setter method for the MAC of the connected node, we get a method that allows generated UART events to trigger a callback to the node process via an RPC callback method (as we will see in more detail in a moment when we look at the Nodes class). This is shown in the following code:

```
    bool Device::write(std::string bytes) {
        if (!deviceState) { return false; }

        // The first byte contains the register to read/write with I2C. Keep it
    as reference.
        if (connType == CONN_I2C && bytes.length() > 0) {
            i2c_register = bytes[0];
        }
        else if (connType == CONN_SPI) {
            // .
        }
        else if (connType == CONN_UART) {
            //
        }
        else { return false; }

        return true;
    }
```

We define a generic method to write to the device, regardless of the type. Here, we only handle the I2C interface to obtain the device register that's being addressed, as shown in the following code:

```
    std::string Device::read(int length) {
        if (!deviceState) { return std::string(); }

        switch (connType) {
            case CONN_SPI:
                return std::string();
                break;
            case CONN_I2C:
            {
                // Get the specified values from the room state instance.
                // Here we hard code a BME280 sensor.
                // Which value we return depends on the register set.
                uint8_t zero = 0x0;
                switch (i2c_register) {
                    case 0xFA: // Temperature. MSB, LSB, XLSB.
                    {
```

```
                                std::string ret =
    std::to_string(roomState->getTemperature()); // MSB
                                ret.append(std::to_string(zero)); // LSB
                                ret.append(std::to_string(zero)); // XLSB
                                return ret;
                                break;
                        }
                        case 0xF7: // Pressure. MSB, LSB, XLSB.
                        {
                                std::string ret =
    std::to_string(roomState->getPressure()); // MSB
                                ret.append(std::to_string(zero)); // LSB
                                ret.append(std::to_string(zero)); // XLSB
                                return ret;
                                break;
                        }
                        case 0xFD: // Humidity. MSB, LSB.
                        {
                                std::string ret =
    std::to_string(roomState->getHumidity()); // MSB
                                ret.append(std::to_string(zero)); // LSB
                                return ret;
                                break;
                        }
                        default:
                                return std::string();
                                break;
                }

                break;
        }
        case CONN_UART:
                //

                break;
        default:
                // Error.
                return std::string();
    };

    return std::string();
}

std::string Device::read() {
    return read(0);
}
```

The `read` methods come with a version that defines a length parameter for the bytes to be read and a version without parameters, instead passing a zero to the first method. This parameter would be useful for a UART, where a fixed buffer size would be used for the data.

For simplicity's sake, we have hardcoded the response for a BME280 combined thermometer, hygrometer, and air pressure meter device. We check the value of the register that was sent over with an earlier `write` command, then return the value appropriate to it, reading the current room values as appropriate.

There are many more devices possible, we would want to implement them in their own configuration files or dedicated classes instead of hardcoding them all here like this.

Custom types for the application are defined in the `types.h` header, as shown in the following code:

```
#include <memory>
#include <thread>
#include <mutex>


enum Connection {
    CONN_NC = 0,
    CONN_SPI = 1,
    CONN_I2C = 2,
    CONN_UART = 3
};


class RoomState {
    float temperature;          // Room temperature
    float humidity;             // Relatively humidity (0.00 - 100.00%)
    uint16_t pressure;          // Air pressure.
    std::mutex tmtx;
    std::mutex hmtx;
    std::mutex pmtx;

public:
    RoomState() :
            temperature(0),
            humidity(0),
            pressure(1000) {
            //
    }

    float getTemperature() {
            std::lock_guard<std::mutex> lk(tmtx);
```

```
            return temperature;
    }

    void setTemperature(float t) {
            std::lock_guard<std::mutex> lk(tmtx);
            temperature = t;
    }

    float getHumidity() {
            std::lock_guard<std::mutex> lk(hmtx);
            return humidity;
    }

    void setHumidity(float h) {
            std::lock_guard<std::mutex> lk(hmtx);
            temperature = h;
    }

    float getPressure() {
            std::lock_guard<std::mutex> lk(pmtx);
            return pressure;
    }

    void setPressure(uint16_t p) {
            std::lock_guard<std::mutex> lk(pmtx);
            pressure = p;
    }
};
```

Here, we see the enumeration for the different connection types, as well as the `RoomState` class, which defines a basic getter/setter-based construction, with a mutex providing thread-safe access to the individual values, as multiple nodes can try to access the same values while the room itself tries to update them.

Next, here's the `Node` class:

```
#include "config.h"
#include "devices/device.h"

#include <string>
#include <vector>
#include <map>


class Node {
    std::string mac;
    bool uart0_active;
```

```
    Device uart0;
    std::map<int, Device> i2c;
    std::map<int, Device> spi;
    std::vector<Device> devices;

  public:
    Node(std::string id, Config &config);
    bool addDevice(Device &&device);

    bool writeUart(std::string bytes);
    bool writeSPI(std::string bytes);
    std::string readSPI();
    bool writeI2C(int i2cAddress, std::string bytes);
    std::string readI2C(int i2cAddress, int length);
};
```

Here's its implementation:

```
#include "node.h"
 #include "nodes.h"

 #include <cstdlib>
 #include <utility>


 Node::Node(std::string id, Config &config) : uart0_active(false) {
    std::string node_cat = "Node_" + id;
    mac = config.getValue<std::string>(node_cat + ".mac", "");

    Nodes::addNode(mac, this);
    std::system("esp8266");
};
```

When a new class instance is created, it obtains its MAC address, adds it to its own local variable, and registers it with the `Nodes` class. A new instance of the node executable (in our case, called `esp8266`) is launched using the native system call, which will cause the OS to start this new process.

As the new process starts, it will connect to the RPC server and obtain the MAC using the RPC functions that we looked at earlier in this section. After this, the class instance and the remote process act as mirror images of each other:

```
bool Node::addDevice(Device &&device) {
    device.setMAC(mac);

    switch (device.connectionType()) {
        case CONN_SPI:
```

```
                    spi.insert(std::pair<int, Device>(device.spiCS(),
std::move(device))));
                break;
            case CONN_I2C:
                i2c.insert(std::pair<int, Device>(device.i2cAddress(),
std::move(device))));
                break;
            case CONN_UART:
                uart0 = std::move(device);
                uart0_active = true;
                break;
            default:
                // Error.
                break;
        }

        return true;
    }
```

When the Room class assigns a new device to the node, we assign our MAC to it to act as an identifier for which node it belongs to. After this, we query the device to see which type of interface it has, so that we can add it to the proper interface, taking into account the CS line (if used) for SPI and the bus address for I2C.

Using move semantics, we ensure that we aren't merely mindlessly making copies of the same device class instance, but essentially shifting ownership of the original instance, thus improving efficiency. Let's look at the following code:

```
bool Node::writeUart(std::string bytes) {
    if (!uart0_active) { return false; }

    uart0.write(bytes);

    return true;
}


bool Node::writeSPI(std::string bytes) {
    if (spi.size() == 1) {
        spi[0].write(bytes);
    }
    else {
        return false;
    }

    return true;
}
```

```
std::string Node::readSPI() {
    if (spi.size() == 1) {
        return spi[0].read();
    }
    else {
        return std::string();
    }
}


bool Node::writeI2C(int i2cAddress, std::string bytes) {
    if (i2c.find(i2cAddress) == i2c.end()) { return false; }

    i2c[i2cAddress].write(bytes);
    return true;
}


std::string Node::readI2C(int i2cAddress, int length) {
    if (i2c.count(i2cAddress) || length < 1) { return std::string(); }

    return i2c[i2cAddress].read(length);
}
```

For the writing and reading functionality, not a lot is involved. Using the CS (SPI), the bus address (I2C), or neither (UART), we know which type of device to access and call its respective methods.

Finally, here's the Nodes class that ties everything together:

```
#include <map>
#include <string>
#include <queue>


class Node;


class Nodes {
    static Node* getNode(std::string mac);

    static std::map<std::string, Node*> nodes;
    static std::queue<std::string> macs;
    static std::map<std::string, int> sessions;

public:
    static bool addNode(std::string mac, Node* node);
    static bool removeNode(std::string mac);
```

```
    static void registerSession(std::string mac, int session);
    static bool writeUart(std::string mac, std::string bytes);
    static bool sendUart(std::string mac, std::string bytes);
    static bool writeSPI(std::string mac, std::string bytes);
    static std::string readSPI(std::string mac);
    static bool writeI2C(std::string mac, int i2cAddress, std::string
bytes);
    static std::string readI2C(std::string mac, int i2cAddress, int
length);
    static void addMAC(std::string mac);
    static std::string getMAC();
};
```

Here's its definition:

```
#include "nodes.h"
 #include "node.h"
 #include <nymph/nymph.h>


// Static initialisations.
std::map<std::string, Node*> Nodes::nodes;
std::queue<std::string> Nodes::macs;
std::map<std::string, int> Nodes::sessions;


Node* Nodes::getNode(std::string mac) {
    std::map<std::string, Node*>::iterator it;
    it = nodes.find(mac);
    if (it == nodes.end()) { return 0; }

    return it->second;
}


bool Nodes::addNode(std::string mac, Node* node) {
    std::pair<std::map<std::string, Node*>::iterator, bool> ret;
    ret = nodes.insert(std::pair<std::string, Node*>(mac, node));
    if (ret.second) { macs.push(mac); }
    return ret.second;
}


bool Nodes::removeNode(std::string mac) {
    std::map<std::string, Node*>::iterator it;
    it = nodes.find(mac);
    if (it == nodes.end()) { return false; }
    nodes.erase(it);
```

```
        return true;
    }
```

With the following methods, we can set and remove node class instances:

```
    void Nodes::registerSession(std::string mac, int session) {
        sessions.insert(std::pair<std::string, int>(mac, session));
    }
```

New MAC and RPC session IDs are registered with the following function:

```
    bool Nodes::writeUart(std::string mac, std::string bytes) {
        Node* node = getNode(mac);
        if (!node) { return false; }

        node->writeUart(bytes);

        return true;
    }


    bool Nodes::sendUart(std::string mac, std::string bytes) {
        std::map<std::string, int>::iterator it;
        it = sessions.find(mac);
        if (it == sessions.end()) { return false; }

        vector<NymphType*> values;
        values.push_back(new NymphString(bytes));
        string result;
        NymphBoolean* world = 0;
        if (!NymphRemoteClient::callCallback(it->second, "serialRxCallback",
    values, result)) {
                //
        }

        return true;
    }


    bool Nodes::writeSPI(std::string mac, std::string bytes) {
        Node* node = getNode(mac);
        if (!node) { return false; }

        node->writeSPI(bytes);

        return true;
    }
```

```
std::string Nodes::readSPI(std::string mac) {
    Node* node = getNode(mac);
    if (!node) { return std::string(); }

    return node->readSPI();
}


bool Nodes::writeI2C(std::string mac, int i2cAddress, std::string bytes) {
    Node* node = getNode(mac);
    if (!node) { return false; }

    node->writeI2C(i2cAddress, bytes);

    return true;
}


std::string Nodes::readI2C(std::string mac, int i2cAddress, int length) {
    Node* node = getNode(mac);
    if (!node) { return std::string(); }

    return node->readI2C(i2cAddress, length);
}
```

The methods for writing and reading from the different interfaces are basically pass-through methods, merely using the MAC address to find the appropriate `Node` instance to call the method on.

Of note here is the `sendUart()` method, which uses the NymphRPC server to call the callback method on the appropriate node process to trigger its UART receive callback, as shown in the following code:

```
void Nodes::addMAC(std::string mac) {
    macs.push(mac);
}


std::string Nodes::getMAC() {
    if (macs.empty()) { return std::string(); }

    std::string val = macs.front();
    macs.pop();
    return val;
}
```

Finally, we got the methods used to set and get the MAC address for new nodes.

With this, we have the basics of the full integration server. In the next section, we will take a look at the firmware and client side of the system before looking at how everything fits together.

Makefile

The Makefile for this part of the project looks as follows:

```
export TOP := $(CURDIR)

GPP = g++
GCC = gcc
MAKEDIR = mkdir -p
RM = rm

OUTPUT = bmac_server
INCLUDE = -I .
FLAGS := $(INCLUDE) -g3 -std=c++17 -U__STRICT_ANSI__
LIB := -lnymphrpc -lPocoNet -lPocoUtil -lPocoFoundation -lPocoJSON
CPPFLAGS := $(FLAGS)
CFLAGS := -g3
CPP_SOURCES := $(wildcard *.cpp) $(wildcard devices/*.cpp)
CPP_OBJECTS := $(addprefix obj/,$(notdir $(CPP_SOURCES:.cpp=.o))

all: makedir $(C_OBJECTS) $(CPP_OBJECTS) bin/$(OUTPUT)

obj/%.o: %.cpp
	$(GPP) -c -o $@ $< $(CPPFLAGS)

bin/$(OUTPUT):
	-rm -f $@
	$(GPP) -o $@ $(C_OBJECTS) $(CPP_OBJECTS) $(LIB)

makedir:
	$(MAKEDIR) bin
	$(MAKEDIR) obj/devices

clean:
	$(RM) $(CPP_OBJECTS)
```

This is a rather simple Makefile as we have no special demands. We gather the source files, determine the names of the resulting object files, and compile all of them before generating a binary out of these object files.

The node

This section covers the firmware for the integration test specifically the reimplementation of the (Arduino) APIs used in the Sming framework.

Most crucial here is that we don't in any way modify the firmware code itself. The only parts that we wish to change from the original firmware image for the ESP8266 MCU are the APIs that our own code interacts with.

This means that we have to first determine the APIs that our code interacts with and reimplement these in a way that is supported on the target (desktop) platform. For our ESP8266-based firmware, this means, for example, that the Wi-Fi network side is left unimplemented, as we are using the local network stack of the OS and therefore don't care about such details.

Similarly, the I2C, SPI, and UART interfaces are implemented as mere stubs that call their respective counterparts on the RPC interface, which we looked at in the previous section. For the MQTT protocol client, we could use the `emqtt` MQTT library that is part of the Sming framework, but as one will quickly find out, this library is meant to be used on embedded systems where the code using it is responsible for connecting it to the network stack.

Our code interacts with the API offered by the `MqttClient` class in Sming. It uses `emqtt` for the MQTT protocol, and inherits from the `TcpClient` class. Following the code down the hierarchy, one will end up at the TCP connection class before diving into the underlying LWIP network library stack.

In order to save ourselves a lot of trouble, it's easiest to just use an alternative MQTT library, such as the Mosquitto client library, which is meant to be run on a desktop OS, and will therefore use the OS-provided sockets API. This will cleanly map to the methods provided by Sming's MQTT client class.

We can leave the header for this class almost entirely untouched, just adding our modifications to integrate the Mosquitto library, as follows:

```
class TcpClient;
#include "../Delegate.h"
#include "../../Wiring/WString.h"
#include "../../Wiring/WHashMap.h"
#include "libmosquitto/cpp/mosquittopp.h"
#include "URL.h"

typedef Delegate<void(String topic, String message)>
MqttStringSubscriptionCallback;
```

```
 typedef Delegate<void(uint16_t msgId, int type)>
MqttMessageDeliveredCallback;
 typedef Delegate<void(TcpClient& client, bool successful)>
TcpClientCompleteDelegate;

 class MqttClient;
 class URL;

 class MqttClient : public mosqpp::mosquittopp {
 public:
    MqttClient(bool autoDestruct = false);
    MqttClient(String serverHost, int serverPort,
MqttStringSubscriptionCallback callback = NULL);
    virtual ~MqttClient();

    void setCallback(MqttStringSubscriptionCallback subscriptionCallback =
NULL);

    void setCompleteDelegate(TcpClientCompleteDelegate completeCb);

    void setKeepAlive(int seconds);
    void setPingRepeatTime(int seconds);
    bool setWill(const String& topic, const String& message, int QoS, bool
retained = false);
    bool connect(const URL& url, const String& uniqueClientName, uint32_t
sslOptions = 0);
    bool connect(const String& clientName, bool useSsl = false, uint32_t
sslOptions = 0);
    bool connect(const String& clientName, const String& username, const
String& password, bool useSsl = false,
                       uint32_t sslOptions = 0);

    bool publish(String topic, String message, bool retained = false);
    bool publishWithQoS(String topic, String message, int QoS, bool
retained = false,
                               MqttMessageDeliveredCallback onDelivery =
NULL);

    bool subscribe(const String& topic);
    bool unsubscribe(const String& topic);

    void on_message(const struct mosquitto_message* message);

 protected:
    void debugPrintResponseType(int type, int len);
    static int staticSendPacket(void* userInfo, const void* buf, unsigned
int count);
```

```
    private:
        bool privateConnect(const String& clientName, const String& username,
    const String& password,
                                    bool useSsl = false, uint32_t sslOptions
    = 0);

        URL url;
        mosqpp::mosquittopp mqtt;
        int waitingSize;
        uint8_t buffer[MQTT_MAX_BUFFER_SIZE + 1];
        uint8_t* current;
        int posHeader;
        MqttStringSubscriptionCallback callback;
        TcpClientCompleteDelegate completed = nullptr;
        int keepAlive = 60;
        int pingRepeatTime = 20;
        unsigned long lastMessage = 0;
        HashMap<uint16_t, MqttMessageDeliveredCallback> onDeliveryQueue;
    };
```

We're including the header file for the C++-based wrapper for the Mosquitto client library here from the version of the Mosquitto library that is included in the project for this chapter. This is because the official version of the library doesn't support building with MinGW.

With the header included, we have the class derive from the Mosquitto MQTT client class instead.

Naturally, the implementation of the Sming MQTT client class has been completely changed, as you can see in the following code:

```
#include "MqttClient.h"
#include "../Clock.h"
#include <algorithm>
#include <cstring>

MqttClient::MqttClient(bool autoDestruct /* = false*/)
{
    memset(buffer, 0, MQTT_MAX_BUFFER_SIZE + 1);
    waitingSize = 0;
    posHeader = 0;
    current = NULL;

    mosqpp::lib_init();
}


MqttClient::MqttClient(String serverHost, int serverPort,
```

```
MqttStringSubscriptionCallback callback /* = NULL*/)
    {
    url.Host = serverHost;
    url.Port = serverPort;
    this->callback = callback;
    waitingSize = 0;
    posHeader = 0;
    current = NULL;

    mosqpp::lib_init();
}
```

The constructor simply initializes the Mosquitto library, with no further input required:

```
MqttClient::~MqttClient() {
    mqtt.loop_stop();
    mosqpp::lib_cleanup();
}
```

In the destructor (shown in the following code) we stop the MQTT client-listening thread that we launched when we connect to an MQTT broker and clean up the resources that were used by the library:

```
void MqttClient::setCallback(MqttStringSubscriptionCallback callback) {
    this->callback = callback;
}

void MqttClient::setCompleteDelegate(TcpClientCompleteDelegate completeCb)
{
    completed = completeCb;
}

void MqttClient::setKeepAlive(int seconds) {
    keepAlive = seconds;
}

void MqttClient::setPingRepeatTime(int seconds) {
    if(pingRepeatTime > keepAlive) {
        pingRepeatTime = keepAlive;
    } else {
        pingRepeatTime = seconds;
    }
}

bool MqttClient::setWill(const String& topic, const String& message, int
QoS, bool retained /* = false*/)
{
    return mqtt.will_set(topic.c_str(), message.length(), message.c_str(),
```

```
QoS, retained);
  }
```

We have a number of utility functions, not all of which are being utilized, but they are still implemented here for the sake of completeness. It's also hard to predict which ones will be required, therefore it's often better to implement more than strictly necessary, especially if they are small functions that take less time to implement than to find out whether that function or method is used at all. Let's look at the following code:

```
bool MqttClient::connect(const URL& url, const String& clientName,
uint32_t sslOptions) {
    this->url = url;
    if(!(url.Protocol == "mqtt" || url.Protocol == "mqtts")) {
        return false;
    }

    waitingSize = 0;
    posHeader = 0;
    current = NULL;

    bool useSsl = (url.Protocol == "mqtts");
    return privateConnect(clientName, url.User, url.Password, useSsl,
sslOptions);
  }

 bool MqttClient::connect(const String& clientName, bool useSsl /* = false
*/, uint32_t sslOptions /* = 0 */)
 {
    return MqttClient::connect(clientName, "", "", useSsl, sslOptions);
 }

 bool MqttClient::connect(const String& clientName, const String& username,
const String& password,
                              bool useSsl /* = false */, uint32_t
sslOptions /* = 0 */)
 {
    return privateConnect(clientName, username, password, useSsl,
sslOptions);
 }
```

The `connect` methods remain the same, as they all use the same `private` method of the class to perform the actual connection operation, as shown in the following code:

```
bool MqttClient::privateConnect(const String& clientName, const String&
username, const String& password,
                              bool useSsl /* = false */,
uint32_t sslOptions /* = 0 */) {
```

```
if (clientName.length() > 0) {
    mqtt.reinitialise(clientName.c_str(), false);
}

if (username.length() > 0) {
    mqtt.username_pw_set(username.c_str(), password.c_str());
}

if (useSsl) {
    //
}

mqtt.connect(url.Host.c_str(), url.Port, keepAlive);
mqtt.loop_start();
return true;
}
```

This is the first section where we directly use the Mosquitto library. We reinitialize the instance either without a password or TLS (anonymous broker access), or with a password, or with TLS (left unimplemented here, as we don't need it).

In this method, we also start the listening thread for the MQTT client, which will handle all incoming messages so that we don't have to further concern ourselves with this aspect of the process. Let's look at the following code:

```
bool MqttClient::publish(String topic, String message, bool retained /* =
false*/) {
    int res = mqtt.publish(0, topic.c_str(), message.length(),
message.c_str(), 0, retained);
    return res > 0;
}


bool MqttClient::publishWithQoS(String topic, String message, int QoS,
bool retained /* = false*/,
                                        MqttMessageDeliveredCallback
onDelivery /* = NULL */)
{
    int res = mqtt.publish(0, topic.c_str(), message.length(),
message.c_str(), QoS, retained);

    return res > 0;
}
```

The MQTT message-publish functionality directly maps to the Mosquitto library's methods:

```
bool MqttClient::subscribe(const String& topic) {
    int res = mqtt.subscribe(0, topic.c_str());
    return res > 0;
}

bool MqttClient::unsubscribe(const String& topic) {
    int res = mqtt.unsubscribe(0, topic.c_str());
    return res > 0;
}
```

Subscribing and unsubscribing both also map easily to the MQTT client instance, as shown in the following code:

```
void MqttClient::on_message(const struct mosquitto_message* message) {
    if (callback) {
            callback(String(message->topic), String((char*) message->payload,
message->payloadlen));
    }
}
```

Finally, we implement the Mosquitto `callback` method for when we receive a new message from the broker. For each received message, we then call the registered `callback` method (from the firmware code) to provide it with the payload and topic.

This takes care of the MQTT client aspect of the firmware. Next, we need to make the rest of the APIs compatible with a desktop OS.

The headers of the Sming framework that the firmware uses are as follows:

```
#include <user_config.h>
 #include <SmingCore/SmingCore.h>
```

The first header file defines some platform-related features that we don't need. The second header is the one that we will add everything that we need to.

To check the firmware's code for API dependencies, we use standard text searching tools to find all function calls, filtering out any that do not call into our code but into the Sming framework. After doing this we can write the following **SmingCore.h** file with these dependencies:

```
#include <cstdint>
 #include <cstdio>
 #include <string>
 #include <iostream>
```

```
#include "wiring/WString.h"
#include "wiring/WVector.h"
#include "wiring/WHashMap.h"
#include "FileSystem.h"
#include "wiring/Stream.h"
#include "Delegate.h"
#include "Network/MqttClient.h"
#include "Timer.h"
#include "WConstants.h"
#include "Clock.h"

#include <nymph/nymph.h>
```

We start off with a combination of standard C library and STL includes, along with a number of headers that define the rest of the API that we are implementing. We also directly use a number of header files that define classes that are used throughout these APIs, but not by the firmware itself.

A class like the `Delegate` class is sufficiently abstract that it can be used as is. As we will see, the `Filesystem` and `Timer` classes required a fair bit of reworking to make them work for our purposes. We already looked at the modifications to the MQTT client earlier.

Naturally, we also include the header file for the NymphRPC library, which will allow us to communicate with the server side of the integration test, as shown in the following code:

```
typedef uint8_t uint8;
 typedef uint16_t uint16;
 typedef uint32_t uint32;
 typedef int8_t int8;
 typedef int16_t int16;
 typedef int32_t int32;
 typedef uint32_t u32_t;
```

For compatibility reasons, we need to define a range of types that are used throughout the firmware code. These are equivalent to the types in `cstdint` from the C library, so we can use simple `typedef`s, as follows:

```
#define UART_ID_0 0 ///< ID of UART 0
 #define UART_ID_1 1 ///< ID of UART 1
 #define SERIAL_BAUD_RATE 115200

 typedef Delegate<void(Stream& source, char arrivedChar, uint16_t
availableCharsCount)> StreamDataReceivedDelegate;

 class SerialStream : public Stream {
    //
```

```
public:
    SerialStream();
    size_t write(uint8_t);
    int available();
    int read();
    void flush();
    int peek();
};

class HardwareSerial {
    int uart;
    uint32_t baud;
    static StreamDataReceivedDelegate HWSDelegate;
    static std::string rxBuffer;

public:
    HardwareSerial(const int uartPort);
    void begin(uint32_t baud = 9600);
    void systemDebugOutput(bool enable);
    void end();
    size_t printf(const char *fmt, ...);
    void print(String str);
    void println(String str);
    void println(const char* str);
    void println(int16_t ch);
    void setCallback(StreamDataReceivedDelegate dataReceivedDelegate);
    static void dataReceivedCallback(NymphMessage* msg, void* data);
    size_t write(const uint8_t* buffer, size_t size);
    size_t readBytes(char *buffer, size_t length);
};

extern HardwareSerial Serial;
```

The first API we fully reimplement is the hardware-based serial device. Since this communicates directly with the virtual interface in the server, we just need to provide the methods here, with the definition in the source file, as we will see in a moment.

We also declare a global instantiation of this serial object class, identical to how the original framework implementation handles it, as shown in the following code:

```
struct rboot_config {
    uint8 current_rom;
    uint32 roms[2];
};

int rboot_get_current_rom();
void rboot_set_current_rom(int slot);
rboot_config rboot_get_config();
```

```
class rBootHttpUpdate;
typedef Delegate<void(rBootHttpUpdate& client, bool result)>
OtaUpdateDelegate;
class rBootHttpUpdate {
    //

public:
    void addItem(int offset, String firmwareFileUrl);
    void setCallback(OtaUpdateDelegate reqUpdateDelegate);
    void start();
};


void spiffs_mount_manual(u32_t offset, int count);
```

The rboot boot manager and SPIFFS filesystem-related functionality has no equivalent on a desktop system, so we declare them here (but as we'll see in a moment, they are left as empty stubs):

```
class StationClass {
    String mac;
    bool enabled;

public:
    void enable(bool enable);
    void enable(bool enable, bool save);
    bool config(const String& ssid, const String& password, bool
autoConnectOnStartup = true,
                                    bool save = true);
    bool connect();
    String getMAC();

    static int handle;
};

extern StationClass WifiStation;


class AccessPointClass {
    bool enabled;

public:
    void enable(bool enable, bool save);
    void enable(bool enable);
};

extern AccessPointClass WifiAccessPoint;
```

```
class IPAddress {
    //
public:
    String toString();
};

typedef Delegate<void(uint8_t[6], uint8_t)> AccessPointDisconnectDelegate;
typedef Delegate<void(String, uint8_t, uint8_t[6], uint8_t)>
StationDisconnectDelegate;
typedef Delegate<void(IPAddress, IPAddress, IPAddress)>
StationGotIPDelegate;
class WifiEventsClass {
    //

public:
    void onStationGotIP(StationGotIPDelegate delegateFunction);
    void onStationDisconnect(StationDisconnectDelegate delegateFunction);
};

extern WifiEventsClass WifiEvents;
```

On the network side, we have to provide all of the class instances and related information that are normally used to connect to a WiFi access point and ensure that we are connected. As we aren't testing WiFi functionality here, these methods are of little use, but are needed to satisfy the firmware code and the compiler:

```
void debugf(const char *fmt, ...);


class WDTClass {
    //

public:
    void alive();
};

extern WDTClass WDT;
```

We then declare the debug-related output function as well as the watchdog class using the following code:

```
class TwoWire {
    uint8_t rxBufferIndex;
    std::string buffer;
    int i2cAddress;

public:
    void pins(int sda, int scl);
```

```
        void begin();
        void beginTransmission(int address);
        size_t write(uint8_t data);
        size_t write(int data);
        size_t endTransmission();
        size_t requestFrom(int address, int length);
        int available();
        int read();
};

extern TwoWire Wire;


class SPISettings {
    //
public:
    //
};

class SPIClass {
    //

public:
    void begin();
    void end();
    void beginTransaction(SPISettings mySettings);
    void endTransaction();
    void transfer(uint8* buffer, size_t numberBytes);
};

extern SPIClass SPI;
```

We declare the two types of communication buses here, as shown in the following code. Again, we declare that there is a global instantiation of each:

```
void pinMode(uint16_t pin, uint8_t mode);
 void digitalWrite(uint16_t pin, uint8_t val);
 uint8_t digitalRead(uint16_t pin);


 uint16_t analogRead(uint16_t pin);
```

Since the firmware contains code that uses the GPIO and ADC pins, the above functions are needed as well.

```
String system_get_sdk_version();
 int system_get_free_heap_size();
 int system_get_cpu_freq();
```

```
int system_get_chip_id();
int spi_flash_get_id();

class SystemClass {
    //

public:
    void restart();
};

extern SystemClass System;


// --- TcpClient ---
class TcpClient {
    //

public:
    //
};


extern void init();
```

Finally, we declare a number of classes and functions that are mostly there to satisfy the compiler as they have no practical use for our purposes, though we could potentially implement advanced test scenarios this way.

Next, we'll look at the implementation of these functions using the following code:

```
#include "SmingCore.h"

#include <iostream>
#include <cstdio>
#include <cstdarg>


int StationClass::handle;
```

The `handle` variable is the one variable we declare as being static in this compile unit. Its purpose is to store the remote server handle ID for future operations after we connect to the RPC server, as shown in the following code:

```
void logFunction(int level, string logStr) {
    std::cout << level << " - " << logStr << std::endl;
}
```

Just like in the server-side code, we define a simple logging function to use with
NymphRPC, as shown in the following code:

```
void debugf(const char *fmt, ...) {
    va_list ap;
    va_start(ap, fmt);
    int written = vfprintf(stdout, fmt, ap);
    va_end(ap);
}
```

We implement the simple debug output function using C-style string formatting features to
fit the function's signature, as shown in the following code:

```
StreamDataReceivedDelegate HardwareSerial::HWSDelegate = nullptr;
std::string HardwareSerial::rxBuffer;
HardwareSerial Serial(0);
```

We define the serial callback delegate along with the serial receive buffer as static, as we
assume the presence of a single UART capable of **receiving data** (RX), which happens to be
the case on the ESP8266 MCU. We also create a single instance of the `HardwareSerial`
class, for UART 0, as shown in the following code:

```
SerialStream::SerialStream() { }
size_t SerialStream::write(uint8_t) { return 1; }
int SerialStream::available() { return 0; }
int SerialStream::read() { return 0; }
void SerialStream::flush() { }
int SerialStream::peek() { return 0; }
```

This class is just there to act as a stub. As none of the code actually uses this object's
methods, we can leave them all unimplemented, as shown in the following code:

```
HardwareSerial::HardwareSerial(const int uartPort) {
    uart = uartPort;
}

void HardwareSerial::begin(uint32_t baud/* = 9600*/) {
    this->baud = baud;
}


void HardwareSerial::systemDebugOutput(bool enable) { }
void HardwareSerial::end() { }
size_t HardwareSerial::printf(const char *fmt, ...) {
    va_list ap;
    va_start(ap, fmt);
        int written = vfprintf(stdout, fmt, ap);
```

```
        va_end(ap);

    return written;
}


void HardwareSerial::print(String str) {
    std::cout << str.c_str();
}


void HardwareSerial::println(String str) {
    std::cout << str.c_str() << std::endl;
}


void HardwareSerial::println(const char* str) {
    std::cout << str << std::endl;
}


void HardwareSerial::println(int16_t ch) {
    std::cout << std::hex << ch << std::endl;
}


void HardwareSerial::setCallback(StreamDataReceivedDelegate
dataReceivedDelegate) {
    HWSDelegate = dataReceivedDelegate;
}
```

A lot of the methods in this class are simple enough that they can be implemented as a simple write to the standard (system) output or with an assignment to a variable. Occasionally a method is left unaltered from the original, though even for the setting of the callback delegate function in the last method in this group, the original code is called into the C-based low-level APIs of the ESP8266's SDK. Let's look at the following code:

```
void HardwareSerial::dataReceivedCallback(NymphMessage* msg, void* data) {
    rxBuffer = ((NymphString*) msg->parameters()[0])->getValue();

    SerialStream stream;
    int length = rxBuffer.length();
    int i = 0;
    HWSDelegate(stream, rxBuffer[i], length - i);
}
```

To receive UART messages, we define a NymphRPC callback function, which for that reason is defined as being static. Since the ESP8266 only has a single UART capable of receiving data this suffices.

When called, this method reads out the payload being received on the UART and calls the `callback` function that the firmware registered previously, as shown in the following code:

```
size_t HardwareSerial::write(const uint8_t* buffer, size_t size) {
    vector<NymphType*> values;
    values.push_back(new NymphString(WifiStation.getMAC().c_str()));
    values.push_back(new NymphString(std::string((const char*) buffer,
size))));
    NymphType* returnValue = 0;
    std::string result;
    if (!NymphRemoteServer::callMethod(StationClass::handle, "writeUart",
values, returnValue, result)) {
        std::cout << "Error calling remote method: " << result <<
std::endl;
        NymphRemoteServer::disconnect(StationClass::handle, result);
        NymphRemoteServer::shutdown();
        return 0;
    }

    if (returnValue->type() != NYMPH_BOOL) {
        std::cout << "Return value wasn't a boolean. Type: " <<
returnValue->type() << std::endl;
        NymphRemoteServer::disconnect(StationClass::handle, result);
        NymphRemoteServer::shutdown();
        return 0;
    }

    return size;
}
```

Writing to the remote UART is done using an RPC call. To do this, we create an STL vector and fill it with the parameters to pass in the proper order—in this case, the node's MAC address and the data that we wish to send on the remote UART.

After this, we use the NymphRPC handle that we got when we connected to call the RPC server and wait for the response from the remote function, as shown in the following code:

```
size_t HardwareSerial::readBytes(char* buffer, size_t length) {
    buffer = rxBuffer.data();
    return rxBuffer.length();
}
```

Reading from the UART is done after we've received data on the UART, after which we can read it out with the following method, just as we would with the original code:

```
int rboot_get_current_rom() { return 0; }
void rboot_set_current_rom(int slot) { }
rboot_config rboot_get_config() {
    rboot_config cfg;
    cfg.current_rom = 0;
    cfg.roms[0] = 0x1000;
    cfg.roms[1] = 0x3000;
    return cfg;
}

void rBootHttpUpdate::addItem(int offset, String firmwareFileUrl) { }
void rBootHttpUpdate::setCallback(OtaUpdateDelegate reqUpdateDelegate) { }
void rBootHttpUpdate::start() { }

void spiffs_mount_manual(u32_t offset, int count) { }
```

Both the rboot boot manager and the SPIFFS filesystem are not used, so they can just return safe values, as shown in the following code. The **over-the-air (OTA)** functionality could potentially be implemented as well, depending on the kind of features of the system one would want to test:

```
StationClass WifiStation;

void StationClass::enable(bool enable) { enabled = enable; }
void StationClass::enable(bool enable, bool save) { enabled = enable; }
String StationClass::getMAC() { return mac; }

bool StationClass::config(const String& ssid, const String& password, bool
autoConnectOnStartup /* = true*/,
                                        bool save /* = true */) {
    //

    return true;
}
```

Since we don't have a Wi-Fi adapter that we want to use directly and are just using the OS's network capabilities, the `WiFiStation` object doesn't do a lot for most of its methods, except for when we actually connect to the RPC server, which is done using the following method:

```
bool StationClass::connect() {
    long timeout = 5000; // 5 seconds.
    NymphRemoteServer::init(logFunction, NYMPH_LOG_LEVEL_TRACE, timeout);
    std::string result;
```

```
    if (!NymphRemoteServer::connect("localhost", 4004,
StationClass::handle, 0, result)) {
        cout << "Connecting to remote server failed: " << result <<
std::endl;
        NymphRemoteServer::disconnect(StationClass::handle, result);
        NymphRemoteServer::shutdown();
        return false;
    }

    vector<NymphType*> values;
    NymphType* returnValue = 0;
    if (!NymphRemoteServer::callMethod(StationClass::handle, "getNewMac",
values, returnValue, result)) {
        std::cout << "Error calling remote method: " << result <<
std::endl;
        NymphRemoteServer::disconnect(StationClass::handle, result);
        NymphRemoteServer::shutdown();
        return false;
    }

    if (returnValue->type() != NYMPH_STRING) {
        std::cout << "Return value wasn't a string. Type: " <<
returnValue->type() << std::endl;
        NymphRemoteServer::disconnect(StationClass::handle, result);
        NymphRemoteServer::shutdown();
        return false;
    }

    std::string macStr = ((NymphString*) returnValue)->getValue();
    mac = String(macStr.data(), macStr.length());

    delete returnValue;
    returnValue = 0;

    // Set the serial interface callback.
    NymphRemoteServer::registerCallback("serialRxCallback",
HardwareSerial::dataReceivedCallback, 0);

    return true;
}
```

This is one of the first methods that gets called in the firmware when it tries to connect to the Wi-Fi access point. Instead of connecting to a Wi-Fi access point, we use this method to connect to the RPC server instead.

We start by initializing the NymphRPC library, calling the initialization method on its `NymphRemoteServer` class, and then connecting to the RPC server using the hardcoded location and port number. Upon successfully connecting to the RPC server, this client will receive a list of the available methods on the RPC server—in this case, all of the methods we registered, as we saw in the previous section on the simulation server.

Next, we request our MAC address from the server, verify that it's a string that we received, and set it for later use. Finally, we locally register the callback for the UART with NymphRPC, as shown in the following code. As we saw in the simulation server's section, the `Nodes` class on the server expects this callback to exist on the client:

```
AccessPointClass WifiAccessPoint;

void AccessPointClass::enable(bool enable, bool save) {
    enabled = enable;
}

void AccessPointClass::enable(bool enable) {
    enabled = enable;
}


WifiEventsClass WifiEvents;

String IPAddress::toString() { return "192.168.0.32"; }

void WifiEventsClass::onStationGotIP(StationGotIPDelegate
delegateFunction) {
    // Immediately call the callback.
    IPAddress ip;
    delegateFunction(ip, ip, ip);
}

void WifiEventsClass::onStationDisconnect(StationDisconnectDelegate
delegateFunction) {
    //
}


WDTClass WDT;

void WDTClass::alive() { }
```

We conclude this networking section with some more stub classes and, finally, the watchdog class, which might make for a nice point for advanced testing, including soft reset testing for long-running code. Of course, such advanced tests would also require that the code runs with the performance of the ESP8266's sub-100 MHz processor.

Of note here is the Wi-Fi events class, where we immediately call the `callback` function for a successful connection to the Wi-Fi access point, or at least pretend to. Without this step, the firmware would forever wait for something to happen. Let's look at the following code:

```
void SPIClass::begin() { }
void SPIClass::end() { }
void SPIClass::beginTransaction(SPISettings mySettings) { }
void SPIClass::endTransaction() { }
void SPIClass::transfer(uint8* buffer, size_t numberBytes) {
    vector<NymphType*> values;
    values.push_back(new NymphString(WifiStation.getMAC().c_str()));
    values.push_back(new NymphString(std::string((char*) buffer,
numberBytes)));
    NymphType* returnValue = 0;
    std::string result;
    if (!NymphRemoteServer::callMethod(StationClass::handle, "writeSPI",
values, returnValue, result)) {
        std::cout << "Error calling remote method: " << result <<
std::endl;
        NymphRemoteServer::disconnect(StationClass::handle, result);
        NymphRemoteServer::shutdown();
        return;
    }

    if (returnValue->type() != NYMPH_BOOL) {
        std::cout << "Return value wasn't a boolean. Type: " <<
returnValue->type() << std::endl;
        NymphRemoteServer::disconnect(StationClass::handle, result);
        NymphRemoteServer::shutdown();
        return;
    }
}

SPIClass SPI;
```

To write on the SPI bus, we again just call the RPC method on the server, getting the response once that call has been completed, as shown in the following code. For simplicity's sake, no SPI read functionality is implemented in this example project:

```
void TwoWire::pins(int sda, int scl) { }
void TwoWire::begin() { }
```

```
  void TwoWire::beginTransmission(int address) { i2cAddress = address; }
  size_t TwoWire::write(uint8_t data) {
     vector<NymphType*> values;
     values.push_back(new NymphString(WifiStation.getMAC().c_str()));
     values.push_back(new NymphSint32(i2cAddress));
     values.push_back(new NymphString(std::to_string(data)));
     NymphType* returnValue = 0;
     std::string result;
     if (!NymphRemoteServer::callMethod(StationClass::handle, "writeI2C",
values, returnValue, result)) {
          std::cout << "Error calling remote method: " << result <<
std::endl;
          NymphRemoteServer::disconnect(StationClass::handle, result);
          NymphRemoteServer::shutdown();
          return 0;
     }

     if (returnValue->type() != NYMPH_BOOL) {
          std::cout << "Return value wasn't a boolean. Type: " <<
returnValue->type() << std::endl;
          NymphRemoteServer::disconnect(StationClass::handle, result);
          NymphRemoteServer::shutdown();
          return 0;
     }

     return 1;
  }


  size_t TwoWire::write(int data) {
     vector<NymphType*> values;
     values.push_back(new NymphString(WifiStation.getMAC().c_str()));
     values.push_back(new NymphSint32(i2cAddress));
     values.push_back(new NymphString(std::to_string(data)));
     NymphType* returnValue = 0;
     std::string result;
     if (!NymphRemoteServer::callMethod(StationClass::handle, "writeI2C",
values, returnValue, result)) {
          std::cout << "Error calling remote method: " << result <<
std::endl;
          NymphRemoteServer::disconnect(StationClass::handle, result);
          NymphRemoteServer::shutdown();
          return 0;
     }

     if (returnValue->type() != NYMPH_BOOL) {
          std::cout << "Return value wasn't a boolean. Type: " <<
returnValue->type() << std::endl;
```

```
            NymphRemoteServer::disconnect(StationClass::handle, result);
            NymphRemoteServer::shutdown();
            return 0;
        }

    return 1;
}
```

After some stub methods in the I2C class, we find the `write` methods. These are essentially the same methods, calling the `remote` method to send the data to the simulated I2C bus on the server, as shown in the following code:

```
size_t TwoWire::endTransmission() { return 0; }
size_t TwoWire::requestFrom(int address, int length) {
    write(address);

    vector<NymphType*> values;
    values.push_back(new NymphString(WifiStation.getMAC().c_str()));
    values.push_back(new NymphSint32(address));
    values.push_back(new NymphSint32(length));
    NymphType* returnValue = 0;
    std::string result;
    if (!NymphRemoteServer::callMethod(StationClass::handle, "readI2C",
values, returnValue, result)) {
            std::cout << "Error calling remote method: " << result <<
std::endl;
            NymphRemoteServer::disconnect(StationClass::handle, result);
            NymphRemoteServer::shutdown();
            exit(1);
    }

    if (returnValue->type() != NYMPH_STRING) {
            std::cout << "Return value wasn't a string. Type: " <<
returnValue->type() << std::endl;
            NymphRemoteServer::disconnect(StationClass::handle, result);
            NymphRemoteServer::shutdown();
            exit(1);
    }

    rxBufferIndex = 0;
    buffer = ((NymphString*) returnValue)->getValue();
    return buffer.size();
}
```

To read from the I2C bus, we use the preceding method, first writing the I2C address we wish to write to, then calling the RPC function to read from the simulated I2C device that should have data available to read, as shown in the following code:

```
int TwoWire::available() {
    return buffer.length() - rxBufferIndex;
}


int TwoWire::read() {
    int value = -1;
    if (rxBufferIndex < buffer.length()) {
        value = buffer.at(rxBufferIndex);
        ++rxBufferIndex;
    }

    return value;
}

TwoWire Wire;
```

The I2C read functionality is essentially the same as it was in the original implementation, as both just interact with a local buffer, as shown in the following code:

```
String system_get_sdk_version() { return "SIM_0.1"; }
int system_get_free_heap_size() { return 20000; }
int system_get_cpu_freq() { return 1200000; }
int system_get_chip_id() { return 42; }
int spi_flash_get_id() { return 42; }

void SystemClass::restart() { }

SystemClass System;
```

Here are more stub implementations that could be of use for specific test scenarios:

```
void pinMode(uint16_t pin, uint8_t mode) { }
void digitalWrite(uint16_t pin, uint8_t val) { }
uint8_t digitalRead(uint16_t pin) { return 1; }

uint16_t analogRead(uint16_t pin) { return 1000; }
```

We left these functions unimplemented, but they could implement GPIO and ADC pins that are connected to virtual GPIO pins on the server side, to control devices and record data that does not use a UART, SPI, or I2C interface. The same would work for PWM functionality.

Moving on to the final part in this source file, we implement the main function as follows:

```
int main() {
    // Start the firmware image.
    init();

    return 0;
}
```

Just like the Sming version of the entry point, we call the global `init()` function in the custom firmware code, which serves as the entrance point there. Conceivably, we could also perform various types of initialization in this main function if we needed to.

The filesystem class methods are implemented using a mixture of C-style file access and C++17-style filesystem operations, as shown in the following code:

```
#include "FileSystem.h"
#include "../Wiring/WString.h"

#include <filesystem>
#include <iostream>
#include <fstream>

namespace fs = std::filesystem;


file_t fileOpen(const String& name, FileOpenFlags flags) {
    file_t res;

    if ((flags & eFO_CreateNewAlways) == eFO_CreateNewAlways) {
        if (fileExist(name)) {
            fileDelete(name);
        }

        flags = (FileOpenFlags)((int)flags & ~eFO_Truncate);
    }

    res = std::fopen(name.c_str(), "r+b");
    return res;
}
```

To simplify this method, we ignore the provided flags and always open the file in full read and write mode (one would only implement the full set of flags if it contributed to the integration test in some way). Let's look at the following code:

```
void fileClose(file_t file) {
    std::fclose(file);
}

size_t fileWrite(file_t file, const void* data, size_t size) {
    int res = std::fwrite((void*) data, size, size, file);
    return res;
}

size_t fileRead(file_t file, void* data, size_t size) {
    int res = std::fread(data, size, size, file);
    return res;
}

int fileSeek(file_t file, int offset, SeekOriginFlags origin) {
    return std::fseek(file, offset, origin);
}

bool fileIsEOF(file_t file) {
    return true;
}

int32_t fileTell(file_t file) {
    return 0;
}

int fileFlush(file_t file) {
    return 0;
}

void fileDelete(const String& name) {
    fs::remove(name.c_str());
}

void fileDelete(file_t file) {
    //
}

bool fileExist(const String& name) {
    std::error_code ec;
    bool ret = fs::is_regular_file(name.c_str(), ec);
    return ret;
}
```

```
int fileLastError(file_t fd) {
    return 0;
}

void fileClearLastError(file_t fd) {
    //
}

void fileSetContent(const String& fileName, const String& content) {
    fileSetContent(fileName, content.c_str());
}

void fileSetContent(const String& fileName, const char* content) {
    file_t file = fileOpen(fileName.c_str(), eFO_CreateNewAlways |
eFO_WriteOnly);
    fileWrite(file, content, strlen(content));
    fileClose(file);
}

uint32_t fileGetSize(const String& fileName) {
    int size = 0;
    try {
        size = fs::file_size(fileName.c_str());
    }
    catch (fs::filesystem_error& e) {
        std::cout << e.what() << std::endl;
    }

    return size;
}

void fileRename(const String& oldName, const String& newName) {
    try {
        fs::rename(oldName.c_str(), newName.c_str());
    }
    catch (fs::filesystem_error& e) {
        std::cout << e.what() << std::endl;
    }
}

Vector<String> fileList() {
    Vector<String> result;
    return result;
}

String fileGetContent(const String& fileName) {
    std::ifstream ifs(fileName.c_str(), std::ios::in | std::ios::binary |
std::ios::ate);
```

```cpp
        std::ifstream::pos_type fileSize = ifs.tellg();
        ifs.seekg(0, std::ios::beg);
        std::vector<char> bytes(fileSize);
        ifs.read(bytes.data(), fileSize);

        return String(bytes.data(), fileSize);
    }

    int fileGetContent(const String& fileName, char* buffer, int bufSize) {
        if (buffer == NULL || bufSize == 0) { return 0; }
        *buffer = 0;

        std::ifstream ifs(fileName.c_str(), std::ios::in | std::ios::binary |
std::ios::ate);

        std::ifstream::pos_type fileSize = ifs.tellg();
        if (fileSize <= 0 || bufSize <= fileSize) {
            return 0;
        }

        buffer[fileSize] = 0;
        ifs.seekg(0, std::ios::beg);
        ifs.read(buffer, fileSize);
        ifs.close();

        return (int) fileSize;
    }
```

These are all standard file operations, so they don't require a lot of explanation. The main reason why both C-style and C++17-style file access are used is because the original API methods assume a C-style way of handling things, and also because of the underlying, C-based SDK functionality.

We would map all API methods to a pure C++17 filesystem functionality, but this would be an additional time investment without any obvious payoff.

The timer functionality uses POCO's `Timer` class in Sming's `SimpleTimer` class to implement an equivalent functionality, as shown in the following code:

```cpp
#include "Poco/Timer.h"
#include <iostream>


typedef void (*os_timer_func_t)(void* timer_arg);

class SimpleTimer {
public:
```

```
    SimpleTimer() : timer(0) {
        cb = new Poco::TimerCallback<SimpleTimer>(*this,
&SimpleTimer::onTimer);
    }

    ~SimpleTimer() {
        stop();
        delete cb;
        if (timer) {
            delete timer;
        }
    }

    __forceinline void startMs(uint32_t milliseconds, bool repeating =
false) {
        stop();
        if (repeating) {
            timer = new Poco::Timer(milliseconds, 0);
        }
        else {
            timer = new Poco::Timer(milliseconds, milliseconds);
        }

        timer->start(*cb);
    }

    __forceinline void startUs(uint32_t microseconds, bool repeating =
false) {
        stop();
        uint32_t milliseconds = microseconds / 1000;
        if (repeating) {
            timer = new Poco::Timer(milliseconds, 0);
        }
        else {
            timer = new Poco::Timer(milliseconds, milliseconds);
        }

        timer->start(*cb);
    }

    __forceinline void stop() {
        timer->stop();
        delete timer;
        timer = 0;
    }

    void setCallback(os_timer_func_t callback, void* arg = nullptr)    {
        stop();
```

```
                userCb = callback;
                userCbArg = arg;
        }

    private:
        void onTimer(Poco::Timer &timer) {
                userCb(userCbArg);
        }

        Poco::Timer* timer;
        Poco::TimerCallback<SimpleTimer>* cb;
        os_timer_func_t userCb;
        void* userCbArg;
    };
```

Finally, for the reimplementation of the `Clock` class, we use STL's chrono functionality, as shown in the following code:

```
#include "Clock.h"
 #include <chrono>

 unsigned long millis() {
     unsigned long now =
std::chrono::duration_cast<std::chrono::milliseconds>(std::chrono::system_c
lock::now().time_since_epoch()).count();
     return now;
 }

 unsigned long micros() {
     unsigned long now =
std::chrono::duration_cast<std::chrono::microseconds>(std::chrono::system_c
lock::now().time_since_epoch()).count();
     return now;
 }

 void delay(uint32_t milliseconds) {
     //
 }

 void delayMicroseconds(uint32_t time) {    //
 }
```

Here, we leave the `delay` functions unimplemented since we don't need them at this point.

Makefile

The Makefile for this part of the project looks like this:

```
GPP = g++
GCC = gcc
MAKEDIR = mkdir -p
RM = rm
AR = ar
ROOT = test/node
OUTPUT = bmac_esp8266
OUTLIB = lib$(OUTPUT).a
INCLUDE = -I $(ROOT)/ \
                -I $(ROOT)/SmingCore/ \
                -I $(ROOT)/SmingCore/network \
                -I $(ROOT)/SmingCore/network/Http \
                -I $(ROOT)/SmingCore/network/Http/Websocket \
                -I $(ROOT)/SmingCore/network/libmosquitto \
                -I $(ROOT)/SmingCore/network/libmosquitto/cpp \
                -I $(ROOT)/SmingCore/wiring \
                -I $(ROOT)/Libraries/BME280 \
                -I $(ROOT)/esp8266/app
FLAGS := $(INCLUDE) -g3 -U__STRICT_ANSI__
LIB := -L$(ROOT)/lib -l$(OUTPUT) -lmosquittopp -lmosquitto  -lnymphrpc \
          -lPocoNet -lPocoUtil -lPocoFoundation -lPocoJSON -lstdc++fs \
          -lssl -lcrypto
LIB_WIN :=   -lws2_32
ifeq ($(OS),Windows_NT)
   LIB := $(LIB) $(LIB_WIN)
endif
include ./esp8266/version
include ./Makefile-user.mk
CPPFLAGS := $(FLAGS) -DVERSION="\"$(VERSION)\"" $(USER_CFLAGS) -std=c++17
-Wl,--gc-sections
CFLAGS := -g3
CPP_SOURCES := $(wildcard $(ROOT)/SmingCore/*.cpp) \
                $(wildcard $(ROOT)/SmingCore/network/*.cpp) \
                $(wildcard $(ROOT)/SmingCore/network/Http/*.cpp) \
                $(wildcard $(ROOT)/SmingCore/wiring/*.cpp) \
                $(wildcard $(ROOT)/Libraries/BME280/*.cpp)
FW_SOURCES := $(wildcard esp8266/app/*.cpp)
CPP_OBJECTS := $(addprefix $(ROOT)/obj/,$(notdir $(CPP_SOURCES:.cpp=.o)))
FW_OBJECTS := $(addprefix $(ROOT)/obj/,$(notdir $(FW_SOURCES:.cpp=.o)))
all: makedir $(FW_OBJECTS) $(CPP_OBJECTS) $(ROOT)/lib/$(OUTLIB)
$(ROOT)/bin/$(OUTPUT)
$(ROOT)/obj/%.o: %.cpp
    $(GPP) -c -o $@ $< $(CPPFLAGS)
$(ROOT)/obj/%.o: %.c
```

```
        $(GCC) -c -o $@ $< $(CFLAGS)
$(ROOT)/lib/$(OUTLIB): $(CPP_OBJECTS)
    -rm -f $@
    $(AR) rcs $@ $^
$(ROOT)/bin/$(OUTPUT):
    -rm -f $@
    $(GPP) -o $@ $(CPPFLAGS) $(FW_SOURCES) $(LIB)
makedir:
    $(MAKEDIR) $(ROOT)/bin
    $(MAKEDIR) $(ROOT)/lib
    $(MAKEDIR) $(ROOT)/obj
    $(MAKEDIR) $(ROOT)/obj/$(ROOT)/SmingCore/network
    $(MAKEDIR) $(ROOT)/obj/$(ROOT)/SmingCore/wiring
    $(MAKEDIR) $(ROOT)/obj/$(ROOT)/Libraries/BME280
    $(MAKEDIR) $(ROOT)/obj/esp8266/app
clean:
    $(RM) $(CPP_OBJECTS) $(FW_OBJECTS)
```

The main thing to note about this Makefile is that it gathers source files from two different source folders, both for the test API and for the firmware source. The former source files are first compiled to object files, which are assembled into an archive. The firmware source is used directly along with this test framework library, though we also have the firmware object files available if we need them.

The reason for creating an archive of the test API before linking it has to do with the way that the linker finds symbols. By using the AR tool, it will create an index of all symbols in the object files inside the archive, ensuring that we will not get any linker errors. Especially for large projects this is often a requirement to have the object files successfully link into a binary.

Compiling to object files first is also helpful with larger projects, as Make will ensure that only files that have actually changed will be recompiled, which can really speed up development time. Since the target firmware source for this project is fairly minimal, we can compile directly from the source files here.

We also include two more Makefiles from this one. The first includes the version number of the firmware source we are compiling with, which is useful since it'll ensure that the produced node binary will report the exact same version as the version installed on an ESP8266 module would. This making validation of a specific firmware version much easier.

The second is the Makefile with user-definable settings, copied *verbatim* from the firmware project Makefile, but with just the variables we need for the firmware source to compile and work, as shown in the following code:

```
WIFI_SSID = MyWi-FiNetwork
WIFI_PWD = MyWi-FiPassword

MQTT_HOST = localhost
# For SSL support, uncomment the following line or compile with this
parameter.
#ENABLE_SSL=1
# MQTT SSL port (for example):
ifdef ENABLE_SSL
MQTT_PORT = 8883
else
MQTT_PORT = 1883
endif

# Uncomment if password authentication is used.
# USE_MQTT_PASSWORD=1
# MQTT username & password (if needed):
# MQTT_USERNAME = esp8266
# MQTT_PWD = ESPassword

# MQTT topic prefix: added to all MQTT subscriptions and publications.
# Can be left empty, but must be defined.
# If not left empty, should end with a '/' to avoid merging with topic
names.
MQTT_PREFIX =

# OTA (update) URL. Only change the host name (and port).
OTA_URL = http://ota.host.net/ota.php?uid=

USER_CFLAGS := $(USER_CFLAGS) -DWIFI_SSID="\"$(WIFI_SSID)"\"
USER_CFLAGS := $(USER_CFLAGS) -DWIFI_PWD="\"$(WIFI_PWD)"\"
USER_CFLAGS := $(USER_CFLAGS) -DMQTT_HOST="\"$(MQTT_HOST)"\"
USER_CFLAGS := $(USER_CFLAGS) -DMQTT_PORT="$(MQTT_PORT)"
USER_CFLAGS := $(USER_CFLAGS) -DMQTT_USERNAME="\"$(MQTT_USERNAME)"\"
USER_CFLAGS := $(USER_CFLAGS) -DOTA_URL="\"$(OTA_URL)"\"
USER_CFLAGS := $(USER_CFLAGS) -DMQTT_PWD="\"$(MQTT_PWD)"\"
ifdef USE_MQTT_PASSWORD
USER_CFLAGS := $(USER_CFLAGS) -
DUSE_MQTT_PASSWORD="\"$(USE_MQTT_PASSWORD)"\"
endif
SER_CFLAGS := $(USER_CFLAGS) -DMQTT_PREFIX="\"$(MQTT_PREFIX)"\"
```

Including this Makefile sets all of these defines to be passed to the compiler. These are all preprocessor statements that are used to set strings or to change which parts of the code will be compiled, such as the SSL code.

However, for simplicity's sake, we aren't implementing SSL functionality for this example project.

Building the project

For the server side, we have the following library dependencies:

- NymphRPC
- POCO

For the node, we have the following dependencies:

- NymphRPC
- POCO
- Mosquitto

The NymphRPC library (described at the beginning of this section) is compiled according to the project's instructions and installed in a place where the linker can find it. The POCO libraries are installed using the system's package manager (Linux, BSD, or MSYS2) or by hand.

For the Mosquitto library dependency, we can compile the `libmosquitto` and `libmosquittopp` library files using the project's library version by using the Makefile in the `test/SmingCore/network/libmosquitto` folder. Again you should install the resulting library files where the linker can find them.

When not using MinGW, one can also use the generally available version via the OS's package manager or similar.

After these steps, we can compile the server and client using the following command-line command from the root of the project:

```
make
```

This should compile both the server and node projects using the top-level Makefile, resulting in an executable for each in their respective `bin/` folder. You should ensure that the executable name and path in the server's `Node` class match that of the node executable's location.

We should now be able to run the project and start to collect test results. The project includes a stripped version of the ESP8266-based BMAC firmware, which we'll be covering in detail in Chapter 9, *Example - Building Monitoring and Control*. Please refer to that chapter to understand how to communicate with the simulated nodes via MQTT, how to turn on modules inside the firmware and how to interpret the data sent over MQTT by the modules.

After setting things up as described in that chapter - requiring at the least an MQTT broker and a suitable MQTT client - and turning on the BME280 module in the simulated node, we expect it to start sending over MQTT the temperature, humidity and air pressure values we set for the room the simulated node is in.

Summary

In this chapter, we looked at how to effectively develop for MCU-based targets in a way that allows us to test them without expensive and long-winded development cycles. We learned how to implement an integration environment that allows us to debug MCU-based applications from the comfort of a desktop OS and the tools it provides.

The reader should now be able to develop integration tests for MCU-based projects and effectively use OS-based tools to profile and debug them before doing final integration work on real hardware. The reader should also be able to perform on-chip debugging, and have a feel for the relative cost of specific software implementations.

In the next chapter, we'll develop a simple infotainment system, based on an SBC platform.

8
Example - Linux-Based Infotainment System

This chapter provides an example of how to implement an infotainment system using a Linux-based **single-board computer** (**SBC**). It also shows how to connect to remote devices using Bluetooth, and how to use online streaming services. The resulting device will be able to play back audio from a variety of sources without a complex UI. In particular, we will be covering the following topics:

- Developing for a Linux-based SBC
- Using Bluetooth under Linux
- Playing back audio from a variety of sources and recording audio
- Using GPIO for both simple input and voice recognition
- Connecting to online streaming audio services

One box that does everything

Infotainment systems have become a common feature in our daily lives, starting with **in-car entertainment** (**ICE**) systems (also known as **In-Vehicle Infotainment** or **IVI**), which evolved from the basic radios and cassette players to include features such as navigation and connecting to smartphones over Bluetooth for access to one's music library, and much more. Another big feature is to provide the driver with hands-free functionality so that they can start a phone call and control the radio without having to take their eyes off the road or their hands off the steering wheel.

As smartphones became more popular, providing their users with constant access to news, weather, and entertainment, the arrival of onboard assistants that use a voice-driven interface, both on smartphones and ICEs, ultimately led to the arrival of speech-driven infotainment systems aimed at in-home use. These usually consist of a speaker and microphone, along with the required hardware for the voice-driven interface and access to the required internet-based services.

This chapter will mostly focus on this type of voice-driven infotainment system. In Chapter 10, *Developing Embedded Systems with Qt*, we will take an in-depth look at adding a graphical user interface.

The goals which we want to achieve here are the following:

- Play music from a Bluetooth source, such as a smartphone
- Play music from an online streaming service
- Play music from the local filesystem, including USB sticks
- Record an audio clip and repeat it when asked
- Control all actions with one's voice, with buttons for some actions

In the next sections, we'll look at these goals and how to accomplish them.

Hardware needed

For this project, any SBC that's capable of running Linux should work. It also needs to have the following features for a full implementation:

- An internet connection (wireless or wired) to access online content.
- Bluetooth functionality (built-in or as an add-on module) to allow the system to act as a Bluetooth speaker.
- Free GPIO input to allow for buttons to be hooked up.
- A functioning microphone input and audio output for the voice input and audio playback, respectively.
- SATA connectivity or similar for connecting storage devices like hard-drives.
- I2C bus peripheral for an I2C display.

For the example code in this chapter we only require the microphone input and audio output, along with some storage for local media files.

To the GPIO pins, we can connect a number of buttons that can be used to control the infotainment system without having to use the voice-activated system. This is convenient for situations where using the voice-activated system would be awkward, such as when pausing or muting music when taking a phone call.

Connecting the buttons will not be demonstrated in this example, but an example can be found in an earlier project in Chapter 3, *Developing for Embedded Linux and Similar Systems*. There, we used the WiringPi library to connect switches to GPIO pins and configured interrupt routines to handle changes on these switches.

One could also connect a small display to the system, if one wanted to show current information, such as the name of the current song or other relevant status information. Cheap displays of 16x2 characters, which can be controlled over an I2C interface, are widely available; these, along with a range of OLED and other small displays, would be suitable for this purpose thanks to their minimal hardware requirements.

In Chapter 3, *Developing for Embedded Linux and Similar Systems*, we had a brief look at what kind of hardware one might want to use for an infotainment system such as this, along with a number of possible user interfaces and storage options. What the right hardware configuration is, of course, depends on one's requirements. If one wants to store a lot of music locally for playback, having a large SATA hard drive connected to the system would be highly convenient.

For the example in this chapter, however, we will make no such assumptions, acting more as an easily extensible starting point. The hardware requirements are therefore very minimal, beyond the obvious need for a microphone and an audio output.

Software requirements

For this project, we are assuming that Linux has been installed on the target SBC, and that the drivers for the hardware functionality, such as the microphone and audio output, have been installed and configured.

Since we use the Qt framework for this project, all dependencies there should be met as well. This means that the shared libraries should be present on the system on which the resulting binary for the project will be run. The Qt framework can be obtained via the package manager of the OS, or via the Qt website at http://qt.io/.

In `Chapter 10`, *Developing Embedded Systems with Qt*, we will look at developing on embedded platforms with Qt in more detail. This chapter will briefly touch upon the use of Qt APIs.

Depending on whether we want to compile the application directly on the SBC or on our development PC, we might have to install the compiler toolchain and further dependencies on the SBC, or the cross-compiling toolchain for Linux on the target SBC (ARM, x86, or other architecture). In `Chapter 6`, *Testing OS-Based Applications*, we looked at cross-compiling for SBC systems, as well as testing the system locally.

As the example project in this chapter doesn't require any special hardware, it can be compiled directly on any system that's supported by the Qt framework. This is the recommended way to test out the code prior to deploying it on the SBC.

Bluetooth audio sources and sinks

Bluetooth is unfortunately a technology that, despite being ubiquitous, suffers from its proprietary nature. As a result, support for the full range of Bluetooth functionality (in the form of profiles) is lacking. The profile that we are interested in for this project is called **Advanced Audio Distribution Profile** (**A2DP**). This is the profile used by everything from Bluetooth headphones to Bluetooth speakers in order to stream audio.

Any device that implements A2DP can stream audio to an A2DP receiver or can themselves act as a receiver (depending on the BT stack implementation). Theoretically, this would allow someone to connect with a smartphone or similar device to our infotainment system and play back music on it, as they would with a standalone Bluetooth speaker.

A receiver in the A2DP profile is an A2DP sink, whereas the other side is the A2DP source. A Bluetooth headphone or speaker device would always be a sink device as they can only consume an audio stream. A PC, SBC, or similar multi-purpose device can be configured to act as either a sink or a source.

As mentioned earlier, the complications surrounding the implementation of a full Bluetooth stack on mainstream OSes has led to lackluster support for anything more than the basic serial communication functionality of Bluetooth.

While FreeBSD, macOS, Windows, and Android all have Bluetooth stacks, they are limited in the number of Bluetooth adapters they can support (just one on Windows, and only USB adapters), the profiles they support (FreeBSD is data-transfer-only), and configurability (Android is essentially only targeted at smartphones).

For Windows 10, A2DP profile support has currently regressed from being functional in Windows 7 to not being functional as of the time of writing due to changes to its Bluetooth stack. With macOS, its Bluetooth stack added A2DP support with version 10.5 of the OS (Leopard, in 2007) and should function.

The BlueZ Bluetooth stack that has become the official Bluetooth stack for Linux was originally developed by Qualcomm and is now included with official Linux kernel distributions. It's one of the most full-featured Bluetooth stacks.

With the move from BlueZ version 4 to 5, ALSA sound API support was dropped, and instead moved to the PulseAudio audio system, along with the renaming of the old APIs. This means that applications and code implemented using the old (version 4) API no longer work. Unfortunately a lot of the example code and tutorials one finds online still targets the version 4, which is something to be aware of, as they work very differently.

BlueZ is configured via the D-Bus Linux system IPC (interprocess communication) system, or by editing configuration files directly. Actually implementing BlueZ support in an application like that in this chapter's project to configure it programmatically would be fairly complicated however, due to the sheer scope of the APIs, as well the limitations in setting configuration options that go beyond just the Bluetooth stack and require access to text-based configuration files. The application would therefore have to run with the correct permissions to access certain properties and files, editing the latter directly or performing those steps manually.

Another complication for the infotainment project is setting up an automatic pairing mode, as otherwise the remote device (smartphone) would be unable to actually connect to the infotainment system. This would require constant interaction with the Bluetooth stack as well, to poll it for any new devices that may have connected in the meantime.

Each new device would have to be checked to see whether it supports the A2DP source mode, in which case it would be added to the audio input for the system. One could then hook into the audio system to make use of that new input.

Due to the complexity and scope of this implementation, it was left out of the example code in this chapter. It could, however, be added to the code. SBCs such as the Raspberry Pi 3 come with a built-in Bluetooth adapter. Others can have a Bluetooth adapter added using a USB device.

Online streaming

There are a number of online streaming services which one could integrate into an infotainment system like the type which are looking at in this chapter. All of them use a similar streaming API (usually an HTTP-based REST API), which requires one to create an account with the service, using which one can obtain an application-specific token that gives one access to that API, allowing one to query it for specific artists, music tracks, albums, and so on.

Using an HTTP client, such as the one found in the Qt framework, it would be fairly easy to implement the necessary control flow. Due to the requirement of having a registered application ID for those streaming services, it was left out of the example code.

The basic sequence to stream from a REST API usually looks like this, with a simple wrapper class around the HTTP calls:

```
#include "soundFoo"
// Create a client object with your app credentials.
client = soundFoo.new('YOUR_CLIENT_ID');
// Fetch track to stream.
track = client.get("/tracks/293")
// Get the tracks streaming URL.
stream_url = client.get(track.stream_url, true);
// stream URL, allow redirects
// Print the tracks stream URL
std::cout << stream_url.location;
```

Voice-driven user interface

This project employs a user interface that is fully controllable by voice commands. For this, it implements a voice-to-text interface powered by the PocketSphinx library (see https://cmusphinx.github.io/) that uses both keyword-spotting and a grammar search in order to recognize and interpret commands given to it.

We use the default US-English language model that comes with the PocketSphinx distribution. This means that any commands spoken should be pronounced with a US-English accent in order to be accurately understood. To change this, one can load a different language model aimed at different languages and accents. Various models are available via the PocketSphinx website, and it is possible to make one's own language model with some effort.

Usage scenarios

We don't want the infotainment system to be activated every single time that the voice user interface recognizes command words when they are not intended as such. The common way to prevent this from happening is by having a keyword that activates the command interface. If no command is recognized after the keyword within a certain amount of time, the system reverts to the keyword-spotting mode.

For this example project, we use the keyword `computer`. After the system spots this keyword, we can use the following commands:

Command	Result
Play Bluetooth	Starts playing from any connected A2DP source device (unimplemented).
Stop Bluetooth	Stops playing from any Bluetooth device.
Play local	Plays the (hardcoded) local music file.
Stop local	Stops playing the local music file, if currently playing.
Play remote	Plays from an online streaming service or server (unimplemented).
Stop remote	Stops playing, if active.
Record message	Records a message. Records until a number of seconds of silence occurs.
Play message	Plays back the recorded message, if any.

Source code

This application has been implemented using the Qt framework, as a GUI application, so that we also get a graphical interface for ease of debugging. This debugging UI was designed using the Qt Designer of the Qt Creator IDE as a single UI file.

We start by creating an instance of the GUI application:

```
#include "mainwindow.h"
#include <QApplication>

int main(int argc, char *argv[]) {
    QApplication a(argc, argv);
    MainWindow w;
    w.show();
    return a.exec();
}
```

This creates an instance of the `MainWindow` class in which we have implemented the application, along with an instance of `QApplication`, which is a wrapper class used by the Qt framework.

Next, this is the `MainWindow` header:

```cpp
#include <QMainWindow>

#include <QAudioRecorder>
#include <QAudioProbe>
#include <QMediaPlayer>


namespace Ui {
    class MainWindow;
}

class MainWindow : public QMainWindow {
    Q_OBJECT
public:
    explicit MainWindow(QWidget *parent = nullptr);
    ~MainWindow();
public slots:
    void playBluetooth();
    void stopBluetooth();
    void playOnlineStream();
    void stopOnlineStream();
    void playLocalFile();
    void stopLocalFile();
    void recordMessage();
    void playMessage();
    void errorString(QString err);
    void quit();
private:
    Ui::MainWindow *ui;
    QMediaPlayer* player;
    QAudioRecorder* audioRecorder;
    QAudioProbe* audioProbe;
    qint64 silence; // Microseconds of silence recorded so far.
private slots:
    void processBuffer(QAudioBuffer);
};
```

Its implementation contains most of the core functionality, declaring the audio recorder and player instances, with just the voice command processing being handled in a separate class:

```
#include "mainwindow.h"
#include "ui_mainwindow.h"

#include "voiceinput.h"

#include <QThread>
#include <QMessageBox>

#include <cmath>


#define MSG_RECORD_MAX_SILENCE_US 5000000

MainWindow::MainWindow(QWidget *parent) : QMainWindow(parent),
    ui(new Ui::MainWindow) {
    ui->setupUi(this);
    // Set up menu connections.
    connect(ui->actionQuit, SIGNAL(triggered()), this, SLOT(quit()));
    // Set up UI connections.
    connect(ui->playBluetoothButton, SIGNAL(pressed), this,
SLOT(playBluetooth));
    connect(ui->stopBluetoothButton, SIGNAL(pressed), this,
SLOT(stopBluetooth));
    connect(ui->playLocalAudioButton, SIGNAL(pressed), this,
SLOT(playLocalFile));
    connect(ui->stopLocalAudioButton, SIGNAL(pressed), this,
SLOT(stopLocalFile));
    connect(ui->playOnlineStreamButton, SIGNAL(pressed), this,
SLOT(playOnlineStream));
    connect(ui->stopOnlineStreamButton, SIGNAL(pressed), this,
SLOT(stopOnlineStream));
    connect(ui->recordMessageButton, SIGNAL(pressed), this,
SLOT(recordMessage));
    connect(ui->playBackMessage, SIGNAL(pressed), this, SLOT(playMessage));
    // Defaults
    silence = 0;
    // Create the audio interface instances.
    player = new QMediaPlayer(this);
    audioRecorder = new QAudioRecorder(this);
    audioProbe = new QAudioProbe(this);
    // Configure the audio recorder.
    QAudioEncoderSettings audioSettings;
    audioSettings.setCodec("audio/amr");
    audioSettings.setQuality(QMultimedia::HighQuality);
    audioRecorder->setEncodingSettings(audioSettings);
```

```
audioRecorder->setOutputLocation(QUrl::fromLocalFile("message/last_message.
amr"));
    // Configure audio probe.
    connect(audioProbe, SIGNAL(audioBufferProbed(QAudioBuffer)), this,
SLOT(processBuffer(QAudioBuffer)));
    audioProbe->setSource(audioRecorder);
    // Start the voice interface in its own thread and set up the
connections.
    QThread* thread = new QThread;
    VoiceInput* vi = new VoiceInput();
    vi->moveToThread(thread);
    connect(thread, SIGNAL(started()), vi, SLOT(run()));
    connect(vi, SIGNAL(finished()), thread, SLOT(quit()));
    connect(vi, SIGNAL(finished()), vi, SLOT(deleteLater()));
    connect(thread, SIGNAL(finished()), thread, SLOT(deleteLater()));
    connect(vi, SIGNAL(error(QString)), this, SLOT(errorString(QString)));
    connect(vi, SIGNAL(playBluetooth), this, SLOT(playBluetooth));
    connect(vi, SIGNAL(stopBluetooth), this, SLOT(stopBluetooth));
    connect(vi, SIGNAL(playLocal), this, SLOT(playLocalFile));
    connect(vi, SIGNAL(stopLocal), this, SLOT(stopLocalFile));
    connect(vi, SIGNAL(playRemote), this, SLOT(playOnlineStream));
    connect(vi, SIGNAL(stopRemote), this, SLOT(stopOnlineStream));
    connect(vi, SIGNAL(recordMessage), this, SLOT(recordMessage));
    connect(vi, SIGNAL(playMessage), this, SLOT(playMessage));
    thread->start();
}
```

In the constructor, we set up all of the UI connections for the buttons in the GUI window that allow us to trigger the application's functionality without having to use the voice user interface. This is useful for testing purposes.

In addition, we create an instance of the audio recorder and media player, along with an audio probe that is linked with the audio recorder, so that we can look at the audio samples it's recording and act on them.

Finally, we create an instance of the voice input interface class and push it onto its own thread before starting it. We connect its signals to specific commands, and other events to their respective slots:

```
MainWindow::~MainWindow() {
    delete ui;
}


void MainWindow::playBluetooth() {
    // Use the link with the BlueZ Bluetooth stack in the Linux kernel to
    // configure it to act as an A2DP sink for smartphones to connect to.
```

```
    }


    // --- STOP BLUETOOTH ---
    void MainWindow::stopBluetooth() {
        //
    }
```

As mentioned in the section on Bluetooth technology, we have left the Bluetooth functionality unimplemented for the reasons explained in that section.

```
    void MainWindow::playOnlineStream() {
        // Connect to remote streaming service's API and start streaming.
    }


    void MainWindow::stopOnlineStream() {
        // Stop streaming from remote service.
    }
```

The same is true for the online streaming functionality. See the section on online streaming earlier in this chapter for details on how to implement this functionality.

```
    void MainWindow::playLocalFile() {
        player->setMedia(QUrl::fromLocalFile("music/coolsong.mp3"));
        player->setVolume(50);
        player->play();
    }


    void MainWindow::stopLocalFile() {
        player->stop();
    }
```

To play a local file, we expect to find an MP3 file present in the hardcoded path. This could, however, also play all of the music in a specific folder with just a few modifications by reading in the filenames and playing them back one by one.

```
    void MainWindow::recordMessage() {
        audioRecorder->record();
    }


    void MainWindow::playMessage() {
        player->setMedia(QUrl::fromLocalFile("message/last_message.arm"));
        player->setVolume(50);
        player->play();
    }
```

In the constructor, we configured the recorder to record to a file in a sub-folder called `message`. This will be overwritten if a new recording is made, allowing one to leave a message that can be played back later. The optional display or another accessory could be used to indicate when a new recording has been made and hasn't been listened to yet:

```
void MainWindow::processBuffer(QAudioBuffer buffer) {
    const quint16 *data = buffer.constData<quint16>();
    // Get RMS of buffer, if silence, add its duration to the counter.
    int samples = buffer.sampleCount();
    double sumsquared = 0;
    for (int i = 0; i < samples; i++) {
        sumsquared += data[i] * data[i];
    }
    double rms = sqrt((double(1) / samples)*(sumsquared));
    if (rms <= 100) {
        silence += buffer.duration();
    }
    if (silence >= MSG_RECORD_MAX_SILENCE_US) {
        silence = 0;
        audioRecorder->stop();
    }
}
```

This method is called by our audio probe whenever the recorder is active. In this function, we calculate the **root-mean square** (**RMS**) value of the audio buffer to determine whether it's filled with silence. Here, silence is relative and might have to be adjusted depending on the recording environment.

After five seconds of silence have been detected, the recording of the message is stopped:

```
void MainWindow::errorString(QString err) {
    QMessageBox::critical(this, tr("Error"), err);
}


void MainWindow::quit() {
    exit(0);
}
```

The remaining methods handle the reporting of error messages that may be emitted elsewhere in the application, as well as terminating the application.

The `VoiceInput` class header defines the functionality for the voice input interface:

```
#include <QObject>
#include <QAudioInput>
```

```
extern "C" {
#include "pocketsphinx.h"
}

class VoiceInput : public QObject {
    Q_OBJECT
    QAudioInput* audioInput;
    QIODevice* audioDevice;
    bool state;
public:
    explicit VoiceInput(QObject *parent = nullptr);
    bool checkState() { return state; }
signals:
    void playBluetooth();
    void stopBluetooth();
    void playLocal();
    void stopLocal();
    void playRemote();
    void stopRemote();
    void recordMessage();
    void playMessage();
    void error(QString err);
public slots:
    void run();
};
```

As PocketSphinx is a C library, we have to make sure that it is used with C-style linkage. Beyond this, we create the class members for the audio input and related IO device that the voice input will use.

Next, the class definition:

```
#include <QDebug>
#include <QThread>

#include "voiceinput.h"

extern "C" {
#include <sphinxbase/err.h>
#include <sphinxbase/ad.h>
}


VoiceInput::VoiceInput(QObject *parent) : QObject(parent) {
    //
}
```

The constructor doesn't do anything special, as the next method does all of the initializing and setting up of the main loop:

```
void VoiceInput::run() {
    const int32 buffsize = 2048;
    int16 adbuf[buffsize];
    uint8 utt_started, in_speech;
    uint32 k = 0;
    char const* hyp;
    static ps_decoder_t *ps;
    state = true;
    QAudioFormat format;
    format.setSampleRate(16000);
    format.setChannelCount(1);
    format.setSampleSize(16);
    format.setCodec("audio/pcm");
    format.setByteOrder(QAudioFormat::LittleEndian);
    format.setSampleType(QAudioFormat::UnSignedInt);
    // Check that the audio device supports this format.
    QAudioDeviceInfo info = QAudioDeviceInfo::defaultInputDevice();
    if (!info.isFormatSupported(format)) {
        qWarning() << "Default format not supported, aborting.";
        state = false;
        return;
    }
    audioInput = new QAudioInput(format, this);
    audioInput->setBufferSize(buffsize * 2);
    audioDevice = audioInput->start();

    if (ps_start_utt(ps) < 0) {
        E_FATAL("Failed to start utterance\n");
    }
    utt_started = FALSE;
    E_INFO("Ready....\n");
```

The first part of this method sets up the audio interface, configuring it to record using the audio format settings PocketSphinx requires: mono, little-endian, 16-bit signed PCM audio at 16,000 Hertz. After checking that the audio input supports this format, we create a new audio input instance:

```
    const char* keyfile = "COMPUTER/3.16227766016838e-13/\n";
    if (ps_set_kws(ps, "keyword_search", keyfile) != 0) {
        return;
    }
    if (ps_set_search(ps, "keyword_search") != 0) {
        return;
    }
    const char* gramfile = "grammar asr;\
```

```
            \
            public <rule> = <action> [<preposition>] [<objects>]
    [<preposition>] [<objects>];\
            \
            <action> = STOP | PLAY | RECORD;\
            \
            <objects> = BLUETOOTH | LOCAL | REMOTE | MESSAGE;\
            \
            <preposition> = FROM | TO;";
        ps_set_jsgf_string(ps, "jsgf", gramfile);
```

Next, we set up the keyword-spotting and JSGF grammar file that will be used during the processing of the audio sample. With the first `ps_set_search()` function call, we start the keyword-spotting search. The following loop will keep processing samples until the utterance `computer` is detected:

```
bool kws = true;
for (;;) {
    if ((k = audioDevice->read((char*) &adbuf, 4096))) {
        E_FATAL("Failed to read audio.\n");
    }
    ps_process_raw(ps, adbuf, k, FALSE, FALSE);
    in_speech = ps_get_in_speech(ps);
    if (in_speech && !utt_started) {
        utt_started = TRUE;
        E_INFO("Listening...\n");
    }
```

Each cycle, we read in another buffer worth of audio samples, to then have PocketSphinx process these samples. It also does silence detection for us to determine whether someone has started speaking into the microphone. If someone is speaking but we haven't started interpreting it yet, we start a new utterance:

```
        if (!in_speech && utt_started) {
            ps_end_utt(ps);
            hyp = ps_get_hyp(ps, nullptr);
            if (hyp != nullptr) {
                // We have a hypothesis.
                if (kws && strstr(hyp, "computer") != nullptr) {
                    if (ps_set_search(ps, "jsgf") != 0) {
                        E_FATAL("ERROR: Cannot switch to jsgf mode.\n");
                    }
                    kws = false;
                    E_INFO("Switched to jsgf mode \n");
                    E_INFO("Mode: %s\n", ps_get_search(ps));
                }
                else if (!kws) {
```

```
                if (hyp != nullptr) {
                    // Check each action.
                    if (strncmp(hyp, "play bluetooth", 14) == 0) {
                        emit playBluetooth();
                    }
                    else if (strncmp(hyp, "stop bluetooth", 14) == 0) {
                        emit stopBluetooth();
                    }
                    else if (strncmp(hyp, "play local", 10) == 0) {
                        emit playLocal();
                    }
                    else if (strncmp(hyp, "stop local", 10) == 0) {
                        emit stopLocal();
                    }
                    else if (strncmp(hyp, "play remote", 11) == 0) {
                        emit stopBluetooth();
                    }
                    else if (strncmp(hyp, "stop remote", 11) == 0) {
                        emit stopBluetooth();
                    }
                    else if (strncmp(hyp, "record message", 14) == 0) {
                        emit stopBluetooth();
                    }
                    else if (strncmp(hyp, "play message", 12) == 0) {
                        emit stopBluetooth();
                    }
                }
                else {
                    if (ps_set_search(ps, "keyword_search") != 0){
                        E_FATAL("ERROR: Cannot switch to kws mode.\n");
                    }
                    kws = true;
                    E_INFO("Switched to kws mode.\n");
                }
            }
        }

        if (ps_start_utt(ps) < 0) {
            E_FATAL("Failed to start utterance\n");
        }
        utt_started = FALSE;
        E_INFO("Ready....\n");
    }
    QThread::msleep(100);
    }
}
```

The rest of the method checks whether we have a usable hypothesis we can analyze. Depending on whether we are in keyword or grammar mode, we check for the detection of the keyword in the former case and switch to grammar mode. If we're already in grammar mode, we try to narrow the utterance down to a specific command, at which point we will emit the relevant signal that will trigger the connected functionality.

A new utterance is started whenever PocketSphinx detects at least one second of silence. After executing a command, the system switches back to keyword-spotting mode.

Building the project

To build the project, the PocketSphinx project has to be built first. In the example project's source code that comes with this chapter, there are two Makefiles underneath the `sphinx` folder, one in the `pocketsphinx` folder and one in the `sphinxbase` folder. With these, the two libraries that form PocketSphinx will be built.

After this, one can build the Qt project, either from Qt Creator or from the command line, by executing the following command:

```
mkdir build
cd build
qmake ..
make
```

Extending the system

In addition to audio formats, one could also add the ability to play back videos and integrate the ability to make and respond to phone calls (using the Bluetooth API). One may want to extend the application to make it more flexible and modular, so that, for example, one could add a module that would add the voice commands and resulting actions.

Having voice output would be convenient as well, making it more aligned with the current commercial offerings. For this, one could use the text-to-speech API that's available in the Qt framework.

It would also be useful to add more *information* to the infotainment system by querying remote APIs for things such as the current weather, news updates, and maybe even running updates on a current football game. The voice-based UI could be used to set up timers and task reminders, integrate a calendar, and much more.

Finally, as can be seen in this chapter's example code, one cannot specify the name of the track that one wants to play, or a specific album or artist name. Allowing such freestyle input is incredibly useful, but comes with its own set of issues.

The main problem is the recognition rate of a voice-to-text system, especially for words it doesn't have in its dictionary. Some of us may already have had the pleasure of raising our voice in trying to make a voice-driven user interface on the phone, in the car, or on our smartphones understand a certain word.

At this point, it's still a big point of research, without a quick and easy solution. One could conceivably brute-force such recognition and get much better accuracy by using an index of local audio filenames and artists, along with other metadata, as part of the dictionary. The same could be done for a remote streaming service, through querying its API. This might add considerable latency to the recognition effort, however.

Summary

In this chapter, we looked at how one can fairly easily construct an SBC-based infotainment system, using voice-to-text to construct a voice-driven user interface. We also looked at ways that we could extend it to add even more functionality.

The reader is expected to be able to implement a similar system at this point, and to extend it to connect it to online and network-based services. The reader should also read up on the implementation of more advanced voice-driven user interfaces, the addition of text-to-speech, and the use of A2DP-based Bluetooth devices.

In the next chapter, we'll be taking a look at how to implement a building-wide monitoring and control system using microcontrollers and the local network.

9
Example - Building Monitoring and Control

The monitoring of conditions within a building, including the temperature, humidity, and CO_2 levels is becoming increasingly more common, with the goal being to adjust heating, cooling, and ventilation systems to keep the occupants of the building as comfortable as possible. In this chapter, such a system is explored and implemented. The following topics will be covered:

- Creating complex firmware for the ESP8266
- Integrating an MCU into an IP-based network
- Adding CO_2 and I2C-based sensors
- Using GPIO and PWM to control relays and DC voltage-controlled fans
- Connecting networked nodes using a central controller

Plants, rooms, and beyond

In Chapter 5, *Example - Soil Humidity Monitor with Wi-Fi*, we looked at developing firmware for the ESP8266 MCU to complement a soil humidity sensor and pump, to ensure that a connected plant would be provided with sufficient water from the water tank.

As we noted in that chapter, the firmware used is highly modular and has the highly flexible MQTT-based interface so that it can be used for a wide variety of modules. This chapter covers the system in which the firmware originated: **Building Management and Control (BMaC)**, originally developed just to monitor rooms for their temperature, humidity, and CO^2 levels, but later expanded to keep tabs on coffee machines and meeting room occupancy, and ultimately to control the air-conditioning throughout the building.

The BMaC project's current development status can be found at the author's GitHub account at `https://github.com/MayaPosch/BMaC`. The version we are covering here is as it exists at this point, with us covering how this system came to be and what it looks like today, and why.

Developmental history

The BMaC project started when sensors were to be added around an office building in order to measure temperature and other parameters, such as relative humidity. After deciding to use ESP8266 MCUs along with DHT22 temperature and humidity sensors, a simple prototype was put together, using a basic firmware written using the Sming framework.

It was found that DHT22 sensors were generally rather bulky and not very precise. The breakout boards used also had an improper resistor mounted on them, leading to the wrong temperature being reported. This sensor type also had the disadvantage of using its own one-wire protocol, instead of a standard interface method.

The DHT22 sensors got swapped out with BME280 MEMS sensors, which measure temperature, humidity, and also air pressure. A CO_2 sensor was added as well, in the form of the MH-Z19. This required the firmware to support these additional sensors too. The sensor readings would be sent as MQTT messages, with a backend service subscribing to these topics, and writing them to a time series database (InfluxDB), for viewing and analysis.

Decisions had to be made when the possibility of reading out the counters for products from the fully automatic Jura coffee machines was considered, and with it whether separate firmware would have to be developed.

Instead of separate firmware, the decision was made to use the same firmware for all ESP8266 nodes. This meant that they needed to have the functionality to somehow enable individual features and to support specific sensors and other features. This led to the development of new firmware, which allowed remote commands, sent over MQTT, to toggle feature modules on or off, along with other management features.

Along with the new firmware, a **command and control** (**C&C**) server was added, used by the individual nodes to retrieve their configuration, along with an administration application to be used to add new nodes and add or edit the node configuration.

With this framework in place, it became possible to add new features quickly. These included the addition of motion sensors, for detecting the presence of people in a room, to ultimately the controlling of air-conditioning units, as the existing centralized control in the office building was found to be inadequate.

The system as a whole can be visualized like this:

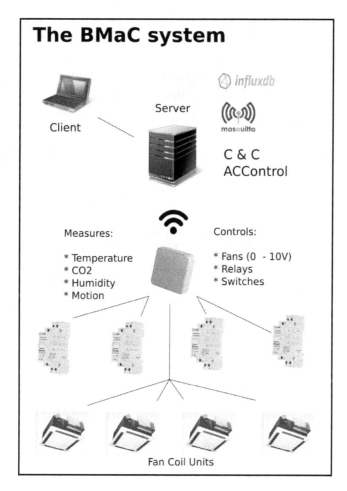

In the upcoming sections, we will be taking a detailed look at each of these aspects.

Functional modules

Here is a list of modules in this firmware:

Name	Feature	Description
THP	Temperature, Humidity, Pressure	Central class for THP sensors. Enables BME280 functionality by default.
CO_2	CO_2 value	Measures CO_2 <indexentry content="functional modules, Building Management and Control (BMaC):CO_2">values using an MH-Z19 or compatible sensor.
Jura	TopTronics EEPROM counters	Reads out the counters for various products from the EEPROM.
JuraTerm	TopTronics remote control	Allows a remote service to send TopTronics (classic, v5-style) commands to a supported coffee machine.
Motion	Motion detection	Uses an HC-SR501 PIR motion sensor or compatible to detect motion.
PWM	PWM output	Sets a pulse-width modulation output on one or more pins.
I/O	I/O expansion	Supports the MCP23008 eight-channel I/O expander module via I2C.
Switch	Persistent switch	Controls a switch that uses a latching relay or equivalent for switching.
Plant	Watering plants	Reads out an analog soil sensor to determine soil humidity, activating a pump when needed.

Firmware source

In this section, we look at the source code for the ESP8266 firmware as used with the BMaC system.

Core

The core of the firmware we already looked at in `Chapter 5`, *Example - Soil Humidity Monitor with Wi-Fi*, including the entry point, the `OtaCore` class, and the `BaseModule` class, which provide all of the functionality needed to make individual modules initialize and to allow them to be enabled and disabled using the MQTT interface.

Modules

Of the firmware modules, we already looked at the plant module in Chapter 5, *Example - Soil Humidity Monitor with Wi-Fi*. Here we will look at the remaining modules, starting with the THP module:

```
#include "base_module.h"
class THPModule {
    public:
    static bool initialize();
    static bool start();
    static bool shutdown();
};
#include "thp_module.h"
#include "dht_module.h"
#include "bme280_module.h"
bool THPModule::initialize() {
    BaseModule::registerModule(MOD_IDX_TEMPERATURE_HUMIDITY,
    THPModule::start, THPModule::shutdown);
    return true;
}
bool THPModule::start() {
    BME280Module::init();
    return true;
}
bool THPModule::shutdown() {
    BME280Module::shutdown();
    return true;
}
```

This module has the provisions to act as a generic interface to a wide variety of temperature, humidity, and air-pressure sensors. As this was not a requirement at the time, it merely acted as a pass-through for the BME280 module. It registers itself with the base module when called and calls the respective functions on the BME280 module when its own are called.

To make it more versatile, the class would be extended to allow for commands to be received—possibly over MQTT as well on its own topic—which would then enable a specific sensor module, or even a collection of them, when using separate temperature and air pressure sensors, for example.

Regardless of whether it is being used or not in this firmware, let's take a look at the DHT module so that we can compare it with the BME280 module later.

```
#include "ota_core.h"

#include <Libraries/DHTesp/DHTesp.h>

#define DHT_PIN 5 // DHT sensor: GPIO5 ('D1' on NodeMCU)


class DHTModule {
    static DHTesp* dht;
    static int dhtPin;
    static Timer dhtTimer;

public:
    static bool init();
    static bool shutdown();
    static void config(String cmd);
    static void readDHT();
};
```

Of note is that while the class is static, any variables that would take up considerable memory—such as library class instances—are defined as pointers. This forms a compromise between having the module available for easy use and going for a more complicated, fully dynamic solution. As most MCUs tend to keep as much of the program code as possible in the ROM until it is used, this should keep both SRAM and ROM usage to a minimum.

```
#include "dht_module.h"

DHTesp* DHTModule::dht = 0;
int DHTModule::dhtPin = DHT_PIN;
Timer DHTModule::dhtTimer;


bool DHTModule::init() {
    if (!OtaCore::claimPin(dhtPin)) { return false; }
    if (!dht) { dht = new DHTesp(); dht->setup(dhtPin, DHTesp::DHT22); }
    dhtTimer.initializeMs(2000, DHTModule::readDHT).start();
    return true;
}
```

To initialize the module, we ensure that we can safely use the **general-purpose input/output** (**GPIO**) pins we intend to use, create a new instance of the sensor class from the library, and set it up before creating the 2-second timer that will perform the scheduled sensor read-out.

Since we create a new instance of the sensor class upon initializing there should never be an existing instance of this class, but we check in case the init() function gets called again a second time for some reason. Calling the initialization function on the timer a second time could also be included in this block, but isn't strictly required as there is no harmful effect from initializing the timer again.

```
bool DHTModule::shutdown() {
    dhtTimer.stop();
    if (!OtaCore::releasePin((ESP8266_pins) dhtPin)) { delete dht; return
false; }
    delete dht;
    dht = 0;
    return true;
}
```

To shut down the module, we stop the timer and release the GPIO pin we were using, before cleaning up all resources we used. As we have claimed the pin we're using previously when we initialized the module we should have no issues releasing it again, but we check to make sure.

```
void DHTModule::config(String cmd) {
    Vector<String> output;
    int numToken = splitString(cmd, '=', output);
    if (output[0] == "set_pin" && numToken > 1) {
        dhtPin = output[1].toInt();
    }
}
```

This is an example of how one could later change the GPIO pin used by a module, here using the old text-based command format that early versions of the BMaC firmware used to use. We could also receive this information via an MQTT topic, or by actively querying the command and control server.

Note that to change the pin used by the sensor one would have to restart the sensor by deleting the class instance and creating a new instance.

```
void DHTModule::readDHT() {
    TempAndHumidity th;
    th = dht->getTempAndHumidity();

    OtaCore::publish("nsa/temperature", OtaCore::getLocation() + ";" +
```

```
    th.temperature);
        OtaCore::publish("nsa/humidity", OtaCore::getLocation() + ";" +
    th.humidity);
      }
```

Next, for the BME280 sensor module, its code looks like this:

```
#include "ota_core.h"

#include <Libraries/BME280/BME280.h>


class BME280Module {
    static BME280* bme280;
    static Timer timer;

public:
    static bool init();
    static bool shutdown();
    static void config(String cmd);
    static void readSensor();
};
```

Finally, it's familiar-looking implementation:

```
#include "bme280_module.h"

BME280* BME280Module::bme280 = 0;
Timer BME280Module::timer;


bool BME280Module::init() {
    if (!OtaCore::starti2c()) { return false; }
    if (!bme280) { bme280 = new BME280(); }

    if (bme280->EnsureConnected()) {
        OtaCore::log(LOG_INFO, "Connected to BME280 sensor.");
        bme280->SoftReset();
        bme280->Initialize();
    }
    else {
        OtaCore::log(LOG_ERROR, "Not connected to BME280 sensor.");
        return false;
    }

    timer.initializeMs(2000, BME280Module::readSensor).start();

    return true;
```

```
    }


    bool BME280Module::shutdown() {
        timer.stop();
        delete bme280;
        bme280 = 0;

        return true;
    }


    void BME280Module::config(String cmd) {
        Vector<String> output;
        int numToken = splitString(cmd, '=', output);
        if (output[0] == "set_pin" && numToken > 1) {
            //
        }
    }


    void BME280Module::readSensor() {
        float t, h, p;
        if (bme280->IsConnected) {
            t = bme280->GetTemperature();
            h = bme280->GetHumidity();
            p = bme280->GetPressure
            OtaCore::publish("nsa/temperature", OtaCore::getLocation() + ";"
+ t);
            OtaCore::publish("nsa/humidity", OtaCore::getLocation() + ";" +
h);
            OtaCore::publish("nsa/pressure", OtaCore::getLocation() + ";" +
p);
        }
        else {
            OtaCore::log(LOG_ERROR, "Disconnected from BME280 sensor.");
        }
    }
```

As we can see, this module was basically copied from the DHT one, and then modified to fit the BME280 sensor. The similarities between those two modules was one of the motivations behind developing the THP module, in order to exploit these similarities.

As with the DHT module, we can see that we rely on an external library to do the heavy lifting for us, with us merely having to call the functions on the library class to set up the sensor and get the data from it.

CO$_2$ module

For the CO$_2$ module, no attempt has been made yet to make it work with multiple types of CO$_2$ sensors. The first CO$_2$ sensor used was the MH-Z14, before it <indexentry content="modules, Building Management and Control (BMaC):CO$_2$ module">switched to the more compact MH-Z19 sensor. Both of these use the same protocol on their **universal asynchronous receiver/transmitter** (**UART**) interface, however.

On the ESP8266 there are two UARTs, though only one is complete, with a receive (RX) and send (TX) line. The second UART only has a TX line. This essentially limits this MCU to a single UART and thus single UART-based sensor.

These sensors also have a single-wire interface in addition to the UART-based interface, where the sensor outputs the current sensor reading using a specific encoding that has to be received and decoded using the specific distance between pulses on that signal wire. This is similar to the DHT-22's single-wire protocol.

Using the UART is obviously significantly easier, and it's what we ended up using with this module:

```
#include "base_module.h"

class CO₂Module {
    static Timer timer;
    static uint8_t readCmd[9];
    static uint8 eventLevel;
    static uint8 eventCountDown;
    static uint8 eventCountUp;

    static void onSerialReceived(Stream &stream, char arrivedChar, unsigned
short availableCharsCount);

public:
    static bool initialize();
    static bool start();
    static bool shutdown();
    static void readCO₂();
    static void config(String cmd);
};
```

We can see here the callback function that will be used with the UART when we receive data. We also have a few other variables whose meaning will <indexentry content="modules, Building Management and Control (BMaC):CO$_2$ module">become clear in a moment:

```
#include "CO₂_module.h"

Timer CO₂Module::timer;
uint8_t CO₂Module::readCmd[9] = {
0xFF,0x01,0x86,0x00,0x00,0x00,0x00,0x00,0x79};
uint8 CO₂Module::eventLevel = 0;
uint8 CO₂Module::eventCountDown = 10;
uint8 CO₂Module::eventCountUp = 0;
```

In the static initializations, we define the command that we will be sending to the CO_2 sensor, which will tell it to send us its currently measured value. We define a number of counters and the related timer instance, which we will be using to analyze the CO_2 levels we receive.

```
bool CO₂Module::initialize() {
    BaseModule::registerModule(MOD_IDX_CO₂, CO₂Module::start,
CO₂Module::shutdown);
    return true;
}


bool CO₂Module::start() {
    if (!OtaCore::claimPin(ESP8266_gpio03)) { return false; }
    if (!OtaCore::claimPin(ESP8266_gpio01)) { return false; }

    Serial.end();
    delay(10);
    Serial.begin(9600);
    Serial.setCallback(&CO₂Module::onSerialReceived);

    timer.initializeMs(30000, CO₂Module::readCO₂).start();
    return true;
}
```

Starting this module triggers the registering of the pins, which we need for the UART, with the UART started at a baud rate of 9,600. Our receive callback is also registered. The pin registration routine in the core class is meant for housekeeping and therefore cannot really fail. In case of an overlapping pin mapping with another module, we might want to release the first pin registration if the second registration fails.

The GPIO pins used by the serial interface are set in the same core class and would have to be modified there. The main reason behind this lack of configurability is that the GPIO pins on the ESP8266 are fairly limited in what features they support, which is why the hardware UART is basically always found on these two pins, leaving the other pins for other functionality.

The timer we start will read out the sensor every 30 seconds, keeping in mind that the first 3 minutes of sensor readings are useless as the sensor takes <indexentry content="modules, Building Management and Control (BMaC):CO$_2$ module">about that long to warm up.

```
bool CO₂Module::shutdown() {
    if (!OtaCore::releasePin(ESP8266_gpio03)) { return false; }
    if (!OtaCore::releasePin(ESP8266_gpio01)) { return false; }

    timer.stop();
    Serial.end();
    return true;
}


void CO₂Module::readCO₂() {
    Serial.write(readCmd, 9);
}
```

Reading out the sensor is as easy as writing the series of bytes we defined during the static initialization phase to the sensor, and waiting for the sensor to respond by sending data back to us into our RX buffer, which will trigger our callback function.

```
void CO₂Module::config(String cmd) {
    Vector<String> output;
    int numToken = splitString(cmd, '=', output);
    if (output[0] == "event" && numToken > 1) {
        //
    }
}
```

The configuration method was also left unimplemented here, but could be used to disable events (explained in the next part) and make various adjustments dynamically:

```
void CO₂Module::onSerialReceived(Stream &stream, char arrivedChar, unsigned
short availableCharsCount) {
    if (availableCharsCount >= 9) {
        char buff[9];
        Serial.readBytes(buff, 9);

        int responseHigh = (int) buff[2];
        int responseLow = (int) buff[3];
        int ppm = (responseHigh * 0xFF) + responseLow;
        String response = OtaCore::getLocation() + ";" + ppm;
        OtaCore::publish("nsa/CO₂", response);

        if (ppm > 1000) { // T3
            if (eventLevel < 2 && eventCountUp < 10) {
```

```
                        if (++eventCountUp == 10) {
                            eventLevel = 2;
                            eventCountDown = 0;
                            eventCountUp = 0;
                            response = OtaCore::getLocation() + ";" +
eventLevel + ";1;" + ppm;

                            OtaCore::publish("nsa/events/CO2", response);
                        }
                    }
                }
                else if (ppm > 850) { // T2
                    if (eventLevel == 0 && eventCountUp < 10) {
                        if (++eventCountUp == 10) {
                            eventLevel = 1;
                            eventCountDown = 0;
                            eventCountUp = 0;
                            response = OtaCore::getLocation() + ";" +
eventLevel + ";1;" + ppm;

                            OtaCore::publish("nsa/events/CO2", response);
                        }
                    }
                    else if (eventLevel == 2 && eventCountDown < 10) {
                        if (++eventCountDown == 10) {
                            eventLevel = 1;
                            eventCountUp = 0;
                            eventCountDown = 0;
                            response = OtaCore::getLocation() + ";" +
eventLevel + ";0;" + ppm;

                            OtaCore::publish("nsa/events/CO2", response);
                        }
                    }
                }
                else if (ppm < 750) { // T1
                    if (eventLevel == 1 && eventCountDown < 10) {
                        if (++eventCountDown == 10) {
                            eventLevel = 0;
                            eventCountDown = 0;
                            eventCountUp = 0;
                            response = OtaCore::getLocation() + ";" +
eventLevel + ";0;" + ppm;

                            OtaCore::publish("nsa/events/CO2", response);
                        }
                    }
                }
            }
        }
    }
```

In the callback, we get the characters as they come in on the RX line. We wait until we have nine characters waiting for us in the RX buffer, which is the <indexentry content="modules, Building Management and Control (BMaC):CO$_2$ module">number of bytes we are expecting to receive from the CO$_2$ sensor. We could also validate the checksum for the received data, for which the MH-Z19 datasheet gives the following C code:

```
char getCheckSum(char* packet) {
    char i, checksum;
    for ( i = 1; i < 8; i++) {
        checksum += packet[i];
    }

    checksum = 0xff - checksum;
    checksum += 1;
    return checksum;
}
```

This routine calculates the checksum for the received data as a single byte, which we can then compare with the value contained in the 9th byte of the received data to see whether the values match.

Returning to our own code, we process the bytes to calculate the **parts per million (PPM)** of the CO$_2$ molecules the sensor detected. This value is immediately published to its respective MQTT topic.

After this, we compare the new PPM value to see whether we have crossed any of the three preset trigger levels, the first one of which indicates a safe CO$_2$ level, the second an elevated CO$_2$ level, and the third a very high CO$_2$ level that requires attention. When we exceed or return to a lower trigger level, an event is published for this on the MQTT topic.

Jura

This is another module which uses the UART. It was used with a number of Jura coffee machines, which used the common TopTronics electronics used by other coffee machine manufacturers as well. To enable reading out these coffee machines, an ESP8266 module was integrated into a small, plastic enclosure which just had a serial connector on one side. This connected with a standard nine-pin serial cable to the so-called service port on the back of the machine.

The serial port on the machine provided 5V when it was powered on, which thus also turned on the ESP8266 node when the coffee machine was on. The plastic enclosure could then be hidden away behind the machine.

The module for this feature looks like this:

```
#include "base_module.h"

class JuraModule {
    static String mqttTxBuffer;
    static Timer timer;

    static bool toCoffeemaker(String cmd);
    static void readStatistics();
    static void onSerialReceived(Stream &stream, char arrivedChar, unsigned
short availableCharsCount);

public:
    static bool initialize();
    static bool start();
    static bool shutdown();
};
```

The only really noticeable thing about this class declaration is the method name involving a
coffee maker. We'll see in a second what it does:

```
#include "jura_module.h"
#include <stdlib.h>
Timer JuraModule::timer;
String JuraModule::mqttTxBuffer;
bool JuraModule::initialize() {
    BaseModule::registerModule(MOD_IDX_JURA, JuraModule::start,
JuraModule::shutdown);
}
bool JuraModule::start() {
    if (!OtaCore::claimPin(ESP8266_gpio03)) { return false; }
    if (!OtaCore::claimPin(ESP8266_gpio01)) { return false; }
    Serial.end();
    delay(10);
    Serial.begin(9600);
    Serial.setCallback(&JuraModule::onSerialReceived);
    timer.initializeMs(60000, JuraModule::readStatistics).start();
    return true;
}
```

As is common, the coffee machine's UART runs at 9,600 baud. We set the serial callback
method, and start a timer for reading out the EEPROM's product counters. Since we are
talking about a coffee machine, reading out the counters more than once a minute is
somewhat silly:

```
bool JuraModule::shutdown() {
    if (!OtaCore::releasePin(ESP8266_gpio03)) { return false; } // RX 0
```

```
        if (!OtaCore::releasePin(ESP8266_gpio01)) { return false; } // TX 0
        timer.stop();
        Serial.end();
        return true;
    }
    void JuraModule::readStatistics() {
        String message = "RT:0000";
        JuraModule::toCoffeemaker(message);
    }
```

To read out the EEPROM's counters, we need to send the command for this to the machine's UART. This command will tell it to send us the contents of the first row in the EEPROM. Unfortunately, the machine's protocol doesn't use plain text, but requires a bit of special encoding, which we do in the next method:

```
    bool JuraModule::toCoffeemaker(String cmd) {
        OtaCore::log(LOG_DEBUG, "Sending command: " + cmd);
        cmd += "\r\n";
        for (int i = 0; i < cmd.length(); ++i) {
            uint8_t ch = static_cast<uint8_t>(cmd[i]);
            uint8_t d0 = 0xFF;
            uint8_t d1 = 0xFF;
            uint8_t d2 = 0xFF;
            uint8_t d3 = 0xFF;
            bitWrite(d0, 2, bitRead(ch, 0));
            bitWrite(d0, 5, bitRead(ch, 1));
            bitWrite(d1, 2, bitRead(ch, 2));
            bitWrite(d1, 5, bitRead(ch, 3));
            bitWrite(d2, 2, bitRead(ch, 4));
            bitWrite(d2, 5, bitRead(ch, 5));
            bitWrite(d3, 2, bitRead(ch, 6));
            bitWrite(d3, 5, bitRead(ch, 7));
            delay(1);
            Serial.write(d0);
            delay(1);
            Serial.write(d1);
            delay(1);
            Serial.write(d2);
            delay(1);
            Serial.write(d3);
            delay(7);
        }
        return true;
    }
```

This method takes in a string, appending the required EOL characters and encoding each byte into four bytes, putting the data bits into each new byte's second and fifth bit, the rest of the bits all being a 1. These four bytes are then sent to the machine's UART with a small delay between each write to ensure correct reception:

```
void JuraModule::onSerialReceived(Stream &stream, char arrivedChar,
unsigned short availableCharsCount) {

    OtaCore::log(LOG_DEBUG, "Receiving UART 0.");
    while(stream.available()){

        delay(1);
        uint8_t d0 = stream.read();
        delay(1);
        uint8_t d1 = stream.read();
        delay(1);
        uint8_t d2 = stream.read();
        delay(1);
        uint8_t d3 = stream.read();
        delay(7);

        uint8_t d4;
        bitWrite(d4, 0, bitRead(d0, 2));
        bitWrite(d4, 1, bitRead(d0, 5));
        bitWrite(d4, 2, bitRead(d1, 2));
        bitWrite(d4, 3, bitRead(d1, 5));
        bitWrite(d4, 4, bitRead(d2, 2));
        bitWrite(d4, 5, bitRead(d2, 5));
        bitWrite(d4, 6, bitRead(d3, 2));
        bitWrite(d4, 7, bitRead(d3, 5));
        OtaCore::log(LOG_TRACE, String(d4));
        mqttTxBuffer += (char) d4;

        if ('\n' == (char) d4) {
            long int espressoCount = strtol(mqttTxBuffer.substring(3,
            7).c_str(), 0, 16);
            long int espresso2Count = strtol(mqttTxBuffer.substring(7,
            11).c_str(), 0, 16);
            long int coffeeCount = strtol(mqttTxBuffer.substring(11,
            15).c_str(), 0, 16);
            long int coffee2Count = strtol(mqttTxBuffer.substring(15,
            19).c_str(), 0, 16);
            OtaCore::publish("nsa/espresso", OtaCore::getLocation() +
            ";" + espressoCount);
            OtaCore::publish("nsa/espresso2", OtaCore::getLocation() +
            ";" + espresso2Count);
            OtaCore::publish("nsa/coffee", OtaCore::getLocation() + ";"
            + coffeeCount);
```

```
                    OtaCore::publish("nsa/coffee2", OtaCore::getLocation() +
                    ";" + coffee2Count);
                    mqttTxBuffer = "";
                }
        }
    }
```

In the serial receive callback, we decode each byte we receive using the same process we used to encode the data we sent to the machine, buffering the decoded bytes until we detect the end of the response (linefeed, LF) character. We then read out the 16-bit counters, which we then publish on the MQTT topic for them.

JuraTerm

The JuraTerm module is similar to the Jura one, but it accepts remote commands, encodes them in the same way as the Jura module, and returns the decoded response. In the project it used to be the Jura class until it got superseded by the new Jura class and this one was delegated to just a terminal class. In a future revision this module's functionality will therefore be merged into the main Jura class.

```
#include "base_module.h"

class JuraTermModule {
    static String mqttTxBuffer;

    static bool toCoffeemaker(String cmd);
    static void onSerialReceived(Stream &stream, char arrivedChar, unsigned
short availableCharsCount);

 public:
    static bool initialize();
    static bool start();
    static bool shutdown();
    static void commandCallback(String message);
};#include "juraterm_module.h"

 String JuraTermModule::mqttTxBuffer;

 bool JuraTermModule::initialize() {
    BaseModule::registerModule(MOD_IDX_JURATERM, JuraTermModule::start,
JuraTermModule::shutdown);
 }


 bool JuraTermModule::start() {
    if (!OtaCore::claimPin(ESP8266_gpio03)) { return false; } // RX 0
```

```
    if (!OtaCore::claimPin(ESP8266_gpio01)) { return false; } // TX 0

    OtaCore::registerTopic("coffee/command/" + OtaCore::getLocation(),
                           JuraTermModule::commandCallback);
    Serial.end();
    delay(10);
    Serial.begin(9600);
    Serial.setCallback(&JuraTermModule::onSerialReceived);

    return true;
}


bool JuraTermModule::shutdown() {
    if (!OtaCore::releasePin(ESP8266_gpio03)) { return false; } // RX 0
    if (!OtaCore::releasePin(ESP8266_gpio01)) { return false; } // TX 0

    Serial.end();
    OtaCore::deregisterTopic("coffee/command/" + OtaCore::getLocation());
    return true;
}


void JuraTermModule::commandCallback(String message) {
    if (message == "AN:0A") { return; }

    JuraTermModule::toCoffeemaker(message);
}
```

When we start this module, we register an MQTT topic to receive commands. This allows us to receive the coffee machine commands. We basically act as a straight pass-through for these commands, except for this one particular command. This command that we filter out would erase the machine's EEPROM, which is something which we are unlikely to want.

Again, we use the same method to encode the command:

```
bool JuraTermModule::toCoffeemaker(String cmd) {
    OtaCore::log(LOG_DEBUG, "Sending command: " + cmd);

    cmd += "\r\n";

    for (int i = 0; i < cmd.length(); ++i) {
        uint8_t ch = static_cast<uint8_t>(cmd[i]);
        uint8_t d0 = 0xFF;
        uint8_t d1 = 0xFF;
        uint8_t d2 = 0xFF;
        uint8_t d3 = 0xFF;
```

```
            bitWrite(d0, 2, bitRead(ch, 0));
            bitWrite(d0, 5, bitRead(ch, 1));
            bitWrite(d1, 2, bitRead(ch, 2));
            bitWrite(d1, 5, bitRead(ch, 3));
            bitWrite(d2, 2, bitRead(ch, 4));
            bitWrite(d2, 5, bitRead(ch, 5));
            bitWrite(d3, 2, bitRead(ch, 6));
            bitWrite(d3, 5, bitRead(ch, 7));

            delay(1);
            Serial.write(d0);
            delay(1);
            Serial.write(d1);
            delay(1);
            Serial.write(d2);
            delay(1);
            Serial.write(d3);
            delay(7);
    }

    return true;
  }


  void JuraTermModule::onSerialReceived(Stream &stream, char arrivedChar,
unsigned short availableCharsCount) {
      OtaCore::log(LOG_DEBUG, "Receiving UART 0.");

    while(stream.available()){
            delay(1);
            uint8_t d0 = stream.read();
            delay(1);
            uint8_t d1 = stream.read();
            delay(1);
            uint8_t d2 = stream.read();
            delay(1);
            uint8_t d3 = stream.read();
            delay(7);

            uint8_t d4;
            bitWrite(d4, 0, bitRead(d0, 2));
            bitWrite(d4, 1, bitRead(d0, 5));
            bitWrite(d4, 2, bitRead(d1, 2));
            bitWrite(d4, 3, bitRead(d1, 5));
            bitWrite(d4, 4, bitRead(d2, 2));
            bitWrite(d4, 5, bitRead(d2, 5));
            bitWrite(d4, 6, bitRead(d3, 2));
            bitWrite(d4, 7, bitRead(d3, 5));
```

```
        OtaCore::log(LOG_TRACE, String(d4));

        mqttTxBuffer += (char) d4;
        if ('\n' == (char) d4) {
            OtaCore::publish("coffee/response", OtaCore::getLocation()
+ ";" + mqttTxBuffer);
            mqttTxBuffer = "";
        }
    }
}
```

Instead of interpreting the data in any way, we merely return the response on its respective MQTT topic.

Motion

The motion module is intended to work with **passive infrared** (**PIR**) sensors. These have onboard logic that determine when a trigger point has been reached, at which point they change an interrupt pin into a high signal. We can use this to determine whether a person is in a room, or is walking through a hallway.

Its code looks as follows:

```
#include "base_module.h"

#define GPIO_PIN 0

class MotionModule {
    static int pin;
    static Timer timer;
    static Timer warmup;
    static bool motion;
    static bool firstLow;

public:
    static bool initialize();
    static bool start();
    static bool shutdown();
    static void config(String cmd);
    static void warmupSensor();
    static void readSensor();
    static void IRAM_ATTR interruptHandler();
};
```

Of note here is that we explicitly move the interrupt handler method into the MCU's SRAM with the IRAM_ATTR keyword, to prevent any delay when the interrupt gets called.

Its implementation is as follows:

```
#include "motion_module.h"
int MotionModule::pin = GPIO_PIN;
Timer MotionModule::timer;
Timer MotionModule::warmup;
bool MotionModule::motion = false;
bool MotionModule::firstLow = true;
bool MotionModule::initialize() {
    BaseModule::registerModule(MOD_IDX_MOTION, MotionModule::start,
    MotionModule::shutdown);
}
bool MotionModule::start() {
    if (!OtaCore::claimPin(ESP8266_gpio00)) { return false; }
    pinMode(pin, INPUT);
    warmup.initializeMs(60000, MotionModule::warmupSensor).start();
    return true;
}
```

A PIR sensor requires warm-up time to stabilize its readings. We give it a minute using the warm-up timer. We also set the mode for the GPIO pin we're using.

```
bool MotionModule::shutdown() {
    if (!OtaCore::releasePin(ESP8266_gpio00)) { return false; } // RX 0

    timer.stop();
    detachInterrupt(pin);

    return true;
}


void MotionModule::config(String cmd) {
    Vector<String> output;
    int numToken = splitString(cmd, '=', output);
    if (output[0] == "set_pin" && numToken > 1) {
        //
    }
}


void MotionModule::warmupSensor() {
    warmup.stop();
    attachInterrupt(pin, &MotionModule::interruptHandler, CHANGE);

    timer.initializeMs(5000, MotionModule::readSensor).start();
}
```

After the sensor has finished warming up, we stop its timer and attach the interrupt to handle any signals from the sensor. We'll check up on the shared variable with the interrupt routine, to see whether the value has changed, publishing the current value every 5 seconds:

```
void MotionModule::readSensor() {
    if (!motion) {
        if (firstLow) { firstLow = false; }
        else {
            OtaCore::publish("nsa/motion", OtaCore::getLocation() +
";0");
            firstLow = true;
        }
    }
    else if (motion) {
        OtaCore::publish("nsa/motion", OtaCore::getLocation() + ";1");
        firstLow = true;
    }
}
```

When checking the current sensor value, we make it a point to ignore the first time that the sensor reports LOW. This in order to ensure that we ignore moments when people do not move a lot in the room. The resulting value is then published on the MQTT topic:

```
void IRAM_ATTR MotionModule::interruptHandler() {
    int val = digitalRead(pin);
    if (val == HIGH) { motion = true; }
    else { motion = false; }
}
```

The interrupt handler merely updates the local Boolean value. Because of the relatively long transition times for most processing circuits for PIR sensor there is quite a bit of time (seconds) before the sensor will detect motion again, creating dead zones. Here we keep track of the last registered value.

PWM

The reason why the PWM module was developed was to have a way to generate an analog output voltage using an external RC filter circuit. This was in order to control the fan of the ceiling-mounted air-conditioning units, whose fan controller accepts a voltage of between 0 and 10 volts.

An interesting feature of this module is that it has its own binary protocol to allow for remote control, which is how the air-conditioning service can directly control the fan speeds via the ceiling-mounted nodes:

```cpp
#include "base_module.h"

#include <HardwarePWM.h>


class PwmModule {
    static HardwarePWM* hw_pwm;
    static Vector<int> duty;
    static uint8 pinNum;
    static Timer timer;
    static uint8* pins;

public:
    static bool initialize();
    static bool start();
    static bool shutdown();
    static void commandCallback(String message);
};
```

The implementation is as follows:

```cpp
#include "pwm_module.h"

HardwarePWM* PwmModule::hw_pwm = 0;
uint8 PwmModule::pinNum = 0;
Timer PwmModule::timer;
uint8* PwmModule::pins = 0;


enum {
    PWM_START = 0x01,
    PWM_STOP = 0x02,
    PWM_SET_DUTY = 0x04,
    PWM_DUTY = 0x08,
    PWM_ACTIVE = 0x10
};
```

We define the commands that will be available with the PWM module here as an enumeration:

```cpp
bool PwmModule::initialize() {
    BaseModule::registerModule(MOD_IDX_PWM, PwmModule::start,
PwmModule::shutdown);
}
```

```
  bool PwmModule::start() {
      OtaCore::registerTopic(MQTT_PREFIX + String("pwm/") +
  OtaCore::getLocation(), PwmModule::commandCallback);

      return true;
  }


  bool PwmModule::shutdown() {
      OtaCore::deregisterTopic(MQTT_PREFIX + String("pwm/") +
  OtaCore::getLocation());

      if (hw_pwm) {
            delete hw_pwm;
            hw_pwm = 0;
      }

      return true;
  }
```

When we start this module, we register the MQTT topic on which the module will be able
to receive commands. When shutting down, we deregister this topic again. We use the
HardwarePWM class from Sming to enable PWM on individual pins.

The rest of the module is simply the command processor:

```
  void PwmModule::commandCallback(String message) {
      OtaCore::log(LOG_DEBUG, "PWM command: " + message);
      if (message.length() < 1) { return; }
      int index = 0;
      uint8 cmd = *((uint8*) &message[index++]);

      if (cmd == PWM_START) {
            if (message.length() < 2) { return; }
            uint8 num = *((uint8*) &message[index++]);

            OtaCore::log(LOG_DEBUG, "Pins to add: " + String(num));

            if (message.length() != (2 + num)) { return; }

            pins = new uint8[num];
            for (int i = 0; i < num; ++i) {
                  pins[i] = *((uint8*) &message[index++]);
                  if (!OtaCore::claimPin(pins[i])) {
                        OtaCore::log(LOG_ERROR, "Pin is already in use: " +
  String(pins[i]));

                        OtaCore::publish("pwm/response",
```

```
OtaCore::getLocation() + ";0", 1);

                    return;
        }

            OtaCore::log(LOG_INFO, "Adding GPIO pin " +
String(pins[i]));
        }

        hw_pwm = new HardwarePWM(pins, num);
        pinNum = num;

        OtaCore::log(LOG_INFO, "Added pins to PWM: " + String(pinNum));

        OtaCore::publish("pwm/response", OtaCore::getLocation() + ";1",
1);
    }
    else if (cmd == PWM_STOP) {
        delete hw_pwm;
        hw_pwm = 0;

        for (int i = 0; i < pinNum; ++i) {
            if (!OtaCore::releasePin(pins[i])) {
                OtaCore::log(LOG_ERROR, "Pin cannot be released: " +
String(pins[i]));

                OtaCore::publish("pwm/response",
OtaCore::getLocation() + ";0", 1);

                return;
        }

            OtaCore::log(LOG_INFO, "Removing GPIO pin " +
String(pins[i]));
        }

        delete[] pins;
        pins = 0;

        OtaCore::publish("pwm/response", OtaCore::getLocation() + ";1");
    }
    else if (cmd == PWM_SET_DUTY) {
        if (message.length() < 3) { return; }

        uint8 pin = *((uint8*) &message[index++]);
        uint8 duty = *((uint8*) &message[index++]);
        bool ret = hw_pwm->setDuty(pin, ((uint32) 222.22 * duty));
        if (!ret) {
```

```
                     OtaCore::publish("pwm/response", OtaCore::getLocation() +
    ";0");

                     return;
              }

              OtaCore::publish("pwm/response", OtaCore::getLocation() + ";1");
       }
    else if (cmd == PWM_DUTY) {
              if (message.length() < 2) { return; }

              uint8 pin = *((uint8*) &message[index++]);
              uint32 duty = hw_pwm->getDuty(pin);

              uint8 dutyp = (duty / 222.22) + 1;
              String res = "";
              res += (char) pin;
              res += (char) dutyp;
              OtaCore::publish("pwm/response", OtaCore::getLocation() + ";" +
    res);
       }
    else if (cmd == PWM_ACTIVE) {
              String res;
              if (pins && pinNum > 0) {
                     res = String((char*) pins, pinNum);
              }

              OtaCore::publish("pwm/response", OtaCore::getLocation() + ";" +
    res);
       }
    }
```

The protocol implemented by the preceding method is the following:

Command	Meaning	Payload	Return value
0x01	Start the module	uint8 (number of pins) uint8* (one byte per pin number)	0x00/0x01
0x02	Stop the module	-	0x00/0x01
0x04	Set the PWM duty level	uint8 (pin number) uint8 (duty cycle, 0 - 100)	0x00/0x01
0x08	Get the PWM duty level	uint8 (pin number).	uint8 (duty level)
0x10	Returns the active pins	-	uint8* (one pin number per byte)

For each command, we parse the string of bytes we receive, checking the number of bytes to see whether we get the expected number, and then interpreting them as commands and their payload. We either return a 0 (failure) or a 1 (success), or a payload with the desired information.

One obvious addition that could be made here would be to add some kind of checksum to the received command, along with sanity checks on the received data. While code like this will work great in a secure environment with encrypted MQTT links and a reliable network connection, other environments may be less forgiving, with corrupted data and false data being injected.

I/O

Sometimes all we need is just a lot of GPIO pins that connect to things like relays, so that we can turn heating valves on or off. This was the reason behind this module. The nodes that were being installed on the ceiling had not just an I2C bus being used for the environmental sensors, but also the UART for CO_2 measurements and four pins for PWM output.

As more GPIO was needed to turn the relays that controlled the valves on the water lines to the air-conditioning units on or off, a dedicated GPIO expander chip was added to the I2C bus to provide eight more GPIO pins.

This module allows for an external service like the air-conditioning service to directly set these new GPIO pins as high or low:

```
#include "base_module.h"

#include <Libraries/MCP23008/MCP23008.h>

class IOModule {
    static MCP23008* mcp;
    static uint8 iodir;
    static uint8 gppu;
    static uint8 gpio;
    static String publishTopic;

public:
    static bool initialize();
    static bool start();
    static bool shutdown();
    static void commandCallback(String message);
};
```

This class wraps the MCP23008 I/O expander device, keeping a local copy of its direction, pull-up, and GPIO state registers for easy updating and control:

```
#include "io_module.h"

#include <Wire.h>

MCP23008* IOModule::mcp = 0;
uint8 IOModule::iodir;
uint8 IOModule::gppu;
uint8 IOModule::gpio;
String IOModule::publishTopic;
```

We keep a local copy of three registers on the I2C GPIO expander device—the I/O direction (`iodir`), pull-up register (`gppu`), and the pin I/O level (`gpio`):

```
enum {
    IO_START = 0x01,
    IO_STOP = 0x02,
    IO_STATE = 0x04,
    IO_SET_MODE = 0x08,
    IO_SET_PULLUP = 0x10,
    IO_WRITE = 0x20,
    IO_READ = 0x40,
    IO_ACTIVE = 0x80
};


enum {
    MCP_OUTPUT = 0,
    MCP_INPUT = 1
};
```

We again define a number of commands in the form of an enumeration, along with one for the pin direction of the GPIO expander:

```
bool IOModule::initialize() {
    BaseModule::registerModule(MOD_IDX_IO, IOModule::start,
IOModule::shutdown);
 }


 bool IOModule::start() {
    publishTopic = "io/response/" + OtaCore::getLocation();
    OtaCore::registerTopic("io/" + OtaCore::getLocation(),
IOModule::commandCallback);
```

```
        OtaCore::starti2c();
}


bool IOModule::shutdown() {
    OtaCore::deregisterTopic("io/" + OtaCore::getLocation());
    if (mcp) {
            delete mcp;
            mcp = 0;
    }
}
```

Initializing and starting the module is similar to the PWM module, with us registering an MQTT topic to receive commands on. The difference here is that since we are using an I2C device, we have to make sure that the I2C functionality has been started already.

Next, we address the command-processing method:

```
void IOModule::commandCallback(String message) {
    OtaCore::log(LOG_DEBUG, "I/O command: " + message);
    uint32 mlen = message.length();
    if (mlen < 1) { return; }
    int index = 0;
    uint8 cmd = *((uint8*) &message[index++]);
    if (cmd == IO_START) {
        if (mlen > 2) {
            OtaCore::log(LOG_INFO, "Enabling I/O Module failed: too
            many parameters.");
            OtaCore::publish(publishTopic, OtaCore::getLocation() +
            ";" + (char) 0x01 + (char) 0x00);
            return;
        }
        // Read out the desired address, or use the default.
        uint8 addr = 0;
        if (mlen == 2) {
            addr = *((uint8*) &message[index++]);
            if (addr > 7) {
            // Report failure. QoS 1.
            OtaCore::log(LOG_INFO, "Enabling I/O Module failed: invalid
            i2c address.");
            OtaCore::publish(publishTopic, OtaCore::getLocation() + ";"
            + (char) 0x01 + (char) 0x00);
            return;
        }
    }
    if (!mcp) {
        mcp = new MCP23008(0x40);
    }
```

```
    // Set all pins to output (0) and low (0)
    mcp->writeIODIR(0x00);
    mcp->writeGPIO(0x00);
    // Read in current chip values.
    iodir = mcp->readIODIR();
    gppu = mcp->readGPPU();
    gpio = mcp->readGPIO();
    // Validate IODIR and GPIO registers.
    if (iodir != 0 || gpio != 0) {
        delete mcp;
        mcp = 0;
        OtaCore::log(LOG_INFO, "Enabling I/O Module failed: not
        connected.");
         OtaCore::publish(publishTopic, OtaCore::getLocation() + ";" +
         (char) 0x01 + (char) 0x00);
         return;
    }
    OtaCore::log(LOG_INFO, "Enabled I/O Module.");
    OtaCore::publish(publishTopic, OtaCore::getLocation() + ";" +
    (char) 0x01 + (char) 0x01);
}
    else if (cmd == IO_STOP) {
        if (mlen > 1) {
            OtaCore::log(LOG_INFO, "Disabling I/O Module failed: too
            many parameters.");
            OtaCore::publish(publishTopic, OtaCore::getLocation() + ";"
            + (char) 0x02 + (char) 0x00);
            return;
        }
        if (mcp) {
            delete mcp;
            mcp = 0;
        }
        OtaCore::log(LOG_INFO, "Disabled I/O Module.");
        OtaCore::publish(publishTopic, OtaCore::getLocation() + ";" +
        (char) 0x02 + (char) 0x01);
    }
    else if (cmd == IO_STATE) {
         if (mlen > 1) {
                OtaCore::log(LOG_INFO, "Reading state failed: too many
parameters.");
                OtaCore::publish(publishTopic, OtaCore::getLocation() + ";"
+
(char) 0x04 + (char) 0x00);
                return;
         }

         OtaCore::publish(publishTopic, OtaCore::getLocation() + ";" +
```

```
(char) 0x04 + (char) 0x01 +
((char) iodir) + ((char) gppu) +
((char) gpio));
    }
    else if (cmd == IO_SET_MODE) {
        if (mlen != 3) {
            OtaCore::log(LOG_INFO, "Reading state failed: incorrect
number of parameters.");
            OtaCore::publish(publishTopic, OtaCore::getLocation() + ";"
+
(char) 0x08 + (char) 0x00);
            return;
        }

        uint8 pnum = *((uint8*) &message[index++]);
        uint8 pstate = *((uint8*) &message[index]);
        if (pnum > 7) {
            OtaCore::log(LOG_INFO, "Setting pin mode failed: unknown
pin.");
            OtaCore::publish(publishTopic, OtaCore::getLocation() + ";"
+
(char) 0x08 + (char) 0x00);
            return;
        }

        if (pstate > 1) {
            // Report failure. QoS 1.
            OtaCore::log(LOG_INFO, "Setting pin mode failed: invalid
pin mode.");
            OtaCore::publish(publishTopic, OtaCore::getLocation() + ";"
+
(char) 0x08 + (char) 0x00);
            return;
        }

        // Set new state of IODIR register.
        if (pstate == MCP_INPUT) { iodir |= 1 << pnum; }
        else { iodir &= ~(1 << pnum); }

        if (mcp) {
            OtaCore::log(LOG_DEBUG, "Setting pinmode in library...");
            mcp->writeIODIR(iodir);
        }

        OtaCore::log(LOG_INFO, "Set pin mode for I/O Module.");
        OtaCore::publish(publishTopic, OtaCore::getLocation() + ";" +
(char) 0x08 + (char) 0x01);
    }
```

```
        else if (cmd == IO_SET_PULLUP) {
            if (mlen != 3) {
                OtaCore::log(LOG_INFO, "Reading state failed: incorrect
number of parameters.");
                OtaCore::publish(publishTopic, OtaCore::getLocation() + ";"
+
(char) 0x10 + (char) 0x00);
                return;
            }

            uint8 pnum = *((uint8*) &message[index++]);
            uint8 pstate = *((uint8*) &message[index]);
            if (pnum > 7) {
                OtaCore::log(LOG_INFO, "Setting pull-up failed: unknown
pin.");
                OtaCore::publish(publishTopic, OtaCore::getLocation() + ";"
+
(char) 0x10 + (char) 0x00);
                return;
            }

            if (pstate > 1) {
                OtaCore::log(LOG_INFO, "Setting pull-up failed: invalid
state.");
                OtaCore::publish(publishTopic, OtaCore::getLocation() + ";"
+
(char) 0x10 + (char) 0x00);
                return;
            }

            if (pstate == HIGH) { gppu |= 1 << pnum; }
            else { gppu &= ~(1 << pnum); }

            if (mcp) {
                OtaCore::log(LOG_DEBUG, "Setting pull-up in library...");
                mcp->writeGPPU(gppu);
            }

            OtaCore::log(LOG_INFO, "Changed pull-up for I/O Module.");
            OtaCore::publish(publishTopic, OtaCore::getLocation() + ";" +
(char) 0x10 + (char) 0x01);
        }
        else if (cmd == IO_WRITE) {
            if (mlen != 3) {
                OtaCore::log(LOG_INFO, "Writing pin failed: incorrect
number of parameters.");
                OtaCore::publish(publishTopic, OtaCore::getLocation() + ";"
+
```

```
(char) 0x20 + (char) 0x00);
                return;
        }
        // Set the new GPIO pin level.
        uint8 pnum = *((uint8*) &message[index++]);
        uint8 pstate = *((uint8*) &message[index]);
        if (pnum > 7) {
                OtaCore::log(LOG_INFO, "Writing pin failed: unknown pin.");
                OtaCore::publish(publishTopic, OtaCore::getLocation() + ";"
+
(char) 0x20 + (char) 0x00);
                return;
        }
        if (pstate > 1) {
                OtaCore::log(LOG_INFO, "Writing pin failed: invalid
state.");
                OtaCore::publish(publishTopic, OtaCore::getLocation() + ";"
+
(char) 0x20 + (char) 0x00);
                return;
        }
        String state = "low";
        if (pstate == HIGH) { gpio |= 1 << pnum; state = "high"; }
        else { gpio &= ~(1 << pnum); }

        OtaCore::log(LOG_DEBUG, "Changed GPIO to: " + ((char) gpio));

        if (mcp) {
                OtaCore::log(LOG_DEBUG, "Setting state to " + state +
                                        " in library for pin " + ((char)
pnum));
                mcp->writeGPIO(gpio);
        }

        OtaCore::log(LOG_INFO, "Wrote pin state for I/O Module.");
        OtaCore::publish(publishTopic, OtaCore::getLocation() + ";" +
(char) 0x20 + (char) 0x01);
    }

    else if (cmd == IO_READ) {

        if (mlen > 2) {
                OtaCore::log(LOG_INFO, "Reading pin failed: too many
                parameters.");
                OtaCore::publish(publishTopic, OtaCore::getLocation()
                                                                (char)
0x40 + (char) 0x00);
                return;
```

```
        }
        // Read the GPIO pin status and return it.
        uint8 pnum = *((uint8*) &message[index]);

    if (pnum > 7) {
        OtaCore::log(LOG_INFO, "Reading pin failed: unknown pin.");
        OtaCore::publish(publishTopic, OtaCore::getLocation() + ";"
        + (char) 0x40 + (char) 0x00);
    }
      uint8 pstate;

    if (mcp) {
        OtaCore::log(LOG_DEBUG, "Reading pin in library...");
        pstate = (mcp->readGPIO() >> pnum) & 0x1;
    }
    OtaCore::log(LOG_INFO, "Read pin state for I/O Module.");
    OtaCore::publish(publishTopic, OtaCore::getLocation() + ";" +
    (char) 0x40 + (char) 0x01 + (char) pnum + (char) pstate);
}

else if (cmd == IO_ACTIVE) {

    if (mlen > 1) {
        OtaCore::log(LOG_INFO, "Reading active status failed: too
        many parameters.");
        OtaCore::publish(publishTopic, OtaCore::getLocation() +
        ";" + (char) 0x80 + (char) 0x00);
        return;
    }
    uint8 active = 0;
    if (mcp) { active = 1; }
    char output[] = { 0x80, 0x01, active };
    OtaCore::publish(publishTopic, OtaCore::getLocation() + ";" +
    String(output, 3));
}
}
```

Its protocol looks as follows:

Command	Meaning	Payload	Return value
0x01	Start the module	uint8 I2C address offset (0-7, optional)	0x01 0x00/0x01
0x02	Stop the module	-	0x02 0x00/0x01
0x04	Returns I/O mode, pull-up, and level state	-	0x04 0x00/0x01 (result) uint8 (iodir register) uint8 (gppu register) uint8 (gpio register)
0x08	Set a pin to a specific mode (In/Out)	uint8 (pin number, 0 - 7) uint8 (0: output, 1: input)	0x08 0x00/0x01
0x10	Set a pin's pull-up resistor (Low/High)	uint8 (pin number, 0 - 7) uint8 (pin pull-up state, 0/1)	0x10 0x00/0x01
0x20	Set a pin to either Low or High	uint8 (pin number, 0-7) uint8 (pin state, 0/1)	0x20 0x00/0x01
0x40	Read the current pin value (Low, High)	uint8 (pin number)	0x40 0x00/0x01 uint8 (pin number) uint8 (pin value)
0x80	Return whether this module has been initialized	-	0x80 0x00/0x01 uint8 (module state, 0/1).

Similar to the protocol for the PWM module, either a Boolean value is returned to indicate success, or the requested payload is returned. We also return the command that was called in the response.

The command is a single byte, allowing for a maximum of eight commands since we are using bit flags. This could be extended to 256 commands if we wanted to.

Possible improvements to this module's code include consolidating duplicated code into (inline) function calls and conceivably the use of a sub-class that would manage the setting and toggling of individual bits with a more higher-level API.

Switch

Since each section of the office had its own central switch that would switch the water in the pipes that flowed to the FCUs, this had to be controllable from the backend server as well. Using a latching relay configuration, it was possible to both switch between heating and cooling configurations, as well as have a memory element that could be read out by the node:

This system was assembled on a single board that was used to replace the original manual switch, using the following module to control it:

```cpp
#include "base_module.h"

class SwitchModule {
    static String publishTopic;

public:
    static bool initialize();
    static bool start();
    static bool shutdown();
    static void commandCallback(String message);
};
```

Its implementation is as follows:

```cpp
#include "switch_module.h"
#include <Wire.h>
#define SW1_SET_PIN 5
#define SW2_SET_PIN 4
#define SW1_READ_PIN 14
#define SW2_READ_PIN 12
String SwitchModule::publishTopic;
enum {
    SWITCH_ONE = 0x01,//Switch the first connected load on, second off.
    SWITCH_TWO = 0x02,//Switch the second connected load on, first off.
    SWITCH_STATE = 0x04,//Returns position of the switch (0x01/0x02).
};
bool SwitchModule::initialize() {
    BaseModule::registerModule(MOD_IDX_SWITCH, SwitchModule::start,
    SwitchModule::shutdown);
}
bool SwitchModule::start() {
    // Register pins.
    if (!OtaCore::claimPin(ESP8266_gpio05)) { return false; }
    if (!OtaCore::claimPin(ESP8266_gpio04)) { return false; }
    if (!OtaCore::claimPin(ESP8266_gpio14)) { return false; }
    if (!OtaCore::claimPin(ESP8266_gpio12)) { return false; }
```

```
      publishTopic = "switch/response/" + OtaCore::getLocation();
      OtaCore::registerTopic("switch/" + OtaCore::getLocation(),
      SwitchModule::commandCallback);
  // Set the pull-ups on the input pins and configure the output pins.
      pinMode(SW1_SET_PIN, OUTPUT);
      pinMode(SW2_SET_PIN, OUTPUT);
      pinMode(SW1_READ_PIN, INPUT_PULLUP);
      pinMode(SW2_READ_PIN, INPUT_PULLUP);
      digitalWrite(SW1_SET_PIN, LOW);
      digitalWrite(SW2_SET_PIN, LOW);
   }
   bool SwitchModule::shutdown() {
      OtaCore::deregisterTopic("switch/" + OtaCore::getLocation());
      // Release the pins.
      if (!OtaCore::releasePin(ESP8266_gpio05)) { return false; }
      if (!OtaCore::releasePin(ESP8266_gpio04)) { return false; }
      if (!OtaCore::releasePin(ESP8266_gpio14)) { return false; }
      if (!OtaCore::releasePin(ESP8266_gpio12)) { return false; }
   }


   void SwitchModule::commandCallback(String message) {
      // Message is the command.
      OtaCore::log(LOG_DEBUG, "Switch command: " + message);

      uint32 mlen = message.length();
      if (mlen < 1) { return; }
      int index = 0;
      uint8 cmd = *((uint8*) &message[index++]);
      if (cmd == SWITCH_ONE) {
            if (mlen > 1) {
                  // Report failure. QoS 1.
                  OtaCore::log(LOG_INFO, "Switching to position 1 failed: too
many parameters.");
                  OtaCore::publish(publishTopic, OtaCore::getLocation() + ";"
+
(char) 0x01 + (char) 0x00);
                  return;
            }

            // Set the relay to its first position (reset condition).
            // This causes pins 3 & 10 on the latching relay to become
active.
            digitalWrite(SW1_SET_PIN, HIGH);
            delay(1000); // Wait 1 second for the relay to switch position.
            digitalWrite(SW1_SET_PIN, LOW);

            OtaCore::log(LOG_INFO, "Switched to position 1.");
```

```
                OtaCore::publish(publishTopic, OtaCore::getLocation() + ";" +
(char) 0x01 + (char) 0x01);
    }
    else if (cmd == SWITCH_TWO) {
        if (mlen > 1) {
            OtaCore::log(LOG_INFO, "Switching to position 2 failed: too
many parameters.");
            OtaCore::publish(publishTopic, OtaCore::getLocation() + ";"
+
(char) 0x02 + (char) 0x00);
            return;
        }

        // Set the relay to its first position (reset condition).
        // This causes pins 3 & 10 on the latching relay to become
active.
        digitalWrite(SW2_SET_PIN, HIGH);
        delay(1000); // Wait 1 second for the relay to switch position.
        digitalWrite(SW2_SET_PIN, LOW);

        OtaCore::log(LOG_INFO, "Switched to position 1.");
        OtaCore::publish(publishTopic, OtaCore::getLocation() + ";" +
(char) 0x02 + (char) 0x01);
    }
    else if (cmd == SWITCH_STATE) {
        if (mlen > 1) {
            OtaCore::log(LOG_INFO, "Reading state failed: too many
parameters.");
            OtaCore::publish(publishTopic, OtaCore::getLocation() + ";"
+
(char) 0x04 + (char) 0x00);
            return;
        }

        // Check the value of the two input pins. If one is low, then
that
        // is the active position.
        uint8 active = 2;
        if (digitalRead(SW1_READ_PIN) == LOW) { active = 0; }
        else if (digitalRead(SW2_READ_PIN) == LOW) { active = 1; }

        if (active > 1) {
            OtaCore::log(LOG_INFO, "Reading state failed: no active
state found.");
            OtaCore::publish(publishTopic, OtaCore::getLocation() + ";"
+
(char) 0x04 + (char) 0x00);
            return;
```

```
        }

            OtaCore::publish(publishTopic, OtaCore::getLocation() + ";" +
(char) 0x04 + (char) 0x01 +
(char) active);
        }
    }
```

This module is very similar to the PWM and I/O modules, with the registering of an MQTT topic to allow communication using its own binary protocol. Here, the device that is being controlled is fairly simple. It is a latching relay with two sides, one of which is connected to the connections that are being switched between, while the other side is used as a one-bit memory cell.

As both sides of this type of relay will switch simultaneously, we can count on the side connected to the MCU to match the position of that on the side connected to the rest of the system. Even after a power failure or reset of the MCU, we can simply read out the values of the pins connected to the relay to find out the state of the system.

The resulting protocol looks like this:

Command	Meaning	Payload	Return value
0x01	Switch to Position 1	-	0x01 0x00/0x01
0x02	Switch to Position 2	-	0x02 0x00/0x01
0x04	Return the current state	-	0x04 0x00/0x01 (result) uint8 (active pin 0x00, 0x01)

Command and control server

As alluded to earlier in this chapter, a so-called **command and control** (C&C) server is essentially a database containing information on individual nodes and their configuration, for use by the nodes themselves and administration tools like the one in the next section.

It also includes an HTTP server, for use with HTTP-based **over-the-air** (OTA) updates. Since the BMaC system is MQTT-based, this server is also written as an MQTT client:

```
#include "listener.h"
#include <iostream>
#include <string>
```

```cpp
using namespace std;

#include <Poco/Util/IniFileConfiguration.h>
#include <Poco/AutoPtr.h>
#include <Poco/Net/HTTPServer.h>

using namespace Poco::Util;
using namespace Poco;
using namespace Poco::Net;

#include "httprequestfactory.h"
int main(int argc, char* argv[]) {
    cout << "Starting MQTT BMaC Command & Control server...\n";
    int rc;
    mosqpp::lib_init();
    cout << "Initialised C++ Mosquitto library.\n";
    string configFile;
    if (argc > 1) { configFile = argv[1]; }
    else { configFile = "config.ini"; }
    AutoPtr<IniFileConfiguration> config(new
IniFileConfiguration(configFile));
    string mqtt_host = config->getString("MQTT.host", "localhost");
    int mqtt_port = config->getInt("MQTT.port", 1883);
    string defaultFirmware = config->getString("Firmware.default",
"ota_unified.bin");
    Listener listener("Command_and_Control", mqtt_host, mqtt_port,
defaultFirmware);
    UInt16 port = config->getInt("HTTP.port", 8080);
    HTTPServerParams* params = new HTTPServerParams;
    params->setMaxQueued(100);
    params->setMaxThreads(10);
    HTTPServer httpd(new RequestHandlerFactory, port, params);
    httpd.start();
    cout << "Created listener, entering loop...\n";
    while(1) {
        rc = listener.loop();
        if (rc){
            cout << "Disconnected. Trying to reconnect...\n";
            listener.reconnect();
        }
    }
    cout << "Cleanup...\n";

    mosqpp::lib_cleanup();

    return 0;
}
```

We're using the Mosquitto C++ MQTT client along with the POCO framework to provide us with the required functionality.

The `Listener` class is next:

```cpp
#include <mosquittopp.h>
#include <string>

using namespace std;

#include <Poco/Data/Session.h>
#include <Poco/Data/SQLite/Connector.h>

using namespace Poco;


class Listener : public mosqpp::mosquittopp {
    Data::Session* session;
    string defaultFirmware;
public:
    Listener(string clientId, string host, int port, string
defaultFirmware);
    ~Listener();
    void on_connect(int rc);
    void on_message(const struct mosquitto_message* message);
    void on_subscribe(int mid, int qos_count, const int* granted_qos);
};
```

We include the headers from POCO for the SQLite database functionality, which forms the database backend for this application. The class itself derives from the Mosquitto C++ class, providing us with all the basic MQTT functionalities along with a few function stubs, which we still have to implement in a moment:

```cpp
#include "listener.h"

#include <iostream>
#include <fstream>
#include <sstream>

using namespace std;

#include <Poco/StringTokenizer.h>
#include <Poco/String.h>
#include <Poco/Net/HTTPSClientSession.h>
#include <Poco/Net/HTTPRequest.h>
#include <Poco/Net/HTTPResponse.h>
#include <Poco/File.h>
```

```
using namespace Poco::Data::Keywords;

struct Node {
    string uid;
    string location;
    UInt32 modules;
    float posx;
    float posy;
};
```

We define a structure for a single node:

```
Listener::Listener(string clientId, string host, int port, string
defaultFirmware) : mosquittopp(clientId.c_str()) {
    int keepalive = 60;
    connect(host.c_str(), port, keepalive);
    Data::SQLite::Connector::registerConnector();
    session = new Poco::Data::Session("SQLite", "nodes.db");
    (*session) << "CREATE TABLE IF NOT EXISTS nodes (uid TEXT UNIQUE, \
            location TEXT, \
            modules INT, \
            posx FLOAT, \
            posy FLOAT)", now;
    (*session) << "CREATE TABLE IF NOT EXISTS firmware (uid TEXT UNIQUE, \
            file TEXT)", now;

    this->defaultFirmware = defaultFirmware;
}
```

In the constructor, we attempt to connect to the MQTT broker, using the provided host and port. We also set up a connection with the SQLite database, and ensure that it has valid nodes and a firmware table:

```
Listener::~Listener() {
    //
}


void Listener::on_connect(int rc) {
    cout << "Connected. Subscribing to topics...\n";
    if (rc == 0) {
        string topic = "cc/config";     // announce by nodes coming online.
        subscribe(0, topic.c_str());
        topic = "cc/ui/config";         // C&C client requesting
configuration.
        subscribe(0, topic.c_str());
        topic = "cc/nodes/new";         // C&C client adding new node.
        subscribe(0, topic.c_str());
```

```
                topic = "cc/nodes/update";     // C&C client updating node.
                subscribe(0, topic.c_str());
                topic = "nsa/events/CO₂";       // CO₂-related events.
                subscribe(0, topic.c_str());
                topic = "cc/firmware";   // C&C client firmware command.
                subscribe(0, topic.c_str());
        }
    else {
            cerr << "Connection failed. Aborting subscribing.\n";
    }
}
```

We reimplement the callback for when a connection has been established with the MQTT broker. In this method, we subscribe to all the MQTT topics in which we are interested.

The next method is called whenever we receive an MQTT message on one of the topics which we subscribed to:

```
void Listener::on_message(const struct mosquitto_message* message) {
    string topic = message->topic;
    string payload = string((const char*) message->payload,
message->payloadlen);
    if (topic == "cc/config") {
            if (payload.length() < 1) {
                    cerr << "Invalid payload: " << payload << ". Reject.\n";
                    return;
            }
```

We validate the payload we receive for each topic. For this first topic, we expect its payload to contain the MAC address of the node which wants to receive its configuration. We make sure that this seems to be the case, then continue:

```
                Data::Statement select(*session);
                Node node;
                node.uid = payload;
                select << "SELECT location, modules FROM nodes WHERE uid=?",
                            into (node.location),
                            into (node.modules),
                            use (payload);
                size_t rows = select.execute();
                if (rows == 1) {
                        string topic = "cc/" + payload;
                        string response = "mod;" + string((const char*)
&node.modules, 4);
                        publish(0, topic.c_str(), response.length(),
response.c_str());
                        response = "loc;" + node.location;
                        publish(0, topic.c_str(), response.length(),
```

```
response.c_str());
        }
        else if (rows < 1) {
                // No node with this UID found.
                cerr << "Error: No data set found for uid " << payload <<
endl;
        }
        else {
                // Multiple data sets were found, which shouldn't be
possible...
                cerr << "Error: Multiple data sets found for uid " <<
payload << "\n";
        }
    }
```

We attempt to find the MAC address in the database, reading out the node's configuration if found and making it the payload for the return message.

The next topics are used with the administration tool:

```
else if (topic == "cc/ui/config") {

    if (payload == "map") {

        ifstream mapFile("map.png", ios::binary);

        if (!mapFile.is_open()) {

            cerr << "Failed to open map file.\n";

            return;

        }
        stringstream ss;
        ss << mapFile.rdbuf();
        string mapData = ss.str();
        publish(0, "cc/ui/config/map", mapData.length(),

        mapData.c_str());

}
```

In the case of this payload string, we return the binary data for a map image that should exist in the local folder. This map contains the layout of the building we are administrating, for displaying in the tool.

```cpp
            else if (payload == "nodes") {
                Data::Statement countQuery(*session);
                int rowCount;
                countQuery << "SELECT COUNT(*) FROM nodes",
                        into(rowCount),
                        now;
                if (rowCount == 0) {
                        cout << "No nodes found in database, returning...\n";
                        return;
                }
                Data::Statement select(*session);
                Node node;
                select << "SELECT uid, location, modules, posx, posy FROM
    nodes",
                                into (node.uid),
                                into (node.location),
                                into (node.modules),
                                into (node.posx),
                                into (node.posy),
                                range(0, 1);
                string header;
                string nodes;
                string nodeStr;
                UInt32 nodeCount = 0;
                while (!select.done()) {
                        select.execute();
                        nodeStr = "NODE";
                        UInt8 length = (UInt8) node.uid.length();
                        nodeStr += string((char*) &length, 1);
                        nodeStr += node.uid;
                        length = (UInt8) node.location.length();
                        nodeStr += string((char*) &length, 1);
                        nodeStr += node.location;
                        nodeStr += string((char*) &node.posx, 4);
                        nodeStr += string((char*) &node.posy, 4);
                        nodeStr += string((char*) &node.modules, 4);
                        UInt32 segSize = nodeStr.length();
                        nodes += string((char*) &segSize, 4);
                        nodes += nodeStr;
                        ++nodeCount;
                }
                UInt64 messageSize = nodes.length() + 9;
                header = string((char*) &messageSize, 8);
                header += "NODES";
```

```
            header += string((char*) &nodeCount, 4);
            header += nodes;
            publish(0, "cc/nodes/all", header.length(), header.c_str());
        }
    }
```

The preceding section reads out every single node in the database and returns it in a binary, serialized format.

Next, we create a new node and add it to the database:

```
else if (topic == "cc/nodes/new") {
    UInt32 index = 0;
    UInt32 msgLength = *((UInt32*) payload.substr(index, 4).data());
    index += 4;
    string signature = payload.substr(index, 4);
    index += 4;
    if (signature != "NODE") {
        cerr << "Invalid node signature.\n";
        return;
    }
    UInt8 uidLength = (UInt8) payload[index++];
    Node node;
    node.uid = payload.substr(index, uidLength);
    index += uidLength;
    UInt8 locationLength = (UInt8) payload[index++];
    node.location = payload.substr(index, locationLength);
    index += locationLength;
    node.posx = *((float*) payload.substr(index, 4).data());
    index += 4;
    node.posy = *((float*) payload.substr(index, 4).data());
    index += 4;
    node.modules = *((UInt32*) payload.substr(index, 4).data());
    cout << "Storing new node for UID: " << node.uid << "\n";
    Data::Statement insert(*session);
    insert << "INSERT INTO nodes VALUES(?, ?, ?, ?, ?)",
                use(node.uid),
                use(node.location),
                use(node.modules),
                use(node.posx),
                use(node.posy),
                now;
    (*session) << "INSERT INTO firmware VALUES(?, ?)",
                use(node.uid),
                use(defaultFirmware),
                now;
}
```

Updating a node's configuration is also possible:

```
else if (topic == "cc/nodes/update") {
        UInt32 index = 0;
        UInt32 msgLength = *((UInt32*) payload.substr(index, 4).data());
        index += 4;
        string signature = payload.substr(index, 4);
        index += 4;
        if (signature != "NODE") {
                cerr << "Invalid node signature.\n";
                return;
        }
        UInt8 uidLength = (UInt8) payload[index++];
        Node node;
        node.uid = payload.substr(index, uidLength);
        index += uidLength;
        UInt8 locationLength = (UInt8) payload[index++];
        node.location = payload.substr(index, locationLength);
        index += locationLength;
        node.posx = *((float*) payload.substr(index, 4).data());
        index += 4;
        node.posy = *((float*) payload.substr(index, 4).data());
        index += 4;
        node.modules = *((UInt32*) payload.substr(index, 4).data());
        cout << "Updating node for UID: " << node.uid << "\n";
        Data::Statement update(*session);
        update << "UPDATE nodes SET location = ?, posx = ?, posy = ?,
modules = ? WHERE uid = ?",
                        use(node.location),
                        use(node.posx),
                        use(node.posy),
                        use(node.modules),
                        use(node.uid),
                        now;
    }
```

Next, we look at the topic handler for deleting a node's configuration:

```
else if (topic == "cc/nodes/delete") {
        cout << "Deleting node with UID: " << payload << "\n";
        Data::Statement del(*session);
        del << "DELETE FROM nodes WHERE uid = ?",
                        use(payload),
                        now;
        (*session) << "DELETE FROM firmware WHERE uid = ?",
                        use(payload),
                        now;
    }
```

When we looked at the CO_2 module of the firmware earlier, we saw that it generated CO_2 events. These also end up here in this example, in order to generate events in JSON format, which we send to some HTTP-based API. We then use the HTTPS client in POCO to send this JSON to the remote server (here set to localhost):

```
else if (topic == "nsa/events/CO₂") {
        StringTokenizer st(payload, ";", StringTokenizer::TOK_TRIM |
StringTokenizer::TOK_IGNORE_EMPTY);
        if (st.count() < 4) {
                cerr << "CO₂ event: Wrong number of arguments. Payload: " <<
payload << "\n";
                return;
        }
        string state = "ok";
        if (st[1] == "1") { state = "warn"; }
        else if (st[1] == "2") { state = "crit"; }
        string increase = (st[2] == "1") ? "true" : "false";
        string json = "{ \"state\": \"" + state + "\", \
                                \"location\": \"" + st[0] + "\", \
                                \"increase\": " + increase + ", \
                                \"ppm\": " + st[3] + " }";
        Net::HTTPSClientSession httpsClient("localhost");
        try {
                Net::HTTPRequest request(Net::HTTPRequest::HTTP_POST,
                                                "/",
Net::HTTPMessage::HTTP_1_1);
                request.setContentLength(json.length());
                request.setContentType("application/json");
                httpsClient.sendRequest(request) << json;
                Net::HTTPResponse response;
                httpsClient.receiveResponse(response);
        }
        catch (Exception& exc) {
                cout << "Exception caught while attempting to connect." <<
std::endl;
                cerr << exc.displayText() << std::endl;
                return;
        }
}
```

Finally, for managing the stored firmware images, we can use the following topic. Which node uses which firmware version can be set in each node's configuration, though as we saw earlier, the default is to use the latest firmware.

Using this topic, we can list the available firmware images or upload a new one:

```
else if (topic == "cc/firmware") {
    if (payload == "list") {
        std::vector<File> files;
        File file("firmware");
        if (!file.isDirectory()) { return; }
        file.list(files);
        string out;
        for (int i = 0; i < files.size(); ++i) {
            if (files[i].isFile()) {
                out += files[i].path();
                out += ";";
            }
        }
        out.pop_back();
        publish(0, "cc/firmware/list", out.length(), out.c_str());
    }
    else {
        StringTokenizer st(payload, ";", StringTokenizer::TOK_TRIM |
StringTokenizer::TOK_IGNORE_EMPTY);
        if (st[0] == "change") {
            if (st.count() != 3) { return; }
            (*session) << "UPDATE firmware SET file = ? WHERE uid
= ?",
                                    use (st[1]),
                                    use (st[2]),
                                    now;
        }
        else if (st[0] == "upload") {
            if (st.count() != 3) { return; }
            // Write file & truncate if exists.
            string filepath = "firmware/" + st[1];
            ofstream outfile("firmware/" + st[1], ofstream::binary
| ofstream::trunc);
            outfile.write(st[2].data(), st[2].size());
            outfile.close();
        }
    }
}
void Listener::on_subscribe(int mid, int qos_count, const int* granted_qos)
{
    //
}
```

On each successful MQTT topic subscription, this method is called, allowing us to do something else if needed.

Next, we look at the HTTP server component, starting with the HTTP request handler factory:

```
#include <Poco/Net/HTTPRequestHandlerFactory.h>
#include <Poco/Net/HTTPServerRequest.h>

using namespace Poco::Net;

#include "datahandler.h"


class RequestHandlerFactory: public HTTPRequestHandlerFactory {
public:
    RequestHandlerFactory() {}
    HTTPRequestHandler* createRequestHandler(const HTTPServerRequest&
request) {
        return new DataHandler();
    }
};
```

This handler will always return an instance of the following class:

```
#include <iostream>
#include <vector>

using namespace std;

#include <Poco/Net/HTTPRequestHandler.h>
#include <Poco/Net/HTTPServerResponse.h>
#include <Poco/Net/HTTPServerRequest.h>
#include <Poco/URI.h>
#include <Poco/File.h>

#include <Poco/Data/Session.h>
#include <Poco/Data/SQLite/Connector.h>

using namespace Poco::Data::Keywords;

using namespace Poco::Net;
using namespace Poco;


class DataHandler: public HTTPRequestHandler {
public:
    void handleRequest(HTTPServerRequest& request, HTTPServerResponse&
```

```
response) {
        cout << "DataHandler: Request from " +
request.clientAddress().toString() << endl;
        URI uri(request.getURI());
        string path = uri.getPath();
        if (path != "/") {
                response.setStatus(HTTPResponse::HTTP_NOT_FOUND);
                ostream& ostr = response.send();
                ostr << "File Not Found: " << path;
                return;
        }
        URI::QueryParameters parts;
        parts = uri.getQueryParameters();
        if (parts.size() > 0 && parts[0].first == "uid") {
                Data::SQLite::Connector::registerConnector();
                Data::Session* session = new Poco::Data::Session("SQLite",
"nodes.db");
                Data::Statement select(*session);
                string filename;
                select << "SELECT file FROM firmware WHERE uid=?",
                                into (filename),
                                use (parts[0].second);
                size_t rows = select.execute();
                if (rows != 1) {
                        response.setStatus(HTTPResponse::HTTP_NOT_FOUND);
                        ostream& ostr = response.send();
                        ostr << "File Not Found: " << parts[0].second;
                        return;
                }
                string fileroot = "firmware/";
                File file(fileroot + filename);
                if (!file.exists() || file.isDirectory()) {
                        response.setStatus(HTTPResponse::HTTP_NOT_FOUND);
                        ostream& ostr = response.send();
                        ostr << "File Not Found.";
                        return;
                }
                string mime = "application/octet-stream";
                try {
                        response.sendFile(file.path(), mime);
                }
                catch (FileNotFoundException &e) {
                        cout << "File not found exception triggered..." <<
endl;
                        cerr << e.displayText() << endl;
                        response.setStatus(HTTPResponse::HTTP_NOT_FOUND);
                        ostream& ostr = response.send();
                        ostr << "File Not Found.";
```

```
                         return;
                }
                catch (OpenFileException &e) {
                        cout << "Open file exception triggered..." << endl;
                        cerr << e.displayText() << endl;
    response.setStatus(HTTPResponse::HTTP_INTERNAL_SERVER_ERROR);
                        ostream& ostr = response.send();
                        ostr << "Internal Server Error. Couldn't open file.";
                        return;
                }
        }
        else {
                response.setStatus(HTTPResponse::HTTP_BAD_REQUEST);
                response.send();
                return;
        }
    }
};
```

This class looks fairly impressive, yet mostly does just an SQLite database lookup for the node ID (MAC address) and returns the appropriate firmware image if found.

Administration tool

Using the APIs implemented by the C&C server, a GUI-based administration tool was created using the Qt5 framework and the Mosquitto MQTT client library was developed, allowing for the basic management of nodes. They were overlaid on top of a layout graphic of buildings.

While basically usable, it was found that a graphical tool was fairly complicated to develop. It was also limited to a single floor of a building, unless one were to have a really large map containing all of the floors with the nodes mapped onto this. This would have been quite clumsy, obviously.

In the source code provided with this chapter, the administration tool can be found as well, to serve as an example of how one could implement it. For the sake of brevity, the code for it has been omitted here.

Air-conditioning service

To control air-conditioning units, a service much like the C&C one was developed, using the same basic template. The interesting parts of its source are the following:

```cpp
#include <string>
#include <vector>

using namespace std;

#include <Poco/Data/Session.h>
#include <Poco/Data/SQLite/Connector.h>

#include <Poco/Net/HTTPClientSession.h>
#include <Poco/Net/HTTPSClientSession.h>

#include <Poco/Timer.h>

using namespace Poco;
using namespace Poco::Net;

class Listener;


struct NodeInfo {
    string uid;
    float posx;
    float posy;
    float current;
    float target;
    bool ch0_state;
    UInt8 ch0_duty;
    bool ch0_valid;
    bool ch1_state;
    UInt8 ch1_duty;
    bool ch1_valid;
    bool ch2_state;
    UInt8 ch2_duty;
    bool ch2_valid;
    bool ch3_state;
    UInt8 ch3_duty;
    bool ch3_valid;
    UInt8 validate;
};


struct ValveInfo {
```

```
    string uid;
    UInt8 ch0_valve;
    UInt8 ch1_valve;
    UInt8 ch2_valve;
    UInt8 ch3_valve;
};


struct SwitchInfo {
    string uid;
    bool state;
};


#include "listener.h"


class Nodes {
    static Data::Session* session;
    static bool initialized;
    static HTTPClientSession* influxClient;
    static string influxDb;
    static bool secure;
    static Listener* listener;
    static Timer* tempTimer;
    static Timer* nodesTimer;
    static Timer* switchTimer;
    static Nodes* selfRef;

public:
    static void init(string influxHost, int influxPort, string influxDb,
string influx_sec, Listener* listener);
    static void stop();
    static bool getNodeInfo(string uid, NodeInfo &info);
    static bool getValveInfo(string uid, ValveInfo &info);
    static bool getSwitchInfo(string uid, SwitchInfo &info);
    static bool setTargetTemperature(string uid, float temp);
    static bool setCurrentTemperature(string uid, float temp);
    static bool setDuty(string uid, UInt8 ch0, UInt8 ch1, UInt8 ch2, UInt8
ch3);
    static bool setValves(string uid, bool ch0, bool ch1, bool ch2, bool
ch3);
    static bool setSwitch(string uid, bool state);
    void updateCurrentTemperatures(Timer& timer);
    void checkNodes(Timer& timer);
```

```
        void checkSwitch(Timer& timer);
        static bool getUIDs(vector<string> &uids);
        static bool getSwitchUIDs(vector<string> &uids);
};
```

The definition for this class in the AC service gives a good overview of the functionality of this class. It's essentially a wrapper around an SQLite database, containing information on nodes, valves, and cooling/heating switches. It also contains the timers that will keep triggering the application to check the status of the system, to compare it to the target state, and to make adjustments if necessary.

This class is used extensively by the `Listener` class of this application for keeping track of the status of nodes and the connected AC units, along with those switches and valves controlling the water flow:

```
#include <mosquittopp.h>

#include <string>
#include <map>

using namespace std;

#include <Poco/Mutex.h>

using namespace Poco;


struct NodeInfo;
struct ValveInfo;
struct SwitchInfo;

  #include "nodes.h"


  class Listener : public mosqpp::mosquittopp {
     map<string, NodeInfo> nodes;
     map<string, ValveInfo> valves;
     map<string, SwitchInfo> switches;
     Mutex nodesLock;
     Mutex valvesLock;
     Mutex switchesLock;
     bool heating;
     Mutex heatingLock;

  public:
     Listener(string clientId, string host, int port);
     ~Listener();
```

```
    void on_connect(int rc);
    void on_message(const struct mosquitto_message* message);
    void on_subscribe(int mid, int qos_count, const int* granted_qos);
    bool checkNodes();
    bool checkSwitch();
};
```

The way that this application works is that the Nodes class timers will cause the Listener class to publish on the topics for the PWM, IO, and Switch modules, inquiring about the state of the devices that are supposed to be active.

This kind of active loop system is common in industrial applications, as it provides constant validation of the system to detect quickly if something isn't working as intended.

InfluxDB for recording sensor readings

Recording the sensor readings and later the statistics read from the coffee machines was a priority from the beginning. The ideal database for this kind of data is a time series database, of which Influx is a common one. The biggest problem with this database is that it does not support MQTT, only offering its HTTP and native interface.

To fix this, a simple MQTT-to-Influx HTTP line protocol bridge was written, again using the Mosquitto client library as well as the POCO framework's HTTP functionality:

```
#include "mth.h"

#include <iostream>

using namespace std;

#include <Poco/Net/HTTPRequest.h>
#include <Poco/Net/HTTPResponse.h>
#include <Poco/StringTokenizer.h>
#include <Poco/String.h>

using namespace Poco;


MtH::MtH(string clientId, string host, int port, string topics, string
influxHost,
                int influxPort, string influxDb, string influx_sec) :
mosquittopp(clientId.c_str()) {
    this->topics   = topics;
    this->influxDb = influxDb;
    if (influx_sec == "true") {
```

```
        cout << "Connecting with HTTPS..." << std::endl;
        influxClient = new Net::HTTPSClientSession(influxHost,
influxPort);
        secure = true;
    }
    else {
        cout << "Connecting with HTTP..." << std::endl;
        influxClient = new Net::HTTPClientSession(influxHost,
influxPort);
        secure = false;
    }

    int keepalive = 60;
    connect(host.c_str(), port, keepalive);
}
```

In the constructor, we connect to the MQTT broker, and create either an HTTP or HTTPS
client, depending on which protocol has been set in the configuration file:

```
MtH::~MtH() {
    delete influxClient;
}


void MtH::on_connect(int rc) {
    cout << "Connected. Subscribing to topics...\n";

    if (rc == 0) {
        StringTokenizer st(topics, ",", StringTokenizer::TOK_TRIM |
StringTokenizer::TOK_IGNORE_EMPTY);
        for (StringTokenizer::Iterator it = st.begin(); it != st.end();
++it) {
            string topic = string(*it);
            cout << "Subscribing to: " << topic << "\n";
            subscribe(0, topic.c_str());

            // Add name of the series to the 'series' map.
            StringTokenizer st1(topic, "/", StringTokenizer::TOK_TRIM |
StringTokenizer::TOK_IGNORE_EMPTY);
            string s = st1[st1.count() - 1]; // Get last item.
            series.insert(std::pair<string, string>(topic, s));
        }
    }
    else {
        cerr << "Connection failed. Aborting subscribing.\n";
    }
}
```

Instead of fixed MQTT topics to subscribe to, we use the topics that are defined in the configuration file, here provided to us as a single string with each topic separated by a comma.

We also create an STL map containing the name of the time series to record for the topic, taking the final part of the MQTT topic after the last slash. One could make this further configurable, but for the topics used in the BMaC system this limitation was no consideration as it not necessary to have more complex topics.

```cpp
void MtH::on_message(const struct mosquitto_message* message) {
    string topic = message->topic;
    map<string, string>::iterator it = series.find(topic);
    if (it == series.end()) {
        cerr << "Topic not found: " << topic << "\n";
        return;
    }

    if (message->payloadlen < 1) {
        cerr << "No payload found. Returning...\n";
        return;
    }

    string payload = string((const char*) message->payload, message-
>payloadlen);
    size_t pos = payload.find(";");
    if (pos == string::npos || pos == 0) {
        cerr << "Invalid payload: " << payload << ". Reject.\n";
        return;
    }

    string uid = payload.substr(0, pos);
    string value = payload.substr(pos + 1);
    string influxMsg;
    influxMsg = series[topic];
    influxMsg += ",location=" + uid;
    influxMsg += " value=" + value;
    try {
        Net::HTTPRequest request(Net::HTTPRequest::HTTP_POST,
        "/write?db=" + influxDb, Net::HTTPMessage::HTTP_1_1);
        request.setContentLength(influxMsg.length());
        request.setContentType("application/x-www-form-urlencoded");
        influxClient->sendRequest(request) << influxMsg;

        Net::HTTPResponse response;
        influxClient->receiveResponse(response);
    }
    catch (Exception& exc) {
```

```
        cout << "Exception caught while attempting to connect." <<
        std::endl;
        cerr << exc.displayText() << std::endl;
        return;
    }
```

When we get a new MQTT message in, we find the name of the Influx time series for it, then create a string to send to the InfluxDB server. The assumption here is that the payload consists of the MAC address of the node which sent the message followed by a semi-colon.

We simply get the part after the semi-colon to set it as the value, and use the MAC as the location. This we then send to the database server.

Security aspects

During the development of this system it became soon obvious that security would be a paramount aspect of the system. For that reason we looked at adding transport layer security (TLS) encryption. This would use the integrated axTLS encryption library in the Sming framework together with AES certificates (host and client) to provide both verification that the host (servers) and clients (nodes) are who they say they are, but also provide a secure encrypted link.

In Chapter 5, *Example - Soil Humidity Monitor with Wi-Fi*, we already looked at the handling of these client certificates and setting up of an encrypted MQTT connection. One detail which is not obvious from that were the troubles which we encountered while setting up this certificate system. As mentioned in Chapter 5, *Example - Soil Humidity Monitor with Wi-Fi*, the ESP8266 does not have enough memory to allocate the default TLS handshake buffers and requires the use of the SSL fragment size extension on the side of the server (host).

Unfortunately we found that the commonly used MQTT broker we were using (Mosquitto) did not support this SSL extension and would therefore require that clients used the default double 16 kB buffer. The first solution to this would be to recompile the Mosquitto broker after making a few changes to its source code to change this setting.

The better solution and the one which we ultimately implemented was to install a proxy software (HAProxy) which functioned as the TLS endpoint, handling the certificates and redirecting the decrypted traffic to the MQTT broker via the local loopback (localhost) interface.

With the SSL fragment size option set to 1-2 kB everything worked as intended and we had a building-wide, wireless monitoring and control system that allowed for secure communications of sensitive information and delicate control commands.

Future developments

There are still many additions that can be made to this system. From the number of sensors that could be supported, further GPIO expander chips, air-conditioning system configurations, room occupancy detection linked into a calendar backend, to clearing out scheduled meetings at an office where nobody showed up, and so on.

There is also the option of switching from ESP8266 as the MCU to a different one, such as ARM-based MCUs, to get wired Ethernet options, along with better debug and development tools. As convenient as it is to have an MCU with Wi-Fi, which one can just stick anywhere and theoretically have it work, the development tools for the ESP8266 aren't that great, and the lack of wired communication options (without using external chips) means that everything either works or doesn't depending on the quality of the Wi-Fi network.

As BMaC involves the automation of a building, it is desirable to have a certain level of reliability, which is hard to guarantee with a Wi-Fi network, though for less crucial components (coffee machine statistics, sensor readings, and so on) this is unlikely to be an issue. Conceivably a hybrid network with both wired and wireless options could be the future.

Summary

In this chapter, we looked at how a building-wide monitoring and management system was developed, what its components looked like, and what lessons were learned during its development.

The reader is expected to understand now how such a large-scale embedded system is constructed and functions, and should be able either to use the BMaC system themselves or implement a similar system.

In the next chapter we will look at developing embedded projects using the Qt framework.

3
Section 3: Integration with other tools and frameworks

After learning how to develop and test embedded systems, you can learn in this part how to develop advanced graphical user interfaces and for hybrid FPGA/SoC platforms.

The following chapters will be covered in this section:

Chapter 10, *Developing Embedded Systems with Qt*

Chapter 11, *Developing for Hybrid SoC/FPGA Systems*

10
Developing Embedded Systems with Qt

Qt (pronounced *cute*) is an advanced C++-based framework that covers a wide range of APIs, allowing you to implement networking, graphical user interfaces, parsing of data formats, the playing back and recording of audio, and much more. This chapter primarily covers the graphical aspect of Qt, and how to create advanced GUIs for embedded devices to provide an attractive and functional UI to users.

The topics covered in this chapter are as follows:

- Creating advanced GUIs with Qt for embedded systems
- Using Qt's 3D designer to create an infotainment UI
- Extending an existing embedded system with a GUI

The power of the right framework

A **framework** is essentially a collection of code aimed at easing the development of software for a specific application. It provides the developer with a range of classes—or the language equivalent—to allow you to implement the application logic without having to worry about interfacing with the underlying hardware, or using the OS's APIs.

In previous chapters, we used a number of frameworks to make our development efforts easier, from the No date Framework (Chapter 4, *Resource-Restricted Embedded Systems*) and CMSIS to Arduino for **microcontrollers** (**MCUs**), and from the low-level POCO framework for cross-platform development to the higher-level Qt framework.

Each of these frameworks has a specific type of system that they are intended for. For No date, CMSIS, and Arduino, the target is MCUs, ranging from 8-bit AVR MCUs to 32-bit ARM MCUs. These target the bare-metal systems, without any intermediate **operating system** (**OS**) or similar. Above those in terms of complexity, we find **real-time OS frameworks** (**RTOS**), which include a full OS in the framework.

Frameworks such as POCO and Qt target OSes in general, from desktop and server platforms to SoC platforms. Here they function primarily as an abstraction layer between the OS-specific APIs, while providing additional functionality alongside this abstraction. This allows you to quickly build up a full-featured application, without having to spend much time on each feature.

This is particularly important for networking functionality, where you do not want to write a TCP sockets-based server from scratch, but ideally just want to instantiate a ready-made class and use it. In the case of Qt, it also provides graphical user interface-related APIs to make the development of cross-platform GUIs easier. Other frameworks that also provide this kind of functionality include GTK+ and WxWidgets. In this chapter, however, we'll just be looking at developing with Qt.

In Chapter 8, *Example - Linux-Based Infotainment System,* we got a good look at how to develop with the Qt framework. There, we mostly ignored the **graphical user interface** (**GUI**) part, even though this is probably the most interesting part of Qt relative to other OS-based frameworks. Being able to use the same GUI across multiple OSes can be incredibly useful and convenient.

This is mostly the case for desktop-based applications, where the GUI is a crucial part of the application, and thus not having to spend the time and trouble of porting it between OSes is a major time saver. For embedded platforms, this is also true, though here you have the option of integrating even deeper into the system than on a desktop system, as we will see in a moment.

We'll also look at the various types of Qt applications that you can develop, starting with a simple **command-line interface** (**CLI**) application.

Qt for command-line use

Even though the graphical user interface is a big selling point of the Qt framework, it is also possible to use it to develop command-line-only applications. For this, we just use the QCoreApplication class to create an input and an event loop handler, as in this example:

```
#include <QCoreApplication>
#include <core.h>

int main(int argc, char *argv[]) {
    QCoreApplication app(argc, argv);
    Core core;

    connect(&core, &Core::done, &app, &app::quit, Qt::QueuedConnection);
    core.start();

    return app.exec();
}
```

Here, our code is implemented in a class called Core. In the main function, we create a QCoreApplication instance, which receives the command-line parameters. We then instantiate an instance of our class.

We connect a signal from our class to the QCoreApplication instance, so that if we signal that we have finished, it will trigger a slot on the latter to clean up and terminate the application.

After this, we call the method on our class to start its functionality and finally start the event loop by calling exec() on the QCoreApplication instance. At this point, we can use signals.

Note here that it is also possible to use Qt4-style connection syntax, instead of the earlier Qt5-style:

```
connect(core, SIGNAL(done()), &app, SLOT(quit()), Qt::QueuedConnection);
```

Functionally, this makes no difference, and using either is fine for most situations.

Our class appears as follows:

```
#include <QObject>

class Core : public QObject {
    Q_OBJECT
public:
    explicit Core(QObject *parent = 0);
```

```
signals:
    void done();
public slots:
    void start();
};
```

Every class in a Qt-based application that wants to make use of the signal-slot architecture of Qt is required to derive from the `QObject` class, and to include the `Q_OBJECT` macro within the class declaration. This is needed for Qt's `qmake preprocessor` tool to know which classes to process before the application code is compiled by the toolchain.

Here is the implementation:

```
#include "core.h"
#include <iostream>

Core::Core(QObject *parent) : QObject(parent) {
    //
}

void hang::start() {
    std::cout << "Start emitting done()" << std::endl;
    emit done();
}
```

Of note is the fact that we can let the constructor of any QObject-derived class know what the encapsulating parent class is, allowing said parent to own these child classes and invoke their destructor when it itself is destroyed.

GUI-based Qt applications

Returning to the Qt-based example project from Chapter 8, *Example - Linux-Based Infotainment System,* we can now compare its main function to the preceding command-line-only version to see what changes once we add a GUI to the project:

```
#include "mainwindow.h"
#include <QApplication>

int main(int argc, char *argv[]) {
    QApplication a(argc, argv);
    MainWindow w;
    w.show();
    return a.exec();
}
```

The most obvious change here is that we use QApplication instead of QCoreApplication. The other big change is that we do not use a completely custom class, but one that derives from QMainWindow:

```cpp
#include <QMainWindow>

#include <QAudioRecorder>
#include <QAudioProbe>
#include <QMediaPlayer>


namespace Ui {
    class MainWindow;
}

class MainWindow : public QMainWindow {
    Q_OBJECT
public:
    explicit MainWindow(QWidget *parent = nullptr);
    ~MainWindow();
public slots:
    void playBluetooth();
    void stopBluetooth();
    void playOnlineStream();
    void stopOnlineStream();
    void playLocalFile();
    void stopLocalFile();
    void recordMessage();
    void playMessage();
    void errorString(QString err);
    void quit();
private:
    Ui::MainWindow *ui;
    QMediaPlayer* player;
    QAudioRecorder* audioRecorder;
    QAudioProbe* audioProbe;
    qint64 silence;
private slots:
    void processBuffer(QAudioBuffer);
};
```

Here, we can see that the `MainWindow` class indeed derives from `QMainWindow`, which also gives it its `show()` method. Of note is the `MainWindow` instance being declared in the UI namespace. This is connected to the auto-generated code that is created when we run the qmake tool on the UI file, as we will see in a moment. Next is the constructor:

```
MainWindow::MainWindow(QWidget *parent)  : QMainWindow(parent),
    ui(new Ui::MainWindow) {
    ui->setupUi(this);
```

The first thing of note here is how we inflate the GUI from the UI description file. This file is usually created by visually laying out the GUI with the Qt Designer tool, which is part of the Qt Creator IDE. This UI file contains a description of each widget's properties, along with the layout applied to them, and so on.

It's also possible to programmatically create these widgets and add them to layouts, of course. This gets quite tedious for larger layouts, however. Generally, you create a single UI file for the main window, and an additional one for each sub window and dialog. These can then be inflated into a window or dialog in a similar fashion:

```
connect(ui->actionQuit, SIGNAL(triggered()), this, SLOT(quit()));
```

Menu actions in the GUI are connected to internal slots by specifying the specific signal on the menu action (`QAction` instance). We can see here that they are in the `ui` object, which is found in the auto-generated source code for the UI file, as we mentioned earlier:

```
    connect(ui->playBluetoothButton, SIGNAL(pressed), this,
SLOT(playBluetooth));
    connect(ui->stopBluetoothButton, SIGNAL(pressed), this,
SLOT(stopBluetooth));
    connect(ui->playLocalAudioButton, SIGNAL(pressed), this,
SLOT(playLocalFile));
    connect(ui->stopLocalAudioButton, SIGNAL(pressed), this,
SLOT(stopLocalFile));
    connect(ui->playOnlineStreamButton, SIGNAL(pressed), this,
SLOT(playOnlineStream));
    connect(ui->stopOnlineStreamButton, SIGNAL(pressed), this,
SLOT(stopOnlineStream));
    connect(ui->recordMessageButton, SIGNAL(pressed), this,
SLOT(recordMessage));
    connect(ui->playBackMessage, SIGNAL(pressed), this, SLOT(playMessage));
```

Button widgets in the GUI are connected in a similar manner, though they of course emit a different signal on account of them being a different type of widget:

```
silence = 0;
// Create the audio interface instances.
player = new QMediaPlayer(this);
audioRecorder = new QAudioRecorder(this);
audioProbe = new QAudioProbe(this);
// Configure the audio recorder.
QAudioEncoderSettings audioSettings;
audioSettings.setCodec("audio/amr");
audioSettings.setQuality(QMultimedia::HighQuality);
audioRecorder->setEncodingSettings(audioSettings);
audioRecorder->setOutputLocation(QUrl::fromLocalFile("message/last_message.
amr"));
// Configure audio probe.
connect(audioProbe, SIGNAL(audioBufferProbed(QAudioBuffer)), this,
SLOT(processBuffer(QAudioBuffer)));
audioProbe→setSource(audioRecorder);
```

We're free to do anything we would do in any other constructor, including setting defaults and creating instances of classes we will need later on:

```
QThread* thread = new QThread;
VoiceInput* vi = new VoiceInput();
vi->moveToThread(thread);
connect(thread, SIGNAL(started()), vi, SLOT(run()));
connect(vi, SIGNAL(finished()), thread, SLOT(quit()));
connect(vi, SIGNAL(finished()), vi, SLOT(deleteLater()));
connect(thread, SIGNAL(finished()), thread, SLOT(deleteLater()));
connect(vi, SIGNAL(error(QString)), this, SLOT(errorString(QString)));
connect(vi, SIGNAL(playBluetooth), this, SLOT(playBluetooth));
connect(vi, SIGNAL(stopBluetooth), this, SLOT(stopBluetooth));
connect(vi, SIGNAL(playLocal), this, SLOT(playLocalFile));
connect(vi, SIGNAL(stopLocal), this, SLOT(stopLocalFile));
connect(vi, SIGNAL(playRemote), this, SLOT(playOnlineStream));
connect(vi, SIGNAL(stopRemote), this, SLOT(stopOnlineStream));
connect(vi, SIGNAL(recordMessage), this, SLOT(recordMessage));
connect(vi, SIGNAL(playMessage), this, SLOT(playMessage));
thread->start();
}
```

One crucial thing to remember here is that this class runs on the UI thread, meaning that we should not do anything intensive in here. That's why we move such class instances off to their own thread, as shown here:

```
MainWindow::~MainWindow() {
    delete ui;
}
```

In the constructor, we delete the UI and all associated elements.

Embedded Qt

A major target of the Qt framework next to desktop systems are **embedded systems**, specifically **Embedded Linux**, where there are a few different ways to use Q. The main point of embedded Qt is to optimize the software stock by allowing you to boot straight into a Qt-optimized environment, and by allowing for a variety of ways to render to the display.

Qt for Embedded Linux supports the following platform plugins for rendering:

Plugin	Description
EGLFS	Provides an interface to OpenGL ES or similar 3D rendering API. Usually, the default configuration for Embedded Linux. More details about EGL can be found at the following address: https://www.khronos.org/egl.
LinuxFB	Writes directly to the framebuffer via Linux's fbdev subsystem. Only software-rendered content is supported. As a result, on some setups the display performance is likely to be limited.
DirectFB	Directly writes to the graphic card's framebuffer using the DirectFB library.
Wayland	Uses the Wayland windowing system. This allows for multiple concurrent windows, but is of course more demanding on the hardware.

In addition to this, Qt for Embedded Linux comes with a variety of APIs for handling touch and pen input, and so on. To optimize the system for a Qt-based application, any unrelated services, processes, and libraries are generally removed, resulting in a system that boots within a matter of seconds into the embedded application.

Custom GUIs with stylesheets

The standard widget-based GUIs that desktop systems tend to use do not lend themselves that readily to customization. As a result, you are generally faced with having to either override the painting function in a `QWidget` instance and handle every single pixel of the widget drawing, or to use stylesheet-based customization.

Qt stylesheets allow you to tweak the look and feel of individual widgets, even dynamically. They are essentially written using **Cascading Style Sheet** (**CSS**) syntax as used with HTML pages. They allow you to change elements of a widget, such as the borders, rounding corners, or the thickness and color of the elements.

QML

Qt Modeling Language (**QML**) is a user interface markup language. It is strongly based on JavaScript and even uses inline JavaScript. It can be used to create dynamic and completely custom user interfaces, and is usually used together with the Qt Quick module.

Later in this chapter, we will take an in-depth look at how a dynamic GUI is created.

3D designer

With Qt 5, the Qt 3D module was introduced, which streamlined access to the OpenGL rendering API. This new module was used as the foundation for the Qt 3D Designer editor and the accompanying runtime. It can be used to create highly dynamic GUIs, featuring a combination of 2D and 3D elements.

It is quite similar to hand-crafted QML-based GUIs, but provides a more streamlined workflow, ease of adding animations, and previewing the project. It's similar to the Qt Designer Studio, which focuses more on 2D GUIs, but this one is not available for free, instead requiring you to purchase a license.

An example of adding a GUI to the infotainment system

In this example, we will be using C++, Qt, and QML to create a graphical user interface that is capable of showing the current track that is playing, performing an audio visualization, indicating the playback progress, and allowing you to toggle different input modes using onscreen buttons.

This example is based on the *Audio Visualizer* example from the Qt documentation. This can be found in the Qt installation folder (if examples got installed), as well as on the Qt site: `https://doc.qt.io/qt-5/qt3d-audio-visualizer-qml-example.html`.

The main difference between this code and the official example is that the `QMediaPlayer` media player was moved into the C++ code, along with a number of other functions. Instead, a number of signals and slots between the QML UI and C++ backend are used in the new `QmlInterface` class for button presses, updating the UI, and interaction with the media player.

A GUI such as this could be wired into the existing infotainment project code to control its functionality, using the GUI in addition to the voice-driven interface.

The GUI we're putting together in this example looks like this in action:

Main

The main source file appears as follows:

```
#include "interface.h"
#include <QtGui/QGuiApplication>
#include <QtGui/QOpenGLContext>
#include <QtQuick/QQuickView>
#include <QtQuick/QQuickItem>
#include <QtQml/QQmlContext>
#include <QObject>

int main(int argc, char* argv[]) {
    QGuiApplication app(argc, argv);
    QSurfaceFormat format;
    if (QOpenGLContext::openGLModuleType() == QOpenGLContext::LibGL) {
        format.setVersion(3, 2);
        format.setProfile(QSurfaceFormat::CoreProfile);
    }
    format.setDepthBufferSize(24);
    format.setStencilBufferSize(8);
```

```
    QQuickView view;
    view.setFormat(format);
    view.create();
    QmlInterface qmlinterface;
    view.rootContext()->setContextProperty("qmlinterface", &qmlinterface);
    view.setSource(QUrl("qrc:/main.qml"));
    qmlinterface.setPlaying();

    view.setResizeMode(QQuickView::SizeRootObjectToView);
    view.setMaximumSize(QSize(1820, 1080));
    view.setMinimumSize(QSize(300, 150));
    view.show();

    return app.exec();
}
```

Our custom class is added to the QML viewer (QQuickView) as a context class. This serves as the proxy between the QML UI and our C++ code, as we will see in a moment. The viewer itself uses an OpenGL surface to render the UI on.

QmlInterface

The header of our custom class features a number of additions to make properties and methods visible to the QML code:

```
#include <QtCore/QObject>
#include <QMediaPlayer>
#include <QByteArray>


class QmlInterface : public QObject {
    Q_OBJECT
    Q_PROPERTY(QString durationTotal READ getDurationTotal NOTIFY
durationTotalChanged)
    Q_PROPERTY(QString durationLeft READ getDurationLeft NOTIFY
durationLeftChanged)
```

The Q_PROPERTY tag tells the qmake parser that this class contains a property (variable) that should be made visible to the QML code, with the parameters specifying the name of the variable, the methods used for reading and writing the variable (if desired), and finally the signal that is emitted whenever the property has changed.

This allows for an automatic update feature to be set up to keep this property synchronized between the C++ code and the QML side:

```
        QString formatDuration(qint64 milliseconds);
        QMediaPlayer mediaPlayer;
        QByteArray magnitudeArray;
        const int millisecondsPerBar = 68;
        QString durationTotal;
        QString durationLeft;
        qint64 trackDuration;
public:
        explicit QmlInterface(QObject *parent = nullptr);

        Q_INVOKABLE bool isHoverEnabled() const;
        Q_INVOKABLE void setPlaying();
        Q_INVOKABLE void setStopped();
        Q_INVOKABLE void setPaused();
        Q_INVOKABLE qint64 duration();
        Q_INVOKABLE qint64 position();
        Q_INVOKABLE double getNextAudioLevel(int offsetMs);
        QString getDurationTotal() { return durationTotal; }
        QString getDurationLeft() { return durationLeft; }

public slots:
        void mediaStatusChanged(QMediaPlayer::MediaStatus status);
        void durationChanged(qint64 duration);
        void positionChanged(qint64 position);
signals:
        void start();
        void stopped();
        void paused();
        void playing();
        void durationTotalChanged();
        void durationLeftChanged();
};
```

Similarly, the Q_INVOKABLE tag ensures that these methods are made visible to the QML side and can be called from there.

Here is the implementation:

```
#include "interface.h"
#include <QtGui/QTouchDevice>
#include <QDebug>
#include <QFile>
#include <QtMath>

QmlInterface::QmlInterface(QObject *parent) : QObject(parent) {
```

```
    // Set track for media player.
    mediaPlayer.setMedia(QUrl("qrc:/music/tiltshifted_lost_neon_sun.mp3"));
    // Load magnitude file for the audio track.
    QFile magFile(":/music/visualization.raw", this);
    magFile.open(QFile::ReadOnly);
    magnitudeArray = magFile.readAll();
    // Media player connections.
    connect(&mediaPlayer,
SIGNAL(mediaStatusChanged(QMediaPlayer::MediaStatus)), this,
SLOT(mediaStatusChanged(QMediaPlayer::MediaStatus)));
    connect(&mediaPlayer, SIGNAL(durationChanged(qint64)), this,
SLOT(durationChanged(qint64)));
    connect(&mediaPlayer, SIGNAL(positionChanged(qint64)), this,
SLOT(positionChanged(qint64)));
}
```

The constructor got changed considerably from the original example project, with the media player instance being created here, along with its connections.

We load the same music file here as was used with the original project. When integrating the code into the infotainment project or a similar project, you would make this dynamic. Similarly, the file that we are also loading here to get the amplitude for the music file with the visualization would likely be omitted in a full integration, instead opting to generate the amplitude values dynamically:

```
bool QmlInterface::isHoverEnabled() const {
#if defined(Q_OS_IOS) || defined(Q_OS_ANDROID) || defined(Q_OS_QNX) ||
defined(Q_OS_WINRT)
    return false;
#else
    bool isTouch = false;
    foreach (const QTouchDevice *dev, QTouchDevice::devices()) {
        if (dev->type() == QTouchDevice::TouchScreen) {
            isTouch = true;
            break;
        }
    }
    bool isMobile = false;
    if (qEnvironmentVariableIsSet("QT_QUICK_CONTROLS_MOBILE")) {
        isMobile = true;
    }
    return !isTouch && !isMobile;
#endif
}
```

This was the only method that previously existed in the QML context class. It's used to detect whether the code runs on a mobile device with a touch screen:

```cpp
void QmlInterface::setPlaying() {
    mediaPlayer.play();
}

void QmlInterface::setStopped() {
    mediaPlayer.stop();
}

void QmlInterface::setPaused() {
    mediaPlayer.pause();
}
```

We got a number of control methods that connect to the buttons in the UI to allow for control of the media player instance:

```cpp
void QmlInterface::mediaStatusChanged(QMediaPlayer::MediaStatus status) {
    if (status == QMediaPlayer::EndOfMedia) {
        emit stopped();
    }
}
```

This slot method is used to detect when the media player has reached the end of the active track, so that the UI can be signaled that it should update to indicate this:

```cpp
void QmlInterface::durationChanged(qint64 duration) {
    qDebug() << "Duration changed: " << duration;
    durationTotal = formatDuration(duration);
    durationLeft = "-" + durationTotal;
    trackDuration = duration;
    emit start();
    emit durationTotalChanged();
    emit durationLeftChanged();
}

void QmlInterface::positionChanged(qint64 position) {
    qDebug() << "Position changed: " << position;
    durationLeft = "-" + formatDuration((trackDuration - position));
    emit durationLeftChanged();
}
```

These two slot methods are connected to the media player instance. The duration slot is required because the length (duration) of a newly loaded track will not be immediately available. Instead, it's an asynchronously updated property.

As a result, we have to wait until the media player has finished with this and emits the signal that it has completed this process.

Next, to allow us to update the time remaining on the current track, we also get constant updates on the current position from the media player so that we can update the UI with the new value.

Both the duration and position properties are updated in the UI using the linkage method we saw in the description of the header file for this class.

Finally, we emit a `start()` signal, which is linked into a slot in the QML code that will start the visualization process, as we will see later on in the QML code:

```
qint64 QmlInterface::duration() {
    qDebug() << "Returning duration value: " << mediaPlayer.duration();
    return mediaPlayer.duration();
}

qint64 QmlInterface::position() {
    qDebug() << "Returning position value: " << mediaPlayer.position();
    return mediaPlayer.position();
}
```

The duration property is also used by the visualization code. Here, we allow it to be obtained directly. Similarly, we make the position property available as well with a direct call:

```
double QmlInterface::getNextAudioLevel(int offsetMs) {
    // Calculate the integer index position in to the magnitude array
    qint64 index = ((mediaPlayer.position() + offsetMs) /
millisecondsPerBar) | 0;

    if (index < 0 || index >= (magnitudeArray.length() / 2)) {
        return 0.0;
    }

    return (((quint16*) magnitudeArray.data())[index] / 63274.0);
}
```

This method was ported from the JavaScript code in the original project, performing the same task of determining the audio level based on the amplitude data we read in previously from the file:

```
QString QmlInterface::formatDuration(qint64 milliseconds) {
    qint64 minutes = floor(milliseconds / 60000);
    milliseconds -= minutes * 60000;
    qint64 seconds = milliseconds / 1000;
```

```
        seconds = round(seconds);
        if (seconds < 10) {
            return QString::number(minutes) + ":0" + QString::number(seconds);
        }
        else {
            return QString::number(minutes) + ":" + QString::number(seconds);
        }
    }
```

Similarly, this method was also ported from the original project's JavaScript code, since we moved the code that relies on it into the C++ code. It takes in the millisecond count for the track duration or position and converts it into a string containing the minutes and seconds, matching the original value.

QML

Moving on, we are done with the C++ side of things and can now look at the QML UI.

First, here is the main QML file:

```
import QtQuick 2.0
import QtQuick.Scene3D 2.0
import QtQuick.Layouts 1.2
import QtMultimedia 5.0

Item {
    id: mainview
    width: 1215
    height: 720
    visible: true
    property bool isHoverEnabled: false
    property int mediaLatencyOffset: 68
```

The QML file consists out of a hierarchy of elements. Here, we define the top element, giving it its dimensions and name:

```
    state: "stopped"
    states: [
        State {
            name: "playing"
            PropertyChanges {
                target: playButtonImage
                source: {
                    if (playButtonMouseArea.containsMouse)
                        "qrc:/images/pausehoverpressed.png"
                    else
```

```
                      "qrc:/images/pausenormal.png"
                }
            }
            PropertyChanges {
                target: stopButtonImage
                source: "qrc:/images/stopnormal.png"
            }
        },
        State {
            name: "paused"
            PropertyChanges {
                target: playButtonImage
                source: {
                    if (playButtonMouseArea.containsMouse)
                        "qrc:/images/playhoverpressed.png"
                    else
                        "qrc:/images/playnormal.png"
                }
            }
            PropertyChanges {
                target: stopButtonImage
                source: "qrc:/images/stopnormal.png"
            }
        },
        State {
            name: "stopped"
            PropertyChanges {
                target: playButtonImage
                source: "qrc:/images/playnormal.png"
            }
            PropertyChanges {
                target: stopButtonImage
                source: "qrc:/images/stopdisabled.png"
            }
        }
    }
]
```

A number of states for the UI are defined, along with the changes that should be triggered if the state should change to it:

```
Connections {
    target: qmlinterface
    onStopped: mainview.state = "stopped"
    onPaused: mainview.state = "paused"
    onPlaying: mainview.state = "started"
    onStart: visualizer.startVisualization()
}
```

These are the connections that link the signals from the C++ side to a local handler. We target our custom class as the source of these signals, then define the handler for each signal we wish to handle by prefixing it and adding the code that should be executed.

Here, we see that the start signal is linked to a handler that triggers the function in the visualization module that starts that module:

```
Component.onCompleted: isHoverEnabled = qmlinterface.isHoverEnabled()

Image {
    id: coverImage
    anchors.fill: parent
    source: "qrc:/images/albumcover.png"
}
```

This `Image` element defines the background image, which we load from the resources that were added to the executable when the project was built:

```
Scene3D {
    anchors.fill: parent

    Visualizer {
        id: visualizer
        animationState: mainview.state
        numberOfBars: 120
        barRotationTimeMs: 8160 // 68 ms per bar
    }
}
```

The 3D scene that will be filled with the visualizer's content is defined:

```
Rectangle {
    id: blackBottomRect
    color: "black"
    width: parent.width
    height: 0.14 * mainview.height
    anchors.bottom: parent.bottom
}

Text {
    text: qmlinterface.durationTotal
    color: "#80C342"
    x: parent.width / 6
    y: mainview.height - mainview.height / 8
    font.pixelSize: 12
}

Text {
```

```
        text: qmlinterface.durationLeft
        color: "#80C342"
        x: parent.width - parent.width / 6
        y: mainview.height - mainview.height / 8
        font.pixelSize: 12
    }
```

These two text elements are linked with the property in our custom C++ class, as we saw earlier. These values will be kept updated with the value in the C++ class instance as it changes:

```
    property int buttonHorizontalMargin: 10
    Rectangle {
        id: playButton
        height: 54
        width: 54
        anchors.bottom: parent.bottom
        anchors.bottomMargin: width
        x: parent.width / 2 - width - buttonHorizontalMargin
        color: "transparent"

        Image {
            id: playButtonImage
            source: "qrc:/images/pausenormal.png"
        }

        MouseArea {
            id: playButtonMouseArea
            anchors.fill: parent
            hoverEnabled: isHoverEnabled
            onClicked: {
                if (mainview.state == 'paused' || mainview.state ==
'stopped')
                    mainview.state = 'playing'
                else
                    mainview.state = 'paused'
            }
            onEntered: {
                if (mainview.state == 'playing')
                    playButtonImage.source =
"qrc:/images/pausehoverpressed.png"
                else
                    playButtonImage.source =
"qrc:/images/playhoverpressed.png"
            }
            onExited: {
                if (mainview.state == 'playing')
                    playButtonImage.source = "qrc:/images/pausenormal.png"
```

```
            else
                playButtonImage.source = "qrc:/images/playnormal.png"
            }
        }
    }

    Rectangle {
        id: stopButton
        height: 54
        width: 54
        anchors.bottom: parent.bottom
        anchors.bottomMargin: width
        x: parent.width / 2 + buttonHorizontalMargin
        color: "transparent"

        Image {
            id: stopButtonImage
            source: "qrc:/images/stopnormal.png"
        }

        MouseArea {
            anchors.fill: parent
            hoverEnabled: isHoverEnabled
            onClicked: mainview.state = 'stopped'
            onEntered: {
                if (mainview.state != 'stopped')
                    stopButtonImage.source =
"qrc:/images/stophoverpressed.png"
            }
            onExited: {
                if (mainview.state != 'stopped')
                    stopButtonImage.source = "qrc:/images/stopnormal.png"
            }
        }
    }
}
```

The rest of the source serves to set up the individual buttons for controlling the playback, with play, stop, and pause buttons, which get swapped over as needed.

Next, we will look at the amplitude bar file:

```
import Qt3D.Core 2.0
import Qt3D.Render 2.0
import Qt3D.Extras 2.0
import QtQuick 2.4 as QQ2

Entity {
```

```
property int rotationTimeMs: 0
property int entityIndex: 0
property int entityCount: 0
property int startAngle: 0 + 360 / entityCount * entityIndex
property bool needsNewMagnitude: true
property real magnitude: 0
property real animWeight: 0

property color lowColor: "black"
property color highColor: "#b3b3b3"
property color barColor: lowColor

property string entityAnimationsState: "stopped"
property bool entityAnimationsPlaying: true

property var entityMesh: null
```

A number of properties are defined before we dive into the animation state change handler:

```
onEntityAnimationsStateChanged: {
    if (animationState == "paused") {
        if (angleAnimation.running)
            angleAnimation.pause()
        if (barColorAnimations.running)
            barColorAnimations.pause()
    } else if (animationState == "playing"){
        needsNewMagnitude = true;
        if (heightDecreaseAnimation.running)
            heightDecreaseAnimation.stop()
        if (angleAnimation.paused) {
            angleAnimation.resume()
        } else if (!entityAnimationsPlaying) {
            magnitude = 0
            angleAnimation.start()
            entityAnimationsPlaying = true
        }
        if (barColorAnimations.paused)
            barColorAnimations.resume()
    } else {
        if (animWeight != 0)
            heightDecreaseAnimation.start()
        needsNewMagnitude = true
        angleAnimation.stop()
        barColorAnimations.stop()
        entityAnimationsPlaying = false
    }
}
```

Every time the audio playback is stopped, paused, or started, the animation has to be updated to match this state change:

```
property Material barMaterial: PhongMaterial {
    diffuse: barColor
    ambient: Qt.darker(barColor)
    specular: "black"
    shininess: 1
}
```

This defines the look of the amplitude bars, using Phong shading:

```
property Transform angleTransform: Transform {
    property real heightIncrease: magnitude * animWeight
    property real barAngle: startAngle

    matrix: {
        var m = Qt.matrix4x4()
        m.rotate(barAngle, Qt.vector3d(0, 1, 0))
        m.translate(Qt.vector3d(1.1, heightIncrease / 2 -
heightIncrease * 0.05, 0))
        m.scale(Qt.vector3d(0.5, heightIncrease * 15, 0.5))
        return m;
    }

    property real compareAngle: barAngle
    onBarAngleChanged: {
        compareAngle = barAngle

        if (compareAngle > 360)
            compareAngle = barAngle - 360

        if (compareAngle > 180) {
            parent.enabled = false
            animWeight = 0
            if (needsNewMagnitude) {
                // Calculate the ms offset where the bar will be at the
center point of the
                // visualization and fetch the correct magnitude for
that point in time.
                var offset = (90.0 + 360.0 - compareAngle) *
(rotationTimeMs / 360.0)
                magnitude = qmlinterface.getNextAudioLevel(offset)
                needsNewMagnitude = false
            }
        } else {
            parent.enabled = true
            // Calculate a power of 2 curve for the bar animation that
```

```
peaks at 90 degrees
                animWeight = Math.min((compareAngle / 90), (180 -
compareAngle) / 90)
                animWeight = animWeight * animWeight
                if (!needsNewMagnitude) {
                    needsNewMagnitude = true
                    barColorAnimations.start()
                }
            }
        }
    }
```

As the amplitude bars move across the screen, they change relative to the camera, so we need to keep calculating the new angle and display height.

In this section, we also replaced the original call to the audio level method with a call to the new method in our C++ class:

```
components: [entityMesh, barMaterial, angleTransform]

QQ2.NumberAnimation {
    id: angleAnimation
    target: angleTransform
    property: "barAngle"
    duration: rotationTimeMs
    loops: QQ2.Animation.Infinite
    running: true
    from: startAngle
    to: 360 + startAngle
}

QQ2.NumberAnimation {
    id: heightDecreaseAnimation
    target: angleTransform
    property: "heightIncrease"
    duration: 400
    running: false
    from: angleTransform.heightIncrease
    to: 0
    onStopped: barColor = lowColor
}

property int animationDuration: angleAnimation.duration / 6

QQ2.SequentialAnimation on barColor {
    id: barColorAnimations
    running: false
```

```
    QQ2.ColorAnimation {
        from: lowColor
        to: highColor
        duration: animationDuration
    }

    QQ2.PauseAnimation {
        duration: animationDuration
    }

    QQ2.ColorAnimation {
        from: highColor
        to: lowColor
        duration: animationDuration
    }
  }
}
```

The rest of the file contains a few more animation transforms.

Finally, here is the visualization module:

```
import Qt3D.Core 2.0
import Qt3D.Render 2.0
import Qt3D.Extras 2.0
import QtQuick 2.2 as QQ2

Entity {
    id: sceneRoot
    property int barRotationTimeMs: 1
    property int numberOfBars: 1
    property string animationState: "stopped"
    property real titleStartAngle: 95
    property real titleStopAngle: 5

    onAnimationStateChanged: {
        if (animationState == "playing") {
            qmlinterface.setPlaying();
            if (progressTransformAnimation.paused)
                progressTransformAnimation.resume()
            else
                progressTransformAnimation.start()
        } else if (animationState == "paused") {
            qmlinterface.setPaused();
            if (progressTransformAnimation.running)
                progressTransformAnimation.pause()
        } else {
            qmlinterface.setStopped();
```

```
            progressTransformAnimation.stop()
            progressTransform.progressAngle =
    progressTransform.defaultStartAngle
        }
    }
```

This section got changed from interacting with the local media player instance to the new one in the C++ code. Beyond that, we left it unchanged. This is the main handler for when anything changes in the scene due to user interaction, or a track starting or ending:

```
QQ2.Item {
    id: stateItem

    state: animationState
    states: [
        QQ2.State {
            name: "playing"
            QQ2.PropertyChanges {
                target: titlePrism
                titleAngle: titleStopAngle
            }
        },
        QQ2.State {
            name: "paused"
            QQ2.PropertyChanges {
                target: titlePrism
                titleAngle: titleStopAngle
            }
        },
        QQ2.State {
            name: "stopped"
            QQ2.PropertyChanges {
                target: titlePrism
                titleAngle: titleStartAngle
            }
        }
    ]

    transitions: QQ2.Transition {
        QQ2.NumberAnimation {
            property: "titleAngle"
            duration: 2000
            running: false
        }
    }
}
```

A number of property changes and transitions are defined for the track title object:

```
function startVisualization() {
    progressTransformAnimation.duration = qmlinterface.duration()
    mainview.state = "playing"
    progressTransformAnimation.start()
}
```

This function is what starts the entire visualization sequence. It uses the track duration, as obtained via our C++ class instance, to determine the dimensions of the progress bar for the track playback animation before starting the visualization animation:

```
Camera {
    id: camera
    projectionType: CameraLens.PerspectiveProjection
    fieldOfView: 45
    aspectRatio: 1820 / 1080
    nearPlane: 0.1
    farPlane: 1000.0
    position: Qt.vector3d(0.014, 0.956, 2.178)
    upVector: Qt.vector3d(0.0, 1.0, 0.0)
    viewCenter: Qt.vector3d(0.0, 0.7, 0.0)
}
```

A camera is defined for the 3D scene:

```
Entity {
    components: [
        DirectionalLight {
            intensity: 0.9
            worldDirection: Qt.vector3d(0, 0.6, -1)
        }
    ]
}

RenderSettings {
    id: external_forward_renderer
    activeFrameGraph: ForwardRenderer {
        camera: camera
        clearColor: "transparent"
    }
}
```

A renderer and light for the scene are created:

```
components: [external_forward_renderer]

CuboidMesh {
    id: barMesh
    xExtent: 0.1
    yExtent: 0.1
    zExtent: 0.1
}
```

A mesh is created for the amplitude bars:

```
NodeInstantiator {
    id: collection
    property int maxCount: parent.numberOfBars
    model: maxCount

    delegate: BarEntity {
        id: cubicEntity
        entityMesh: barMesh
        rotationTimeMs: sceneRoot.barRotationTimeMs
        entityIndex: index
        entityCount: sceneRoot.numberOfBars
        entityAnimationsState: animationState
        magnitude: 0
    }
}
```

The number of bars, along with other properties, is defined:

```
Entity {
    id: titlePrism
    property real titleAngle: titleStartAngle

    Entity {
        id: titlePlane

        PlaneMesh {
            id: titlePlaneMesh
            width: 550
            height: 100
        }

        Transform {
            id: titlePlaneTransform
            scale: 0.003
            translation: Qt.vector3d(0, 0.11, 0)
```

```
        }

        NormalDiffuseMapAlphaMaterial {
            id: titlePlaneMaterial
            diffuse: TextureLoader { source:
"qrc:/images/demotitle.png" }
            normal: TextureLoader { source: "qrc:/images/normalmap.png"
}

            shininess: 1.0
        }

        components: [titlePlaneMesh, titlePlaneMaterial,
titlePlaneTransform]
    }
```

This plane contains the title object whenever there's no track playing:

```
        Entity {
            id: songTitlePlane

            PlaneMesh {
                id: songPlaneMesh
                width: 550
                height: 100
            }

            Transform {
                id: songPlaneTransform
                scale: 0.003
                rotationX: 90
                translation: Qt.vector3d(0, -0.03, 0.13)
            }

            property Material songPlaneMaterial:
NormalDiffuseMapAlphaMaterial {
                diffuse: TextureLoader { source:
"qrc:/images/songtitle.png" }
                normal: TextureLoader { source: "qrc:/images/normalmap.png"
}

                shininess: 1.0
            }

            components: [songPlaneMesh, songPlaneMaterial,
songPlaneTransform]
        }
```

This plane contains the song title whenever a track is active:

```
property Transform titlePrismPlaneTransform: Transform {
    matrix: {
        var m = Qt.matrix4x4()
        m.translate(Qt.vector3d(-0.5, 1.3, -0.4))
        m.rotate(titlePrism.titleAngle, Qt.vector3d(1, 0, 0))
        return m;
    }
}

components: [titlePlane, songTitlePlane, titlePrismPlaneTransform]
}
```

To transform the planes between playing and non-playing transitions, this transform is used:

```
Mesh {
    id: circleMesh
    source: "qrc:/meshes/circle.obj"
}

Entity {
    id: circleEntity
    property Material circleMaterial: PhongAlphaMaterial {
        alpha: 0.4
        ambient: "black"
        diffuse: "black"
        specular: "black"
        shininess: 10000
    }

    components: [circleMesh, circleMaterial]
}
```

A circle mesh that provides a reflection effect is added:

```
Mesh {
    id: progressMesh
    source: "qrc:/meshes/progressbar.obj"
}

Transform {
    id: progressTransform
    property real defaultStartAngle: -90
    property real progressAngle: defaultStartAngle
    rotationY: progressAngle
}

Entity {
    property Material progressMaterial: PhongMaterial {
        ambient: "purple"
        diffuse: "white"
    }

    components: [progressMesh, progressMaterial, progressTransform]
}

QQ2.NumberAnimation {
    id: progressTransformAnimation
    target: progressTransform
    property: "progressAngle"
    duration: 0
    running: false
    from: progressTransform.defaultStartAngle
    to: -270
    onStopped: if (animationState != "stopped") animationState =
"stopped"
    }
}
```

Finally, this mesh creates the progress bar, which moves from the left to the right to indicate playback progress.

The entire project is compiled by running qmake followed by make, or by opening the project in Qt Creator and building it from there. When run, it will automatically start playing the included song and show the amplitude visualization, while being controllable via the buttons in the UI.

Summary

In this chapter, we looked at the myriad ways in which the Qt framework can be used to develop for embedded systems. We briefly looked at how it compares with other frameworks and how Qt is optimized for these embedded platforms, before working through an example of a QML-based GUI that could be added to the infotainment system we previously created.

You should now be able to create basic Qt applications, both purely command line-based and with a GUI. You should also have a clear idea of which options Qt offers to develop GUIs with.

In the next chapter, we will be taking a look at the next evolution of embedded platforms, using **field-programmable gate arrays** (**FPGAs**) to add custom, hardware-based functionality to speed up embedded platforms.

11
Developing for Hybrid SoC/FPGA Systems

In addition to standard CPU-based embedded systems, an increasingly common approach has been to combine CPUs in the form of SoCs with **Field Programmable Gate Arrays (FGPAs)**. This allows CPU-intensive algorithms and processing, including DSP and image processing, to be implemented on the FPGA part of the system, with the CPU side handling less intensive tasks, such as user interaction, storage, and networking.

In this chapter, we will cover the following topics:

- How to communicate with the FPGA side of a hybrid FPGA/SoC system
- Learning how a variety of algorithms are implemented in FPGA and used from the SoC side
- How to implement a basic oscilloscope on a hybrid FPGA/SoC system

Going extremely parallel

When it comes to performance, executing a single instruction at a time on a single-core processor is essentially the slowest way you can implement an algorithm or other functionality. From here, you can scale this singular execution flow to multiple flows using simultaneous scheduling on a single processor core's individual functional units.

The next step to increase performance is to add more cores, which of course complicates the scheduling even more, and introduces potential latency issues with critical tasks being postponed because less critical tasks are blocking resources. The use of general purpose processors is also very limiting for certain tasks, especially those that are embarrassingly parallel.

For tasks where a single large dataset has to be processed using the same algorithm applied to each element in the set, the use of **general-purpose graphical processor unit-based processing (GPGPU)** has become very popular, along with the use of **Digital Signal Processors (DSPs)** to massively speed up a range of operations by using specialized hardware.

On the other side of this issue are the tasks, which are massively parallel, but involve many dissimilar operations being performed on incoming data, internal data, or both. This is level of complexity that it would be extremely hard to get any reasonable performance for if implemented purely in software for a range of microprocessor cores.

The use of expensive DSP hardware might help here, but even that would not be optimized for the task. Traditionally, this would be the point where a company might consider having a custom **integrated circuit (IC)** designed and produced as an **application-specific integrated circuit (ASIC)**. The costs for this are, however, extremely high, and only realistic for large-volume production where it could compete with other options.

Over time, different solutions were invented to make such custom hardware implementations more realistic, one of which was the development of the programmable logic chip. A system like the Commodore 64, for example, contained a **PLA** (short for **Programmable Logic Array**, originally a Signetics 82S100) chip, which was a one-time programmable array of combinatorial logic elements. It allowed the processor to reconfigure the on-board routing of the address bus to change what parts of the DRAM memory chips, ROM chips, and other peripherals were in the active addressing space.

After programming the PLA, it functioned in essentially the same way as a large number of 74-logic chips (discrete logic chips), but in a fraction of the space required for such a discrete solution. This approach essentially gave Commodore their very own custom ASIC, but without having to invest money in having to design and produce it. Instead, they used an off-the-shelf part, and were free to make improvements to the logic burned into the PLA chip during the lifetime of the Commodore 64.

Over time, PLAs (also referred to as PALs) became more advanced, developing into **Complex Programmable Logic Devices (CPLDs)**, which are based around macrocells, which allow for the implementation of more advanced features instead of just simple combinatorial logic. These eventually evolved into FPGAs, which again add more advanced features and peripherals.

These days, FPGAs are found almost everywhere where some kind of advanced processing or control is required. Video and audio-processing equipment often use FPGAs alongside DSPs, with an MCU or SoC handling the user interface and other low-priority functionality.

Today, devices such as oscilloscopes are implemented with an analog (and digital, if supported) frontend, with DSPs doing the raw converting of data and the initial processing of this data prior to handing it over to one or more FPGAs , which perform further processing and analysis of the data. After processing, this data can be stored in a buffer (the "digital storage" part of a **digital storage oscilloscope** (**DSO**) as well as handed over to the frontend, where the software running on the SoC will render it in the user interface and allow the user to input commands manipulation the displayed data.

In this chapter, we will look at a basic oscilloscope project that will be implemented using simple hardware and an FPGA programmed using VHDL code.

Hardware description languages

As the complexity of **Very Large Scale Integrated** (**VLSI**) circuits increased over the past decades, it became more and more crucial to find ways to improve the development process, including the ability to verify the design. This led to the development of **hardware description languages** (**HDLs**), of which today VHDL and Verilog are the two most commonly used ones.

The main purpose of HDLs is to allow a developer to easily describe hardware circuits of the type that would be integrated into ASICs or used to program FPGAs with. In addition, these HDLs also make it possible to simulate the design and to validate its functional correctness.

In this chapter, we will look at an example that uses VHDL for the side of the programming that is implemented on the FPGA. **VHSIC Hardware Description Language** (**VHDL**) as a language first appeared in 1983, when it was developed by the US Department of Defense. It was intended to act as a way to document the behavior of ASICs that suppliers would provide with equipment.

Over time, the idea was broached that these documentation files could be used to simulate the behavior of the ASICs. This development was soon followed by the development of synthesis tools, to create a functional hardware implementation that could be used to create ASICs.

VHDL is heavily based on the Ada programming language, which itself also has its roots in the US military. Although VHDL is primarily used as an HDL, it can also be used as a generic programming language, much like Ada and its kin.

FPGA architecture

Though not every FPGA is structured the same way, the general principle remains the same: they are arrays of logic elements that can be configured to form specific circuits. The complexity of these **logic elements (LEs)** therefore determines what kind of logic circuits can be formed, which has to be taken into account when writing VHDL code for a specific FPGA architecture.

The terms **logic elements (LEs)** and **logic cells (LCs)** are used interchangeably. An LE consists of one or more **look-up tables (LUTs)**, with an LUT usually having between four and six inputs. Regardless of the exact configuration, each LE is surrounded by interconnection logic, which allows different LEs to be connected to each other, and the LE itself is programmed to a specific configuration, thus forming the intended circuit.

This potential pitfalls of developing for FPGAs include the strong assumption by FPGA manufacturers that FPGAs will be used with clocked designs (using a central clock source and clock domains), instead of combinatorial (unclocked) logic. In general, it's a good idea to familiarize yourself with a target FPGA system prior to including it in a new project to see how well it can support the features that you need.

Hybrid FPGA/SoC chips

Although systems that include both an FPGA and SoC have been very common for years, a more recent addition has been hybrid FPGA/SoC chips, which include the dies for both an FPGA and an SoC (usually ARM based) in the same package. These are then linked together with a bus so that both can efficiently communicate with each other using memory-mapped I/O and similar.

Common examples of such FPGAs currently include Altera (now Intel), Cyclone V SoC, and Xilinx Zynq. The Cyclone V SoC's block diagram from the official datasheet gives a good overview of how such a system works:

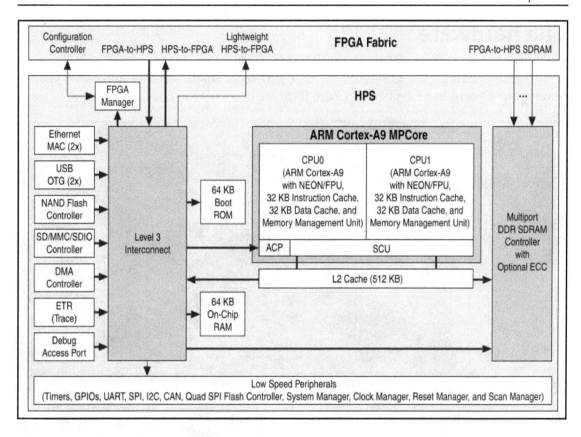

Here, we can see that there are a number of ways that the **Hard Processor System** (**HPS**) and FPGA sides can communicate with each other, such as via a shared SDRAM controller, two point-to-point links, and a number of other interfaces. For the Cyclone V SoC, either the FPGA or SoC side can be the first side that boots when the system starts, allowing for a wide range of system configuration options.

Example – basic oscilloscope

This example gives a basic overview of how one could use an FPGA in an embedded project. It uses the FPGA to sample an input and measure a voltage or similar, the way an oscilloscope would. The resulting ADC data is then sent over a serial link to a C++/Qt-based application, which displays the data.

The hardware

For the project, we will use a Fleasystems FleaFPGA Ohm board (`http://fleasystems.com/fleaFPGA_Ohm.html`). This is a small, sub-$50, sub-€40 FPGA development board in a Raspberry Pi Zero form factor:

It has the following specifications:

- **Lattice ECP5 FPGA** with 24K LUT elements and 112KB Block RAM.
- **256-Mbit SDRAM**, 16 bits wide and 167 MHz clock.
- **8-Mbit SPI Flash ROM** for FPGA configuration storage.
- 25 MHz Crystal oscillator.
- **HDMI video** out (up to 1080p30 or 720p60 screen modes possible).
- **µSD card slot**.
- Two micro USB host ports with alternate PS/2 host port functionality.

- 29 user GPIO, including 4 x medium-speed ADC inputs and 12 x LVDS signal pairs available from the (Raspberry Pi compatible) 40-pin expansion, and 2-pin reset headers, respectively.
- One micro USB slave port. Provides +5V supply feed to the Ohm, serial console/UART communications, as well as access to the on-board JTAG programming interface (for configuring the ECP5 FPGA).
- Provision for an external JTAG programming pod to allow real-time debugging.

To this board, we connect circuit which will allow us to connect an oscilloscope probe:

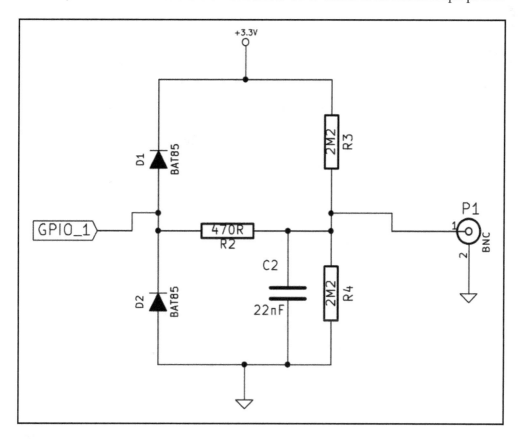

This circuit will be connected to pin number 29 on the Ohm board's GPIO header, corresponding to GPIO 5. It allows us to measure 0 to 3V DC signals, and 1.5V AC (RMS), in 1 x probe measurement mode. Bandwidth is a little over 10 MHz.

The VHDL code

In this section, we will take a look at the top-level entity in the VHDL project, to get an idea of what it does. This starts with the standard library includes for VHDL as shown:

```
library IEEE;
use IEEE.STD_LOGIC_1164.ALL;
use IEEE.std_logic_unsigned.ALL;
use IEEE.numeric_std.all;

entity FleaFPGA_Ohm_A5 is
    port(
    sys_clock          : in        std_logic;   -- 25MHz clock input from
external xtal oscillator.
    sys_reset          : in        std_logic;   -- master reset input from
reset header.
```

This maps to the underlying FPGA's system clock and reset line. We can also see the way that port mapping works, defining the direction of the entity port and the type. Here, the type is `std_logic`, which is a standard logic signal of either a binary one or zero:

```
    n_led1                   : buffer     std_logic;
    LVDS_Red           : out        std_logic_vector(0 downto 0);
    LVDS_Green         : out        std_logic_vector(0 downto 0);
    LVDS_Blue          : out        std_logic_vector(0 downto 0);
    LVDS_ck                  : out        std_logic_vector(0 downto 0);
    slave_tx_o         : out        std_logic;
    slave_rx_i         : in         std_logic;
    slave_cts_i        : in         std_logic;   -- Receive signal from #RTS
pin on FT230x
```

We also use the status LED on the board, map the HDMI's video pins (LVDS signaling), and the UART interface, which uses the FDTI USB-UART chip on the board. The latter is what we will be using to send the data from the FPGA to the C++ application.

Next, the Raspberry Pi compatible header mapping, as shown in the following code:

```
    GPIO_2                   : inout      std_logic;
    GPIO_3                   : inout      std_logic;
    GPIO_4                   : inout      std_logic;
    -- GPIO_5                : inout      std_logic;
    GPIO_6                   : inout      std_logic;
    GPIO_7                   : inout      std_logic;
    GPIO_8                   : inout      std_logic;
    GPIO_9                   : inout      std_logic;
    GPIO_10                  : inout      std_logic;
    GPIO_11                  : inout      std_logic;
```

```
GPIO_12                    : inout          std_logic;
GPIO_13                    : inout          std_logic;
GPIO_14                    : inout          std_logic;
GPIO_15                    : inout          std_logic;
GPIO_16                    : inout          std_logic;
GPIO_17                    : inout          std_logic;
GPIO_18                    : inout          std_logic;
GPIO_19                    : inout          std_logic;
GPIO_20                    : in        std_logic;
GPIO_21                    : in        std_logic;
GPIO_22                    : inout          std_logic;
GPIO_23                    : inout          std_logic;
GPIO_24                    : inout          std_logic;
GPIO_25                    : inout          std_logic;
GPIO_26                    : inout          std_logic;
GPIO_27                    : inout          std_logic;
GPIO_IDSD        : inout          std_logic;
GPIO_IDSC        : inout          std_logic;
```

The reason that GPIO 5 is commented out is because we want to use it for the ADC functionality and not general-purpose input/output.

Instead, we enable the sigma-delta-capable ADC3 peripheral to work on that pin as follows:

```
--ADC0_input        : in        std_logic;
--ADC0_error        : buffer    std_logic;
--ADC1_input        : in        std_logic;
--ADC1_error        : buffer    std_logic;
--ADC2_input        : in        std_logic;
--ADC2_error        : buffer    std_logic;
ADC3_input   : in          std_logic;
ADC3_error   : buffer      std_logic;
```

Here, we see that we have another three ADC peripherals that we could use if we wanted to add additional channels to the oscilloscope , as shown in the following code:

```
mmc_dat1            : in        std_logic;
mmc_dat2            : in        std_logic;
mmc_n_cs            : out       std_logic;
mmc_clk             : out       std_logic;
mmc_mosi            : out       std_logic;
mmc_miso            : in        std_logic;

PS2_enable          : out       std_logic;
PS2_clk1            : inout          std_logic;
PS2_data1           : inout          std_logic;
PS2_clk2            : inout          std_logic;
PS2_data2           : inout          std_logic
```

```
    );
end FleaFPGA_Ohm_A5;
```

The entity definition for the top-level ends with the MMC (SD card) and PS2 interfaces.

Next is the architecture definition of the module. This part is akin to the source file of a C++ application, with the entity definition functioning like a header as shown:

```
architecture arch of FleaFPGA_Ohm_A5 is
    signal clk_dvi   : std_logic := '0';
    signal clk_dvin  : std_logic := '0';
    signal clk_vga   : std_logic := '0';
    signal clk_50    : std_logic := '0';
    signal clk_pcs   : std_logic := '0';

    signal vga_red   : std_logic_vector(3 downto 0) := (others => '0');
    signal vga_green : std_logic_vector(3 downto 0) := (others => '0');
    signal vga_blue  : std_logic_vector(3 downto 0) := (others => '0');
    signal ADC_lowspeed_raw   : std_logic_vector(7 downto 0) := (others =>
'0');
    signal red    : std_logic_vector(7 downto 0) := (others => '0');
    signal green  : std_logic_vector(7 downto 0) := (others => '0');
    signal blue   : std_logic_vector(7 downto 0) := (others => '0');
    signal hsync  : std_logic := '0';
    signal vsync  : std_logic := '0';
    signal blank  : std_logic := '0';
```

A number of signals are defined here. These allow us to connect the ports, entities, processes, and other elements of a VHDL module with each other.

We can see that some signals are defined here for VGA support. This allows compatibility with VGA-enabled FPGA boards, but parts of it are also compatible with the HDMI (or a DVI) peripheral, as we will see in a moment. Let's look at the following code:

```
begin
  Dram_CKE <= '0';     -- DRAM Clock disable.
  Dram_n_cs <= '1';    -- DRAM Chip disable.
  PS2_enable <= '1';   -- Configures both USB host ports for legacy PS/2 mode.
  mmc_n_cs <= '1';     -- Micro SD card chip disable.
```

With the begin keyword, we indicate that this is the point where we want to start executing the commands in the architecture definition. Everything after this keyword and the terminating keyword (end architecture) will be executed simultaneously, unless a block of instructions is encapsulated within a process (not shown in this code).

We disable a number of hardware features by writing to the appropriate pins. We omitted the DRAM (external memory) section in the earlier entity definition for brevity's sake. The DRAM and SD card functionality are disabled, while PS2 (keyboard, mouse) functionality is enabled. This allows us to connect a PS2 input device if we wanted to:

```
user_module1 : entity work.FleaFPGA_DSO
    port map(
            rst => not sys_reset,
            clk => clk_50,
            ADC_1 => n_led1,
            ADC_lowspeed_raw => ADC_lowspeed_raw,
            Sampler_Q => ADC3_error,
            Sampler_D => ADC3_input,
            Green_out => vga_green,
            Red_out => vga_red,
            Blue_out => vga_blue,
            VGA_HS => hsync,
            VGA_VS => vsync,
            blank => blank,
            samplerate_adj => GPIO_20,
            trigger_adj => GPIO_21
        );
```

Here, we define that we will be using an instance of the FleaFPGA Digital Storage Oscilloscope module. Only the first channel is mapped, though the module could support four channels. This simplification helps to demonstrate the principle of operation.

The DSO module is responsible for reading out the data from the ADC as it samples the signal we're measuring with the probe, and both renders it to a local cache for display on a local (HDMI or VGA) monitor and send it over the serial interface to the UART module (shown at the end of this section). . Let's look at the following code:

```
red <= vga_red & "0000";
green <= vga_green & "0000";
blue <= vga_blue & "0000";
```

Here, the final colors for the display output are determined with the HDMI output signal:

```
u0 : entity work.DVI_clkgen
port map(
        CLKI            =>      sys_clock,
        CLKOP           =>      clk_dvi,
        CLKOS                =>    clk_dvin,
        CLKOS2               =>    clk_vga,
        CLKOS3               =>    clk_50
        );
```

```
u100 : entity work.dvid PORT MAP(
    clk        => clk_dvi,
    clk_n      => clk_dvin,
    clk_pixel  => clk_vga,
    red_p      => red,
    green_p    => green,
    blue_p     => blue,
    blank      => blank,
    hsync      => hsync,
    vsync      => vsync,
    -- outputs to TMDS drivers
    red_s      => LVDS_Red,
    green_s    => LVDS_Green,
    blue_s     => LVDS_Blue,
    clock_s    => LVDS_ck
);
```

This whole section serves to output the video signal that gets generated by the DSO module, allowing us to also use the FPGA board as a standalone oscilloscope unit:

```
myuart : entity work.simple_uart

    port map(
            clk => clk_50,
            reset => sys_reset, -- active low
            txdata => ADC_lowspeed_raw,
            --txready => ser_txready,
            txgo => open,
            --rxdata => ser_rxdata,
            --rxint => ser_rxint,
            txint => open,
            rxd => slave_rx_i,
            txd => slave_tx_o
        );
end architecture;
```

Finally, the simple UART implementation that allows the DSO module to communicate with our C++ application.

The UART is configured to work at a baud rate of 19,200, 8 bits, 1 stop bit, and no parity. After building this VHDL project and programming the FPGA board with it, we can connect to it over this serial connection.

The C++ code

While the VHDL code implements a simple display output with basic input options, if we want to have a large (high-resolution) display, perform signal analysis, make recordings of multiple minutes or even hours, and so on, it will be very convenient to be able to do this on an SBC.

The following code is written as a C++/Qt graphical application that takes in the raw ADC data from the FPGA board and displays it in a graph. While barebones, it provides the framework for a full-featured, SoC-based system.

First, the header is shown, as follows:

```
#include <QMainWindow>

#include <QSerialPort>
#include <QChartView>
#include <QLineSeries>


namespace Ui {
    class MainWindow;
}

class MainWindow : public QMainWindow {
    Q_OBJECT
public:
    explicit MainWindow(QWidget *parent = nullptr);
    ~MainWindow();
public slots:
    void connectUart();
    void disconnectUart();
    void about();
    void quit();
private:
    Ui::MainWindow *ui;
    QSerialPort serialPort;
    QtCharts::QLineSeries* series;
    quint64 counter = 0;
private slots:
    void uartReady();
};
```

Here, we can see that we will be using the serial port implementation in Qt, along with the QChart module, for the visualization part.

The implementation is shown in the following code:

```
#include "mainwindow.h"
#include "ui_mainwindow.h"

#include <QSerialPortInfo>
#include <QInputDialog>
#include <QMessageBox>

MainWindow::MainWindow(QWidget *parent) : QMainWindow(parent),
    ui(new Ui::MainWindow) {
    ui->setupUi(this);
    // Menu connections.
    connect(ui->actionQuit, SIGNAL(triggered()), this, SLOT(quit()));
    connect(ui->actionConnect, SIGNAL(triggered()), this,
SLOT(connectUart()));
    connect(ui->actionDisconnect, SIGNAL(triggered()), this,
SLOT(disconnectUart()));
    connect(ui->actionInfo, SIGNAL(triggered()), this, SLOT(about()));
    // Other connections
    connect(&serialPort, SIGNAL(readyRead()), this, SLOT(uartReady()));
    // Configure the chart view.
    QChart* chart = ui->chartView->chart();
    chart->setTheme(QChart::ChartThemeBlueIcy);
    chart->createDefaultAxes();
    series = new QtCharts::QLineSeries(chart);
    chart->setAnimationOptions(QChart::NoAnimation);
    chart->addSeries(series);
}
```

In the constructor, we create the connections with the menu options in the GUI, which allow us to quit the application, connect to a serial port, disconnect from a serial port if we are connected, or get information about the application.

We connect the serial port instance to a slot that will be called whenever new data is ready to be read.

Finally, we configure the chart view in the GUI, obtaining a reference to the QChart instance inside the QChartView widget. On this reference, we set a theme for the chart, add default axes, and finally, add an empty series, which we will be filling up with the incoming data from the FPGA , as shown in the following code:

```
MainWindow::~MainWindow() {
    delete ui;
}
```

```
void MainWindow::connectUart() {
    QList<QSerialPortInfo> comInfo = QSerialPortInfo::availablePorts();
    QStringList comNames;
    for (QSerialPortInfo com: comInfo) {
        comNames.append(com.portName());
    }
    if (comNames.size() < 1) {
        QMessageBox::warning(this, tr("No serial port found"), tr("No
serial port was found on the system. Please check all connections and try
again."));
        return;
    }
    QString comPort = QInputDialog::getItem(this, tr("Select serial port"),
tr("Available ports:"), comNames, 0, false);
    if (comPort.isEmpty()) { return; }
    serialPort.setPortName(comPort);
    if (!serialPort.open(QSerialPort::ReadOnly)) {
        QMessageBox::critical(this, tr("Error"), tr("Failed to open the
serial port."));
        return;
    }
    serialPort.setBaudRate(19200);
    serialPort.setParity(QSerialPort::NoParity);
    serialPort.setStopBits(QSerialPort::OneStop);
    serialPort.setDataBits(QSerialPort::Data8);
}
```

When the user wishes to connect to the FPGA via the UART, the serial connection on which the FPGA is connected has to be selected, after which a connection will be established, with the 19,200 baud, 8N1 settings we established previously in the VHDL section of the project.

For a fixed configuration where the serial port is always the same, one could consider automating the following part when the system boots:

```
void MainWindow::disconnectUart() {
    serialPort.close();
}
```

Disconnecting from the serial port is quite straightforward:

```
void MainWindow::uartReady() {
    QByteArray data = serialPort.readAll();
    for (qint8 value: data) {
        series->append(counter++, value);
    }
}
```

When the UART receives new data from the FPGA board, this slot gets called. In it, we read all of the data from the UART buffer, appending it to the series that we added to the graph widget, which updates the displayed trace. The counter variable is used to provide an increasing time base for the graph. This functions as a simplistic timestamp here.

At some point, we should start removing data from the series to prevent it from getting too large, along with the ability to search through it and save the data. The counter-based timestamp could report the actual time at which we received the signal, though ideally this should be part of the data that we received from the FPGA:

```
void MainWindow::about() {
    QMessageBox::aboutQt(this, tr("About"));
}


void MainWindow::quit() {
    exit(0);
}
```

We end with a few simple slots. For the information dialog, we simply show the standard Qt information dialog. This could be replaced with a custom help or information dialog.

Building the project

The VHDL project can be built and programmed onto the Ohm FPGA board using the free Lattice Semiconductor Diamond IDE software (http://www.latticesemi.com/latticediamond). Programming the board requires that the FleaFPGA JTAG utility from https://github.com/Basman74/FleaFPGA-Ohm is installed so that Diamond can use it.

By following the instructions for the FleaFPGA Ohm board as described in the quick start guide, it should be relatively easy to get that part of the project up and running. For the C++ side, one has to make sure that the FPGA board and SBC (or equivalent) are connected so that the latter can access the UART on the former.

With this in place, simply compiling the C++ project with the Qt framework (directly on the SBC or preferably cross-compiling on a desktop system) suffices. After this, one can run the application with the flashed FPGA board active, connect to the UART, and observe the trace being drawn on the application window.

Summary

In this chapter, we looked at what role FPGAs play in embedded development, how they have changed in importance over the past decades, and how they are now being used. We looked at a simple implementation of an oscilloscope that uses both an FPGA and an SBC-based component. Having read through this chapter, you should now know when to pick an FPGA for a new embedded project and understand how one can use and communicate with such a device.

Best Practices

As with every software project, there are a number of common issues and pitfalls. With embedded development, the hardware aspect is added to this, creating a unique set of issues. From resource management issues to interrupt troubles and weird behavior induced by hardware issues, this appendix shows you how to prevent and handle many of these issues. In addition, it shows you a variety of optimization approaches and what to be wary of. In this appendix, we'll cover the following topics:

- Safe ways to optimize your embedded code
- How to avoid and fix a variety of common software- and hardware-related issues
- Recognizing the imperfect world of hardware and how to integrate this into your design

All the best-laid plans

As with any project, there's the inevitable divide between the intended design and how it functions in reality. Even with the best planning and bountiful experience, there will always be unforeseen or unnoticed issues. The best you can do is to be as well-prepared as possible.

The first step is to have access to all of the available information for the target platform, understand the tools that are available, and have a solid development and testing plan. We ran through many of these aspects in this book already.

In this appendix, we'll summarize a number of best practices that should help you avoid some of the more common issues.

Working with the hardware

Each target platform has its own quirks and characteristics. Much of this is due to the development history of that platform. For a platform such as AVR, it's fairly coherent, as it was developed by a single company (Atmel) over many years, so it's fairly consistent between different chips and the tools that are used for the platform.

A platform such as ESP8266 (and to some extent its ESP32 successor) was never designed to be used as a generic MCU system, which shows in its rather sketchy and fragmented software ecosystem. Though things have gotten better over the past few years, with various frameworks and open source tools smoothing over the roughest spots, it's a platform where it's easy to make mistakes due to a lack of documentation, issues with tools, and a lack of on-chip debugging.

The ARM MCUs (Cortex-M) are being produced by a wide range of manufacturers in a dizzying number of configurations. Though programming these MCUs tends to be fairly consistent, using tools such as OpenOCD, the peripherals added to each MCU tend to be wildly different between manufacturers, as we will look at in the next section.

Finally, ARM SoCs and similar find themselves in a position similar to ARM MCUs, but with significantly more complicated architectures and fewer peripherals than their MCU brethren. To this, ARM SoCs add a complex initialization routine, requiring comprehensive bootloaders, which is why most people opt to use a ready-made Linux image or similar for the SoC, and develop for that instead.

Here, there's no real right or wrong answer. Most of it comes down to what works for the project, but it's essential that you have a good overview of the hardware platforms you work with.

The confusing world of peripherals

A highly amusing reality with ARM MCUs is that they have different and often incompatible peripherals, mapped to highly different areas in the memory space. Worst of all here are timer peripherals, which come in a variety of complexities, with them in general being able to generate any desired output signal on a GPIO pin, including PWM, as well as work as interrupt-based timers to control the execution of the firmware.

Configuring timer peripherals and similar complex peripherals isn't for the fainthearted. Similarly, using a built-in MAC with an external PHY (Ethernet physical interface) requires a lot of in-depth knowledge to know how to configure them. Reading the datasheets and application notes is essential here.

Relying on autogenerated code by tools such as ST's CubeMX software for their STM32 range of ARM MCUs can lead to you wrestling with non-functional code because you forgot to tick a few boxes in CubeMX editor due to not being aware of what those options were for.

There's nothing wrong with using such auto-generating tools, or high-level libraries provided by the manufacturer, as they can make life significantly easier. It's however crucial to accept the risks that come with this decision, as it requires one to trust that the provided code is correct, or to spend time validating that it is indeed correct.

To make the use of peripherals across different MCUs and SoCs less confusing, one has to add a level of abstraction somewhere to allow for portability of the code. The key is to ensure that this does indeed make life easier and not just add another potential issue that may derail the current project or a future project.

Knowing your tools

While working on an embedded project, you have to know which tools exist for the target platform and how they work. This ranges from programming an MCU via JTAG or other interface and starting a debugging session for on-chip debugging, to the limitations of on-chip debugging. It pays to read the manual or documentation for a tool before using it and doing some reading up on the experiences of other developers with these tools.

We looked at a number of these tools in previous chapters, both for MCU and SoC platforms, along with ways to validate an MCU design before even flashing it on the target hardware.

Choosing asynchronous methods

Many hardware devices and operations take time to finish. It therefore makes sense to choose asynchronous actions using interrupts and timers instead of blocking operations.

When doing bare-metal programming, you'll tend to use a single loop with interrupt routines and timers that allow you to respond to and poll for events. If programmed in a fully asynchronous manner, this main loop will efficiently work through the tasks while the interrupt handlers update the data that has to be processed.

Even on SoC platforms, the use of asynchronous methods is a good idea, as things such as network operations and other I/O operations may take longer than desirable. Having ways to deal with operations not completing is another issue that pops up.

Reading the datasheet

Especially for MCUs, the datasheet gives us a lot of valuable information about how the hardware works, such as how to configure the internal system clock, how individual peripherals work, and available registers and their meaning.

Even if you use an existing board instead of a custom hardware system, it pays to understand the underlying hardware, even if it's from a cursory read of the MCU or SoC datasheet.

Keeping interrupt handlers short

The very nature of an interrupt dictates that it interrupts the regular execution of the processor, switching to the interrupt handler instead. Any microsecond that we spend in the interrupt handler code is a microsecond during which we aren't running the other routines or handling other interrupts.

To prevent any issues arising from this, interrupt handlers (ISRs) should be kept as short as possible, ideally merely updating a single value in a quick and safe manner before ending the ISR and resuming normal operation.

8-bit means 8 bits

Not surprisingly, the use of 16-bit and 32-bit integers on 8-bit MCUs is pretty slow. This is because the system has to perform multiple operations on the same integer value, as it can only fit 8 bits into its registers at a time.

Similarly, the use of floating-point variables on a system without a floating-point unit (FPU) means that such operations are highly suitable for slowing a system down to a crawl as the integer-only processor struggles to keep up with a flow of instructions aimed at simulating floating-point operations.

Don't reinvent the wheel

If a library or framework exists that's of a good quality and available for your target platform and project license, use it instead of writing your own implementation.

Keep a library of commonly used snippets and examples as a reference-not only for yourself, but also for other team members. It's easier to remember where you can find an example of a feature than it is to remember the exact implementation details of that feature.

Think before you optimize

The trick to optimizing code is that you should never attempt to do this without having a full understanding of what the change you're proposing will affect. Just having a feeling or a vague idea of how it might be a good idea isn't good enough.

While SoC-based platforms with a full OS tend to give you a bit more leeway, for MCU platforms, it's essential that you understand what the addition of a single keyword or use of a different data structure to store some information will mean.

The worst thing to do here is to assume that optimizations that you've used on SBCs and desktop systems will have a similar effect on an MCU platform. Due to the modified Harvard architecture and various quirks of platforms such as AVR, these are most likely to backfire or, if you're lucky, just be ineffective.

Here, the application notes provided for the (MCU) platform are useful to understand how the hardware can be optimized. The take-away message here is to do your research before making optimizations, just as one doesn't just start writing code without considering the project design.

Requirements are not optional

Writing embedded software without having a firm set of requirements for the project is like starting to build a new house without a clear idea of how many rooms it should have, where the windows and doors should be, and where the plumbing and wiring should run.

While you can totally start writing working code and hammer out a functioning prototype in no time, the reality is that these prototypes are usually put into production without having had time to fully consider the life cycle of the product, or those who will have to keep patching up the firmware over the coming years to add features that the original firmware code was never designed for.

After completing the requirements that the product has to fulfill, these are then translated into an architecture (the overall structure of the application), which is then translated into a design (what will be implemented). The design is then translated into the actual code.

The advantages of this approach are that not only do you need to answer a lot of questions about *why* something is done a particular way, it also generates a lot of documentation, which can then be used practically as is once the project is completed.

Additionally, in an embedded project having the full set of requirements can save a lot of money and time as it allows one to pick the right MCU or SoC for the project without having to spend more money on a more powerful than needed chip 'just in case'. It also prevents embarrassing mid-project discoveries where a feature which had been 'forgotten' about suddenly necessitates a change in the hardware design.

Documentation saves lives

It's become somewhat of a running joke that programmers don't like to write documentation and thus refer to the code that they've written as *self-documenting code*. The reality is that without clear documentation of the design requirements, architecture overview, design plans, and with the API documentation, you risk the future of the project and both one's fellow developers and the end-users who rely on the software to function.

Following procedures and doing all the boring paperwork before you can start writing the first line of code may seem like a complete killjoy. Unfortunately, the reality is that, without this effort, this knowledge will remain locked in the heads of the project's developers, which complicates the integration of the firmware into the rest of an embedded project and makes future maintenance, especially if moved to a different team, a daunting prospect.

The simple fact is that no code is self-documenting, and even if it were, no hardware engineer is going to go through thousands of lines of code to figure out what kind of signal is being put out on a specific GPIO pin when a particular input condition for the MCU occurs.

Testing code means trying to destroy it

A common mistake when writing tests is to write test scenarios that you expect will work. That's missing the point. While it's wonderful that a particular parsing routine did what it should do when it's handed perfectly formatted data, that's not very helpful in a real-life scenario.

While you can get perfect data, it's equally likely that you'll get completely corrupted or even garbage data in your code. The goal is to ensure that no matter what horrible things you do to the input data, it will never have a negative effect on the rest of the system.

All input should be validated and sanity checked. If something doesn't seem right, it should be rejected rather than you allowing it to cause issues elsewhere in the code later on.

Summary

In this appendix, we ran through a number of common issues and pitfalls that are likely to occur when working on an embedded software design.

The reader should now know what phases exist in projects, along with the reasons behind documenting every step of the project.

Other Books You May Enjoy

If you enjoyed this book, you may be interested in these other books by Packt:

C++ High Performance
Viktor Sehr, Björn Andrist

ISBN: 9781787120952

- Benefits of modern C++ constructs and techniques
- Identify hardware bottlenecks, such as CPU cache misses, to boost performance
- Write specialized data structures for performance-critical code
- Use modern metaprogramming techniques to reduce runtime calculations
- Achieve efficient memory management using custom memory allocators
- Reduce boilerplate code using reflection techniques
- Reap the benefits of lock-free concurrent programming
- Perform under-the-hood optimizations with preserved readability using proxy objects
- Gain insights into subtle optimizations used by STL algorithms
- Utilize the Range V3 library for expressive C++ code
- Parallelize your code over CPU and GPU, without compromising readability

The Modern C++ Challenge
Marius Bancila

ISBN: 9781788993869

- Serialize and deserialize JSON and XML data
- Perform encryption and signing to facilitate secure communication between parties
- Embed and use SQLite databases in your applications
- Use threads and asynchronous functions to implement generic purpose parallel algorithms
- Compress and decompress files to/from a ZIP archive
- Implement data structures such as circular buffer and priority queue
- Implement general purpose algorithms as well as algorithms that solve specific problems
- Create client-server applications that communicate over TCP/IP
- Consume HTTP REST services
- Use design patterns to solve real-world problems

Leave a review - let other readers know what you think

Please share your thoughts on this book with others by leaving a review on the site that you bought it from. If you purchased the book from Amazon, please leave us an honest review on this book's Amazon page. This is vital so that other potential readers can see and use your unbiased opinion to make purchasing decisions, we can understand what our customers think about our products, and our authors can see your feedback on the title that they have worked with Packt to create. It will only take a few minutes of your time, but is valuable to other potential customers, our authors, and Packt. Thank you!

Index

U

Unified Programming and Debug Interface (UPDI)
122, 124
user-defined types (UDTs) 49

V

vacuum fluorescent displays (VFD) 12
Valgrind
  reference 214
  used, for testing 214, 215
vector graphics file (SVG) 115
very large-scale integrated (VLSI) 411
VHSIC Hardware Description Language (VHDL)
411
virtual base classes 50, 51
virtual functions
  reference 50
voice-driven infotainment system
  extending 311, 312
  hardware requisites 296, 297
  online streaming, integrating 300
  project, building 311
  software requisites 297
  source code 301, 303, 304, 305, 306, 307,
  308, 309, 311

usage scenarios 301
user interface 300

W

Wi-Fi-enabled soil humidity monitor
  compiling 192
  complications 194
  configuration 192, 193
  creating 152
  enhancement 194
  firmware 157
  flashing 192
  hardware requisites 152, 153, 154, 155, 156
  plant module code 159
  Sming, setting up 157, 158
  using 193
wireless access point (WAP) 167
WiringPi
  reference 73

Y

Yocto Project
  reference 57

Z

Z80-based 29